CLARK
2008

The Origins of
FBI Counterintelligence

The Origins of
FBI Counterintelligence

Raymond J. Batvinis

University Press of Kansas

Published by the University Press of Kansas (Lawrence, Kansas 66045), which was organized by the Kansas Board of Regents and is operated and funded by Emporia State University, Fort Hays State University, Kansas State University, Pittsburg State University, the University of Kansas, and Wichita State University

Library of Congress Cataloging-in-Publication Data

Batvinis, Raymond J.
The origins of FBI counterintelligence / Raymond J. Batvinis.
p. cm. — (Modern war studies)
Includes bibliographical references and index.
ISBN-13: 978-0-7006-1495-0 (cloth : alk. paper)
1. United States. Federal Bureau of Investigation—History.
2. Intelligence service—United States—History—20th century.
3. United States—History—1933-1945. I. Title.
HV8144.F43B48 2007
327.1273009—dc22
2006034427

British Library Cataloguing-in-Publication Data is available.

Printed in the United States of America
10 9 8 7 6 5 4 3 2 1

The paper used in this publication meets the minimum requirements of the American National Standard for Permanence of Paper for Printed Library Materials Z39.48-1992.

CONTENTS

A photo section appears following page 150.

PREFACE

There is an adage in the writing world that says, "write what you know about." I tried to keep that in mind when I set out to choose a topic for my doctoral dissertation, which I started in 1996 and is the basis for this book.

I have always had a keen interest in American history. I received my bachelor's degree in history in 1968 and my master's degree two years later. I then served as a special agent of the FBI for twenty-five years, which included an assignment in the training unit of the FBI's Intelligence Division (today known as the Counterintelligence Division). After new-agent training, my first assignment was at the Cleveland office of the FBI. In April 1974 I was transferred to the Washington, D.C., field office, where I was initially assigned to the Applicant Squad, conducting background investigations on prospective U.S. government employees who required national security clearance. There I had my first encounter with older, more senior FBI agents—men who had served in the military or with the Bureau during the Second World War. I was surprised to learn that these agents had not carried out conventional FBI assignments during the war; instead, they had worked undercover in Central and South America as part of the FBI's little known and highly classified Special Intelligence Service. It still bothers me, even today, that I did not take advantage of the opportunity to ask them about their fascinating stories of undercover life and wartime intelligence and counterintelligence in foreign capitals. I suppose in fairness to myself, I was settling into a new home and a new job, learning a new task, and preparing for the birth of our second child, who came along in November 1974.

After nine months of what seemed like countless neighborhood checks, reference interviews, employment inquiries, and education verifications, I was reassigned to the office's huge and mysterious foreign counterintelligence program. I expected to stay there for only a few months, after which I hoped to finagle a switch to a more traditional criminal squad. In fact, I remained on the counterintelligence side of the house for the rest of my FBI career. During the next two and a half decades, I did all the things one does in the counterintelligence business: conduct surveillances, cultivate sources, develop and operate double agents, direct espionage investigations, and conduct and coordinate joint investigations with the military services, the CIA, the NSA, and foreign intelligence and security services. For a good part of my career, I even had the rare privilege of serving as the first-line supervisor for many of the FBI's finest professional counterintelligence investigators and support employees, working on a number of this country's most important national security matters. It was a wonderful experience and a perfect blend of traditional criminal investigative work and foreign intelligence work.

A work of this type could not be undertaken without the encouragement and help of numerous people. First to be recognized are the professors who supported me during my doctoral studies at the Catholic University of America. They include John Wakelyn, the history department chairman who urged me to start down the road, and professors Catherine Cline, Jerry Z. Mueller, Gary Gerstle, and Larry Poos. A special note of gratitude is extended to Professor Harold Langley, a World War II veteran, Smithsonian Institution naval historian, and my dissertation adviser. His encouragement and patience are the mark of a great teacher.

Others include Mike Warner, who is currently serving as the chief historian for the new Office of the Director of National Intelligence; Robert "Lou" Benson of the NSA; John Fox, the historian of the FBI; and FBI colleagues of many years, including Tom Reilly, Hank Flynn, Dave Major, and Les Wiser. A special note of thanks to Julian "Jay" Koerner for his enlightening interview of the late Joseph Santoiana, creator of the FBI's first Spanish- and Portuguese-language training program in 1941. I am also grateful to the scholars and historians who read key parts of the manuscript and offered helpful comments, including David Kahn, Nigel West, Katie Sibley, Athan Theoharis, and Tim Naftali.

Major sources of information on the FBI's Special Intelligence Service were the dozens of special agents and FBI support personnel who served in the SIS and allowed me to interview them about their experiences. Their names are listed in the bibliography, and I will forever be grateful for their kindness. In particular, I want to single out my friend, mentor, and confidant, the late Kenneth Crosby, who served with great pride as an SIS agent in Argentina. He was a wonderful person whose zest for life infected everyone around him.

No researcher, regardless of skill or experience, can negotiate the bewildering world of original documents without the assistance of skilled librarians and archivists. I will always be indebted to circulation librarian Lillian Blake, reference librarian Bill McQuade, and many others at the Admiral Chester Nimitz Library at the U.S. Naval Academy; the staff of the Bentley Library at the University of Michigan; the James Cabell Library at Virginia Commonwealth University in Richmond; Eugenia Ryner, chief librarian at the FBI Academy Library, Quantico, Virginia; the J. D. Williams Library at the University of Mississippi in Oxford; the National Archives and Records Administration, College Park, Maryland; the Library of Congress; and the Franklin D. Roosevelt Library at Hyde Park, New York. I also want to thank the staff of the U.S. Army Historical Center at Carlisle, Pennsylvania; the British Public Records Office; the Naval Historical Center; the Naval Historical Foundation; and the J. Edgar Hoover Center for Law Enforcement. I am grateful to the directors of the Eleanor and Franklin Roosevelt Institute for awarding me a Beeke-Levy Research Grant for research at the Roosevelt Library.

I want to extend my appreciation to Mike Briggs, executive editor at the University Press of Kansas, for his faith in this project and in me.

In the end, it all comes down to family, and mine is wonderful: my children, Maura and Peter; my son-in-law, Doug; and my two junior historians, Brenna and Kaitlyn. I owe you so much, and I love you. And most important is Maryalice, whose support never wavered and whose love made it all possible.

ABBREVIATIONS

Abwehr	German Military Intelligence Service
ACLU	American Civil Liberties Union
APL	American Protective League
AWOL	absent without leave
BOI	Bureau of Investigation
BSC	British Security Coordination
CCA	Comprehensive Communications Act of 1934
CIA	Central Intelligence Agency
CPGB	Communist Party of Great Britain
DAB	German-American Workers Organization (Deutsche-Americanische Berufagemeinschaft)
DNI	director of naval intelligence
DOJ	Department of Justice
FARA	Foreign Agents Registration Act
FBI	Federal Bureau of Investigation
FCC	Federal Communications Commission
GC&CS	Government Codes and Cypher School (U.K.)
GID	General Intelligence Division
GRU	Soviet Military Intelligence Agency (Glavnoye Razvedyvatelnoye Upravlenie)
ID	Identification Division
IIC	Interdepartmental Intelligence Conference
IRA	Irish Republican Army
IWW	International Workers of the World
MI5	British Security Service
MI6	British Secret Intelligence Service
MID	Military Intelligence Division, U.S. War Department
NDC	National Defense Conference (FBI)
NKVD	People's Commissariat for Internal Affairs
NSA	National Security Agency

xii   ABBREVIATIONS

OGPU	Unified State Political Directorate
ONI	Office of Naval Intelligence
RCMP	Royal Canadian Mounted Police
RSS	Radio Signals Service
SAC	special agent in charge
SIS	Special Intelligence Service (FBI)
WCD	War College Division

INTRODUCTION

This is the story of how the counterintelligence structure within the U.S. government was organized in the critical years before the Second World War. It traces how the Federal Bureau of Investigation, a relatively small investigative agency within the Department of Justice, evolved from a law enforcement agency with virtually no counterespionage mandate into the United States' first organized, sustained counterespionage service; then into the first counterintelligence service; and then into the first organized civilian foreign intelligence service.

To fully understand the narrative, one must first grasp how the term *counterintelligence* is used in this study. Throughout history, what we refer to today as counterintelligence was in fact the defense of the realm—an essential element in the protection of the sovereign and the preservation of his power. It was the king's instrument for maintaining political stability. His spies remained vigilant for treasonous subjects who might threaten the kingdom's internal security, as well as for outsiders who slipped into the kingdom unnoticed, seeking information that could benefit foreign enemies.

History is full of stories of what happens to spies and traitors who are caught. Remember the fate of William Wallace (depicted in the movie *Braveheart*), who led the Scottish people in a revolt for independence against the British king. For his treachery, he was hung by the neck until near death, then disemboweled and his insides burned, after which he was drawn and quartered and his limbs publicly displayed throughout the kingdom as a warning to anyone with similar inclinations. Even Shakespeare understood the seriousness of this business: Henry V condemns his three most trusted aides to death for their traitorous acts. The twentieth century witnessed its own barbarity toward spies. One example was Eli Cohen, a brilliant Israeli spy who penetrated the highest echelons of the Syrian political and military leadership, acquiring priceless information that contributed to Israel's success in the Golan Heights during the Six-Day War in 1967. Cohen was

1

discovered by Syrian counterintelligence and executed, and his body was left hanging for days in the main square of Damascus, again as a warning.

But what is counterintelligence in the modern sense? Simply stated, it is the relentless effort of a government to identify, penetrate, and ultimately neutralize the activities of a foreign intelligence service that is attempting to acquire critical political, military, industrial, financial, and economic secrets. Foreign intelligence officers often work undercover as diplomats assigned to embassies and consulates; even more difficult to ferret out are the espionage agents, intelligence officers, and terrorists who live quietly and anonymously in the United States, blending into the very fabric of society. To accomplish this mission in today's world, the government must have a counterintelligence service made up of highly competent, motivated, and trained professionals with the imagination and initiative to pursue often tedious and time-consuming investigations.

For years, the United States had no counterintelligence service. After the First World War and the governmental abuse of civil liberties that followed, this important national security function was shut down. In effect, for fifteen years the United States had only a weak, unfocused counterintelligence structure and no coherent policies or strategies for dealing with the growing foreign espionage menace.

What follows is an examination of the reemergence of U.S. counterintelligence through the work of a small federal investigative agency with virtually no experience in conventional counterespionage practices. It traces the factors that led to the sudden awareness of the intelligence threat facing the nation, the reaction to that threat and the steps taken to confront it, and the success that eventually emerged out of some dismal early counterespionage failures.

Among the issues discussed are the challenges faced in developing new coordination guidelines; the secret and not-so-secret examination of bank and financial records of foreign governments; the factors leading up to President Franklin Roosevelt's authorization of FBI foreign counterintelligence wiretapping; the unique and highly secret foreign assignments undertaken by FBI agents before the Second World War; and the president's remarkable decision, in the wake of isolationism, to secretly establish and fund this nation's first organized foreign intelligence service and then dispatch undercover agents to foreign capitals to steal vital secrets—all without Congress's knowledge or assent. It concludes with a new look at the case that broke the back of pre–World War II German espionage and prepared the United States' counterintelligence structure for the wartime challenges it was about to confront.

CHAPTER ONE

Rumrich

He was a U.S. Army deserter when he was arrested on February 14, 1938, and charged with spying for Germany. His name: Guenther Gustave Maria Rumrich.

Guenther was born in June 1911 in Chicago, Illinois, to Alfonso Rumrich, secretary to the imperial Austrian consulate general, and his wife, Jolan. Guenther was two years old when his father was transferred to Bremen, Germany; a year later, the family moved to Budapest, Hungary. He later lived with his parents and sister in Italy and Russia and was educated between 1919 and 1928 in Czechoslovakia and Germany. Young Guenther elected to affirm his American citizenship in April 1929 when he applied for and received a U.S. passport at the U.S. consulate in Prague. He returned to the United States five months later and joined the army in January 1930, serving briefly in New York City at the general dispensary on Whitehall Street and the surgeon's office on Governors Island. Five months later he went absent without leave (AWOL) but surrendered to the military in August 1930. After serving six months in prison and forfeiting two-thirds of his salary, he was released and returned to duty, again assigned to Governors Island and the station hospital at Fort Hamilton, Brooklyn. Thirty-three months after enlisting, he was promoted to the rank of sergeant and was discharged on April 27, 1933. Rumrich reenlisted the next day and spent the next two years assigned to the station hospital at Fort Clayton in the Panama Canal Zone, followed by a stint at Fort Missoula, Montana.[1]

Rumrich went AWOL from Fort Missoula on January 2, 1936, and soon got lost among the throngs in New York City. Settling in Brooklyn, he began working at a string of low-level jobs, including restaurant dishwasher, language instructor at the Berlitz School of Languages, and technician with the Denver Chemical Manufacturing Company on Varick Street in Lower Manhattan. In April 1937, his wife, whom he had met in Montana, joined him, and they settled in an apartment in the Bronx.[2]

At some point, Rumrich stumbled across a copy of *Geheime Macht,* the memoirs of Colonel Walter Nicolai, head of the German foreign military intelligence service during the First World War. He was so impressed by the colonel's exploits that Rumrich decided to offer his services to Germany and sent a letter to Nicolai through the German daily newspaper *Voelkischer Beobachter.* Describing himself as a "high official in the United States Army" with access to important military information, Rumrich asked Nicolai to forward his offer to the "proper authorities." Taking a cue from Nicolai's book, he suggested that the Germans contact him by inserting an advertisement in the *New York Times* public notices section addressed to "Theodore Koener—Letter received, please send reply and address to Sanders, Hamburg 1, Postbox 629, Germany." Over the next four months Rumrich waited patiently while his letter made its way to the Abwehr, the foreign intelligence service of the German military high command. The advertisement was eventually placed, and on May 3, 1936, Rumrich met a German agent in a New York City restaurant, where he was quickly assessed and signed up as an Abwehr agent. Over the next twenty-one months, the success that had eluded Rumrich during his six years in the military was countered by the volumes of sensitive military data he stole and smuggled to Germany. When he finally sat down with the FBI and told his story, the U.S. government's approach to countering espionage would change forever.[3]

Rumrich's value as a productive Abwehr agent grew steadily until his fortunes ended abruptly with his arrest in February 1938. Increasing carelessness and audacity doomed Rumrich's brief career as a spy. At first, he would cautiously pick up information of value to the Abwehr using tactics that raised no suspicion and attracted no attention. Success and the financial rewards of espionage, however, led him to contrive high-risk ploys that would soon prove disastrous.

In late 1937 Rumrich received instructions to acquire information concerning venereal disease among U.S. military troops. A critical concern for any military commander is readiness for combat. General George Patton, commander of the Third Army, was in England in the spring of 1944, preparing for the invasion of Europe. He mused about the problem in his diary. "I can't get anyone to realize," he wrote, "that even without fighting, a unit is always about 8% below strength due to sickness etc., and that a unit 15% low in manpower is at least 30% low in efficiency." One way for a foreign intelligence service to assess foreign troop readiness in the 1930s was the acquisition of intelligence concerning the percentage of soldiers medically incapacitated by illness, injury, or disease. With the majority of the United States' 138,000 military members serving overseas, facts and figures concerning venereal disease among American troops were critical for German military planning.[4]

Venereal disease was such a serious problem in terms of lost duty time that in 1925 the surgeon general, writing in the War Department's annual report, had described it as "the most important sanitary problem in the Army." Only respiratory conditions caused more hospitalizations at the time. U.S. military authorities began taking strong measures to control the problem. Intensive educational programs designed to warn soldiers about the dangers of venereal disease, as well as harsher measures such as loss of pay, reduction in rank, and even court-martial of infected soldiers, became standard military practice. Beginning in the mid-1920s, statistical data collected on the progress of venereal disease prevention efforts were turned into reports for War Department planning purposes. It was these reports that Rumrich was ordered to secure.[5]

Rumrich had an advantage in his pursuit of army medical intelligence. Having served in a series of medical units in New York City, Panama, and Montana, he knew which information was valuable, where it was located, and how easily he could acquire it. Assuming the role of a senior American military officer, Rumrich threw caution to the wind and simply telephoned the medical section at Fort Hamilton in Brooklyn. Identifying himself as a specialist with the U.S. Army Medical Corps, he told the duty officer that he had arrived in New York City for a conference on military readiness and discovered that he had left some important statistics on venereal disease at his office in Washington, D.C. Aware of the lax security assigned to this type of information, he brazenly ordered the Fort Hamilton medical staff to deliver the data to him at the Manhattan hotel where he was staying. Without any verification of the caller's identity, the sensitive documents were taken by a soldier to the Hotel Taft and handed over to Rumrich. Within days, this valuable information concerning the status of U.S. war-fighting capabilities and the readiness of American military units stationed throughout the world was on its way across the Atlantic into the waiting hands of German military authorities.[6]

Rumrich's brilliant intelligence coup only whetted the Abwehr's appetite for more. His new mission—one that meant potentially greater rewards for

Germany but that increased his risk of discovery—was to obtain blank U.S. passports. These were valuable commodities for both the Abwehr and the Soviet intelligence services, and acquiring them was a top priority for both. Using sophisticated technology available only in the most modern laboratories, blank passports could be forged so as to appear genuine even to experts examining them with the naked eye. Because few Americans traveled abroad during the 1920s and 1930s, customs and immigration officials at border crossings were not adequately trained to spot forgeries, making passports valuable false identity documents for espionage agents across Europe and Asia. The U.S. Department of State's Passport Office, keenly aware of the espionage value of passports, placed a high level of security on them, making theft almost impossible.[7]

Rumrich's previous gambit as a "senior American military official" had been so successful that he decided to try it again. Using a more audacious variation, he called the Passport Office in New York City from a telephone booth at Grand Central Station and identified himself to the incredulous clerk as Cordell Hull, the U.S. secretary of state. Using a hushed voice for dramatic effect, he explained that he was in New York City incognito and ordered the delivery of thirty-five blank passports to Mr. Edward Weston, supposedly an assistant secretary of state, staying at the McAlpin Hotel in Midtown Manhattan. The dumbfounded clerk could not conceive of such a bizarre request. A quick check confirmed that Hull was in Washington, D.C., and the State Department had no assistant secretaries named Weston. A package containing blank passport applications, rather than the blank passports Rumrich had requested, was readied and sent on its way under the close observation of State Department investigators and the New York City Police Department. Rumrich was arrested by police officers on February 14, 1938, when he took possession of the package.

With Rumrich in custody, State Department officials immediately began questioning the lawfulness of the arrest. Although posing as a U.S. government official was illegal, ordering blank passport applications, even under these strange circumstances, was not. Even more troublesome for the bureaucrats was the potential embarrassment to the State Department if Secretary of State Cordell Hull was subpoenaed to testify at a high-profile court proceeding in New York City against someone whose crime was questionable. Unaware that it had one of Germany's most important spies sitting in jail, State Department officials saw only two options: turn Rumrich over to the military as a deserter, or release him.[8]

Crown

In July 1937 British postal authorities received a report concerning the suspicious behavior of a woman living in Dundee, a sleepy little farming town in central Scotland. Daily shipments of mail and packages postmarked from countries in South America, Europe, and Asia were arriving at the obscure address, along with daily postings from the Dundee resident back to these and other foreign addresses. People in Dundee regularly sent and received a steady and predictable stream of mail consisting of bills, family and business letters, packages, and so forth, but nothing reaching the magnitude of this person's activities. The volume of mail soon caught the attention of the curious postman who handled the route. On the surface, nothing illegal was happening, but given British anxiety over Adolf Hitler's increasingly threatening behavior on the Continent, the postman passed his suspicions on to his superiors. The report was quickly forwarded through the British Postal Service, eventually making its way to London and the headquarters of the British Security Service, known as MI5, which launched an inquiry.[9]

Who was this anonymous person living quietly in Scotland? MI5 quickly identified her as Mrs. Jessie Wallace Jordan, a hairdresser in her early fifties who worked in a local beauty shop. She lived in a tiny flat on Kinlock Street in a working-class neighborhood, kept to herself, maintained a modest lifestyle on a meager income, and rarely traveled. With such blandly predictable behavior—except for her unusual mailing activities—and no friends or contacts that raised any security concerns, there was no reason for anyone to suspect that Mrs. Jordan was an espionage agent.[10]

Surface impressions can be misleading, however, as British authorities soon discovered. A deeper probe by MI5 officers over the next few months gradually uncovered a link between this obscure beautician and espionage. Although she had been born in Scotland and was a British citizen, Jordan had been living in Dundee only since 1937, after residing in Germany for thirty years. Before the First World War she had met and married a German traveling through Scotland, moved with him to Germany, and acquired German citizenship. Her husband had served in the German army during the war, receiving wounds that later proved fatal. A second marriage in Germany had ended in divorce. A closer look at her travel patterns only deepened MI5's concerns. Jordan had told friends that she had broken all ties with Germany and that her only close relatives lived in Scotland; yet an investigation of her travel patterns uncovered a number of unexplained trips to Germany in 1937 that she had not mentioned to anyone.[11]

MI5 veterans had long suspected the Germans and the Russians of conducting espionage in Great Britain, but in the nearly two decades since the end of the First World War, the understaffed and underfunded security service had unearthed little meaningful evidence. In January 1938, however, MI5 arrested four spies involved in a Soviet ring that had been quietly stealing blueprints for naval weapons from the Woolwich Arsenal. Now, with the Dundee investigation, another act of espionage in the British Isles may have been uncovered, and like any sophisticated counterintelligence service, MI5 began thinking beyond Mrs. Jordan. By secretly examining the contents of her mail and tracking her mailing patterns, MI5 hoped to find other spies operating in Great Britain, particularly moles burrowed deep within the British government and the military establishment. Even more significantly, the possibility loomed that Britain's knowledge of German espionage could reach beyond its borders, offering the British a unique opportunity to identify, penetrate, and neutralize German and Russian intelligence operations throughout the world.[12]

Surveillance of Jordan soon began producing encouraging results. Letters from the United States, France, Holland, and South America arrived with regularity. Her mailing habits, as one historian later described them, were equally prolific, "with bulging envelopes [sent] to all sorts of faraway places." Over time, a careful examination of her mail led investigators to conclude that the letters and packages were not intended for Mrs. Jordan; rather, they were destined for Germany and its intelligence establishment, as well as intelligence agents in other parts of the world. Mrs. Jordan, as MI5 suspected, was a "mail drop," or, in British counterintelligence terminology, a "live letter box." She was a "cut-out"—an anonymous person living an obscure existence who received and forwarded mail without examining the contents, motivated by a sense of loyalty, financial compensation, or both. Regardless of her reasons, Jordan was clearly spying for the Germans, and the British began reaping valuable information about German agents and operating methods throughout the world.[13]

MI5's initial strategy called for discreet and indefinite surveillance of Jordan's mail. Then, when it was satisfied that enough information had been acquired, it would develop a scheme to quietly intercede and gain control of the operation, without the knowledge of the Germans or the Russians. On January 17, 1938, however, MI5 plans collapsed when Jordan received a letter postmarked from New York City. Calling himself "Crown," the author began with a warning about local custom regarding forms of address. Expressing concern that "nothing arouses even the faintest sort of suspicion," he informed his German bosses that the Scottish custom was to address a married woman using the first name of her husband, regardless of his presence in the house. Crown worried that although he might appear to be a "stickler," "'Mrs. Jessie Jordan' was a trifle away from the usual designation." His next paragraph, however, stopped the British investigation in its tracks. There, Crown outlined his plan for the theft of "details regarding the coast defense operations and bases on the Atlantic coast." These records, he explained, were kept in the office of a Colonel Eglin, the commander of Fort Totten in New York. Crown proposed a scheme in which he would pose as the "aide de camp of the commanding general of the Second Corps" and order Eglin to appear at an "emergency staff meeting" at the McAlpin Hotel in Manhattan on January 31 or February 1 with the material. Eglin would be instructed to follow specific procedures for delivery, discuss the planned meeting with no one, and undertake no verification of these orders because the meeting was a "military secret." The letter's tone then turned sinister. After ensuring that Eglin was alone and had the required material, Crown would "over power him and remove [the] papers," making "every effort to leave clues that would point to communistic perpetrators."[14]

A direct threat on the life of an American military officer left the British with no options. The U.S. government would have to be warned, a step that would expose the Jordan investigation and possibly end it. The concerns of the British government were captured by Guy Liddell, a senior officer of MI5. In an aide-mémoire he prepared after an official visit to the United States in March and April 1938, Liddell wrote that the plot "could have been merely designed by this agent in order to obtain money, since if it did not materialize he would be discredited with his employers." He noted that "although the plan to overpower Colonel Eglin at the McAlpin Hotel, New York, appeared extremely crude, the matter could not be dismissed lightly since we [MI5] were positive that its details had been communicated by a German agent to the German Intelligence Service."[15]

On January 29, 1938, Colonel Raymond E. Lee, the U.S. embassy's military attaché in London, was briefed on the matter and given a paraphrased copy of Crown's letter. Wasting no time, Lee cabled the War Department, which quickly determined that Colonel H. W. T. Eglin, the base commander, was in no danger and had received no such instructions. Next the War

Department requested FBI assistance to observe activities around the Mc-Alpin Hotel, looking for the mysterious Crown and awaiting his telephone call to the colonel.[16]

Two weeks later, on February 14, a surprised FBI and War Department learned about Rumrich's arrest in the blank passport scam, an event that probably would have gone unnoticed, except that a note containing details of the Eglin plot had been found in a search of his home. Under questioning by military authorities, Rumrich quickly admitted planning the document theft and the elimination of Eglin. He was turned over to the FBI on February 19, 1938. Everyone now realized that Crown and Rumrich were the same person.[17]

Crown's Revelations

Confusion and surprise characterized conditions at FBI headquarters and the Department of Justice upon learning of Rumrich's arrest for espionage. FBI director J. Edgar Hoover, who was vacationing in Miami, was unaware of the case and was reluctant to get the FBI involved. Attorney General Homer Cummings, like Hoover, knew nothing of the arrest and ordered an immediate clamp on all news releases concerning the investigation. A stickler for clear lines of authority and responsibility, Hoover abhorred the messy jurisdictional issues this case presented. In his view, it was already seriously flawed because of the complete absence of coordination among the State Department, War Department, FBI, New York City Police Department, and British Security Service. The espionage charges would surely be dismissed for lack of merit, and Rumrich would end up facing only the charge of desertion. Despite pressure from the War Department to pursue the matter because of the threat to Colonel Eglin, Hoover continued to resist. He argued that the case was already in the hands of the Department of State; leaks by the New York City Police Department to the press had compromised the case, reducing the chances of a successful prosecution; and little could be achieved because the conspirators were now undoubtedly aware of the ring's exposure.[18]

In the end, Hoover relented to military pressure, and Rumrich's prosecution for espionage and for impersonating Hull was authorized by U.S. attorney Lamar Hardy. Leon Turrou, a thirty-eight-year-old, ten-year veteran working in the FBI's New York field office, was assigned to the case. Turrou was chosen because of his previous experience with the attempted sabotage of the navy dirigible the USS *Akron* by a fanatic Communist and because of his fluency in German, Russian, French, and Italian. Turrou started the investigation with a series of illuminating interviews with a talkative Rumrich that soon revealed the vast extent of the Abwehr spy network in the United States. Details about how Rumrich had begun spying, his methods of keeping in contact with his Abwehr masters in Europe, leads to other spies in the United States and Canada, and a catalog of his successes and the ease with which he was able to obtain military and government secrets all cascaded out in rich detail.[19]

The chatty spy, hoping to save himself, outlined Abwehr methods for passing on instructions, receiving messages, and checking on agents around the world. He identified Karl Schleuter, then in Germany and a steward on the steamship the SS *Bremen,* as the courier who had carried his information to Germany. Once on the Abwehr payroll, Rumrich had learned that Otto Maurer, an official of the Hamburg-America Steamship Lines, had placed the original advertisement in the *New York Times* signaling German interest in Rumrich. Maurer acted on instructions from a Kapitan-Lieutenant Dreschel, assigned to the office of the marine superintendent of Hamburg-America, and Dreschel's orders came from Captain Heinrich Lorentz, chief officer of the German cruise ship *Europa,* which made weekly crossings of the Atlantic Ocean between Europe and the United States. Maurer, Dreschel, and Lorentz answered to Erich Pfeiffer, an Abwehr intelligence officer assigned to Bremen, Germany. Messages and packages between Rumrich and Pfeiffer were carried by ordinary crew members, particularly Schleuter. Sending and receiving mail and packages from mail drops was an alternative method of communication designed to enhance the security of the operation. Jordan's address in Scotland was not Rumrich's only mail drop; he also used two addresses in Germany supplied by his superiors.

After further questioning by Turrou, Rumrich revealed the identities of two people he had tried, unsuccessfully, to recruit as spies: a U.S. Navy Department employee with access to code and cipher information, and a seaman in Newport News, Virginia. He was more successful, however, with Erich Glaser, an army private assigned to the Eighteenth Reconnaissance Squadron at Mitchell Field in New York, who had already supplied him with important army air force and navy codes and ciphers. Glaser's information passed through Rumrich to Johanna Hoffmann, a hairdresser on the *Europa,* for transmittal to Germany. Turrou also learned that Hoffmann was due to arrive in New York City sometime in the next few days.[20]

As for Rumrich, his twenty-one-month espionage career produced some impressive results. A stunned Turrou learned that the spy's reports to the Abwehr had covered a broad range of useful topics. Rumrich routinely frequented taverns and bars along the docks and wharves, casually chatting for hours with unsuspecting sailors, merchant seamen, longshoremen, and stevedores interested only in a few drinks and some relaxed conversation. In this way, Rumrich picked up an important answer to a seemingly innocuous question here, a valuable tidbit there, or an interesting piece of gossip somewhere else. When assembled and combined with his own observations, these disparate pieces of seemingly irrelevant data created a clear picture of ship destinations and descriptions, warship movement and construction, and the volumes, types, and destinations of cargoes moving in and out of the port of New York City. Rumrich also admitted that he had stolen copies of confidential ship-to-shore communication codes, information concerning the navy's Atlantic Fleet movements, and contingency plans for the installation of antiaircraft weapons in the New York metropolitan area. All were now hopelessly lost to Germany.[21]

Greibl

A search of Rumrich's home uncovered the names of Ignatz Greibl and Willy Lonkowski. Rumrich acknowledged that in May 1936, after his initial meeting with the Abwehr courier who signed him up, he had been introduced to both men, whom he characterized as key agents in the Abwehr's U.S. operations. Turrou then interviewed Greibl and learned that he was a physician, born, raised, and educated in Munich, who had immigrated to the United States in 1925. Supported by his wife, Maria, a nurse he had met while serving in the German army, Greibl continued his medical studies at Long Island Medical College and later at Fordham University. He started a medical practice in Bangor, Maine, and later moved back to New York City, settling in the Yorkville section of Manhattan. A much more difficult interrogation subject than Rumrich, the wily physician cleverly deflected Turrou's direct questions about espionage, claiming that he was merely a doctor dedicated to the needs of his patients. With no admissions by Greibl, Turrou was forced to let him go.[22]

What Greibl did not tell Turrou was that he was the linchpin of the whole organization. Less than halfway into President Franklin Roosevelt's first term in office, Greibl wrote a personal letter to Joseph Goebbels, Hitler's minister of propaganda, offering his services to the Reich. Like Rumrich's letter, Greibl's offer eventually found its way to the Abwehr. Within months, an agent assigned to a ship crew met Greibl in New York, assessed his value for intelligence collection, signed him up, and introduced him to Lonkowski. Greibl was, in Rumrich's opinion, a true German nationalist, an immigrant so heartened by the success stories coming out of Germany that he wanted to make a personal contribution to his native land. This passion led him to join the German Society of Literature and Arts in the United States and to assume a leadership role in a New York pro-Nazi organization called the Friends of New Germany. U.S. officials first encountered Greibl in 1934 when, as convention chairman, he gave the opening speech before twenty thousand German Americans at a swastika-clad Madison Square Garden on German Day. He roused the audience with fiery rhetoric demanding that U.S. political leaders increase German representation in the government so that "within ten years all government offices will have Germans in them." At the end of his remarks he thrilled the screaming listeners by announcing that he would immediately send a cablegram to the "Great Awakener of the German people," referring to Hitler, pledging the audience's loyalty.[23]

The Yorkville section of Manhattan was one of the largest German colonies in the United States at the time, and German American physicians were a rare commodity. The high status accorded to Greibl in the community allowed him exceptional access to information that was not available to the average person. German immigrants living in the area preferred his medical services because he spoke their language, had a similar background and common cultural experiences, and shared their sense of pride over the successes of the new Germany. The strong doctor-patient bond contributed to patients' willingness to discuss personal issues that they would be unlikely to confide to an American doctor. Dr. Greibl exploited this relationship and gently pried into the private lives of his patients without raising any suspicions. Taking medical histories could prove very productive. Information about a patient's job, place of employment, capacity to pay medical bills, and, most important, attitudes, feelings, and loyalties toward Germany and the new Nazi leadership was easily elicited. Depending on the patient's potential value to German rearmament and access to valuable military information, a decision would be made whether to risk approaching that person for recruitment into the Abwehr espionage network.

One such agent recruited by Greibl was Christian F. Danielsen, a marine engineer living in Maine. Danielsen's forty-year residency in the United States and American citizenship were not enough to resist the lure of Greibl's approach. He agreed to work as an agent because he had children still living in Germany and "a more than nostalgic attachment to the old country." Employed at the Bath Iron Works in Bangor, Danielsen soon began supplying the Germans with secret blueprints of destroyers and other warships that the company was designing and building for the navy. Every month or so, he traveled to New York and personally delivered his cache of secrets to Greibl. In this careful yet deliberate manner, the Abwehr maintained a successful international military-industrial espionage organization with access to a wide variety of valuable technical information. The Greibl-Lonkowski ring was a diverse and highly effective group of spies that included, as one historian described it, a "Swiss born Captain in the United States Army who supplied details of new infantry weapons, a draftsman in a firm of naval architects in New York, a designer of guns in Montreal, an engineer in the metallurgical laboratory of the Federal Shipbuilding and Dry Dock Company at Kearny, New Jersey, contacts in the navy yards in Boston, and Newport News, Virginia and in a number of scattered aircraft factories."[24]

With the U.S. government oblivious to these losses between 1934 and 1940, the Abwehr's U.S.-based agents filched a steady stream of the latest technical advances coming off the industrial drawing boards. To illustrate the magnitude of these losses, one need only examine the period between January and July 1935. During these seven months, Abwehr agents delivered into German hands the plans for every plane built at the Sikorsky aircraft plant in Farmingdale, New York; blueprints for the FLG-2 and the SBU-1 carrier-based scout bomber under production by the Vought Company for the U.S. Navy; specifications for a bomber manufactured by the Boeing Company; and a plane produced by the Douglas Aircraft Corporation. Assorted classified U.S. Army maps, details of an anodizing process and certain military-related experiments with chromium, blueprints for three new navy destroyers, communication devices manufactured by the Lear Radio Corporation, and reports on tactical exercises being conducted by the navy at Mitchell Field in New York were also passed along.[25]

Lonkowski, Gudenberg, and Voss

The focus of the Rumrich interviews turned next to Lonkowski. Born in Silesia before the turn of the twentieth century, Lonkowski had been educated in German technical schools and served in the German army as an aircraft mechanic during the First World War. He held occasional postwar jobs in Germany's tiny aircraft industry before reentering the army, where his talents were quickly spotted by German military intelligence. As one of the few persons knowledgeable about airpower, his ability to move about Europe, studying foreign aircraft development, became critical. In 1922 he traveled to France using an alias to assess the state of aviation development there and returned to Germany with a large cache of valuable information. That success led to other foreign intelligence assignments and eventually to his most important Abwehr mission. In 1927, with a false passport and a new alias, Lonkowski was ordered to the United States to steal U.S. aircraft industry secrets. Topping the German wish list were new and more efficient airplane motors under commercial development and new propeller designs being tested by the Westinghouse Corporation.[26] After settling into a routine in the United States, Lonkowski was surprised to discover a benign counterintelligence environment. Government agents never questioned him, never inquired about his personal history, and showed no interest in his associates, his loyalties, or his comings and goings. In general, he found American industrial conditions rather inviting for an experienced, cautious, and enterprising spy. Lonkowski's aircraft technical skills were in great demand, and with no background investigation to worry about and no industrial security procedures in place to determine employee suitability, he soon obtained an entry-level technical position at the Ireland Aircraft Corporation on Long Island. His good work habits and common sense soon caught the attention of Ireland management, leading to a promotion to the personnel department, where he took control of the hiring and firing of workers. This allowed Lonkowski to plant two other Abwehr agents, whom he had recruited before leaving Germany, at the Ireland Corporation.[27]

Werner Georg Gudenberg and Otto Herman Voss reached the United States in 1928 and, thanks to Lonkowski, immediately started working at Ireland. However, three spies at the same location were unnecessary, so the small espionage ring gradually expanded. Thirty-three-year-old Gudenberg, a World War I veteran of the German army, obtained work at the Curtiss

Airplane and Motor Company in Buffalo, New York. Curtiss was conducting experimental research on lightweight aluminum airframes at the time. Voss, also thirty-three, had served in Finland and France during the war. After the armistice he spent another two years in the volunteer corps of the German army, followed by attendance at a technical school until 1922. He eventually settled in Baltimore, Maryland, where he worked for the Seversky Aircraft Company manufacturing airplane propellers for the U.S. Navy. Gudenberg and Voss sent their stolen military secrets to Lonkowski, who packaged them for transatlantic shipment via courier to Berlin. The success of this efficient little ring was remarkable. It had smuggled volumes of sensitive technical data to Germany by 1932, including the design for a "fireproof plane" and "the world's most advanced power air-cooled motor" under development for the army by the Wright Aeronautical Corporation. Also stolen were plans for a "pursuit plane said to be capable of 'landing either on a ship or on water' that were still on the drawing boards of the Curtiss Aeroplane and Motor Company."[28]

Having successfully completed his mission, Lonkowski was anxious to return home to Germany. He was set to sail for Europe on September 27, 1935, when he was detained by U.S. Customs Service officers, who had discovered material in his bags suggesting his involvement in espionage. Lonkowski was later released and returned to his home on Long Island when the documents were deemed to be inconsequential. Before authorities could get wise to his activities, Lonkowski contacted Greibl, who wasted no time taking him to Canada, where he anonymously boarded another ship bound for Europe.[29]

Glaser

Erich Glaser became the next focus of Turrou's attention. Born in 1909 in Leipzig, Germany, he immigrated to the United States in 1930 and joined the army fifteen months later. His military service record included a stint in the Panama Canal Zone, reenlistment in 1934, and another three years in the Philippines until his discharge in 1937. After only a short time as a civilian, Glaser reenlisted in January 1938 and served in the air corps at Mitchell Field until his arrest. Glaser and Rumrich originally met in the Panama Canal Zone, and he later lived with Rumrich and his wife for a time in the Bronx. As noted earlier, Rumrich identified Glaser as one of his agents and provided a full description of his espionage-related thefts. Faced with accusations of supplying highly sensitive cipher and code data to the Germans, Glaser made a complete confession.[30]

Hoffmann

Ten days after Rumrich's arrest, Johanna Hoffmann, the hairdresser-courier, arrived in New York City aboard the *Europa*. Turrou confronted her with Rumrich's accusations, along with incriminating letters addressed to Greibl found during a search of her belongings. Alone and trapped, Hoffmann too admitted spying for the Germans and described her role as a courier, carrying military secrets between Greibl and her intelligence bosses in Germany and delivering messages, money, and instructions on her return to the United States. She identified other crew members doing spy work and defended her activities, explaining that refusal to assist the Abwehr would have meant the loss of her job. Another letter found in Hoffmann's belongings was traced to one of Lonkowski's agents, Otto Voss.[31]

Having returned from Baltimore to the New York area, Voss was now working for the Sikorsky Airplane Company in Farmingdale. Turrou quickly located and interrogated Voss, who admitted his involvement in the spy ring and implicated additional participants, including Lonkowski and Carl Eitel, both of whom were safely in Germany.[32]

At the end of World War II, Eitel found himself interned at Camp 020 in England, where he was interrogated by British officials. His revelations offer insights into the Abwehr recruitment of German citizens for espionage. Eitel was born in Mulhouse, Germany, in 1900 and joined the German army toward the end of the First World War. Later as a civilian he held various midlevel hotel service positions in Germany and France before signing on as a wine steward aboard the Norddeutsche-Lloyd Lines' SS *Bremen* in 1928. Promotion to chief wine steward in the ship's Ritz Carleton Grill Room soon followed.[33] In the spring of 1930, Eitel was approached by a stranger aboard the ship who asked the steward to pick up some magazines, technical journals, and newspapers for him the next time he visited the United States. After months of collecting this material for the man, Eitel was given a "typewritten list of magazines, newspapers, and books which were more urgently required by his people." Included on this list were commonly available periodicals such as *Popular Mechanics, Popular Science,* and the *Army and Navy Journal,* which, Eitel later told his interrogators, were of interest to the Germans "since they disclosed advance information on technical developments in many spheres." Fully aware that he was being used to collect low-level intelligence, and seeing no harm in it, Eitel continued to follow orders. He even joined the Nazi Party and became a member of the *Bremen*'s political cell led by Wilhelm Boehnke, who held the rank of Orstgrupenfuhrer. The power of this position was clearly displayed when Eitel observed Boehnke, the ship's baker, summon the captain to his cabin for a confidential discussion.

Gradually the demands on Eitel shifted from acquiring publicly available magazines and journals to obtaining sensitive information bordering on espionage. Military fortifications and installations around the ports of Cherbourg and New York City—including commercial ship movements; types and numbers of aircraft, airfields, and seaplane bases; and warship movements—became Eitel's new targets. Realizing that his continued employment depended on his cooperation with the Abwehr, he later told his British interrogators that he reluctantly agreed to the new demands and set about acquiring the information through observation, conversation, and the purchase of public source material. On one trip home, Eitels' contact introduced him to Erich Pfeiffer, head of the Abwehr's Bremen station. After commending him on his success, Pfeiffer issued new orders: on future visits to New York, Eitel was to make every effort to "establish some contact . . . with an individual either serving in the U.S. Navy or having some indirect connection with it." Filled with dread, Eitel reluctantly accepted this new assignment because, as he told his interrogators, turning Pfeiffer down would have cost him his job. Collecting magazines and newspapers was one thing, but trying to convince Americans to spy on their country was a dangerous undertaking that he was neither equipped nor trained to do. Owing to fear, lack of skill, or both, Eitel never recruited an American spy. However, by 1935 he routinely carried messages, orders, and stolen secrets between Greibl, Lonkowski, Voss, and Gudenberg in New York and Pfeiffer in Bremen.[34]

Greibl Reappears

A few weeks later, concerned about what government investigators were learning about the spy ring and his role in it, Greibl appeared, unannounced, at the New York office of the FBI. Hoping to ingratiate himself with his interrogators, he began volunteering details of German espionage in the United States, his role in the conspiracy, and the structure and personalities of the setup. He began by describing the Deutsche-Americanische Berufagemeinschaft (DAB), the principal German bund organization in the United States. Originally an organization of German white-collar workers, the DAB was, in fact, a branch of the German Labor Front, which supervised practically all labor and professional associations in Germany. He also offered details surrounding the 1937 visit to the United States of Frederick ("Fritz") Wiedemann, a wartime comrade of Hitler and one of his three personal adjutants. The ostensible purpose of the trip was sightseeing and visiting old friends, but according to Greibl, Wiedemann's real mission was to meet with Fritz Kuhn, the leader of the German-American Bund. Wiedemann tried to dissuade Kuhn from demanding that German citizens living in the United States give up membership in the German-American Bund, which, in Greibl's view, constituted a large percentage of the organization's steadily increasing membership.

Professing complete innocence, yet faced with the collective accusations of Rumrich, Voss, Hoffmann, and Glaser, who identified him as the ring leader, Greibl slowly began conceding some involvement. "[I] never had anything to do with espionage activities," he told Turrou, "although certain curious circumstances had brought [me] in contact with a number of other people who appeared to be doing some work of the kind."[35] The more he talked, however, the more the particulars of his spying activities emerged. He provided additional details of Voss's espionage thefts, as well as the loss to German agents of valuable information from Kallmorgen Optical Company in Brooklyn, New York; Gibbs and Cox, a naval architecture company, and Sperry Gyroscope Company, both in New York City; and an unnamed shipbuilding company in Newport News, Virginia. Next, he identified a civilian naval employee named Agnes Driscoll, a woman unknown to the FBI, who had sold a "secret decoding device" to Germany for $7,000. The more he talked, the more Turrou suspected that, just as Rumrich had reported, Greibl was in fact the head of German military intelligence collection in the United States. Confronted with these suspicions and the FBI's awareness of his 1934 letter offering his services as a spy, Greibl prevaricated, evading direct responses while minimizing his involvement with partial and misleading admissions. Finally, Greibl acknowledged his assistance to German intelligence but claimed that it had only begun in January 1937, when he had sailed to Europe aboard the *Europa* with his mistress, Kay Moog. Karl Schleuter, the ship steward, had introduced him to Kapitan-Lieutenant Menzel and another crew member named von Bonin, and only later did he learn that both were Abwehr officers. Von Bonin was particularly interested in Moog, whom he brazenly encouraged to move from her home in New York City to Washington, D.C., rent an apartment there, and "become acquainted with various government officials from whom she would extract information." Further FBI questioning produced the names Karl Weigand and Karl Frederich Wilhelm Herman, the latter perhaps the most important conspirator identified by Greibl. Herman, as head of "the Gestapo in New York," would be available to assist Greibl whenever he was needed.[36]

Greibl found himself trapped by his own admissions and the growing mountain of evidence against him. Facing arrest, conviction, and a lengthy imprisonment, he began stalling for time to plan his next move. Securing the chief FBI investigator's trust by offering his assistance in the investigation was Greibl's only option, and the gullible Turrou accepted. Under Turrou's direction, Greibl learned details from Herman about German espionage in the United States, including that "Weigand" was a fictitious name for Theodor Scheutz, a steward aboard the Hamburg-America Lines' SS *New York*. Greibl also met with Dreschel of Hamburg-America, and their conversation, electronically recorded by the FBI in a New York City hotel room, produced even more information. Rumrich's arrest in February 1938 shocked the Abwehr, forcing a temporary halt to its transatlantic courier operations. Scheutz, at sea aboard the SS *New York,* abruptly left the ship at Havana, Cuba, after receiving a telegram from Germany warning him of the arrest.[37]

A search of Herman's residence produced a large cache of incriminating evidence, including the names of Rumrich and Voss. Armed with Greibl's evidence against Herman and Dreschel, Turrou interviewed both men, and they quickly confessed. Herman described his role and furnished the names of additional persons cooperating with the German intelligence services. Like Eitel, he too claimed that the Abwehr had forced him to cooperate and that failure to obey instructions would have meant the immediate loss of his job. Turning on Herman, Dreschel told his interrogators that he had been required to issue special passes in "very exceptional cases" that allowed the holder to board any German ship and gain access to any crew member after immigration officers had departed, permitting the safe acquisition and transmittal of secret information destined for Greibl or Germany.

Dreschel had also been ordered to allow Greibl to use Norddeutsche-Lloyd Lines' telegraph system for communicating with Pfeiffer in Bremen, and Dreschel's ship had been used to smuggle Abwehr agents in and out of the United States. One such instance involved the hasty departure of a person named "Spanknoebel," whom Dreschel described as the principal organizer of Nazi groups in the United States. He then ran off a list of German agents in the United States that included Wilhelm Boening, a machinist and New York resident, and Johann Baptiste Unkel, a spy who had already supplied the Abwehr with complete plans of military fortifications in the Panama Canal Zone. Boening was described as the head of the Ordnungsdienst, a uniformed Nazi militia group made up of about twenty thousand Americans of German origin, which conducted military-type drills throughout the United States.[38]

Collapse

Success followed success as Turrou, with seemingly no effort, gained admissions from practically everyone he interviewed. In the ninety days since the Rumrich arrest, he had assembled volumes of information concerning German espionage in the United States; spies were being identified on an almost daily basis, along with full descriptions of the huge quantities of military and industrial secrets lost to Germany. Turrou then made a tactical decision that drastically altered the direction of the case and created an unexpected publicity nightmare and public policy debacle for the FBI and the U.S. government.

Since joining the FBI ten years earlier, Turrou had served in a number of field offices and investigated a variety of criminal matters, including some high-profile cases. For instance, Turrou had found the ransom money paid by Charles Lindbergh in the kidnapping of his son in Bruno Richard Hauptmann's garage. Later, at Turrou's urging, Hauptmann had provided incriminating handwriting samples that were compared with and matched to the ransom note. Turrou was also assigned to investigate the machine gun slaying of gangster Frank Nash, two police officers, and an FBI agent outside the Kansas City train station on the morning of June 17, 1933—a shooting that became known around the world as the "Kansas City Massacre." Turrou's experience did not equip him, however, to understand foreign intelligence methods or the investigation of espionage. He approached the

German spy ring case like any conventional investigation. After assembling all the facts, he began informing the suspects that a grand jury would be convened on May 5, 1938, to examine all the charges and that each of them would be served with a subpoena, requiring their appearance to give testimony. When that date arrived, both FBI director Hoover and Lamar Hardy, the U.S. government's chief prosecutor in New York, were dismayed to learn that fourteen of the eighteen identified ring members had fled the country. The four who remained were those originally jailed in February. U.S. officials should not have been surprised; both Hoover and Turrou knew from Dreschel's admissions that German shipping lines and crews were under Abwehr orders to facilitate the escape of agents who found themselves in trouble.[39]

Gudenberg, Lonkowski's agent, escaped prosecution by stowing away on the Hamburg-America Lines' SS *Hamburg,* leaving a wife and child in the care of his brother-in-law in Bristol, Pennsylvania. Greibl turned up safely in Germany, where he publicly accused Turrou of misinforming him about the date of the grand jury, claiming that it had been rescheduled for May 12, 1938. Both Greibl and coconspirator Karl Schleuter stowed away on the SS *Bremen,* which departed for Germany on May 11, 1938; neither man ever returned to the United States.[40]

The initial success of the Rumrich-Greibl espionage investigation suddenly collapsed into a huge publicity disaster for the FBI's bumbling counterspies. The New York press laid the blame for the escape of the fourteen fugitive spies on Hoover's doorstep. Under the Roosevelt administration, Hoover and the FBI had skyrocketed to national fame. The federalization of crime fighting had thrust the Bureau into the American consciousness with headline-grabbing solutions to thousands of cases, including the kidnappings of prominent Americans, bank robberies, and extortion, not to mention the capture of glamorous fugitives. Hoover and his agents pursued scientific law enforcement and had achieved a national stature; they conveyed a polished image and the message that there was no crime the FBI could not solve. Now, behind the scenes, a different reality was unfolding. In spite of the mounting evidence of foreign espionage the Bureau had collected, FBI officials were acutely aware of how badly they had mishandled the case. Doctrine that had worked so successfully in the war against fugitives, bank robbers, and embezzlers during the 1930s had failed in this case. The FBI was now up against a very different investigative problem. With suspects disappearing and major newspapers serving up a daily dose of criticism, the staff at FBI headquarters began instituting efforts to better inform special agents in charge (SACs) about this new criminal phenomenon, as well as rank-and-file investigative agents. New training methods were needed, and it was hoped that this could begin with a nationwide SAC conference planned for the summer of 1938.

One FBI official, in an internal memorandum, described the new and unexpected challenge facing the FBI. This new adversary was "shrewd and cunning." Unlike the motivation of homegrown criminals, the goal of espionage agents was to assist "their native land," rather than the "financial remuneration obtained." As a consequence, "the investigation of an espionage case presents, to some extent, a different type of problem than is ordinarily encountered in other cases investigated by the Bureau."[41]

No less a figure than Reed Vetterli, SAC of the FBI's New York office and Turrou's boss, weighed in on the Bureau's poor performance. Vetterli was an experienced investigator and no stranger to major cases. He had moved up quickly through the ranks, working many cases throughout the country. In June 1935, serving as SAC of the Kansas City FBI office, he had been wounded during the Kansas City Massacre and later testified at the trial of the triggerman, Adam Richetti. The thirty-four-year-old Vetterli did not mince words in his critique of the FBI's performance, calling it a "rather feeble" effort consisting mainly of interviews and interrogations, followed by more interviews and interrogations. Such "precipitous" actions, he noted, seriously disadvantaged FBI investigators. They had acted only on what an interviewee knew or was willing to disclose, while at the same time providing the suspect with more information about the investigation than he originally knew. In effect, the FBI had relied mainly on the word of one suspected spy who turned on a coconspirator, rather than employing a full array of investigative tools to produce independent, verifiable evidence that could be used in court. Espionage agents, in Vetterli's view, were smart enough "to become citizens of the U.S. and claim allegiance to this country, when in reality . . . in a number of instances, this is all a sham and artifice and merely an effort to further allay our suspicion with respect to them." Then, risking the wrath of FBI headquarters for his honesty, he warned his Washington bosses that the German agents investigated in the Rumrich case had little regard for FBI prowess and "probably have laughed time and again at our efforts in connection with the instant case."[42]

For Hoover, 1938 was not shaping up as a banner year. In February personal tragedy struck when his mother, Annie, whom he had lived with and cared for since joining the Department of Justice twenty-one years earlier, suddenly died.[43] Now the FBI's first big espionage case, which had begun with such promise, was threatened with dismissal because Hoover's chief investigator had allowed fourteen of its principal subjects to escape right under his nose. And the loss of the spies was only the start of Hoover's nightmare. Adding to his woes was the embarrassing public revelation in June that Turrou had been dismissed from the FBI "with prejudice." The charge: violating the "G-man oath which binds all agents not to disclose any service information." Hoover learned that Turrou had been leaking information about the investigation to New York newspaper sources and had drafted a series of articles about the case for publication in the *New York Post*. Turrou's treachery infuriated Hoover, particularly because it violated a nondisclosure agreement the agent had signed years earlier upon entering FBI service. While the New York media frenzied over the flap, Hardy sought a court order enjoining the press from publicizing what one paper called the "authentic inside story" by the FBI's "former star G-man." For his part, Turrou challenged Hoover, denying that he had ever signed a nondisclosure agreement and claiming that he had every right to use information derived from an ongoing federal investigation for his own purposes. Simon Rifkind, Turrou's attorney, accused the government of a double standard concerning the publication of information about criminal cases, offering as evidence a book of "clippings from every newspaper in the city" and claiming that "one of the most prolific sources of news contained in these clippings was J. Edgar Hoover, who was Mr. Turrou's Chief."[44]

Adding to this already lively controversy were new accusations about Turrou and, by inference, the FBI during the ongoing prosecution of the four spies still in custody. George Dix, the attorney for Johanna Hoffmann, accused Turrou of accepting a bribe from Greibl in exchange for helping him slip out of the country—an accusation that Turrou was later forced to vigorously deny in a sworn affidavit.[45]

The Rumrich fiasco soon took on national proportions, making its way directly to the Oval Office. President Roosevelt had no choice but to weigh in on the matter when J. David Stern, publisher of the *New York Post,* sent him a letter on June 23, 1938, accusing the Department of Justice of muzzling the press and conspiring with his competitors to prevent the publication of Turrou's articles. "Rival newspapers and certain other interests," Stern warned the president, "have persuaded the Department of Justice to hold up the publication of a series of articles on Nazi espionage in this country." Yet in his opinion, "all of the important facts already have been printed in all newspapers. The specious plea has been presented that publication of these articles might obstruct justice."[46]

Speaking to a group of reporters in the Oval Office the next day, the president roundly criticized the press and, by implication, Stern, for their behavior in such a sensitive matter. Accusing the newspaper of questionable "patriotism and ethics" for signing a contract with Turrou, a "government employee" with access to privileged information garnered strictly through his work as a FBI agent, the president denounced the publication of the details of the case before a grand jury or a trial jury had heard the evidence.[47]

With the press screaming and the principal espionage suspects now in Europe, the Department of Justice and U.S. attorney Hardy took steps to repair some of the damage. In May, Hardy issued material witness arrest warrants for Boehnke, who had recruited Kay Moog, as well as couriers Walter Otto, Lutz Leiswitz, Johann Hart, and other ship crew members. Unfortunately, all of them had already fled to Europe. On June 2, 1938, the FBI arrested Heinrich Lorentz, captain of the Norddeutsche-Lloyd liner *Chemitz*, and Frans Friske, former captain of the Hamburg-America liner *Hindenburg*. Both were charged as material witnesses to espionage and jailed. By the next day, both had been released on $2,500 bail and soon escaped to Europe by ship, prompting Hoover to publicly point the finger of blame at Hardy for their disappearance.[48]

With the flight of Greibl, Gudenberg, Schleuter, Friske, Lorentz, and at least fourteen suspected agents, and with the successful prosecution of the few remaining suspects in jeopardy, Hardy decided on a desperate new tactic. He ordered the arrest of Maria Greibl, the doctor's wife, as a material witness, just as she was preparing to leave the country to join her husband in Germany. Having exhausted all options, but with no credible evidence against her, Hardy hoped to use her detention as leverage to prompt her husband's speedy return to the United States. But if Hardy thought that Mrs. Greibl, who was no stranger to controversy, would sit quietly in jail, he was badly mistaken. Five years earlier, George Medalie, then U.S attorney for New York, had ordered her to appear before a grand jury to explain why a certain German, who had come to the United States to organize support for Hitler, had been a house guest of the Greibls. She had brazenly refused, claimed that she was innocent of any wrongdoing, and publicly charged that she could not expect unbiased treatment from Medalie because he was Jewish. Mrs. Greibl showed the same grit this time. Claiming bewilderment over the accusations of spying, she announced publicly that her husband was an innocent man who had gone to Austria on family business and would return to the United States within the next three weeks. She summoned reporters to her jail cell and told them that her arrest was actually a "frame up by his [Dr. Greibl's] enemies," vowing that "nothing could turn [her] against him." She then portrayed herself as a victim of Hardy's incompetence and cruelty. In response to questioning, she told reporters that Dr. Greibl had been "hounded" by investigators and then speculated that if he were, in fact, in Germany, "there is no safer place for him."[49]

The publicity disaster for Hardy and Hoover continued when Seward Collins, editor of the *America Review,* joined the fight on Mrs. Greibl's behalf. Collins, a power in the New York publishing world, took on the Roosevelt administration directly by accusing the government of holding the doctor's wife "hostage" in its efforts to force his return to the United States—a practice that was tantamount to "torturing the relatives of accused persons as in Stalin's Russia." With an eye toward getting Mrs. Greibl's exclusive story, Collins secured her release from jail by personally putting up $50,000 bail on June 11, 1938. Collins was soon disappointed, however, for within days of her release, she too skipped bail and quietly boarded a ship bound for Europe.[50]

The Trial

The trial of the three remaining conspirators (Rumrich had already pleaded guilty)—Otto Voss, Erich Glaser, and Johanna Hoffmann—began on October 18, 1938, in the Federal Court Building in Manhattan and was front-page news for the next three days. Voss was charged with sketching and supplying information on the construction of aircraft wings, fuel and gasoline compartments, and bomb racks built at the Sikorsky Airplane Corporation in Farmingdale, New York. Hoffmann was accused of serving as a courier, transmitting "restricted code used for communication between military aircraft and its station." Glaser was charged with providing army and navy radio telephone-telegraph procedure manuals to the Abwehr.[51]

Insights into FBI knowledge of the extent and nature of German espionage in the United States acquired since the arrest of Rumrich can be gleaned, in part, from the testimony of witnesses during the trial. Hardy gave the opening statement for the government and accused Hoffmann,

Voss, and Glaser of enabling the "far-seeing eye" of the German government to infiltrate U.S. military and industrial research centers. After outlining the techniques used by the ring to steal information, he laid out for the jury the clever methods used to smuggle those secrets out of the country through couriers aboard transatlantic ships. The prosecution's first witness was Guenther Rumrich, who had made a deal with the government in exchange for his testimony. With rich detail, Hardy's star witness explained to a packed New York courtroom how he had volunteered his services to the Abwehr and the elaborate steps taken to contact him and sign him up as an agent. The jurors learned that Rumrich had been ordered to obtain genuine White House stationery so that it could be taken back to Germany and used to forge fictitious presidential orders requesting copies of the blueprints of the *Enterprise,* the country's newest aircraft carrier. The important role of shipboard agents was also explained to the enthralled jury. Their duties were not limited to carrying secrets back and forth across the Atlantic; these German agents also opened sealed transatlantic mailbags using sophisticated techniques. Each piece of mail underwent careful examination, and any information of value was recorded and passed on to German military and political planners. The letters and packages were then resealed so that the recipients would be unaware that any tampering had occurred. Led by Hardy's careful questioning, Rumrich testified that his intelligence chief often bragged that the Abwehr had spies in all U.S. aircraft plants and that their list of achievements was extensive. Among the information obtained were a navy signal code used to communicate between the fleet and land batteries, the number of coast artillery regiments stationed in the Panama Canal Zone, secret and confidential military booklets, the army mobilization and defense plans for units on the East Coast of the United States, and much more.[52]

The two-month trial had its humorous moments. In another stinging jab at the FBI's already sagging counterespionage reputation, the German government arrogantly dismissed any concern over the matter, claiming that the Americans themselves had little concern. A German foreign ministry spokesman publicly claimed that his government viewed the entire issue with "equanimity," adding that the Americans "have no great enthusiasm over the spy case because the very man who dug up the information on which the charges were based since has tried to sell his story for publication" (referring to Turrou). Next it was George Dix, Hoffmann's attorney, who went after the FBI and Turrou. He called the already discredited agent to testify as a defense witness. Dix's strategy was to cast his client as the victim and Turrou as the overreaching government investigator interested only in enriching himself from the sale of his story. Under withering and often embarrassing questioning, the former FBI agent was repeatedly forced to defend himself against accusations of conducting flawed investigations, tampering with witnesses, and accepting bribes from Greibl. If this did not leave Turrou sufficiently demoralized, Dix had one more trick up his sleeve. After finishing with Turrou, Hoffmann's attorney surprised the packed courtroom by calling a new witness to the stand to attack the former FBI agent's credibility. This witness offered no new information that was relevant to the case but stunned everyone by publicly accusing Leon Turrou, the FBI's star G-man, of being an impostor. The witness testified that he knew Turrou as "Leon Petrov." Furthermore, before the First World War, the man he knew as Petrov had undergone treatment in the psychiatric ward at Kings County Hospital in New York City. Then, with Turrou's accuser sitting in the witness chair and his chilling accusations still hanging in the air, the trial judge, over Hardy's vigorous objections, allowed Dix to enter Petrov's psychiatric file into evidence. Summoning his finest theatrical skills, Dix then read aloud many of the file's most sensational details, making certain that he emphasized Petrov's final diagnosis as "undifferentiated depression."[53]

After six weeks of testimony, 3,500 pages of transcripts, and the introduction of 195 evidentiary exhibits, the three hapless German spies were convicted and sentenced to prison. Voss received the harshest sentence—a six-year term; Hoffmann got four years in prison, and Glaser was sentenced to two years. Rumrich—perhaps the greediest, most venal, and most impulsive of the group, and the one who, in the end, brought down the ring—received a mere two years in prison in consideration for his testimony.[54]

CHAPTER TWO

A Look Back

The FBI investigation of German espionage that had begun so promisingly with Rumrich quickly collapsed into a theatrical farce, played out daily for the entire world to witness. After six years of headline-grabbing arrests of dangerous gangsters, kidnappers, murderers, bank robbers, and corrupt politicians, Hoover suddenly saw his image of invincibility fading on the international stage. Why did Hoover's new tactics and investigative doctrine of scientific law enforcement, introduced with such fanfare, produce such poor results? The investigation was a high priority for the FBI, with a large cadre of special agents in the New York office working on the case. During the case's six-month life, the FBI discovered information about German espionage tactics, assessed the huge loss of critical military and industrial secrets acquired by the Germans, uncovered and caught numerous ring members, and developed leads on other potential spies in the United States and around the world. Why, then, did so many of the conspirators escape right under Hoover's nose, leaving the FBI with only a few unfortunate, low-level simpletons holding the bag when the trial began in the fall of 1938?

Military Intelligence Division

With U.S. entry into the First World War, the U.S. Army experienced its largest buildup ever. From just under 98,000 members in 1914, the Regular Army ballooned to 4 million by war's end. The need for an improved and robust military intelligence capability was reflected in this wartime expansion. During the years leading up to the First World War, the Military Intelligence Division (MID) of the War Department's General Staff had steadily declined in skill, importance, and quality of personnel and intelligence output. Until the middle of the first decade of the twentieth century, the MID had a reputation as a small but independent segment of the General Staff that produced first-rate information for military planners. During the nation's westward expansion, the MID took the initiative by ordering adjutant generals of the states and territories to provide Washington with up-to-date information on National Guard and militia units under their command. The attaché system was established in 1889, with trained officers initially assigned to five European capitals: St. Petersburg, Vienna, Berlin, London, and Paris. Each had specific orders concerning what information to look for and send back to Washington. By the start of the Spanish-American War in 1898, the MID had twenty officers assigned to headquarters; these officers examined the reports of sixteen attachés and another forty intelligence officers assigned to the militia. The MID's assessment contained exact figures on the number of Spanish soldiers in Cuba, as well as a complete picture of the island's Spanish fortifications. Years later, President Theodore Roosevelt, wary of Japan's growing ambitions in Asia, ordered daily MID reports on that country's worldwide movements. The MID, in turn, produced useful intelligence in support of the United States' "Great White Fleet"—a round-the-world cruise of naval vessels dispatched by Roosevelt as a display of U.S. sea power. It also started an aggressive program that produced high-quality maps of the world for War Department use before the outbreak of the First World War.[1]

A turning point in MID fortunes began in mid-1907, when the War Department began a bureaucratic shuffle that quickly stalled any progress the MID had made over the preceding decades. With the relocation of the War College Division (WCD) from a site near War Department headquarters (now the Old Executive Office Building, adjacent to the White House) to the Washington Barracks (now Fort Leslie J. McNair), the MID began a rapid decline. Because the WCD was so dependent on MID-produced maps, charts, and graphs, a decision was made to colocate the MID with the WCD. Concerned army officers who supported an autonomous intelligence structure launched vigorous protests, charging that the new structure would result in the MID becoming a function of the WCD. They insisted that the MID retain its independence so that its product could be readily available to wider War Department components, the White House, and the Navy and State Departments. These complaints were swept aside, and within months, the WCD and MID were merged into one unit—an unworkable arrangement that soon resulted in a significant curtailment of information collection during the decade before the war.[2]

Eleven years later, the situation had changed very little for the MID. Despite the efforts of many of the military's best and brightest officers—including Colonel Ralph Van Deman, a Harvard graduate and the man considered the father of military intelligence—to convince the General Staff of the importance of an independent MID in modern warfare, it still languished as an army backwater. So serious was this problem that General Peyton March commented on it when he became chief of staff in 1918. Oddly, by that time, the MID had become an independent division again, and the military intelligence situation had improved somewhat, necessitated by U.S. involvement in the war in Europe. Nevertheless, March noted that the MID was still considered an "unimportant section of the General Staff." He complained that "every other army of importance in the world had a General Staff division devoted to gathering military intelligence, and on a par with the other General Staff functions of military plans, operations and supply." Mincing no words, a bewildered March complained that the United States had entered the First World War with an MID staff of "two officers and two clerks," and he described the situation as "unbelievable."[3]

By war's end, the MID had grown in size to 282 officers, 29 sergeants, and nearly 1,000 civilians. This staff provided information for War Department purposes and at the same time covered "the world in furnishing information to the State Department, the Department of Justice, and other government departments and bureaus and war boards." These numbers, however, are somewhat misleading, because they fail to reflect the actual number of career officers assigned to the MID. In fact, during the war the MID never had more than six regular officers working there at any one time. The remainder were drawn from civilians commissioned as officers in the Regular Army only for the war's duration.[4]

Security and counterintelligence (also known as negative intelligence) became important functions of the wartime MID. Colonel Van Deman, who had assumed command of the MID in 1915, established a strong security apparatus in response to growing complaints in 1917 about acts of foreign espionage, subversion, and sabotage that were reportedly occurring throughout the United States. In the wake of the frenzied anti-German sentiment gripping the nation, dozens of private superpatriotic organizations sprang up, devoted to chasing spies, anarchists, saboteurs, and industrial agitators. Van Deman recognized the considerable benefit to the army in these efforts, and he supported the consolidation of such groups under an umbrella organization known as the American Protective League (APL). Later, he coordinated their efforts, even providing groups with confidential MID-produced reports and distributing often unverified APL reports to other governmental agencies.[5]

By the end of the war, the United States was exhausted and wanted a return to normalcy. In 1920 Congress passed the National Defense Act, which drastically reduced the Regular Army to only 280,000 and the National Guard force to 445,000. With the army once again truncated, intelligence gathering was soon forgotten. By 1920 the MID had withered to 80 officers and 160 civilians. This reduction was largely due to congressional action, but the MID's blemished reputation—caused by public backlash over its close ties to APL excesses and its role in the mass arrests of aliens suspected of Communist affiliation and radical agitation authorized by Attorney General A. Mitchell Palmer (the Palmer Red Raids)—also played a role. The MID once again became a meaningless army backwater that was avoided by talented and ambitious officers. In an army where promotions became increasingly rare, career officers viewed intelligence assignments as dead-end jobs; the MID was a "second-class citizen" in the army structure and a "dumping ground" for poor performers. Cuts were so severe that by 1936 it had dwindled in size and importance to a mere 18 officers, no enlisted personnel, 48 civilians, and a budget of $87,000.[6]

The ultimate insult was yet to come. General John J. Pershing, who led U.S. forces in Europe during the First World War, became the army chief of staff in 1920. The army was made up of nine corps areas in the United States, Hawaii, the Philippines, and Panama, with four principal divisions within the General Staff. By law, each division was commanded by an assistant chief of staff with the rank of brigadier general. Pershing, however, envisioned a five-division staff made up of Personnel, Intelligence, Operations and Training, Supply, and War Plans. The economy-minded Congress authorized Pershing's five-part system but sidestepped its own law by failing to appropriate funds for an additional brigadier general slot. With five divisions and only four brigadier generals authorized, the MID was once again reduced in status: for the next two decades, it would be commanded by a lieutenant colonel. The MID's security and counterespionage components experienced the severest consequences. Army counterintelligence went out of business completely when the countersubversion squad was disbanded in 1920 and the Negative Intelligence Branch of the MID, which supervised and conducted army counterintelligence investigations, was eliminated in 1921. It would not reemerge until eighteen years later—five months before the new war in Europe exploded.[7]

Office of Naval Intelligence

The Office of Naval Intelligence (ONI), the intelligence arm of the U.S. Navy, was formed in 1882. For the next seventeen years it collected, collated, and distributed information for the use of war planners without a formal budget or congressional authorization. Its primary purpose during these years was the promotion of naval expansion by alerting lawmakers to advances being made by foreign navies. The handful of attachés assigned to major foreign capitals began acquiring blueprints, technical reports, articles, and equipment specimens in an effort to convince policy makers of the need to convert the U.S. Navy from an antiquated fleet of wooden sailing vessels to a high-tech fleet of steam-powered steel ships. The United States' smashing victory over the Spanish navy during the Spanish-American War confirmed the ONI's value and encouraged the passage in 1899 of legislation making it a formal organization within the navy bureaucracy. A year later, in the lingering euphoria of victory, it merged with the Naval War College and the Secretary of the Navy's General Board, forming a primitive version of the Office of Chief of Naval Operations. However, with modern warships a reality, Spain defeated, and President Theodore Roosevelt (an aggressive supporter of naval expansion) out of office, the ONI experienced a severe decline because of dwindling interest in new naval technologies and war planning intelligence.[8]

The increased demands of World War I once again propelled the ONI to the forefront of naval planning. ONI staffers were the first to recognize the threat in Europe and urge preparedness on navy leadership. The war also forced the ONI to enter the new world of counterespionage. Although its primary duty was the collection of information in support of war planners, the ONI was also responsible for protecting the navy from foreign espionage. This new function got a jump-start when Congress passed President Woodrow Wilson's legislation authorizing the ONI to pursue spies, saboteurs, and subversives by using surveillance, informants, wiretapping, surreptitious entries, code breaking, and the opening of mail. Operating with few precedents, vague or nonexistent policies, and little direction from navy brass, ONI investigators often went far beyond traditional boundaries. Like the MID, the ONI, in furtherance of its mission of protecting the military, routinely intruded on the lives of civilians—both U.S. citizens and aliens—who were suspected of threatening the nation's internal security through anarchism and radical political activities. The ONI's small cadre of regular officers was augmented with 3,000 reserve officers, volunteers, and enlisted personnel, who, in the view of one historian, "tended to view intelligence with less restraint than regular officers."[9]

ONI investigators followed hundreds of suspected radicals, including the prominent socialist John Reed and his wife, even stealing documents from them dealing with the Bolshevik Revolution. The leadership and members of the radical Industrial Workers of the World (IWW), known as the Wobblies, were also targets of ONI investigations. Unfortunately, the poorly trained and ill-equipped ONI and MID personnel, many with no investigative background, often produced unverified reports filled with wild speculation that were nevertheless routinely distributed throughout the government. In one case, a vague informant report supplied by the MID to Rear Admiral Albert Parker Niblack, director of the ONI, alleged a nationwide terrorist plot led by prominent radicals Emma Goldman, Mollie Steiner, Alexander Berkman, Jack Abrams, and "several other Anarchists." Characterizing his source as "reliable," Niblack warned other navy commands that the terrorists were a collection of German and Russian Jews, Mexican bandits, IWW subversives, and a Japanese "master spy" named Kato Kamato and that their plot would "surpass anything that ever happened in this country."[10]

At its peak during the war, the ONI had 306 officers assigned to its headquarters in Washington with another 500 working at the branch office in New York City. Repeating the cycle that had followed the Spanish-American War, the postwar navy was again reduced, as new priorities focused on economy and budget restraints. Within two years of the armistice, only 42 officers remained at the ONI, with many facing imminent detachment; operational budgets were also materially cut. Ship commanders were ordered to drastically reduce intelligence collection and limit expenditures to no more than $15 per month. By 1931 the ONI had been reduced even further, with a staff of 18 naval and marine officers and 38 civilians—a complement that one historian described as "barely adequate for routine work."[11]

Captain Luke McNamee took command of the ONI in 1923. A highly intelligent and shrewd officer, McNamee set out to reverse the decline in naval fortunes by linking the importance of a robust sea power to the growth and prosperity of the U.S. economy in the 1920s. Writing in the May 1923 edition of the *Proceedings of the Naval Institute*, he resurrected the theses of the great nineteenth-century naval theorist Alfred Thayer Mahan, arguing for a strong navy that would support the growing commerce and international trade of U.S. companies. Published on the heels of the recently completed Washington Naval Conference, convened to solve the escalating international naval race, McNamee's article criticized government officials and civilians for their "Alice in Wonderland thinking" and for trying to strip the nation of a navy that could protect its vital commerce. He then accused these unidentified persons of treasonous behavior, charging that Bolshevism was influencing their demands for reductions in the navy. McNamee warned readers that he was repeating "no idle rumor, when I tell you that much of this propaganda has a sinister foreign source, its object the overthrow of our government and the ultimate dictatorship of the proletariat."[12]

Six years later, retired naval intelligence officer Captain Dudley Wright Knox, who had served as head of the ONI's naval library and historical archives for years, picked up on McNamee's theme in another article in the *Proceedings*. Knox, whose influence on the ONI and naval intelligence policy was significant, wrote about sinister foreign influences burrowing into American life spreading pacifism, subversion, and harmful influences on naval preparedness. "From what has been set forth it is clearly indicated that large sums of money are being spent by many powerful organizations in which foreigners play a prominent role to propagandize the country through the press, the church, the stage, the movie, the schools and colleges, the lecture platforms, and virtually every agency of communication."[13]

With McNamee and Knox providing the philosophical underpinnings, the ONI set out to prove that the signers of the Washington Naval Treaty, particularly the Japanese, were violating its provisions. It was this search that drove their intelligence and counterintelligence efforts during the late 1920s and 1930s. In a poorly coordinated and somewhat haphazard fashion, the ONI used a variety of secretive means, including informants, undercover agents, banking sources, and illegal surreptitious entries—all in the hope of acquiring proof to support the contention that more resources were needed for naval preparedness.

Observation of pacifist and anarchist groups intensified, including organizations such as the Bonus Marchers, the Communist Party of America, the National Council for Prevention of War, the National Federation of Churches, and the Women's League for Peace and Freedom. Captain Haynes Ellis, who took over as head of the ONI in 1931, mobilized every available resource, including intelligence officers, volunteer informants, retired officers, vigilante societies, and professors of naval sciences on college campuses such as Yale, Georgia Tech, Harvard, and Northwestern to spy on "ultra-pacifist" students.[14]

Nightly break-ins became a routine feature of local ONI intelligence and counterintelligence collections in the 1920s and 1930s. These local operations, which were often haphazard and poorly coordinated with headquarters, were generally lacking in an overall national strategic purpose or objective as well. Targets included foreign diplomatic establishments, along with the homes and offices of American citizens and aliens alike. In one case the ONI received information that a Japanese spy had entered New York City to steal the navy's aeronautical secrets. Using techniques developed during the First World War, ONI agents broke into a series of private offices and ransacked luggage, searching for signs of the mysterious agent. A safe was cracked at the Japanese consulate in New York in the hope of acquiring codebooks and evidence of Japanese espionage in the United States. For five consecutive nights in September 1929, ONI agents, accompanied by two detectives, two photographers, a locksmith, and a lookout, broke into the office of the Japanese inspector of naval machinery in New York City. Throughout the night they photographed documents from the safe and then left the office and the safe's contents just as they had found them. The photographs revealed the latest Japanese military aircraft, artillery shells, and codebooks. ONI agents also entered the headquarters of the Communist Party of America, and many similar operations were conducted in San Francisco, South America, and the Panama Canal Zone.[15]

The ONI routinely cooperated with the FBI on a case-by-case basis in counterespionage matters. In 1935 Lieutenant Cecil H. Coggins, a young medical officer assigned to the naval dispensary at Long Beach, California, also worked informally for the ONI's local district intelligence officer. Coggins had long suspected that Japanese naval officers, assigned to the United States as English language students, were using financial inducements to obtain military secrets. After some investigation, Coggins discovered that a former navy yeoman, Harry Thomas Thompson, had sold top-secret engineering, gunnery, and other critical data to an unknown agent of the Japanese Imperial Navy. The ONI, with the assistance of the local FBI office and the local police, mounted its "first real counterespionage investigation" in an effort to prove Thompson's guilt, locate the original source of the data, and identify the recipient of the material. The recipient was Toshio Miyazaki, a language student and Japanese naval officer. The investigation failed to uncover who provided the data to Thompson, and Miyazaki fled the country and escaped prosecution. As for Thompson, who was a civilian and not under navy jurisdiction, he was arrested by the FBI, convicted of espionage in 1937, and imprisoned at the McNeil Island Federal Penitentiary.[16]

Another case of ONI-FBI cooperation involved a former naval officer named John Semer Farnsworth. A graduate of the U.S. Naval Academy, Farnsworth had been dismissed from the navy in 1926 for begging from enlisted men to support his inflated lifestyle. After years of anonymity, Farnsworth suddenly turned up at naval bases on the West Coast, where he reestablished connections with old shipmates still on active duty. This time there was no financial desperation. In fact, it was just the opposite; Farnsworth flaunted his success by flashing rolls of money and picking up dinner tabs. An ONI investigation began when an old friend reported that their innocent conversations had shifted to probing questions about new warship designs, weapons, and tactics. Even more ominous were Farnsworth's odd requests to borrow code and signal books, blueprints, maps, and other secret Navy Department information. Because the navy had no legal jurisdiction over Farnsworth, who had been a civilian for the past eleven years, the ONI and FBI teamed up to investigate his activities. After months of surveillance, nothing meaningful was uncovered. Farnsworth, however, learned of the investigation, began drinking heavily, and, in a moment of panic, contrived a ploy to save himself: he told a local newspaper reporter that he was actually a double agent for the United States. The journalist reported Farnsworth to the ONI, and the FBI arrested him; he was convicted in federal court on February 26, 1937, for passing national defense information to the Japanese government and sentenced to a term in the Atlanta Federal Penitentiary.[17]

Bombs

In early 1919 the Bureau of Investigation (BOI), the forerunner of the modern-day Federal Bureau of Investigation, uncovered a plot to assassinate President Woodrow Wilson after his return from the Versailles Peace Conference. Fourteen Spaniards from New York City and Philadelphia, calling themselves Groupa Pro Prenza, were identified and arrested by the U.S. Secret Service. On May 1, 1919, a series of violent marches occurred in London and Berlin, celebrating the Communist Internationale; there was also some serious rioting in Paris, Buenos Aires, Cleveland, Boston, and New

York City. More disturbing was the discovery of mail bombs designed to detonate at their destination. The premature detonation of a device mailed to U.S. Senator Thomas Hardwick of Georgia, which severely injured an employee, and the discovery of another delivered to Seattle Mayor Ole Hanson spawned a massive nationwide investigation that uncovered an additional twenty-nine bombs moving through the mails. Addressees included prominent Americans from every walk of life. Targeted government officials included Supreme Court Justice Oliver Wendell Holmes, who had written opinions sustaining the convictions of radical labor agitators; Secretary of Labor William B. Wilson, who oversaw immigration matters; Anthony Caminetti, commissioner general of the Immigration Service; Senator Lee Overman, chairman of a committee investigating radical activities; and Representative John L. Burnett, chairman of the House Immigration Committee. Others targets were Frank Nebeker, special assistant to the attorney general; international financiers J. P. Morgan and John D. Rockefeller; William M. Wood, president of the American Woolen Company of Massachusetts; and Frederick Bullmers, editor of the *Daily News* of Jackson, Mississippi.[18]

A month later, more powerful bombs designed to explode at the residences of the intended victims were discovered by authorities. Nine of these devices actually made it to their destinations and detonated. An explosion occurred on the front steps of Attorney General Palmer, killing the bomber. Another killed a watchman in front of the home of Judge Charles C. Notts of the General Sessions Court, who had sentenced two men in connection with a plot to bomb St. Patrick's Cathedral in New York. Other targets included Judge W. P. Thompson of Pittsburgh, who had presided over the trial of labor activist Carlo Tresca; Max Gold, a silk manufacturer from Patterson, New Jersey; and Representative Leland W. Powers from Massachusetts. Leaflets found at the bombing sites revealed that the attacks were politically motivated. Entitled "Plain Words" and signed simply "The Anarchist Fighters," they warned that there "will have to be bloodshed; we [will] not dodge; there will have to be murder; we will kill because it is necessary; there will have to be destruction; we will destroy to rid the world of your tyrannical institutions."[19]

William J. Flynn, director of the BOI, took charge of the nationwide investigation. He convened a conference of police chiefs and detectives from around the country to develop a coordinated investigative approach. The plan decided on was twofold: investigators would monitor the organizations and individuals suspected of involvement, and they would examine the physical evidence recovered at the crime scenes in an attempt to identify the bombers. Flynn's investigation eventually led to the identification of various Italian groups, including the El Arieto Society, with a membership of approximately 12, and the L'era Nuovo Group, with 25 members; the 10,000-member Communist Labor Party; the Communist Party of America, with 40,000 members; the Union of Russian Workers, numbering 4,000 members; and the IWW, with 300,000 members.[20]

General Intelligence Division

Following the discovery of the mail bombs and the bombing of Palmer's Georgetown home, investigations of anarchists and radicals intensified throughout the country. A major step in this effort was the Department of Justice's establishment of a records system containing detailed information on radicals and anarchists for intelligence purposes and later use in prosecutions. Palmer assigned direction of the project to his special assistant, J. Edgar Hoover, on August 20, 1920.[21]

Hoover created what later became known as the General Intelligence Division (GID) of the Department of Justice by reconstituting old files collected on Germans opposed to U.S. entry into the First World War and adding new records on radicals and potential anarchists collected by major police departments around the country. The GID eventually comprised more than 150,000 index cards containing a wide variety of detailed information. There were cards on persons, organizations, societies, publications, and associations that posed potential threats. The index system was broken down alphabetically and geographically, to identify "social conditions existing in certain localities." A card was prepared for each major U.S. city containing the names of key organizations and their principal officers. The cards were updated continually, offering the Department of Justice a current assessment of the changing situation throughout the country.[22]

Later the GID added records of international movements and international economic disturbances. It included data on prominent anarchists; political movements such as the Communist Party of the United States, the Communist Labor Party, and the Union of Russian Workers; and major labor disruptions such as the steel and coal strikes of 1919. Biographic sketches were kept on all authors, publishers, and editors with radical connections, expanding the GID files to 250,000 information-filled cards. Foreign-language newspapers, journals, and books from twenty-seven countries, including Italy, France, Romania, Lithuania, and Portugal—"particularly noticeable for [their] strong radical leanings"—were also cataloged. Information on African Americans agitating for improved political and economic rights was also accumulated; prominent figures such as W. E. B. DuBois, an early leader of black nationalism, were singled out by Hoover as a "major menace" to the status quo.[23]

Harlan Fiske Stone

At Plymouth Notch, a sleepy little farming village in central Vermont, Vice President Calvin Coolidge and his wife, Grace Anne, were vacationing at his family home. Early in the morning of August 2, 1923, his father awakened him with news that would change his life forever. President Warren G. Harding had died of a stroke during the night while traveling in California. Coolidge got up, dressed quickly, and walked across town to a local store, where he telephoned Charles Evans Hughes, Harding's secretary of state. Hughes offered Coolidge further details of Harding's death and then urged him to take the oath of office as soon as possible. The vice president then walked back home, where his father, a justice of the peace, swore him in as the thirtieth president of the United States. As momentous as the morning's events were, Coolidge's first presidential act was to return to bed.

Coolidge needed his sleep, because the cabinet team he inherited was a cauldron of graft and corruption. Harding's own personal flaws were legendary. His wealthy wife, Florence, was reportedly responsible for forging his political career during their long and often stormy marriage. She regularly competed with other women for her husband's attention. Harding had several romantic affairs, including a relationship with Nan Britton, a woman thirty years his junior, that produced a child. Harding's political judgments were equally questionable. As the newly elected president in 1920, he had surrounded himself with unqualified advisers who had little or no knowledge of government. As one critic noted, Harding preferred his "best friend" to the "best man" for the job. Secretary of the Interior Albert B. Fall went to federal prison for accepting bribes in exchange for awarding leases of the naval oil reserves at Teapot Dome, Wyoming. Edwin N. Denby, the secretary of the navy, resigned in disgrace for consenting to the transfer of the oil reserves. Last to go was another presidential crony from Ohio, Attorney General Harry Daugherty, Harding's campaign manager. Coolidge dismissed him in March 1924 on the eve of a congressional investigation of his shady financial relationship with Prohibition violators and his own involvement in the Teapot Dome affair. Reestablishing public confidence in governmental integrity and Republican Party leadership became the dominant theme of Coolidge's first year as president.

A key appointment was the selection of Harlan Fiske Stone as Daugherty's replacement. Coolidge's new attorney general had a background similar to the president's. He was a fellow Yankee and a Republican, born on October 11, 1872, in the little village of Chesterfield, Vermont. Like the president, Stone attended Amherst College, graduating Phi Beta Kappa. In 1898 he graduated from Columbia University Law School and entered law practice in New York City. At heart, however, Stone was a teacher and a jurist, with little interest in legal fees, clients, and litigation. This would explain the year he spent after law school teaching high school history in Brooklyn and his continuing relationship with Columbia, first as an adjunct professor, then as a full-time faculty member, and finally his prestigious appointment in 1910 as the law school's dean. Years later, when asked why he had chosen to serve as Coolidge's attorney general rather than accepting a lucrative offer from a prominent New York City law firm, he replied, "I am interested in the law. Money, as money, does not particularly appeal to me."[24]

Stone's liberal views on the issue of immigration and aliens frequently brought him into conflict with his Columbia University colleagues, particularly his boss Nicholas Murray Butler, chancellor of the university. Stone and Butler, who differed widely on the connection between the law and social conditions, often battled about the law's impact on immigrant groups. In the words of one person who knew them both, Stone always "cherished an exceedingly low opinion" of Columbia's chancellor. They often disagreed over academic freedom and in one instance were at loggerheads over Butler's belief that the political persuasion and patriotism of law professors should be factors in making tenure decisions.[25]

Stone was first propelled onto the national stage when he served on a board of inquiry established in the spring of 1918 to examine liberalized policies toward conscientious objectors in the wake of the recently passed Selective Service Act. Butler considered all conscientious objectors "cowards, slackers and half-wits." Stone, in contrast, was a realist who believed that although some would use objection to war as an excuse to evade military service, there were others with genuine moral and religious convictions. After interviewing more than 350 conscientious objectors housed at Fort Leavenworth, Kansas, he recommended clemency for 150 "without delay" and the release of most of the remainder "in a reasonable time and certainly as soon as peace is declared." In 1920 he threw his prestige behind the National Popular Government League, which dedicated itself to denouncing governmental actions in the so-called Palmer Red Raids. In a letter to Congress that demanded an investigation into the actions of the Department of Justice, Stone acknowledged the government's right to deport aliens but questioned Palmer's belief that aliens have no rights under U.S. law. The "undisputed facts," according to Stone, were that agents of the BOI had violated the "express provisions" of federal statutes by arresting aliens without warrants. Any system, he feared, that gave government the power to "restrain [the] liberty of individuals without proper safeguards like those which exist in criminal cases" and "without adequate authority for judicial review of the action of the administrative officer risks abuse of power and intolerable injustice and cruelty to individuals."[26]

Then, for the first time in the nation's history, Stone introduced a new concept concerning aliens. He asserted that an alien who has been admitted to the United States by the immigration authorities was "a person" within the United States and therefore "entitled to the protection of the due process of law guaranteed by the Constitution to persons in the United States." The only logical conclusion, in his opinion, was a "firm but impartial adherence to the law by those in authority, and ceaseless and untiring efforts to educate and enlighten these men and especially the class to whom they make their appeal together with the fullest discussion and most searching analysis of the doctrines which they preach." Stone's letter prompted a firestorm in Washington. Senator Smith Brookhart of Iowa pushed through a resolution bearing his name ordering a congressional investigation into Department of Justice abuses. As part of the investigation, Brookhart demanded that Attorney General Daugherty turn over politically damaging documents, including those related to the attorney general's own shady dealings with Fall and Denby.[27]

Among Stone's first priorities as attorney general was reforming the BOI. Since its formation in 1908, it had been riddled with cronyism, nepotism, and overall incompetence, routinely serving the political interests of the Harding administration by investigating the activities of its opponents and covering up the questionable behavior of administration officials. There were no professional or educational standards for the selection of investigators, and it was not uncommon for drunkards, relatives of politicians in need of a job, incompetents, and even some with criminal backgrounds to serve in BOI ranks.[28]

The first step was removal of its colorful director, William Burns, chosen by Daugherty in 1921 as Flynn's replacement. Burns's qualifications for the job included his Republican Party connections, his boyhood friendship with Daugherty, his ownership of the William J. Burns International Detective Agency, strong lobbying by corporate clients, and a lengthy record of questionable tactics used against organized labor. Later, as director of the BOI, Burns reinforced his antilabor credentials by swearing before Congress that the domestic labor disturbances of the early 1920s were Communist inspired and instigated by Moscow. Information that Burns supplied to the State Department concerning Moscow-backed agitation in the United States was instrumental in curtailing diplomatic recognition of the new Soviet state. Burns also conspired with Daugherty to intimidate Harding administration critics through intrusive investigations. Senator Burton K. Wheeler of Montana was investigated for representing a private client before a federal agency, a charge that culminated in Wheeler's indictment. The case was universally viewed as a frame-up, and the facts were aired out at Wheeler's trial, where the jury issued Daugherty and Burns a stinging rebuke by declaring the senator not guilty.[29]

Stone chose J. Edgar Hoover as acting director of the BOI on May 10, 1924—the day after he fired Burns. The attorney general knew little about Hoover except that he had served in the Department of Justice as an attorney since July 1917, had been a special assistant to the attorney general, and had been reassigned as Burns's secretary and executive assistant in August 1921 as part of a Daugherty-directed shake-up. As an interim appointment, until the attorney general could find a permanent director, Hoover was required to report directly to Stone. The next day, Stone gave Hoover his instructions, with reformation of the BOI at the top of the priority list. Stone set down his demands in a six-point document that would serve as Hoover's "North Star" for the next fifteen years. Five points addressed personnel issues, such as weeding out incompetent and unreliable employees, dismissing the so-called dollar-a-year men (wealthy Americans who took influential government positions at a salary of a dollar a year), and hiring no new agents without Stone's express authorization.[30]

The sixth point, however, had the longest-lasting effect on the new acting director of the BOI and the nation. Hoover was ordered to immediately discontinue any so-called intelligence-type investigations. Instead, all future inquiries conducted by special agents of the BOI had to be confined "strictly . . . to violations of federal law" and under the direction of the attorney general "or under the direction of an Assistant Attorney General regularly conducting the work of the Department of Justice." The order halted all Department of Justice and BOI countersubversion investigations. No American citizen or alien could be investigated based on race, ethnicity, religion, political beliefs and activities, or vague relationships or connections with someone involved in atypical political movements. Even investigations of Americans with questionable connections to foreign governments or suspicious agents of foreign companies, consulates, or embassies were to be avoided. Stone's new principle also ended the GID and the cataloging of domestic intelligence data. Now, an investigation could be initiated only when a specific violation of a federal statute could be alleged. Stone would consider no exceptions to this rule. At the same time, exchanges of potentially consequential information among the BOI, MID, and ONI ended. With the MID's Negative Intelligence Branch disbanded, it could supply reports to Bureau field offices "only upon a specific request" of MID headquarters in Washington. With that decision, any chance of developing a functional counterintelligence information-sharing system capable of protecting U.S. interests from foreign intelligence aggression was delayed for another fifteen years.[31]

Consequences of the Stone Doctrine

Hoover never wavered from Stone's orders, even well after the attorney general's appointment to the Supreme Court. During the ensuing years, a number of allegations brought to the attention of the BOI and the Department of Justice were turned down for investigation based on the so-called Stone Doctrine. In 1933, with the threat of fascism rapidly growing in Europe, U.S. immigration officials, at the urging of President Roosevelt, requested BOI assistance in a joint investigation of "Nazi propaganda in this country." Hoover, who was willing to assist, nevertheless questioned whether the matter had been discussed with the Department of State or whether the Postal Service had conducted an investigation of possible postal law violations based on the "mailing of Nazi literature." When told that the Immigration and Naturalization Service had conferred with the State Department on the matter, Hoover replied that he could take no action without evidence of a

violation of law, orders from the attorney general, or a request for investigation from the State Department. "If State Department, at the instance of the
President or upon its own instance," Hoover noted, "desired an investigation
to be made of this propaganda, it should direct a written communication to
that effect, to the Attorney General for his consideration." He then emphasized that until such a specific request was made "through proper channels
there was no action which this Division [Division of Investigation] could
take in this matter."[32]

Another instance involved Charles Feinberg, vice president and editor
of the *American Hebrew and Jewish Tribune* in New York City. Meeting with
Hoover's staff in 1933, Feinberg urged an investigation of William Dudley
Pelley, head of the right-wing extremist group the Silver Shirts of America,
and Colonel Edwin Emerson. Both were avowed fascists who were distributing a pamphlet entitled *Liberation,* which attacked Jews in America and
criticized Roosevelt's policies. Feinberg's complaint was forwarded to the
Justice Department, which found no violation of federal law and ordered
no investigation.[33]

Potentially valuable relationships with foreign law enforcement agencies also suffered from the counterintelligence limitations placed on the
Department of Justice during this period. In 1934 the Turkish government
requested, through the State Department, FBI assistance in the sharing of
information about criminal, terrorism, and presidential assassination issues.
Hoover understood that new advances in transportation were shrinking the
world and making foreign liaison more important. "It will not be long before
the earth swings on a vastly smaller axis. Europe and Asia are coming closer
every day. We need cooperation." Hoover envisioned a day when a criminal
could "rob a bank in New York on one day and eat dinner in Paris the next
night." Yet, despite the obvious need for international cooperation, Hoover
was forced to concede that the FBI had little information to offer concerning
radical political activities and that because of Department of Justice policies
that restricted the investigation of such matters unless there was a potential
violation of federal law, his hands were tied. In explaining the absurdity of
the existing situation, he warned, "It follows, of course, that information
of this kind (advocating the overthrow of the Government) is of no value
when existing laws do not permit a prosecution of the persons engaged in
advocating the overthrow of the Government." Hoover explained that if details concerning a plot to overthrow the U.S. government by a foreign police
or counterintelligence service were uncovered, the FBI would be "powerless

to act upon the information furnished unless it constituted some violation of a Federal Statute within the Bureau's jurisdiction."[34]

The case of Heinz Spanknoebel illustrates the problem facing counter-intelligence during the 1930s. A German immigrant, Spanknoebel was a fanatic Nazi and the founder of Friends of the New Germany, an amalgam of members of the Teutonia Association and the GAU-USA, a unit of Hitler's Nazi Party. In an attempt to drum up support for his new party, Spanknoebel traveled throughout the United States publicly denouncing communism and racial mixing and exhorting his German American audiences to preserve their German heritage. His new party later formed the nucleus of the German-American Bund headed by Fritz Kuhn. Spanknoebel's activities soon caught the attention of Congressman Samuel Dickstein of Brooklyn, New York, who accused Spanknoebel of being a Hitler henchman and demanded his arrest for inflammatory anti-Jewish and racial remarks. Even before Dickstein weighed in on the matter, State Department officials had requested a Justice Department investigation of Spanknoebel for failing to register as an agent of the German government, a potential violation of federal law. Although no violation was uncovered, Dickstein's pressure forced the Department of Justice to charge Spanknoebel, which led to the issuance of a U.S. commissioner's warrant for his arrest as an agent of a foreign power. The arrest warrant opened the way for an FBI fugitive investigation, but before any arrest could be made, Spanknoebel fled to Germany at the end of 1933.[35]

Growing White House concern over the extent of Nazi propaganda in the United States prompted the president to convene an emergency meeting in May 1934 of key agencies to discuss the problem. Suspicions were increasing that this was not a homegrown U.S. movement but rather a scheme being financed and directed by the German government through its Washington embassy and various consulates throughout the country. President Roosevelt, aware of the strict limitations on intelligence investigations, recognized that only immigration laws applied in this situation, making the Immigration Service the lead agency for any potential investigation. The combined efforts of the Secret Service, Immigration Service, and Department of Justice would be exploited, with the FBI serving as the "clearing house" for all information collected.[36]

Hoover wasted no time. In an effort to technically comply with existing guidelines and policies governing FBI investigations, Hoover relied on the fact that the Immigration Service (an agency of the Department of Labor)

had ordered the investigation of possible immigration law violations. By doing so, however, the rules governing FBI investigations began to shift. Broader
and more sweeping informational inquiries designed to keep the president
updated on the activities of Nazi groups in United States were added to the
case-by-case investigation of alleged violations of federal statutes. Governmental agencies would now survey "anti-racial and anti-American activities,
having any possible connections with the official representatives of the German Government in the United States." Reminding his subordinates of the
secret nature of such investigations (only the directors of the Secret Service
and the Immigration Service and the attorney general would be briefed),
Hoover issued orders to assign a "competent supervisor" at headquarters to
oversee these "so-called intelligence investigations." A general survey would
be prepared and sent to the White House on a regular basis, and a report
was ordered to be prepared for the attorney general as soon as possible,
together with "confidential instructions" for all field offices outlining the
requirements for these new and highly confidential investigations.[37]

For the next twenty-eight months, intelligence investigations of Nazi activities were carried out by the Secret Service, the FBI, and the Immigration
Service. Investigative targets of the FBI included a wide variety of right-wing
groups and persons, such as the German-American Bund, headed by Fritz
Kuhn; William Dudley Pelley, leader of the Silver Shirts movement; the Citizens Protection League; the German-American Republican League; the National Committee Against Communism; and the Protestant Civic Welfare
Federation based in New York City, which distributed literature published
by the Independent Republican National Christian-Gentile Committee. In
June 1936 the Memphis, Tennessee, police provided Hoover with information concerning the formation of a new political party called the Constitutional Party. Police officials had received a report from local chamber
of commerce officials. Typical of unsolicited information was a list passed
from Assistant Attorney General Joseph Keenan to Hoover containing the
"Names of Nazi Members whose activities bear watching."[38] Investigation
consisted of discreet and limited reviews of public literature and newspapers, record and informant checks, law enforcement sources, and local contacts to acquire a broad picture of Nazi and fascist groups in the area. Field
offices then sent the results of their investigations to Washington, where the
results were indexed, cataloged, matched against Bureau files, analyzed, and
distilled into reports for dissemination to the White House, State Department, Secret Service, and Immigration Service.[39]

What had started as a limited intelligence investigation of Nazi-sponsored propaganda in May 1934 expanded after an Oval Office briefing of the president by Hoover on August 24, 1936. Roosevelt had previously received an FBI memorandum reporting that General Smedley Butler, a U.S. Marine Corp veteran and two-time winner of the Medal of Honor, had been encouraged by Father Charles Coughlin, an anti-Semitic Roman Catholic priest who hosted a popular Detroit radio program, to form a militia and lead an expedition to Mexico. The president was becoming increasingly concerned about the growth of fascism and communism and their effect on the economic and political life of the country. Hoover described the activities of Harry Bridges, West Coast leader of the dock workers' union, and his increasing influence on union activities in ports on the Gulf and Atlantic coasts. Next he outlined the growing influence of John L. Lewis, head of the United Mine Workers Union, and of the Newspaper Guild led by Heywood Broun. Bridges, whose union was "practically controlled" by the Communist Party, was pressuring ship owners to extend a contract set to expire in September 1936 to April 1937, when the United Mine Workers' contract would also expire. Hoover accused Broun's organization, which was also characterized as being heavily influenced by the Communist Party, of putting the *Seattle Post Intelligencer* out of business and infiltrating other newspapers around the country. He warned the president that the goal of the Communist Party was to control all three unions and thus cripple U.S. shipping, the economy, and the newspaper industry.[40]

FDR, operating on only vague and anecdotal information, insisted on more specific details—a "broad picture of the general movement and its activities as may affect the economic and political life of the country as a whole." Hoover told the president that the acquisition of such information was currently spread among a number of agencies, each of which used the data for its own specific investigative needs. There was no one particular agency responsible for collecting and analyzing the data in a manner that would be useful for the White House. Given the restrictions on FBI activities, broader types of intelligence investigations required a directive from the State Department. The president was reluctant to issue a formal investigative order to the FBI through the State Department, fearing that a leak to the press might be politically embarrassing to the White House. Instead, he suggested an informal order contained in a confidential memorandum that he would keep in the White House safe. The next afternoon, FDR and Hoover met again to discuss the issue, this time with Secretary of State Cordell Hull.

Under instructions from the president, Hull ordered Hoover to "quite confidentially" begin investigating Communist Party activities, links between the party and Moscow, and the activities of Constantin Oumansky, Soviet ambassador to the United States. Following a briefing by Hoover days later, Attorney General Homer Cummings instructed him to proceed with the investigation and coordinate his inquiries with MID and ONI officials.[41]

Hoover turned to special agent George E. Starr to set up the new filing system at headquarters. A Maryland native, Starr had been hired by the BOI on Hoover's personal recommendation in January 1920. He was fluent in Russian, German, French, and Spanish; had served with the U.S. Navy; had been a dock worker, an investigator for the New York State legislature, and an officer in the Panama Canal Zone Police Service; and had spent two years with the MID. Hoover had originally used Starr to establish the GID in 1920 and again in 1934 to set up the file system on Nazi propaganda.

This time, Starr had an even bigger task. Working under Edward Tamm, Hoover's senior assistant, Starr created a detailed filing system of subversive information subdivided by categories such as activities in the maritime industry; government affairs; the steel industry; the coal industry; the Newspaper Guild; the clothing, garment, and fur industries; general strikes; the armed forces of the United States; educational institutions; the Communist Party and affiliated organizations; fascist organizations; antifascist movements; and labor organizations. Starr indexed the new information, matching it with the original GID index cards and miscellaneous information volunteered to the FBI and indexed since the termination of the GID in 1924. The new records highlighted the identities of people who were prominent in subversive circles at the time. Moving quickly to set up the system, Starr established a daily register of changing developments in the various categories, which he sent to Hoover and formed the basis of the ongoing briefings of the president.[42]

Reality

The Stone Doctrine dramatically shifted the FBI focus away from the investigation of subversives and curtailed any possibility of detecting foreign espionage in the United States unless prima facie evidence was brought to the FBI's attention. Another obstacle was the historic American notion that policy concerning espionage, diplomacy, and foreign diplomats, embassies, and consulates was the exclusive purview of the Department of State, which would decide what cases were worthy of investigation. Assuming that sufficient facts existed to start an investigation, FBI policy regarding espionage matters, reflecting State Department policy control and Justice Department oversight, also stalled efforts to unearth the activities of German, Soviet, and Japanese agents in the United States before they had an opportunity to do damage. For example, if FBI agents determined that an "employee of another Governmental organization" was linked in any way to a possible espionage matter, or if the investigation revealed that participants in an espionage conspiracy included a "representative of a foreign diplomatic or consular service," the investigation had to be stopped; further investigation could be pursued only after acquiring State Department authorization.[43]

In June 1938 legislation was passed requiring certain persons employed by agencies to disseminate propaganda in the United States and for other purposes to register with the Department of Justice. Yet FBI policy demanded that if violations of this law were detected, FBI field offices could not investigate. Instead, the information had to be sent to FBI headquarters for referral to the Department of State.[44] The structure of local FBI field offices reflected this reality. There were no counterespionage squads, even in large cities such as New York, Chicago, or Los Angeles; nor was there a special agent designated for such matters. In fact, counterespionage had sunk to such a low priority that these investigations were handled by the bank robbery squad, or they were bunched together with falsified passport applications. The standard for opening and investigating a case was so high that interest among local field offices understandably waned, and such cases were ignored in favor of more immediate problems. If allegations of spying by military personnel—either uniformed or civilian—were encountered, field offices could only pass the information on to Washington for referral to the director of ONI or the War Department. As for nonmilitary civilians, Hoover reminded his field offices that the FBI had "primary jurisdiction" in these matters. Nevertheless, investigation was prohibited except when there were specific allegations indicating that the "suspects have in their possession or are furnishing information which would be detrimental to the national defense or [have] furnished to a foreign power information detrimental to the interests of the United States Government."[45]

When special agent Leon Turrou confronted Guenther Rumrich in February 1938, the U.S. counterintelligence structure was dysfunctional. The MID's Negative Intelligence Branch was out of business, and the ONI was focusing only on navy matters. There was little exchange of information between the FBI and the military services, no agency focusing on the larger threat posed by foreign intelligence services, and no comprehension of the strategies and tactics being used by those services.

As for the FBI, it was grossly unprepared for the task at hand. Its operating rules made it difficult to acquire a picture of the catastrophic losses suffered by U.S. industry and the military and the foreign intelligence threat facing them. There was no coherent doctrine to counter that threat; the FBI had conducted no training of its staff and had no experts in the fields of counterespionage and counterintelligence. Eleven years later, after the Second World War and in the midst of the cold war, Turrou summed it up simply and clearly: "In 1938 [the FBI] had no counterespionage service. The ferreting out of spies by the FBI had had no precedent."[46]

CHAPTER THREE

Controversy and Confusion

Public reaction to the indictments, convictions, and revelations of stolen military and industrial secrets was generally unanimous. Most newspapers condemned Germany's action. "Modest increases" in counterespionage budgets were urged on the Roosevelt administration by the *New York Times,* because the FBI and the military were busier pursuing spies "than at any time since the World War." The *Washington Post* applauded the government's handling of the case "without kid gloves," charging that the nation had grown "too complacent" about the threat. Getting to the core of the issue, the paper urged improved coordination among governmental agencies, pointing to the capture of only four of the eighteen ring members as clear evidence of the absence of an "effective counterespionage system."[1]

The president came under increasing public pressure to do something about the spy problem. Texas congressman Martin C. Dies, a bitter Roosevelt critic, used every opportunity to attack the president and his New Deal policies. As chairman of the Special House Un-American Activities Committee, Dies decried the threat of fascist and communist subversion and routinely criticized the State Department for foot-dragging on the investigations of spies. Fueling his accusations was the arrests, on the opening day of the Rumrich trial, of several Germans on espionage charges in the Panama Canal Zone. The secretary to the local German consul and two ship crew members were accused of photographing gun emplacements and a rock that could be used as an aiming point because of its proximity to a weapons battery.[2]

Two months later, Mikhail Gorin and Kenneth Drummond were arrested on similar charges. A Soviet government official and an NKVD intelligence officer, Gorin had arrived in the United States in 1936 to take up duties at the Amtorg Trading Corporation in New York City. Following his reassignment as head of the Los Angeles bureau of Intourist, the Soviet government's official tourist service, he recruited Hafis Salich, a Russian American employee of the ONI who began supplying him with valuable naval secrets. Drummond, a twenty-one-year-old aircraft inspector, stole blueprints of a new airplane under development by the Northrop Division of the Douglas Aircraft Corporation, which he tried to peddle to the Japanese consulate in Los Angeles, a Japanese ship captain, and a Japanese attorney. At his sentencing he proclaimed his innocence, arguing that he was a whistle-blower intent on exposing the weaknesses in the defense industry by demonstrating to the world "how easy it [was] to steal such data." He hoped that everyone would realize "how lax are the safety measures of aircraft companies building government planes." As for his approach to the Japanese, Drummond told the court that he simply wanted to complete his example. He received a two-year prison sentence.[3]

In the wake of the nationwide uproar, Roosevelt moved quickly to convince the nation that his administration was taking foreign espionage seriously and vigorously pursuing measures to meet the challenge. In early October 1938 he discussed the "spy situation" at a White House press conference, acknowledging the federal government's "very definite responsibility" for combating the "continuance of foreign government spying on our national defenses." Four days later, however, when asked by reporters what steps he was taking to improve counterespionage enforcement, the president conceded an inadequate level of coordination within his administration and said that he was "trying to get some better method of cooperation."[4]

At a White House cabinet meeting on October 14, 1938, Roosevelt raised his concerns with Attorney General Homer Cummings. Cummings told the president that, in his view, the government already had a "well defined system" and that changes in the existing structure were unnecessary. The counterespionage agencies—the MID, headed by Colonel Warren McCabe; the ONI, led by Admiral Ralston S. Holmes; and the FBI under Hoover— had been quietly coordinating behind the scenes for many years. "All are in frequent contact," Cummings noted, and "are operating in harmony." The president questioned this assessment and ordered Cummings to chair a committee of FBI, MID, and ONI representatives to study the coordination problem and report to him as soon as possible.[5]

Hoover's Report

Throwing himself into the task, the FBI director drew heavily on his twenty years of experience in internal security matters. The one truth he wanted to convey in the report he was about to prepare for the president was that internal security and counterespionage must be a civilian governmental responsibility concentrated in a single agency. The military must focus its attention on war fighting without other distractions. In an internal FBI memorandum prepared in 1938, Hoover elucidated this point: the "Army and Navy must bend every effort toward winning the war," he wrote, with "investigative activities and protective measures handled by one central agency, the Bureau."[6]

Hoover's proposed changes were radical in scope and unprecedented in a peacetime environment. They represented a seismic shift in national security thinking, in effect, serving as the genesis for what we now refer to as the *intelligence community*. The plan called for the replacement of the unworkable, fragmented system of overlapping jurisdictions and investigative duplication with a new structure that concentrated all counterespionage investigations in the FBI. All espionage-related "complaints, referrals, and information," Hoover suggested, should be channeled into the FBI so they can be "catalogued, associated with information already available with efficiency and a minimum of effort."[7]

Instituting such sweeping changes was sure to provoke bureaucratic warfare and might exceed what was politically palatable for the Roosevelt administration. These changes included FBI takeover of the Federal Communications Commission, along with its monitoring of cable transmissions, radio stations, and transmitting stations, and FBI assumption of the functions and responsibilities of the Immigration and Naturalization Service, then under the Department of Labor, and the U.S. Customs Service, subordinated at the time to the Department of the Treasury. Turning to the serious deficiencies in industrial plant protection exposed by the Rumrich investigation, Hoover pointed out that during the First World War, the military services had been concerned more with sabotage than with espionage; possessing ample manpower, they had handled this responsibility effectively. With the huge postwar military drawdown of staffing and budgets, far less attention was being paid to industrial security. These factors, combined with aggressive foreign espionage penetration of U.S. factories and military research facilities, led Hoover to recommend FBI oversight of the physical and personnel security function of these installations "in its entirety." Such a move would require FBI review of all existing and planned government contracts involving companies doing business with the military and the insertion of a clause in any new contracts requiring company officials to "accept and carry out regulations of the Bureau as to guards, devices, and plans for protection of plant property and work in process for the Government against espionage, acts of war, fire, and enemy aliens." Addressing the level of personnel needed for these new and expanded FBI functions, Hoover estimated that at least 5,000 FBI agents should be hired immediately, with that number increasing to "10,000 to 17,000 as rapidly as possible."[8]

Next Hoover turned his sights on the Department of State and its traditional role as the coordinator of counterespionage investigations. He urged that U.S. passport violations, a traditional State Department responsibility, be taken over by the FBI. Illegal passport activities in foreign countries would remain under the State Department's jurisdiction, in cooperation with the FBI. The monitoring and tracking of aliens entering the United States were also examined. Hoover suggested an FBI role in the issuance of visas to foreign visitors, a historic function of the State Department. Though insisting that U.S. entry or departure decisions regarding foreign persons would remain under State Department jurisdiction, Hoover recommended that in certain cases approval be obtained from the MID, ONI, and FBI.[9]

Harboring doubts about how seriously the State Department viewed security matters, Hoover next made an audacious recommendation that was calculated to wrest control of counterintelligence policy away from the State Department and shift it into the collective hands of the FBI, ONI, and MID. Hoover recommended that agents of foreign countries be investigated by the FBI "without notifying the Secretary of State," a move that would permit the FBI to investigate anyone, including foreign diplomats assigned to the United States and State Department employees, without prior notification or coordination with department officials.[10]

Cummings's Report

Six days after receiving his orders from the president, Cummings submitted his report. The October 20, 1938, letter outlined the history of the relationship among the three services, the roles they played in the national defense setup, and Cummings's own thoughts on necessary changes. Initially, he described the "General Intelligence Section" of the FBI, which collected and correlated for "ready reference" information dealing with subversive or intelligence matters. Categories of information collected included "maritime," "industry," "general strike," "organized labor," "Negroes," and "Fascisti," with more than 2,500 names in the index dealing with the activities of communism, fascism, and various types of foreign espionage. The president was told that the FBI had developed an extensive library that included daily, weekly, and monthly publications, as well as pamphlets and books dealing with general intelligence activities, all of which were classified as to name and subject for reference and research purposes. Cummings explained that the FBI had for some time collected "information dealing with various forms of activities of either a subversive or so-called intelligence type." His letter also cited the three key targets of the MID and ONI: subversive activities that undermine the loyalty and efficiency of naval and civilian personnel involved in construction or maintenance, sabotage, and espionage.[11]

Concerning any proposed expansion, the report noted that a well-developed structure of counterespionage coordination and cooperation already existed. That structure, developed over a period of years, was, in Cummings's opinion, "working as satisfactorily as could be expected under the limitations of personnel and appropriations as have existed in the past." Speaking for McCabe and Holmes, he rejected the need for any expansion beyond the MID-ONI-FBI structure. Other agencies were "less interested" in counterespionage and general intelligence, he explained, emphasizing that the "more circumscribed the program is the more effective it will be and [the] less danger there is of its becoming a matter of general public knowledge."[12]

Cummings next turned his attention to the requirements of expansion. Fearing criticism or objections from "ill-informed persons or individuals having some ulterior motive," he sought to strike a balance between expansion, on the one hand, and the "utmost need of secrecy," on the other. New legislative remedies, in his view, would be "undesirable." They would immediately "draw attention to the . . . proposed development of a special counter-espionage drive of great magnitude." From a legal perspective, expansion of the FBI's responsibility would require no new legislation. For years, he noted, the annual appropriations legislation had included the wording "for such investigations regarding official matters under the control of the Department of Justice and the Department of State as may be directed by the Attorney General." This wording was "sufficiently broad to cover any expansion" of the FBI's responsibilities into counterespionage activities.[13]

Cummings then suggested a framework for making changes in the existing coordination structure. He reminded the president that for fiscal year 1940, the ONI had requested a total of $39,000 for domestic intelligence work, which the attorney general believed would be sufficient. Next he suggested a $35,000 increase in the MID budget and consideration that the two agencies colocate to the same building, for smoother and more efficient interaction. Turning his attention to the FBI, Cummings made a number of sweeping recommendations designed to address the specialized character of general intelligence work. For some time, ONI officers had attended FBI training schools for new special agents, and ten of them had already successfully completed the course. In Cummings's view, the specialized material taught by the FBI could be particularly useful "to larger groups of Officers from both the MID and ONI" because it covered "not only general investigative work but also special matters dealing with general intelligence work." In anticipation of the extraterritorial nature of the emerging threat from foreign intelligence, he suggested expansion of the FBI presence beyond the continental United States by reopening offices in the Hawaiian Islands, Alaska, and Puerto Rico. Other measures urged on the president were legislation that better defined the new realities of espionage; designation of a liaison officer from each of the three services to maintain daily contact; use of the FBI as a clearinghouse for intelligence and counterespionage information, in close coordination with the MID and ONI; and assignment of primary civilian investigative responsibility in the field to the FBI. Cummings also recommended that other governmental agencies be "instructed" to promptly refer any relevant information that came to their attention to these intelligence services and to "cooperate fully" with them.

Cummings finally turned his attention to a critical issue looming over everyone in the economically strapped nation's capital: money. He told the president that implementation of these recommendations would require an immediate $300,000 increase in FBI funding to cover the expansion that he believed was "necessary and desirable." This would permit the assignment of additional agents, qualified in the field of intelligence investigation, to cities throughout the country where the army and navy maintained a significant presence. At the same time, the nation's chief law enforcement officer was fully aware that such a huge funding increase would far exceed the FBI's congressionally authorized budget.[14]

Roosevelt's Decision

By November 1, 1938, Roosevelt had completed his review of Hoover's plan and ordered the FBI director to meet with him in secret to discuss it.

Roosevelt approved Hoover's overall concept but turned down his manpower requests, which were clearly beyond the administration's political and fiscal capabilities. The plan for closer MID, ONI, and FBI coordination of counterespionage matters was also approved, with modest funding increases. With the FBI operational budget for fiscal year 1939 already at more than $6 million, Roosevelt, without any congressional consultation, secretly ordered an additional emergency counterespionage appropriation of $600,000, a figure that exceeded the authorized FBI budget by almost 10 percent.[15]

Hoover wasted no time putting the funds to work. He immediately undertook a hiring program, hoping to add 140 special agents to his existing complement of 587, a 24 percent increase. To support the investigations of these new special agents, an additional 40 clerical employees were hired, bringing the total to 284. When fully staffed, the FBI would increase its total personnel complement from 831 to a new high of just over 1,000 employees, an increase of more than 15 percent.

During the ensuing months, the FBI, ONI, and MID met frequently to discuss budget issues, streamlined information sharing, and systems for case referrals. With relations among the three agencies progressing quickly in Washington, Hoover moved to ensure that FBI field offices developed similar lines of communication with military intelligence officials at the local level. In February 1939 he ordered his special agents in charge throughout the country to immediately establish liaison on matters of espionage, counterespionage, and sabotage with the local military commanders; he also insisted that a special agent from each field office be assigned to serve as a liaison officer. Two new committees were set up the next month, chaired by senior FBI officials, to coordinate espionage and counterespionage policies with the MID and ONI and to systematize investigations.[16]

Presidential blessing for the new FBI-military arrangement was still confidential; not even other governmental agencies were aware of it. With heightened tensions concerning espionage, and with other agencies showing an interest in pursuing these matters, the Department of Justice made the announcement that the FBI would have exclusive jurisdiction over espionage and subversive matters. In a letter prepared by Assistant Attorney General Joseph B. Keenan (at Hoover's request) and sent on February 7, 1939, the U.S. Postal Service, Secret Service, Internal Revenue Service, Coast Guard, and Customs Service were informed about the new arrangement. Keenan, a Harvard Law School graduate, had served under Cummings since September 1933 (and in 1946 he would be appointed by President Harry Truman as chief counsel for the prosecution in the trials of Japanese war criminals in Tokyo). Keenan's letter announced that the FBI, in cooperation with the MID, had begun investigating "espionage and subversive" activities. To ensure that allegations and complaints were "handled expeditiously," he asked agency heads to instruct their local personnel to refer information concerning such matters to the local field offices of the FBI. To emphasize a unified front, Keenan concluded the letter by noting that he was authorized to announce that the "Chief of Military Intelligence of the War Department is desirous of having the foregoing arrangement become effective."[17]

This announcement prompted an immediate firestorm within the government. Later, when Keenan's letter, Hoover's secret report, and the ongoing FBI discussions with the military were fully outlined, outraged agencies quickly closed ranks. Fearing budget reductions and the loss of personnel and responsibilities, they quickly formed a battle line in a war of titanic proportions that would be fought over the next four months behind the scenes in the offices and conference rooms of Washington.

Messersmith

Leading the fight against Hoover and the military was George Strauser Messersmith, a newly appointed assistant secretary of state. A native of Pennsylvania, Messersmith had spent his early career in Delaware as a teacher and school administrator. Before the outbreak of World War I he joined the State Department as a foreign service officer, serving at a number of diplomatic posts in the Caribbean and South America. He was vice-consul in Germany from 1930 to 1934 and minister to Austria from 1934 to July 1937, where he was one of the first Americans to sound the warning about the nature of Hitler's regime and the menace it posed to the world.[18]

Among Messersmith's new duties as assistant secretary of state was intelligence liaison with the MID, ONI, FBI, and Department of Justice. His previous foreign assignments had exposed him to espionage indirectly, providing him with some understanding of the counterintelligence business. His first encounter had occurred on the Dutch West Indies island of Curaçao. The United States had just entered the war when Messersmith became involved in the ouster of the German consul, who was suspected of being the head of German espionage in South America. With wartime censorship of all communications, German agents had to come up with imaginative ploys and clever cipher systems to get vital information to Europe. Based on a tip, Messersmith discovered that insurance policies being sent through the international mail contained concealed intelligence messages written in a sophisticated German code. Such policies were generally immune from the prying eyes of censors, but closer examination led to discovery of the identities of German agents sending vital information between South America and Germany. The thrill of this accomplishment remained a great source of pride to Messersmith. More than a quarter of a century later, he still recalled that the "principal [German] agents in practically every part of the country had been spotted at the same hour," and the "net [was] drawn in at least a score of cities in the United States and in several cities of Cuba." He also assisted in the successful theft of codebooks used by the fast German sea raider *Karlsruhe*. The codes were later exploited by American and British ships combating German submarines in the north Atlantic. Before leaving Curaçao, Messersmith uncovered another German intelligence operation involving an Austrian agent who was posing as an Italian count and spying on American interests. Two decades later, while assigned in Europe, he participated in other intelligence ventures, including direct assistance to anti-Nazi propagandists.[19]

Like the rest of the government, Messersmith had been surprised by the Rumrich case and its revelations of widespread spying. Two months after the convictions, he expressed a concern shared by many senior State Department officials about the new phenomenon of secret intelligence collection in the United States. In a private letter to a colleague, he complained that the United States has "as many German agents . . . today as we had between 1914 and 1917." The critical difference, in his view, was that they were committing espionage and not "direct sabotage." Describing espionage as "un-American," he wrote that legislation was under consideration requiring the registration of aliens, as well as statutes providing for the "rapid cancellation of naturalization of persons engaged in political activities or showing evidence of dual allegiance." He was hopeful that the legislative proposals would become law, but even if they failed, they would still serve as a strong deterrent to spying. In his words, the "psychological effects on certain aliens and naturalized citizens will be enormous."[20]

Messersmith privately believed that the time had come for the government to be "on guard" against foreign spying and to take "definite action." He urged the secretary of state to create some type of interdepartmental

committee "without delay" to review the situation and make recommendations to the president for improving the existing structure. Although Hoover
counseled secrecy in such matters, Messersmith believed that public exposure of the intergovernmental debate on national security improvements
would have a salutary effect on the situation and discourage anyone hoping
to emulate Rumrich and his gang. "I see no reason why any secret should be
made that such a committee has been appointed," he wrote to the secretary
of state. Public knowledge of the committee's existence would swiftly curb
espionage because the "very fact that it is known" would have a "very whole-
some effect on those who are fostering these activities."[21]

For the Department of State, improved coordination did not translate
into loss of its control of counterespionage policy. Espionage had always
been seen as a necessary, if unpleasant, function of international statecraft,
and in the United States, it was no different. Any changes in the government's approach to the new threat from foreign spying would ultimately
have to be sanctioned and dictated by its foreign policy makers and not by
other organs of the government that lacked an understanding of the political sensitivities involved in the foreign policy process. The keenest insights
into the nature of the bureaucratic struggle raging within the government
were offered by a foreign observer reporting to his superiors. Guy Liddell,
an Englishman of culture, was fluent in French, a war hero and winner of
the Military Cross for gallantry in action, well read, and an accomplished
cellist; he also possessed well-developed social contacts among the leading
members of British society and, in the words of one knowledgeable writer,
was "an exceptional intelligence officer, in every way."[22] He had years of
professional experience, having joined Scotland Yard in 1919 as a Special
Branch counterintelligence officer and later becoming a senior MI5 officer.
Before the Second World War Liddell had served as the head of MI5's B
Division, responsible for a number of significant Soviet and German espionage investigations. His study of the MASK decrypts, intercepted Comintern wireless traffic exchanged between Moscow and the Communist Party
of Great Britain (CPGB), deepened his concern about the espionage threat
from Russia. The arrest of Percy Glading, the CPGB national organizer, in
February 1938 convinced him of the seriousness of the threat.[23]

At the time of his visit to the United States in the spring of 1938, Liddell
was the deputy director of MI5's Counterespionage Branch. His secret mission was twofold: coordinate the Jordan aspect of the Rumrich case with the
FBI and the military, and explore approaches for counterintelligence liaison

with the U.S. government. Liddell analyzed the counterintelligence conditions in the U.S. government in a report he later prepared for Sir Robert
Vansitart, the permanent undersecretary of state. The State Department's
investigative staff was small and concentrated only on passport violations,
he noted, while the Secret Service focused mainly on presidential protection and the investigation of "revenue frauds." The scope of FBI activities,
however, was "gradually widening" into the investigation of criminal matters and espionage. He observed that although the FBI had "no charter (to
collect counterintelligence information) it has on the quiet been going thoroughly into Soviet activities." Bureau officials told Liddell in confidence that
they had acquired a "mass of information about the Soviet trading organization 'Amtorg'" and were closely following the activities of the Communist
Party, the American labor leader John L. Lewis, and the Congress of Industrial Organizations. Based on his conversations with the FBI director, Liddell reported that Hoover "rather sensed that trouble was ahead and that he
did not intend to be caught unawares."[24]

Liddell then turned his attention to the most important issue—international cooperation among foreign counterintelligence services. A key to
successful counterespionage is the effective use of open and covert liaison
with foreign intelligence and security services. Direct contact allows services to share ideas and observations on many facets of an adversary service, including operational doctrine, personalities, changing organizational
structure, and so forth. Good liaison also facilitates the passage of valuable information between services, including leads on agents, intelligence
officers, and cases. Direct contact encourages an atmosphere of trust that
considerably increases a counterintelligence service's capacity to neutralize
spying. In some instances, however, a country's domestic political climate
or its foreign policy may dictate that liaison relationships with security and
intelligence services of different countries be kept confidential. Such covert relationships allow security services to obtain information that may
be essential to the nation's security while avoiding political embarrassment
through public exposure of the relationship.

During his visit to Canada, Liddell learned from Stewart T. Wood, the
commissioner of the Royal Canadian Mounted Police (RCMP), that Hoover
was sharing counterintelligence and security information with his Canadian
colleagues. Wood and Hoover had been professional and personal friends
for some time. Both had attended the 1937 convention of the International
World Police held in Montreal, after which Wood had been Hoover's guest

during a visit to Washington, D.C. Wood maintained close contact with Hoover, and anything he wished to learn about "these matters he could write to him [Hoover] personally." The commissioner's questions, however, were always "based more on criminal than political lines." Liddell noted that when "members of the C.I.O. visit Canada, the Canadians get over the difficulty by asking for their criminal records."[25]

There was no such information-sharing mechanism with the British. State Department control prevented a direct relationship between the FBI and the counterintelligence services of friendly countries. This meant that all leads in foreign countries developed by FBI investigation had to be forwarded to that country's security service through State Department channels. In the case of Great Britain, this cumbersome process required that both criminal and counterespionage investigative leads be sent from the FBI to State Department headquarters and then to the U.S. embassy in London. From there, the request for investigation would be sent to the British Foreign Office and then passed to the British Security Service or Scotland Yard. When the investigation was completed, the results would be returned in the same manner.[26]

Liddell criticized the State Department's unshakeable hold on counterintelligence liaison. The U.S. military services and the FBI were "more than anxious to establish a liaison with us, which could cover not only Soviet, German, and Italian activities, but also those of the Japanese." He then reported that despite this rigid control of international police contact, Hoover was able to circumvent State Department restrictions. While quietly admiring Hoover's cunning, Liddell cautioned that "quite obviously the State Department wishes to keep the strings in their own hands." He complained that British counterintelligence leads sent to the United States through State Department channels often were not passed on to the FBI for investigation. Instead, they were handled by State Department investigators, who were "not in a position to go very much beyond obtaining passport particulars." Likewise, investigative reports prepared by the Bureau for the British often had sections containing information of "a delicate nature" excised or edited "from a political angle." Liddell puzzled over "how to give effect to such liaison with us, which could cover not only Soviet, German, and Italian activities but also those of the Japanese. The difficulty is to know how to give effect to any such liaison without causing offence to the State Department, with whom we have been in touch via the Counsellor of the American Embassy here ever since the war." He concluded that the State Department's attitude was "not to allow those soldiers and policemen to get loose on their own. If we do not exercise a restrained hand they may lead us into deep water politically and there may be repercussions in Congress."[27]

With no hint of a solution in sight, an exasperated Roosevelt finally ordered Messersmith to bring the warring governmental agencies together to hammer out an agreement. Involved in the proceedings was Mathew McGuire, assistant attorney general under Frank Murphy, Cummings's successor. The forty-year-old McGuire, a native of St. John's, Canada, had been educated at Holy Cross College and held a law degree from Boston University. He had previously served as Cummings's special assistant for five years (and in 1941, President Roosevelt would appoint him to a judgeship on the U.S. District Court for the District of Columbia). McGuire informed Edward Tamm, Hoover's assistant, that Messersmith wanted a meeting of all parties in the matter "but did not want the FBI present." Tamm reminded him that the president had already authorized an increase in the FBI budget for espionage investigations and suggested that the FBI's absence from such a meeting would be highly unusual. Tamm then warned McGuire what would happen if the FBI was excluded: Hoover would "immediately go to the White House, explain the ridiculousness of the situation and undoubtedly will receive a decision in his favor." He then urged McGuire not to let the "opposition know about this vantage."[28]

With the Treasury Department and the Postal Service led by the State Department on one side, and the Department of Justice, MID, and ONI led by the FBI on the other, Messersmith convened a meeting of the parties at the State Department on the afternoon of March 20, 1939. In attendance were McGuire; Admiral Holmes, director of the ONI; Colonel McCabe, head of the MID; Elmer Irey of the Treasury Department; and a representative from the Postal Service. Hoover snubbed Messersmith and sent Tamm as his representative. The stormy session began with Messersmith noting that the president wanted all parties to develop a system that would allow for "absolute coordination" of all information developed by governmental agencies in connection with espionage issues. He then insisted that coordination of "all espionage investigations" remain under State Department control, with Messersmith's deputy, Fletcher Warren, handling the day-to-day responsibilities. Warren would examine each complaint, assess the logical agency to handle it, and forward it to that agency for investigation. Tamm promptly objected. With the backing of Holmes, McCabe, and McGuire, he called the plan inefficient and cumbersome and pointed out that it would increase the danger of serious delays in responding to threats that required immediate attention. Tamm then reminded everyone that the FBI had been conducting espionage, sabotage, and counterespionage investigations since the First World War and was currently actively engaged in an increasing number of such matters. Tempers soon flared when someone criticized "the quality of the services of the Department of Justice in this situation." An angry Tamm wasted no time responding to the criticism. To hammer home his point about FBI competence, he reminded them that the State Department had recently considered the FBI "sufficiently qualified" to order a special agent to travel to Brazil to set up a "secret police system of a type similar to that considered necessary in the United States for dealing with espionage cases." FBI agent Edward Thompson had been in Rio de Janeiro for three months, providing counterintelligence instruction to Brazilian police officials and assisting in the construction of a security service. Thompson's assignment had been endorsed by Undersecretary of State Sumner Welles and personally approved by the president. Tamm also reminded Messersmith that in 1938 officials in the Dominican Republic had requested Bureau assistance in investigating German subversion. Any criticism of the Bureau's performance, in Tamm's view, was a criticism of the president, Welles, and the State Department. Tamm also reminded the participants that Roosevelt had already indicated his preference for the FBI to handle these matters, as evidenced by his appropriation of funds.[29]

In the end, the meeting produced a compromise of sorts that temporarily satisfied all parties while postponing major jurisdictional changes that were only weeks away. A subcommittee of all the governmental departments was formed for the purpose of exchanging information on espionage matters, with the initial gathering taking place at the State Department on March 24, 1939. Hoover later told Murphy that all future gatherings would be held at FBI headquarters and expressed confidence "that it will be possible in a very short time to effect complete arrangement along the lines we discussed."[30]

Not one to waste time, Hoover quickly undertook an aggressive campaign designed to make it clear that counterintelligence and the FBI were synonymous. Hoover informed Murphy about the espionage convictions and prison sentences of Gorin and Salich, highlighting a letter from the prosecuting attorney in the case praising the "outstanding" work of FBI investigator Glen Dierst. Next Hoover recounted the activities of Fritz Wiedemann, who had assumed the post of German consul general in San Francisco in March

1939. A month later, Messersmith had requested as much information on Wiedemann as possible, but in such a manner that "there would be no indication that we are looking into his activities." On April 21, 1939, the FBI learned that two army soldiers stationed at the Presidio in San Francisco had engaged in sexual acts with Rudolf Huebner, the German vice-consul. Huebner had tried to acquire information from them concerning a new automatic rifle that the army was considering as a replacement for the Springfield 30.06. On May 1, 1939, Messersmith requested a confidential FBI investigation of Baron Edgar von Spiegel, German consul in New Orleans, who was pressuring the president of the University of Tampa to accept the services of a German language professor. Hoover also reported a State Department inquiry to the FBI on April 6, 1939, concerning the Baroness Martha Maria Steiner, described as a German national who was suspected of being a "narcotics smuggler and perhaps engaged in espionage." Further complicating the matter was her use of the Attorney General Murphy's name as a reference for her travel visa to the United States.[31]

The last nail in the coffin of the status quo came on May 30, 1939, when President Roosevelt, in the spirit of fostering closer diplomatic relations with the Colombian government, personally approved an urgent State Department request for the temporary assignment of FBI special agent Edward Thompson to Bogota (from Rio de Janeiro, where he was working with the Brazilian police). The Colombian government, with a view toward assisting in the defense of the Panama Canal, sought Thompson's expertise "in advising in the organization of an office similar to the Bureau" that would exercise "surveillance over the activities of aliens in Colombia."[32]

With mounting evidence of the inefficiency and unworkability of the espionage, counterespionage, and sabotage structure, Murphy weighed into the fray on June 17, 1939, with a personal appeal to the president. The existing structure, in his view, was merely "an informal committee" made up of State, Justice, Postal Service, Treasury, War, and Navy representatives that provided no real coordination of investigations. Instead, it was simply an inefficient "clearing house for data or information concerning such matters," with each agency conducting its own espionage, counterespionage, and sabotage investigations while the FBI, MID, and ONI handled the bulk of the inquiries. The existing setup was "neither effective nor desirable," and in Murphy's opinion, it left open the possibility of a dangerously slow response to emergencies. Murphy then urged the president to abandon the current structure and replace it with a committee made up of the FBI, MID,

and ONI that would meet regularly and coordinate and investigate all espionage, counterespionage, and sabotage matters for the government.[33]

The president recognized that decentralization had failed. After six
months of bitter haggling and frustration, Roosevelt acknowledged that the
State Department was ill suited and ill equipped to coordinate counterespionage matters. Siding with Murphy, Hoover, and the military services,
the president issued a confidential directive to his cabinet on June 26, 1939,
ordering the creation of the first counterintelligence policy board in the
nation's history. It read as follows:

> It is my desire that the investigation of all espionage, and sabotage mat-
> ters be controlled and handled by the Federal Bureau of Investigation of
> the Department of Justice, the Military Intelligence Division of the War
> Department, and the Office of Naval Intelligence in the Navy Depart-
> ment. The directors of these departments are to function as a committee
> to coordinate their activities. No investigation should be conducted by
> any investigative agency of the Government into matters involving actu-
> ally or potentially any espionage, counterespionage, or sabotage except
> by these three agencies mentioned above.[34]

Eight months earlier, in November 1938, while Cummings and Hoover
were exploring consolidation of the counterintelligence community, Hull
had urged the president to consolidate the Foreign Agriculture Service and
the Foreign Commerce Service under the State Department's own Foreign
Service. Ironically, Messersmith, in a lengthy memorandum prepared for
the White House, argued that consolidation would lead to greater efficiency,
less confusion on the part of foreign governments concerning who is in
charge, and clearer lines of authority related to centralization. With regard
to Hull's leadership of this new organizational structure, Messersmith noted
that "succeeding Presidents have recognized that the person at the head of
the *premier Department of this Government* must be a man of the highest
qualifications."[35]

The stroke of Roosevelt's pen creating the Interdepartmental Intelligence
Conference was a huge blow to the prestige and historical authority of the
government's "premier Department." Concerned about the impact on the
State Department's leadership, the president felt compelled to ease the blow
by sending Hull a note and reminding him that the new structure "does not
mean that the intelligence work of the State Department should cease in any
way." The State Department would continue to collect information, as it had

in the past, with the proviso that now the "directors of the three agencies [FBI, MID, ONI] should be constantly kept in touch by the State Department with the work it is doing."[36]

This was a landmark directive for U.S. counterintelligence. For the first time in U.S. history, a new structure composed of specialized agencies with core competencies in such matters would focus on, direct, and coordinate all espionage, counterespionage, and sabotage investigations involving the federal government. Six months after the Rumrich convictions, the United States had in place its first counterintelligence coordinating committee. From this point forward, committee members would travel a bumpy road marked by frustration and finger-pointing, as well as collegiality, cooperation, and brilliant successes. And this road would bring the U.S. government into the Second World War with a new, transformed, and improved counterintelligence apparatus.

CHAPTER FOUR

Interdepartmental Intelligence Conference

Before President Roosevelt's coordination order, the three new agencies of the Interdepartmental Intelligence Conference (IIC) operated independently and met on an irregular basis. Exchange of information was sporadic and poorly defined because of legal and institutional issues left over from the constitutional excesses following the First World War. The June 1939 order changed everything. The FBI, MID, and ONI leadership now met weekly in a large conference room in J. Edgar Hoover's office at the Department of Justice (DOJ) Building in Washington. Discussions focused on items from a formalized agenda that had been prepared beforehand by subordinate staff. From the IIC's earliest days, all the participants had a basic idea of the coordination problems confronting them. Two committees secretly established in February 1939 by the MID, ONI, and FBI had been meeting for months at FBI offices. Both committees were composed of senior managers from the three agencies. The Committee on Investigations, chaired by Stanley J. Tracy, oversaw investigations affecting the military services, and the Committee on Espionage and Counterespionage, headed by W. Richard Glavin, addressed questions of policy formulation.[1]

Hoover's selection of Tracy and Glavin was no accident. Born in Ogden, Utah, in 1900, Tracy received a bachelor's degree in 1922 and a law degree in 1925, both from George Washington University. Before becoming an FBI agent in 1933, he served in the War Department and the Treasury Department. After a brief investigative field assignment, he was promoted to FBI headquarters in 1934. Ten months later Hoover brought Tracy into his inner sanctum, reassigning him to his personal office staff, where he still served when appointed to chair the Committee on Investigations. In September 1941 he was promoted again, this time to assistant director of the Identification Division and later the Technical Laboratory. Glavin, a native of Mahoney, Pennsylvania, graduated from Southeastern University in Washington, D.C., and then worked for the Postal Telegraph Company. This was followed by five years of service in the Marine Corps, where he taught general business subjects at the Marine Corps Institute. Glavin joined the FBI in April 1931, and in May 1941 he too was promoted to assistant director. The committees chaired by Tracy and Glavin met weekly on a wide range of issues affecting interagency coordination, such as duplication and overlapping of investigations, coordination questions, jurisdictional issues, legal matters, and new policies that would govern the actions and decisions of the three agencies.[2]

The April 9, 1940, meeting was a typical IIC session. Among the agenda items considered was a list of factories that had been visited by Fritz Wiedemann, the German consul general in San Francisco; procedures and policies governing aliens crossing U.S. borders, and an ONI request for information concerning the level of sabotage protection afforded California oil properties. Occasionally, matters less substantive and more personal in nature came up for discussion. For instance, at the May 14, 1940, meeting, Colonel J. M. Churchill of the MID requested an autographed photo of Hoover and the April graduating class of the FBI National Police Academy, which included some MID officers.[3]

An important aspect of cooperation among the new counterintelligence czars was their personal relationships with one another. As part of a class room exercise, Major Cyrus Searcy, a student at the U.S. Army War College, was assigned to study the question of coordination among the MID, ONI, and FBI in the event of war. His January 1939 report was generally a positive one. In wartime, the young officer concluded, "there undoubtedly will arise many occasions when the interests of these three services will be in conflict. Personalities will then, as always, play an important role."[4]

From the beginning, Hoover's attempts to wrest control of intelligence and counterintelligence policy away from the State Department poisoned his relationship with Messersmith. His personal relationship with the new MID chief was not much better. On April 17, 1939, the War Department established a separate Counterintelligence Branch after an eighteen-year hiatus.[5] With war in Europe now a reality, the War Department decided to upgrade the status of the MID's commanding officer from the traditional field-grade rank of colonel to a general officer level. On April 30, 1940, eleven days before the German invasion of France, Brigadier General Sherman Miles replaced the retiring Colonel Warren McCabe as the assistant chief of staff for intelligence. Miles had the army in his blood, having been born into a family with a long and distinguished military pedigree. His grand-uncle was William Tecumseh Sherman. His father, Nelson Miles, had served as a major general in the Civil War and later commanded the U.S. Army during the late 1890s. General Leonard Wood, President William McKinley's assistant surgeon and a member of Theodore Roosevelt's Rough Riders in Cuba, was married to Miles's cousin. Miles was a West Point graduate (class of 1905) and a close friend of General George S. Patton, Major General Ulysses S. Grant III, Lady Nancy Astor, and many prominent personalities from the world of art and theater, including Edith Wharton, winner of the Pulitzer Prize for *The Age of Innocence,* and screen actor Douglas Fairbanks Jr.[6]

Miles was thirteen years older than Hoover and had considerable experience in military intelligence but none in counterintelligence. His World War I service included combat action at St. Mihiel, France, and the Meuse-Argonne offensive. Later he authored a number of papers and studies on military matters, including "Notes on the Dardanelles Campaign of 1915." In 1919 he was part of a team of experts sent to Zagreb, Sarajevo, and Belgrade to report on developments in the Balkans following the collapse of the Hapsburg Empire. A European historian later recorded that Miles, a lieutenant colonel at the time, played an important role in this mission, "settling the border question between [Germany], Austria, and the newly created Kingdom of the Slovenes, Croats, and Serbs." Miles also saw military attaché service in Bucharest (1912–1914), Moscow (1914–1916), Turkey (1922–1925), and London from 1939 until his MID appointment in April 1940. In 1939 he was promoted to the rank of major general. Three years later, Miles's career would be derailed by the intelligence failure in connection with the Japanese air attack on Pearl Harbor. In 1942 he was replaced as head of the MID and spent the remainder of the war in a backwater post as head of the Volunteer Service Corps.[7]

The FBI director was wary of the general and his new role. After a history of warm relations with Colonel Churchill, Hoover's attitude toward Miles was cordial but formal. Repeatedly insisting that counterintelligence in the United States was essentially a civilian function, Hoover continually pressured the MID and ONI to concentrate their counterintelligence resources on military personnel and installations. Such an approach, in his view, would minimize duplication, improve coordination, and keep the military out of civilian matters. With his new field-grade rank, professional and personal connections, and family background, Miles was unaccustomed to challenges from bureaucrats like Hoover. In his view, Hoover was inexperienced in these matters, as well as inflexible and high-handed in his attitude toward the army. Complicating this relationship was the awkward juxtaposition of the roles of the two men. Hoover was chairman of the IIC, but at the same time, he served as a reserve lieutenant colonel in the MID, which subordinated him to Miles in the military hierarchy. Frustrated by this paradox, Miles never missed a chance to tweak Hoover by addressing his correspondence to the FBI director as "Lt. Col. Hoover."[8]

Eventually their contentious relationship erupted beyond the confines of the IIC, escalating up their respective chains of command to Secretary of War Henry Stimson and Attorney General Robert Jackson. Stimson, whose disdain for Hoover rivaled that of Miles, was often forced to intervene in the many conflicts between the two counterintelligence chiefs. Hoover's direct access to President Roosevelt infuriated Stimson and aroused his suspicion that the FBI director was using his White House access to influence interagency battles. In his private musings, Stimson accused Hoover of acting like a "prima donna" and behaving in a "childlike" manner rather than as a responsible government official. Stimson's anger and frustration led to fear that Hoover would "poison the mind of the president." After a year of futile struggle, the secretary of war despaired of ever achieving a satisfactory relationship between the two men, and at one point he even considered replacing Miles with someone who could get along with Hoover.[9]

Jackson (who would later serve as an associate justice of the Supreme Court and, after the Second World War, as U.S. representative and chief of counsel for the prosecution at the International Military Tribunal and war crimes trials in Nuremberg, Germany) admired Hoover's skills and abilities. However, he found that the FBI director's strong will made him "a difficult person to deal with." Jackson understood that the investigation of foreign espionage was moving the IIC into uncharted waters where a clash with civil liberties was a real danger. Hoover understood this as well, and Jackson appreciated the director's restraint in using his agents for these matters. As attorney general, Jackson, who had little background in espionage or counterintelligence, often sought Hoover's advice and frequently supported him on tough policy questions.[10]

One controversy that typified the philosophical differences between the military and the FBI arose during the spring of 1941. Miles and his two civilian bosses, Assistant Secretary of War John McCloy and Undersecretary of War Robert Patterson, approached Hoover with a request that FBI agents be assigned to a secret squad that would investigate labor unrest in war-related industries using means that clearly exceeded the rules of law. McCloy later claimed that his intention was not the surveillance of labor leaders but rather the prevention of violence, arson, work stoppages, and slowdowns by "foreign spies and saboteurs."[11]

Rebuffed by Hoover, McCloy and Patterson appealed to Jackson, who turned them down cold. An incensed Jackson informed the president about Patterson and McCloy's approach and their accusations that the FBI was confining "its investigations *within the limits of law.*" Both men, the president learned, had urged the creation of a "suicide squad" that would ignore conventional methods and be "unrestrained in wiretapping, in stealing evidence, in conducting unlimited searches and seizures, use of Dictaphones, etc., etc." Jackson's adamant opposition, as expressed to the president, ended the matter. Years later, in a manuscript that Jackson was working on before his sudden death, he praised Hoover for remaining within the bounds of the law. "I think he had no desire to abuse it," Jackson wrote. "The fact that he refused to go into labor matters at the request of the War Department and supervise labor conversations showed a restraint in the use of his powers for which, I may say, he was never given credit outside."[12]

Hoover's relationship with other IIC members was in marked contrast to his battles with General Miles. This was particularly so with Rear Admiral Walter S. Anderson, the director of naval intelligence (DNI), and Assistant Secretary of State Adolf Berle. Born in 1882 in Carlinville, Illinois, and a 1903 Naval Academy graduate, Anderson served during the First World War aboard the battleship *Arizona*. His first taste of intelligence gathering occurred in Japan in 1908 while sailing between Kobe and Yokkaichi aboard a Japanese ship named the *Tenyu Maru*. Permitted by the ship's captain to inspect the vessel, Anderson later provided his commanding officer with a detailed report on the functioning of the "turbine propelling machine and oil burning boilers." Five years later he dabbled in the newspaper business when Acting Secretary of the Navy Franklin D. Roosevelt authorized then Lieutenant Anderson to serve as a newspaper correspondent for the *New York Herald*. Ten years later, Commander Anderson blended his interest in journalism and his navy career in an article entitled "Light Cruisers—Our Navy's Needs," which appeared in the *Chicago Herald Examiner* in early 1923.[13] During the mid 1930s he served as naval attaché in London, followed by promotion to rear admiral in 1936. He took over command of the ONI in June 1939, where he remained until his transfer to Pearl Harbor as commander of battleships for the Pacific Fleet, with the USS *West Virginia* as his flagship.[14]

Although jurisdictional issues and bureaucratic controversies regularly produced differences of opinion between Hoover and Anderson, their close personal relationship helped them find common ground and reach mutually agreeable compromises. Anderson, who had no experience in counterintelligence and security, looked to Hoover for guidance and leadership and cooperated closely with him. In April 1940 Anderson and a senior FBI official met with representatives of the National Industrial Conference Board in New York to discuss the plant protection program; the following September they met again, along with Hugh Clegg, the recently appointed assistant director of the FBI's National Defense Division. In the feuds between Hoover and Miles over the direction of counterintelligence policy, Anderson continually sided with Hoover. As DNI, he ordered his local agents to share their information with FBI field offices and to assist local FBI agents in the surveillance of Japanese Americans and Japanese visitors. In addition, Anderson sent language expert Arthur McCallum to provide the FBI with linguistic support. Anderson's role as DNI offered him frequent and direct Oval Office access, an advantage that permitted him to lobby the president for legislation that would permit government wiretapping, registration of all alien-owned fishing vessels based in U.S. ports, and restriction of photography near U.S. military installations.[15]

Hoover reciprocated in kind. ONI personnel attended a four-week FBI training course focusing on counterintelligence issues. Radio intercepts from FBI stations in Latin America were routinely supplied to the ONI, together with a steady stream of updates from a special agent team sent to Quito, Ecuador, to aid the naval attaché in an operation against a Nazi agent. Hoover valued this collaboration. "Our relationship in intelligence has been an ideal one," Hoover later noted, and "I feel that greater progress has been made in real coordination and cooperation of the Intelligence agencies during this period than anytime heretofore." Writing to Secretary of the Navy Frank Knox, Hoover "exceedingly" regretted Anderson's transfer. "No Director of Naval Intelligence," Hoover effused, "has been more cooperative than Admiral Anderson." Decades later, reflecting on his tenure as DNI, Anderson characterized the cooperation between the FBI and the ONI as "excellent," noting that he "conceived a very high and warm regard" for all IIC members, "especially for J. Edgar Hoover."[16]

Assistant Secretary of State Adolf Berle succeeded Messersmith in the spring of 1940 as the State Department liaison for intelligence matters. Berle had served as an army intelligence officer during the First World War and later assisted the U.S. delegation at the Versailles peace negotiations. Back in civilian life, he achieved international renown as an economist and professor at Columbia University in New York City. As an early member of Roosevelt's "brain trust," he had no career connections with the State Department, which made him less parochial in his outlook and, in Hoover's view, more supportive of the Bureau's position in discussions with State Department officials. The FBI director kept Berle regularly informed concerning IIC matters, always hopeful that he could pressure the department's leadership to make decisions favorable to the FBI.[17]

Berle shared Hoover's anticommunist outlook and later supported him during the wiretapping controversy that erupted in the spring of 1940. One of Hoover's proudest accomplishments was the creation of the FBI National Police Academy in Washington, D.C. Upon completion of the course of study, graduates attended a ceremony that included a keynote speech given by a prestigious public figure. In selecting speakers, Hoover chose only persons he considered friendly and loyal to the Bureau's mission. His fondness for Berle was evident when he invited the assistant secretary to serve as guest speaker at the graduation ceremonies for the academy's fourteenth session. In addition to demonstrating his trust in Berle, it highlighted the importance the FBI placed on state, local, and federal law enforcement relations as the country moved closer to war. "We consider these men a reserve force available to the bureau in times of national emergency," Hoover told Berle in his invitation, and "I know that you will be most interested in this phase of the academy's work in as much as it is so closely related to our problems of national defense."[18]

The August 24, 1939, nonaggression pact between Germany and the Soviet Union and the German invasion of Poland strengthened the IIC and the FBI's role in counterintelligence. Roosevelt's Executive Order 8247, declaring a national emergency, clarified any lingering questions concerning counterintelligence jurisdiction by ordering the FBI to "take charge of investigative work in matters relating to espionage, sabotage, and violations of neutrality regulations." To meet these new demands, the White House authorized an increase in FBI staffing for fiscal year 1940, adding 150 special agents, which necessitated a supplemental budget increase of $1,475,000. Another 100-agent increase was authorized in fiscal year 1941, at a new total cost of $2,693,000. By the end of 1939, however, espionage complaints coming into FBI field offices around the country had ballooned to a level far exceeding the Justice Department's original estimates, hindering the FBI's ability to handle them in a timely manner. Statistics for January 1940 indicated a rapidly growing backlog of complaints awaiting investigation and at least 12,000 industrial plants requiring surveys. With the original case and staffing projections no longer relevant, Attorney General Frank Murphy was forced to request new appropriations doubling the number of special agents hired over the remaining six months of fiscal years 1940 and 1941.[19]

Foreign Liaison

The creation of the IIC also prompted changes in FBI relations with foreign security services. No longer did the Canadians have to conceal their real purposes when requesting information from Hoover. Within days of the president's secret order of June 26, 1939, creating the IIC, Hoover's staff began pressuring him for an expansion of the confidential relationship between the RCMP and the FBI. Before the new IIC order, the FBI and RCMP secretly exchanged information on matters of espionage, sabotage, and subversion "when it was believed that the information would be of interest to that organization." The RCMP was also quietly investigating leads supplied by the FBI in certain espionage cases. In November 1939 Hoover began a direct and open exchange of information with the RCMP on a variety of sensitive matters, such as the names of suspicious travelers moving back and forth across the U.S.-Canadian border or arriving from Europe or the Far East, war industries protection, international money transfers, and suspected enemy agents and saboteurs. Following U.S. entry into the Second World War, the FBI and RCMP exchanged representatives who had direct access to each other's raw investigative files. This new relationship significantly improved the counterintelligence environment in North America and would pay major benefits during the war.[20]

The same could not be said for liaison with the British. Even with the president's emergency proclamation and a critical need for better communication between the FBI and the British services, the State Department was still worried about critics accusing the administration of warmongering. Tentative steps at contact between the FBI and the British Secret Intelligence Service (MI6) were quickly dashed by State Department officials. In early September 1939 Sir James Paget, an MI6 officer stationed in New York under cover as the British passport control officer, approached Hoover and the War Department seeking a mechanism for the direct exchange of information. When the State Department learned of this move, Assistant

Secretary of State James Dunn immediately sent a cautionary note to the British, reminding them that all intelligence and police information must be transmitted through the U.S. embassy in London. Herschel Johnson, a foreign service officer stationed in London, was serving as the intelligence liaison for the State Department. Johnson called Guy Liddell to the embassy and handed Dunn's note to him personally. An obviously frustrated Liddell later vented his private feelings in his diary. The State Department wanted all such information "bottle-necked" through the embassy, he recorded. The excuse, he wrote, was worry "about liberal exchange through the police and military owing to the delicate international situation."[21]

Fingerprints

Another step forward in the IIC relationship was the role of the FBI's Identification Division (ID). By the start of the war it had sole responsibility for collecting, processing, and filing cards containing the fingerprints of tens of millions of Americans. An understanding of the importance of the ID in the counterintelligence structure requires a brief look at the history of fingerprinting. As the science of fingerprinting evolved in the late nineteenth and early twentieth centuries, so did the general acceptance of the fact that each human being's fingerprints are unique. In 1901 a fingerprint classification system was successfully introduced in England and Wales by Sir Edward Henry. The Henry system was a categorization of fingerprint patterns based on the consideration of all ten fingers as a unit. This revolutionary new classification system, using a combination of letters and numbers, detailed the general patterns of skin ridges on human fingers. When filed in the proper sequence, the system facilitated ready reference and quick retrieval. Police agencies throughout Europe and the United States gradually began to recognize the utility of fingerprints and the Henry system in professional police work. Latent prints—finger impressions left on evidence at a crime scene—could be lifted and later matched with a person's complete set of fingerprint impressions. If the latent print matched the fingerprints of a person on file, that could be used in court as evidence. As the use of latent print evidence became increasingly accepted by police agencies, many of the convictions achieved through this new technique were appealed to state and federal appellate courts, based on the claim that the science of fingerprinting was invalid and subject to flawed conclusions. In all these instances, however, the scientific accuracy of human fingerprint identification was upheld, and the acceptance of such evidence gradually became a standard practice in U.S. courts.[22]

In October 1923 the fingerprint cards and records of the Bureau of Investigation, maintained at Leavenworth Penitentiary in Kansas, were transferred to the DOJ in Washington, D.C. Nine months later, in July 1924, Congress ordered these records combined with material held by the Association of Chiefs of Police and consolidated under the jurisdiction of J. Edgar Hoover, who in May 1924 assumed the duties of acting director of the Bureau of Investigation. Known as the National Division of Identification and Information, it started with more than 800,000 fingerprint cards and records administered by twenty-five employees.[23]

By 1930 the number of fingerprint records on file had grown to over 2 million. That same year Congress authorized the new division to begin collecting and compiling crime statistics from across the entire nation. In September the first monthly bulletin containing these figures was published and distributed to state and local police agencies throughout the country. A year later Hoover initiated an international exchange of fingerprint data with a number of nations in the Western Hemisphere and Europe. As the reputation of the new division grew, so did its role in helping the Bureau forge stronger bonds of cooperation at all levels of law enforcement. It was also a source of great pride for Hoover. He frequently touted its successes, as well as the growing importance of forensic science in the solution of complicated criminal cases. He believed, however, that this new technique was not the exclusive purview of the federal government; to be fully effective, it must be embraced by police agencies at all levels nationwide. In 1936, one year after the first class graduated from the National Police Academy, Hoover inaugurated a series of courses, taught by FBI personnel, to instruct police officers in the technique of taking a person's fingerprints, classifying them for future identification and retrieval, and maintaining local identification records.[24]

On March 27, 1936, the FBI reached the milestone of 100,000 fingerprint cards in its Civil Section. This category was separate and distinct from the cards containing the prints of men and women arrested throughout the country on criminal charges. Established in 1933, the Civil Section of the ID served as the repository for the fingerprint cards of noncriminals, which generally originated from state and local agencies as part of the employment process. When the FBI received a set of fingerprints from an originating agency, an examiner would search all fingerprint files to determine whether the ID had ever received an identical set of prints. If no record was found, the originating agency was so informed; if a match was found, the originating agency would be informed of the contents of the record in the ID files. Because fingerprints of the same person might be submitted repeatedly, a single identification record containing a summary of all submissions, both civil and criminal, was constructed for future use by the FBI and all submitting agencies.[25]

Recording, classifying, searching, and responding to the receipt of millions of fingerprint records on a daily basis was both tedious and labor-intensive, and each function was critical to the next. Failure to match a new print card with an identical set on file could have serious consequences: a person with a serious criminal record could be drafted into the military, a human body discovered without identification could remain anonymous forever, or a criminal using an assumed name might never have his true identity uncovered.

The cases of Joseph Bullay, Joseph Wendling, and Evo Orsi illustrate how the system worked. All three were fingerprinted in accord with the Alien Registration Act of 1940. Bullay had been a fugitive for ten years for failing to comply with orders of the Ohio State Board of Parole. Wendling had been sentenced in 1910 to life in prison for murder, escaped and was recaptured in 1919, and was eventually released in 1935 on the condition that he leave the United States. When he was readmitted to the country in 1936, he failed to maintain the required contact with immigration authorities, and a warrant was issued for his arrest. Orsi had a lengthy arrest record during the 1930s and had been wanted since 1938 for probation violation by the Santa Barbara, California, sheriff's office. All three men were arrested when their new fingerprint cards were matched with their existing ID records.[26]

A curious incident that illustrates the value of this process occurred during the war and involved Guenther Rumrich. Following his release from prison, he was essentially homeless and unable to get a job because of his conviction. Desperate, he changed his name, moved to the Pacific Northwest, and got a low-level job as a time keeper at the Kaiser shipbuilding plant near Tacoma, Washington. Under the rules in place for war manufacturing facilities, Rumrich was fingerprinted as a routine part of his employment application. Eventually these prints were sent to Washington, where they were classified and matched with Rumrich's fingerprints taken by the FBI when he was arrested in February 1938. Kaiser officials were quickly notified, and Rumrich was fired.[27]

The ease with which Lonkowski, Gudenberg, and other Rumrich conspirators had obtained employment at U.S. defense plants stunned military authorities. No background investigation, no records check, and no questioning of any kind were necessary for a person to acquire a job that immediately offered direct access to the nation's most sensitive military-industrial secrets. The Rumrich case changed this procedure forever. The Roosevelt administration ordered the fingerprinting of all War Department employees and those working in related industries. Although exact figures are not available, conclusions concerning the explosive growth of the ID can be drawn from the fact that the Bureau had more than 5 million fingerprint cards on file in July 1935; only 19,000 of these cards were in the Civil Section. By the time of the Pearl Harbor attack, however, the total number of civil fingerprint submissions had grown to nearly 9 million prints, with 1.5 million records received in fiscal year 1938 alone.[28]

Although the growth of the ID between 1935 and 1940 was certainly remarkable, it paled in comparison to the acceleration that occurred after the summer of 1940. All applicants for federal government employment, as well as all active-duty military personnel, were fingerprinted. Added to this were the new requirements of the Immigration Act, signed by the president at the end of June 1940, and the new Selective Service Act. All new aliens arriving in the United States were fingerprinted, along with 3.5 million residents with noncitizen status. In addition, the military draft necessitated the fingerprinting of 1.5 million young men facing mandatory military service. The pressure on the Bureau's manpower became staggering. The national defense role of the IIC expanded the FBI's responsibilities from a small law enforcement service into a twenty-four-hour-a-day operation reaching throughout the government and private industry.

A confidential report prepared for the White House in October 1940 by Hoover told the whole story. The ID had doubled in size during the previous year. It received 12,000 new military-related fingerprint cards daily, and comparisons of those submissions were reported back to the originating agencies within thirty-six hours of receipt. Another 2,000 fingerprint cards were received daily from the Immigration Bureau, with more than 12,000 received between November 4 and 9, 1940, alone. By the end of 1940 the ID reached a new high of 14 million fingerprint cards—a figure that continued to increase at a dizzying rate as war drew closer. On the eve of Pearl Harbor the average daily inflow of fingerprint cards was 25,000, and the total number of cards on file skyrocketed to 24 million. Keeping pace with these growing demands meant continued pressure on the White House for more resources. In a special 1940 budget request, Hoover proposed hiring 500 additional fingerprint examiners to handle the burgeoning workload. As a result, the size of the ID doubled during fiscal year 1940 and more than doubled in fiscal year 1941.[29]

Counterespionage Training

With the responsibility for civilian counterintelligence squarely on the shoulders of the FBI, Hoover wasted no time preparing his field investigators for the new cases that were now dramatically increasing. The job of developing a training course was assigned to one of his closest associates and longest-serving agents, inspector and assistant director for training Hugh H. Clegg. A Mississippi native, Clegg received a degree in 1920 from Millsap College in Jackson, Mississippi, and a law degree from George Washington University in 1926. His manner was always courtly, but as one later observer noted, he appeared as "tough as a gangster." During the 1930s he participated in some of the FBI's most noted cases, including the Kansas City Massacre and the failed arrest attempt of John Dillinger at Little Bohemia, Wisconsin, where special agent Carter Baum was murdered. Education was a significant aspect of Clegg's background. While at Millsap he had taught Latin and chemistry, and he later taught for two years at Bennett Academy in Mathiston, Mississippi. During the 1930s he established the course of instruction for new agents entering the FBI and the curriculum at the FBI National Police Academy.[30]

Clegg designed a course of instruction to educate special agents and managers about all aspects of foreign intelligence services, including the covert movement of funds through the worldwide banking system and new ways to fight it.[31] On July 17, 1939, less than two months after the president's restructuring order, the FBI held its first in-service training in Washington, D.C. It was a four-week course broken into two segments. Lectures reflected the new realities facing the U.S. national security establishment. Students studied espionage investigations, counterespionage and sabotage, subversive movements, and neutrality act investigations. Other topics focused on more refined intelligence and investigative techniques. "Chemistry problems in neutrality, espionage, and sabotage investigations, document identification, sound recording, methods of concealing messages, secret codes and secret writing, detection of secret inks, photographic aspects of espionage work," and "technical equipment" were also studied. The FBI's new plant survey program also required instructional attention. A total of twenty-four topics were taught, ranging from basic plant protection policy to combustibles, acids, abrasives, explosives, and arson; from latent fingerprints to crime scene searches.[32]

General Intelligence Division

When the IIC was formed in June 1939, the FBI had only one division at headquarters managing all investigations nationwide. In addition to espionage, sabotage, and internal security, Division One, as it was known, supervised more than seventy other categories of investigative violations, ranging from bank robbery, kidnapping, and extortion to violations of the Migratory Bird Act. The new national security cases, expanded military and foreign intelligence liaison, and related responsibilities soon overwhelmed the existing bureaucratic structure, rendering it unworkable.

With the volume of complaints and investigations and the intensity of coordination increasing at a spiraling rate, Hoover reorganized the FBI's headquarters structure in an attempt to better address these new interorganizational demands. In November 1939 the national supervision of espionage, sabotage, and internal security matters was removed from Division One and reassigned to the new General Intelligence Division (GID), known within the FBI as Division Five. Hoover entrusted the leadership of the new division to another close aide, Edward Tamm. Together with his number-one man C. H. "Kit" Carson, Tamm now oversaw all counterespionage investigative matters that in any way affected the MID, the ONI, and the State Department.[33]

For efficiency, the new division was organized into four sections: espionage and sabotage, selective service and foreign funds, internal security, and plant survey. Within the Sabotage Section an FBI supervisor was assigned, for the first time, as the day-to-day coordinator of the FBI-IIC meetings, while a second supervisor handled direct day-to-day liaison with the MID, ONI, and State Department. Original staffing figures for the new division are unavailable. By February 1941, however, sixteen months after its creation, Division Five reached a total supervisory complement of forty-eight FBI agents.[34]

Plant Survey Program

The inclusion of the Plant Survey Section in the GID reflected another new and major role for the FBI. A year before the president's emergency order, the military services had asked Hoover to assume responsibility for investigating conditions in the approximately 12,000 industrial plants that had sprung up in response to the nation's growing military rearmament. Staffing difficulties and constitutional concerns over the separation of military and civilian industrial relationships drove the decision to minimize direct navy and army involvement in plant security matters. As a consequence, by the fall of 1939, a nationwide plant survey program managed by the FBI was under way. FBI agents with special training began visiting industrial plant managers, inspecting their sites, looking for weaknesses, and offering recommendations for protecting factories against sabotage and espionage. Depending on the size of the facility, these inspections often required more than one agent and could take several days or weeks to complete.[35]

Typical of these plant inspections was the one performed in January 1940 at the North American Aviation Company's facility in Ingleside, California. It took one agent eleven days to complete and addressed everything from physical security to labor-management relations. Fences, lighting, parking, dining areas, entry and exit systems, protective devices, and guard systems were afforded the same emphasis as the numerical breakdown of foreign-born employees, who were now vetted for the first time concerning their loyalties. The results of the investigation were then incorporated into a report that was forwarded to the GID in Washington. Findings included the improper filing of blueprints in unlocked drawers, draftsmen exchanging documents without proper recordation, transformers and substations at danger points, no special protection given to machinery within the plant, and office wastepaper baskets emptied and material burned by the janitorial staff.[36]

Along with other observations and recommendations for necessary changes and improvements, such reports were then passed on to the MID or the ONI, depending on which service had a contract with the particular plant. The special agent who conducted the survey also discussed the results with local plant officials. By June 1940, 800 surveys were under way, and more than 200 had been completed. Industrial mishaps were also recorded, and appropriate steps were taken when the number and frequency of unexplained incidents rose at a particular plant. Within a year, these surveys were augmented by special agents of the FBI and ONI posing as workers in key industrial defense plants, for the purpose of ferreting out possible saboteurs.[37]

At the same time, the navy and army leadership began pressuring defense companies doing business with the government to tighten up security at their plants and factories. In 1939 the Wright Aircraft Company, which had contracts with the military, entered into an agreement with the Soviet Union's Stalin Aircraft Plant that included provisions for the exchange of inspectors at each facility. The U.S. military began exercising more vigilance regarding these inspection visits, and in late 1939, Chief of Naval Operations Harold Stark ordered his subordinates to inform Wright executives that the navy could no longer "look with favor" on Soviet engineers being permanently "stationed in the company's plant." He charged that there were routinely twenty or thirty Russian visitors at these facilities, ostensibly for the purpose of exchanging information on civilian aircraft construction, yet they were allowed to wander throughout the plant unescorted, observing the production and development of military aircraft engines. In fact, in the wake of the national defense buildup, and with the events of the past year still fresh in everyone's mind, the navy demanded that Russian technicians no longer be "admitted to the company's plant," suggesting that the company consider instituting a policy of "casual one day visits."[38]

Gradually, the experiences and lessons gathered from these surveys were collected by the Bureau and published in a series of monographs that were distributed by the tens of thousands to industrial plant managers throughout the nation. *Suggestions for Protection of Industrial Facilities,* produced in December 1941, was typical of these instructional bulletins and contained a wide range of useful ideas about strengthening security in industrial plants. Topics such as personnel, physical property, confidential documents, identification systems, and guard forces were covered. Plant managers were warned that foreign agents would "make every effort to obtain employment in an important plant or a plant producing confidential material," and they were cautioned to view unexplained employee absenteeism "with suspicion" and institute an inquiry into the individual's activities. Among the commonsense personnel security measures recommended was the performance of a background investigation on all applicants for employment, particularly "a statement as to the employee's whereabouts and activities during the period from 1914 to 1918, inclusive." All applicants and current employees should be fingerprinted and the prints sent to the FBI for retention. "This is especially true," the bulletin noted, "where the employee is found to have secretly traveled to another city or a foreign country." Also, rather than disposing of trash as junk and removing it intact from the plant area, it recommended that all wastepaper be incinerated or shredded.[39]

Coordination and Investigation

Allegations of espionage were often spurious, with little factual basis. Charges were frequently based on flimsy evidence or mere suspicion based on a person's German background, poor English-speaking ability, favorable remarks about Hitler and Nazism, wall posters touting Germany's achievements, aloofness from neighbors and coworkers, or remarks that someone considered unpatriotic. These types of complaints flooded into FBI offices around the country by the thousands. In general, some investigation was required to resolve a complaint. If the accusation contained no supporting facts, which was frequently the case, the FBI conducted no further investigation, and the matter was referred to the appropriate military service for informational purposes. In most cases, the MID or ONI would index the person's name for possible future reference, and no action would be taken.

Not all allegations, however, could be indexed, filed, and dismissed by IIC member agencies. Many complaints included information requiring further investigation to satisfactorily resolve the issue. In other instances, even if there was little basis to the accusation, the nature of the allegation could not be ignored. The investigation of Robert Brunner was typical of such cases. An army sergeant assigned to the Quartermaster Corps, Brunner kept flattering posters of Hitler on his walls and offered Nazi literature to someone who later complained to the FBI. Another involved a seaman named Robert Charles Simpson who was reported to the FBI in February 1940 by a Miami, Florida, photo shop owner who had developed photographs taken by Simpson as his ship passed through the Panama Canal. In another case, perhaps driven by the discovery of Mrs. Jesse Jordan's role in the Rumrich-Abwehr correspondence, the FBI launched an investigation of a physician named Arthur Schramm. A resident of Los Angeles, California, Schramm was suspected of harboring pro-Nazi views and had received letters from around the United States and from foreign countries. Another such case involved a report received about a Japanese American living in

Seattle, Washington. His neighbors suspected that he was involved in espionage because he maintained a powerful radio transmitter at his home. During the course of the investigation, the FBI contacted the Federal Communications Commission (FCC) to determine whether lists of radio operators were maintained. The FBI's closing report was submitted to the ONI because of its primary jurisdiction for the West Coast and Pacific Ocean activities. The FCC's position, the report noted, was that "as a rule amateur radio operators are not listed by nationality but in the case of the Japanese a separate list is maintained of all persons of this nationality who have amateur licenses." The Bureau's investigation of such cases generally included a close examination of the person's mail for thirty days, followed by additional surveillance, interviews of witnesses, and, if warranted, an interview of the subject.[40]

During the thirty months between the president's June 1939 order centralizing counterintelligence activities and the Japanese attack on Pearl Harbor in December 1941, the new and untested IIC structure contributed to the successful resolution of a number of important espionage cases, including that of Frederick Duquesne, which is examined in detail in chapter 11. A major factor in the successful U.S. response to foreign espionage was improved access to records contained in each IIC member's files. Names of persons, groups, organizations, and corporations were now being collected and indexed at an accelerated rate by each IIC member, and these files could now be searched, on request, by other members.

Four cases that highlight this improvement in coordination involved Jones Orin York, Paul Borchardt, Itaru Tachibana, and Frederick Rutland. York, born in Illinois in 1893, was a divorced aircraft technician who had worked at Northrop Corporation and the Lockheed Airplane Company. A would-be inventor bent on getting rich, York met Stanislaw Shumovsky in the early 1930s when the Russian was leading a commercial delegation visiting Lockheed. York hoped to interest Shumovsky in a new aircraft engine that he had designed. Instead, Shumovsky, a Soviet intelligence officer (who later enrolled as a graduate student at the Massachusetts Institute of Technology as a cover), exploited York's greed and recruited him in 1934 as an espionage agent.[41]

York came to FBI attention four years later through the Gorin investigation. Following the arrests of Gorin and Salich, York panicked, abruptly left his job at Lockheed without explanation, and disappeared. Eventually, he was traced to an isolated campsite in New Hampshire, where he was living under the name R. L. DuBoise. The FBI investigation of York and the hunt for his whereabouts involved close coordination with MID and ONI representatives on the national and local levels. Frequent meetings were held and files were exchanged, including ONI files on Shumovsky's activities and FBI reports on the progress of the investigation.[42]

Paul Borchardt was a German Jew by birth and a Roman Catholic by faith, an explorer, and an authority on the Libyan desert. He had worked in the Middle East during the First World War as a German agent under the name Abdul Hamil Battota. In 1933 he was discharged from the directorship of the Military Geographical School after a year of service because of his Jewish ancestry. His army connections protected his unofficial teaching position until April 1939, when he was forced to leave Germany and immigrate to England. Despite good social connections and strong backing from British pacifist groups, Borchardt's offer to serve the War Office and the Admiralty as an operative in the Middle East was rejected.[43]

In February 1940 the State Department informed the MID that a visa had been issued to Borchardt, who was leaving London to assume a teaching position at Seton Hall College in New Jersey. A year later Borchardt came to the FBI's attention when an informant, working in the German consulate in New York City, discovered his name on a piece of wastepaper that had not been completely incinerated. An investigation was started, and with the help of MID information, Borchardt was soon linked to five others involved in a spy ring headed by Kurt Frederick Ludwig, an American-born German agent who was arrested and charged with spying in August 1941. Borchardt was closely watched by the FBI until December 8, 1941, when he was arrested and charged with violating U.S. espionage laws.[44]

The IIC focus was not just on German and Soviet activities. For a number of years the United States and Japan had an exchange agreement involving the assignment of American military officers to Japan for two years to study the language and culture, with an equal number of Japanese officers sent to the United States to study English. The five Japanese officers visiting the United States in 1939 were technically assigned as "language student[s]" to the Japanese embassy in Washington, D.C., but without diplomatic status. In fact, they rarely visited Washington but regularly received funds from the embassy, which each officer used to finance unsupervised and unregulated travel throughout the United States. One prominent student who took advantage of this arrangement between the wars was a Japanese naval officer named Isoroku Yamamoto—the same Yamamoto who later rose to the rank of admiral and planned the surprise attack on Pearl Harbor.[45]

Itaru Tachibana, a thirty-seven-year-old lieutenant commander in the
Japanese navy, arrived in the United States in July 1939. He became the focus of an FBI investigation in 1940 when the Los Angeles office of the ONI
reported his language-student status and his residence at a local hotel. The
case took off in March 1941 when Los Angeles resident Al Blake told the FBI
about a conversation he had recently had with Toraichia Kono, a Japanese
American friend. Kono had casually asked Blake about his selective service
status and expressed disappointment when he learned that Blake was a military veteran. Kono suggested that a friend who was an official of "the Imperial Japanese Navy was prepared to pay $50,000 for U.S. Navy information."
Blake expressed interest in the proposition and quickly fabricated a story
about a friend in Honolulu aboard the USS *Pennsylvania* who might also be
interested in making some "easy money."[46]

Kono, born in Japan in 1885, had immigrated to the United States at the
age of fifteen. He later studied auto mechanics, married, had children, and
worked in a variety of jobs up and down the California coast. For a number
of years he served as a valet and chauffeur for the silent film star Charlie
Chaplin, accompanying him on a trip to Japan in the early in 1930s and later
being fired for reasons unknown. At the time he and Blake met, the fifty-six-
year-old Kono was doing odd jobs at local produce markets.[47]

Blake's story intrigued the FBI. However, unaccustomed to handling
these types of cases, the Los Angeles office was concerned about the legal
question of entrapment. Entrapment issues arise when a law enforcement
agency lures an individual into the commission of a crime for the purpose of
prosecuting that person for it. A defense attorney could claim that the arrest
was invalid because no crime would have occurred if the situation had not
been created and manipulated by the law enforcement agency.[48] Nevertheless, Blake was urged to continue his relationship with Kono and to provide
regular reports to the FBI in Los Angeles. For reasons that are unclear, Blake
reported his next contact with Kono to the ONI, which assumed control of
the case. Over the next few weeks, Kono introduced Blake to Tachibana,
who was using the name Yamato. At Kono's and Tachibana's urging, Blake
agreed to travel to Honolulu to meet with his "friend." Under the ONI's
watchful eye, Blake twice traveled to Hawaii, where ONI officers gave him
documents to pass on to Kono and Tachibana. The material contained confidential information on target practice conducted by the USS *Phoenix* and
the movements of the cruiser the USS *Indianapolis*. By late May 1941, Kono

had bought the information from Blake for $3,600, which he claimed had come from Tachibana.[49]

The Tachibana investigation highlighted the problems facing the new IIC setup. The ONI, which directed this phase of the investigation, was an intelligence collection service with no authority to arrest civilians; it had arrest authority only in areas under naval jurisdiction. In addition, it had little experience or training in the collection of evidence, the legal considerations of importance to federal prosecutors, or the preparation of witnesses and evidence for trial. Yet as the case progressed, it became clear that both Tachibana and Kono were violating federal espionage laws. Furthermore, Blake's testimony about his role as a government informant, the part played by the ONI in directing his activities, the significance of the sensitive navy information supplied by the ONI for Blake to give to Kono and Tachibana, and the ONI's growing evidence of a wider espionage conspiracy would all be critical factors in any subsequent prosecution. The seriousness of this situation was quickly recognized, and in early May 1941, while Blake was in Honolulu, the ONI briefed the FBI's Los Angeles office with a view toward developing a partnership. Examination of the evidence and a series of meetings involving the FBI, the ONI, and the U.S. attorney for Los Angeles led the U.S. attorney to authorize the arrest and prosecution of both Tachibana and Kono on espionage charges.[50]

Within days the Department of Justice was informed of this decision, and the Department of State was briefed on the matter. On May 13, however, the U.S. attorney was overruled by the State Department. In a telephone call to Tamm, Berle refused to discuss the details of his decision but insisted that the department had "good reasons for making this request." Despite the fact that Kono was a U.S. citizen and Tachibana had no diplomatic immunity protecting him from federal law, the State Department cited ongoing diplomatic tensions between the United States and Japan as the reason for not pursuing charges against the two men. On May 22 Berle was again asked for an opinion concerning prosecution, and Tamm reminded him that Tachibana had already given money to Blake, through Kono, for a second trip to Honolulu to acquire additional confidential navy information. Berle referred the matter to the Secretary of State Cordell Hull, who overruled him on May 24, expressing no opposition to the FBI-ONI actions. His support, however, was contingent on three important assurances: that convictions could be obtained; that the FBI, DOJ, and ONI were "certain of their facts"; and that the arrests were necessary. Five days later, Attorney General Robert Jackson authorized the arrest of Tachibana and Kono; less than a month later, on June 7, 1941, both men were arrested and charged with committing espionage for Japan.[51]

On June 3, 1941, just four days before the arrest of Tachibana and Kono, another lieutenant commander of the Japanese Imperial Navy, Sadatomo Okada, was arrested for speeding by the Bakersfield, California, Police Department. Okada had been under investigation by the ONI since December 1940 as a possible espionage agent while he was living in Seattle, Washington. But in April 1941, after consultation with the FBI in Washington, ONI officials had been forced to drop any plans to prosecute Okada because of insufficient evidence against him. However, a search of his suitcase after his traffic arrest uncovered national defense material that Okada later admitted to ONI agents was destined for Tachibana in Los Angeles. Okada's situation only worsened after Tachibana's arrest, when a search of his room revealed compelling evidence of collaboration between the two naval officers. Further investigation soon implicated another coconspirator, Wataru Yamada, an engineering officer in the Japanese navy who was also living and studying on the West Coast. Yamada was already in the FBI's files. He had accompanied Tachibana from California to Washington in May 1941 when the latter had delivered Blake's material to the Japanese embassy.[52]

With evidence of espionage mounting against Yamada and Okada, the Department of State was again asked for its position concerning prosecution. Once again Berle supported the arrests and prosecutions, based on Hull's previous provisos. Both men were arrested by agents of the ONI and FBI on June 22, 1940. With Tachibana free on bail and Kono in jail, the next question was the course of the prosecution. The Department of State was consulted again, and this time, the new IIC learned what can occur when law enforcement, counterintelligence, and diplomacy collide. In spite of Tachibana's admissions, his lack of diplomatic immunity, and the overall strength of the government's case, Hull reversed himself, urging no further prosecution because of the worsening relationship between Japan and the United States. Instead, he recommended that Tachibana be permitted to return to Japan quietly; as for Okada, he insisted that no prosecution be undertaken without "additional consultation" with the State Department. Hull had no objection to the prosecution of Kono, "provided he entered a plea of guilty." The espionage charges against Yamada were dropped for lack of sufficient evidence. Diplomacy had trumped the process of law. On June

21, 1941, two weeks after his arrest, Tachibana sailed from San Francisco for Japan following the dismissal of the charges against him, as did Yamada and Okada on July 5. With Tachibana, Okada, and Yamada now unavailable, the case against Kono was irreparably weakened, forcing the government to dismiss the charges against him too. He quickly returned to life in Los Angeles until his arrest on December 7, 1941; he spent the rest of the war in prison.[53]

Frederick Rutland, a British citizen, was living in Beverly Hills, California, in 1941 and operating an investment firm in Los Angeles. During the First World War, Rutland had served in the Royal Naval Air Service, receiving the Distinguished Service Cross for his contributions to improved aerial cooperation in fleet action during the Battle of Jutland. Later he was awarded the Albert Medal First Class, bestowed on those who have "in saving or endeavoring to save lives of others from shipwreck or other perils of the sea endangered their own lives"; the First Class rating was reserved for "cases of extreme and heroic daring." After the war Rutland left the British navy and moved to Japan, where he consulted for the Mitsubishi Aircraft Company as part of the Japanese pursuit of a modern naval air arm. By the time he arrived in California in 1937, he had already traveled to South America in search of business opportunities; returned to England in 1931, where he worked in automobile sales; and traveled back to Japan on two or three occasions.[54]

Rutland was also a Japanese agent working for Tachibana. His motivation for spying is still in question today. One biographer, writing decades after the war ended, described him as a man of action, a loyal British subject, yet an "old-fashioned type of mercenary, ready to work for anyone reasonably congenial who would pay him well, provided that he was not expected to work against his country." Although the ONI was following Japanese intelligence activities on the West Coast, it had not developed sufficient evidence against Rutland to take any action. When Tachibana was arrested, a panicky Rutland quickly offered his services to the FBI, claiming that his "extremely good commercial connections" with the Japanese government could be useful for gathering information. When the FBI rejected his offer, he turned to John Maude, an MI5 officer assigned to the British embassy in Washington. Maude considered using him as a double agent—an idea that was quickly quashed when the FBI and ONI advised him of Rutland's predicament. With enough evidence in hand to prosecute Rutland, the FBI and DOJ began considering his arrest on espionage charges. However, in the interest of avoiding the "scandal of bringing to trial an ex-member of the British air force," a decision was made to encourage Rutland to return to England voluntarily. Maude, with FBI backing, led Rutland to believe that he was being considered as a British double agent against the Japanese and urged him to return to England, where the plan could be further developed. Jumping at the opportunity, Rutland fled the United States and arrived in England in October 1941, where he was placed under continuous surveillance until his arrest on December 11, 1941, under the Emergency Regulation (18b) for "Hostile Associations."[55]

Custodial Detention

In May 1940, as the Low Countries and France began their six-week journey toward defeat at the hands of the German army, President Roosevelt moved quickly to tighten the rules concerning immigration and resident aliens. Roosevelt undertook a wide-ranging reappraisal of the United States' alien control policy. Since the decree of a national emergency in September 1939, there had been a growing debate within the administration over tightening immigration restrictions and transferring the Immigration Bureau from the Department of Labor to the Department of Justice. Frances Perkins, Roosevelt's secretary of labor and the nation's first female cabinet secretary, was a loyal New Deal disciple. She had helped promote much of the groundbreaking labor legislation during her seven years as secretary. Perkins did not, however, agree with the president on immigration policy. On September 4, 1939, just days after the German army invaded Poland, the president gathered his cabinet at the White House and polled them on the idea of issuing a national emergency decree. Perkins offered no comment. The following day she wrote a lengthy memorandum for the president detailing her analysis of the European crisis and its impact on the United States. "There is no emergency in the sense in which it is intended," she wrote, and "we are not attacked by enemies or famine or pestilence and we are not at war." She then warned Roosevelt that his current course of action was ill-advised and would only bring with it "greater infringement on civil rights and personal freedom."[56]

Throughout the fall of 1939, Perkins came under increasing pressure to strengthen the oversight of the Immigration Bureau in light of the emergency conditions prevailing in the country. Hoover, the recently appointed chairman of the IIC, urged her repeatedly to begin fingerprinting aliens to obtain some type of estimate of the number of aliens living in the United States. Such a step, in the FBI director's view, would also help locate dangerous aliens if war became a reality and custodial detention was required. Perkins flatly rejected Hoover's suggestions. She feared that mandatory fingerprinting of aliens would criminalize millions of innocent people living in the United States.

The State Department was equally frustrated over the Labor Department's poor administration of immigration policy. Undersecretary of State Sumner Welles complained that the government had no accurate information concerning aliens entering, residing in, or leaving the United States. Current immigration policy exempted certain categories of aliens from the requirement of undergoing consular examination for a visa. Welles criticized the lack of effective checks on nonimmigrant aliens such as transients, visitors, and seamen during their stay in the United States and an absence of procedures that would ensure the departure of foreign government officials and their families after the termination of their duties. The State Department pressed for withdrawal of the exceptions for visa requirements, as well as the immediate registration and fingerprinting of all aliens. Undoubtedly mindful of the role played by seamen in the Rumrich case, the fingerprinting and registration of all alien seamen arriving in the United States and issuance of identification documents to them were jointly recommended by the IIC and the State Department. The documents would be deposited with a government official on the sailor's arrival and returned to him on his departure from the United States.[57]

In late May 1940, when Roosevelt moved the Immigration Bureau to the DOJ, Perkins relinquished control without complaint. Her easy acquiescence stemmed from her long-held view that immigration matters were incompatible with the other responsibilities of the Department of Labor and her belief that the Immigration Bureau should be moved to another cabinet department. Perkins would have preferred that it be transferred to the Department of the Interior, however, remarking that the DOJ was "a bad place for it." Immigration should be treated, in her opinion "as one of the humanitarian functions of the government."[58]

Congressional blessing for the move meant that unprecedented authority was concentrated in the principal criminal investigative and prosecutorial arm of the federal government. The attorney general of the United States was now directly responsible for overseeing all immigration matters, as well as initiating and shaping new policies. He could establish yearly immigration quotas, develop workable and humane mechanisms for alien controls, and coordinate with other governmental agencies to establish, assess, and update lists of aliens who would be subject to arrest, custodial detention, and deportation in the event of war. To aid in this effort, with the stroke of a pen, the DOJ absorbed thousands of lawyers, immigration officers assigned to ports of entry throughout the United States, and other bureaucrats. This shift represented not only a significant expansion of influence over a wide range of governmental policies but also a huge increase in the department's size.[59]

During the summer of 1940 Congress passed the Alien Registration Act, which required all aliens residing in the United States to register with the government. The program was run by the Alien Registration Unit of the DOJ in conjunction with the Postal Service and the FBI. Aliens were required to go to designated post offices, fill out a detailed form, and undergo fingerprinting. The required information included name, date and place of birth, a physical description, occupation and employer, club memberships, and previous arrests. This information was forwarded to the DOJ for processing, and the fingerprint cards were sent to the Identification Division of the FBI for records checks and cataloging. Eventually, almost 5 million persons complied with the registration program.[60]

At the same time, Hoover began compiling a list of aliens and citizens living and working in United States who would be subject to arrest if the nation suddenly found itself at war. In May 1940 he ordered all special agents in charge to identify individuals in their regions who could be candidates for such detention and provide their names to headquarters with supporting documentation. By the end of 1940 this list, which became known as the Custodial Detention Index, was essentially complete. Meanwhile, a new organization within the DOJ called the Special Defense Unit began developing its own alien enemy list. Using criteria based on the British model, aliens were classified into three categories, which became known as the ABC List: (A) leaders of nonpolitical cultural organizations (e.g., Japanese military *kais*, the Federation of Italian War Veterans, the German-American Bund) considered dangerous because they were influential in their ethnic communities or because their work could facilitate espionage; (B) potentially dangerous members of such organizations; and (C) donors and non-dues-paying supporters of such organizations who merited close observation. The combined ABC List and Custodial Detention Index was continually updated and broken down by geographic region in anticipation of quick dissemination to FBI offices for immediate arrests when hostilities began.[61]

Following the Pearl Harbor attack, one of President Roosevelt's first actions was to issue a series of proclamations designating Japanese, German, and Italian nationals as enemy aliens. Pursuant to his orders, presidential warrants were authorized for the immediate arrest and detention of thousands of aliens included on the FBI and DOJ lists. Based on these warrants, more than 2,400 aliens who were considered dangerous were arrested and interned in the week following the attack. Eventually, a total of 31,275 citizens and aliens would be interned.[62]

Agreements

On May 10, 1940, the frenetic activities of the IIC had been under way for eleven months, when suddenly, the nation was confronted with the shock of a hot war in Europe. Codification of individual IIC roles was needed, and less than a month after the German invasion of France, these roles were defined and made permanent. On May 29, 1940, a Memorandum on Division of Duties between Military Intelligence Division, Office of Naval Intelligence, and the Federal Bureau of Investigation was signed by the IIC principals. It was a comprehensive document that formalized individual responsibilities and information-sharing protocols for peacetime and wartime. All parties agreed to the continuation of weekly meetings, the establishment of full-time liaison officers, and the formalization of the FBI's plant protection duties. The FBI survey program was expanded to include navy and army construction yards, arsenals, and ammunition dumps; the investigation of "aliens employed in military aircraft plants"; and the registration of agents of foreign principals requested by the War Department. The memorandum also codified FBI investigative jurisdiction for civilians suspected of committing espionage and sabotage; the ONI and MID would be responsible for investigating similar allegations against civilian employees and uniformed personnel in their respective services. All vaguely agreed that the FBI should "stay in close touch" with "un-American groups" that might be attempting to disrupt the mission of the military services and the "national defense program." Information derived from these investigations would, in turn, be provided to the military services on a regular basis.[63]

On June 5 the document was amended. An addendum stipulated that the FBI would keep the MID and ONI informed about developments affecting industrial plants engaged in army and navy contracts, vital utilities, critical points in the transportation system, and actual or strongly presumptive espionage or sabotage, including the names of individuals definitely known to be connected with subversive groups. The May 29 agreement had stipulated that the FBI was responsible for investigating all cases in these categories "directed from foreign countries on those occasions and in these situations in which the State, War or Navy Departments specifically request investigation of a designated group or set of circumstances." By consensus, this proviso was withdrawn, probably under pressure from Hoover, who believed that it restricted the FBI's initiation of espionage investigations to only those instances when the War, Navy, or State Department made a specific request. Hoover, Miles, and Anderson agreed that the provision "did not establish an adequate coverage of cases in this category in the foreign field" and that "further study of this matter was needed."[64]

On February 7, 1941, the policy directive of May 1940 was further refined with regard to the jurisdictions of the three services. Hoover, as director of the FBI, was designated ex officio chairman of the IIC; representatives of the ONI and MID were the other two permanent members, with "other officials [added] as may be considered necessary from time to time." The IIC's mandate was now the coordination of "all matters of procedure and policy in connection with the handling of national defense investigations and related intelligence operations." At the same time, the IIC divided up the world for jurisdictional purposes. The FBI could now initiate counterespionage investigations in all matters within the United States and U.S. territories, with the exception of the Panama Canal Zone. The MID would cover all Continental military installations as well as the Panama Canal Zone, Republic of Panama, and Philippine Islands, regardless of the subject's military or civilian status; the ONI assumed the same duties on all naval installations as well as Guam, American Samoa, Palmyra Atoll, Midway, and Johnson Island.[65]

MID, ONI, and FBI agreement to these new jurisdictional boundaries reflected a major shift in national security thinking. For the first time in the nation's history, a more structural rationality was applied to the investigation of foreign intelligence attacks against U.S. interests both at home and in U.S. possessions. It affirmed the dominant role of the FBI in the foreign counterintelligence establishment but provided each IIC member with a starting point that enabled it to focus on who it was and was not responsible for investigating. If the person was a civilian—whether citizen or alien—living in the United States, investigative responsibility fell to the FBI. Civilian War Department employees and uniformed military services personnel were investigated by the ONI or MID. Allegations could now be forwarded to the proper agency for investigation, and any issues that did not fit neatly into this scheme could be resolved at the weekly meetings of the principals or by the new liaison officers.[66]

The May 29 agreement and the June 5 addendum were watersheds in the future direction of the FBI. An often overlooked feature of this document was the agreement of all three parties to the FBI's establishment of "a counterintelligence service" the purpose of which was to keep "close check upon the Intelligence activities of representatives of all foreign governments." In national security cases, the high standard set by the so-called Stone doctrine in 1924 required an allegation of criminality before opening a national security case; this new agreement eliminated that standard. The FBI was now authorized to move aggressively into areas that were previously off-limits to governmental investigators, laying the foundation for the FBI to assume the role and functions of a professional counterintelligence service. "Keeping a close check upon the Intelligence activities of representatives of all foreign governments" now meant "cases of actual or strongly presumptive espionage and sabotage." Investigations of foreign intelligence officers posing as diplomats and other foreign nationals assigned to the United States in an official capacity could be conducted without a prior allegation of spying. Investigations could now be instituted to determine whether they were in fact gathering intelligence or engaging in criminal behavior.[67]

Under the new policy, the FBI significantly stepped up its counterintelligence effort. The next eighteen months witnessed an accelerated use of electronic and visual surveillance of embassies, consulates, private residences, and business fronts throughout the country. For the first time, the Bureau began large-scale efforts to quietly monitor the movements of diplomats suspected of being intelligence officers, identify their contacts, and determine the nature of the relationship. Now, a year and a half before U.S. entry into the Second World War, the U.S. government had in place a new and unprecedented surveillance structure that opened up opportunities to uncover espionage activities and develop human sources of information that could report on the activities and personalities of foreign diplomatic personnel.

CHAPTER FIVE

Following the Money

Henry Morgenthau, Franklin Roosevelt's close friend and Dutchess County, New York, neighbor, served as his secretary of the treasury from 1934 to 1945. Though slightly younger than the president, Morgenthau shared his values, was intensely loyal to him, and never wavered in his support of New Deal economic policies. Like Roosevelt, he viewed isolationism as harmful for the nation's long-term domestic and international interests, and he believed that the United States must forcefully assert itself in the world. Early in his cabinet tenure, Morgenthau recognized the menace emerging in Europe and Asia and chafed at the United States' helplessness in dealing with the spiraling international violence.

Suspicion and mistrust toward Germany was a Morgenthau family tradition. His grandfather, a German Jewish immigrant, had witnessed firsthand Prussian cruelty and the mistreatment of minorities. His father had served from 1914 to 1916 as Woodrow Wilson's ambassador to Turkey, and the future secretary of the treasury had accompanied his father on three trips to Istanbul, acting on each occasion as his secretary. In later conversations with his biographer, he commented that his inherited feelings of hostility had been further shaped through conversations with German diplomats during these visits. In his view, Germans' indifference to the brutalities and human devastation of the European war was rivaled only by their sinister motives and worldwide ambitions. He recalled casually listening to a chattering German military officer at an embassy reception one evening. Unaware that young Morgenthau understood German, the officer started "damning Americans in foul language." He made "a great impression on me," Morgenthau later said, instilling feelings that never abated. Years later, while reminiscing about his family, Henry Morgenthau III recalled a trip to Europe during the summer of 1938 aboard a Dutch steamship. One night in the ship's dining room, the secretary of the treasury and his family were attended by "an especially efficient [German] steward" assigned to their table.

Morgenthau, his son remembered, kept a watchful eye on the steward, believing that he might be a spy.[1]

Morgenthau's enmity only hardened in late June 1916 following the massive explosion at the Black Tom Island Munitions Depot in New York City and a fire, just weeks later, at the Kingsland Munitions Plant in New Jersey. An uncoordinated federal, state, and local investigation, marked by competition and mistrust, quickly stalled due to rivalries among the agencies involved. It was evident, however, that both incidents had been deliberate acts of sabotage carried out by agents of the German government. Yet the evidence was so weak that no criminal charges were ever filed.

Years later, as Roosevelt's new treasury secretary, Morgenthau's life again intersected with Black Tom Island and Kingsland—this time, in an official capacity. The Treasury Department was following closely an investigation being conducted by New York lawyer John J. McCloy. Originally hired by the insurance companies saddled with paying millions of dollars in damage and death claims resulting from the explosions, McCloy set out to prove that both incidents had been acts of sabotage. If he was successful, he could collect financial damages for his clients through the Mixed Claims Commission, established in 1922 to settle U.S.-German war-related financial disputes and determine indemnity payments for the victims. After an exhaustive search of German archival records and interviews of German operatives in the United States, Ireland, and Europe, McCloy clearly established that Black Tom Island and Kingsland had been acts of sabotage. Both crimes had been planned by the German government in the hope of stanching the flow of wartime munitions and supplies to Great Britain and France. Equally revealing to the new treasury secretary was the Germans' use of secret agents recruited from ethnic groups in the United States with historical antagonisms against Britain and France.[2]

At the end of the First World War, Great Britain and France were virtually bankrupt, which prevented them from repaying their war-related debts to the United States. As for Russia, U.S. loans obtained under Czar Nicholas II were renounced by the Bolshevik government following the October Revolution. Meanwhile, a defeated Germany found it impossible to pay its crushing reparations to the victorious Allies. Congress, ignoring the economic, financial, and political realities that crippled postwar Europe, reacted violently to this failure to meet what it viewed as legitimate obligations. It resurrected the Logan Act, originally passed in 1799, which forbade unauthorized contact by a U.S. citizen with any foreign government for the purpose of influencing its conduct in a controversy with the U.S. government. Next it passed the Johnson Debt Default Act, which, in a direct rebuke to European "deadbeats," prevented the United States from issuing any further loans to any foreign nation that had failed to repay its debts. As an extra sting, Congress imposed higher than normal tariffs on all imports to the United States from such countries.

The Treasury Department, which acquired enforcement responsibility for these new laws, had a keen interest in the successful resolution of McCloy's investigation. A favorable financial settlement for victimized American insurers would mean increased federal tax revenues at a time when corporate failures, business slowdowns, and unemployment were eroding tax receipts. At the same time, the U.S. government carefully monitored the many legal decisions emerging from this high-profile litigation, in anticipation of the impact on future international debt issues. As the case slowly progressed through the courts during the 1930s, and as more information was unearthed, Morgenthau's suspicions of German espionage tactics only intensified. Routine briefings by McCloy offered strong proof of German recruitment of Americans for espionage and sabotage. One such conspirator was Hans Hanfstangel, an American citizen of German parentage and former Harvard University student who later worked in his family's New York City publishing firm. The family's personal and business connections gave him access to many luminaries, including J. P. Morgan, Henry Ford, and a young New York legislator named Franklin Roosevelt. Years later, while Hanfstangel was serving as the foreign press spokesman for Hitler, President Roosevelt tried to persuade his old friend "Putzi" to caution Hitler against any "rashness and hotheadedness."[3]

Economic Defense

Hitler's increasing aggression, combined with McCloy's revelations, served as a constant reminder of the need to protect the nation's secrets. Morgenthau insisted on steady vigilance against German espionage in the United States, including the use of all the resources the Roosevelt administration could muster. McCloy warned him that German diplomats had routinely paid money to their secret agents in the United States during the First World War. This secret funding of sabotage and intelligence collection offered anonymity and deflected suspicion from the German government.[4] Energized by these revelations of illegal payments and the movement of money through legitimate banking channels, Morgenthau began to examine the connections between a government's intentions and the international movement of its funds. Uncovering these linkages meant carefully tracking the worldwide movement of Axis funds in a manner that would benefit not only Morgenthau's department but also a wide range of governmental interests. In a letter to Vice President John Nance Garner, he laid out the objectives of his economic defense plan as follows:

> Obtain continuing reports from and about individuals and concerns with a view to be constantly informed as to their activities whether in an economic or financial field or in the field of propaganda or subversive activities. Some of this information thus obtained will be of assistance to other agencies such as the FBI in the carrying out of their functions and through this channel an agency such as the FBI may be able to obtain the desired information without revealing their hand.[5]

Morgenthau kept himself informed, through regular reports from Hoover, on the full extent of foreign money moving through U.S. banks.[6] The FBI's ability to provide such timely data to the Treasury Department had some interesting origins. Starting in May 1924, when he was acting director of the BOI, Hoover began carving out a special role in the investigation of bank fraud, embezzlement, and bankruptcy matters. Throughout the 1920s banks failed at an average rate of 500 per year, spiking to 659 in 1929 on the eve of the stock market collapse. The bank failure rate then leveled off until late 1930, when 600 banks closed in the last sixty days of the year, bringing the total to 1,352—more than double that of 1929. Another 522 banks failed in a single month in 1931, and by the end of the year, 2,294 banks had ceased operations—nearly twice as many as in 1930 and an all-time U.S. record. Among the most prominent victims was the Bank of the United States, with more than 400,000 customers and deposits in excess of $280 million.

This extraordinary pressure on U.S. financial institutions often led bankers and businessmen to commit financial crimes in an effort to remain solvent and avoid closing their doors. This, in turn, led to a rise in the reported cases of bank fraud and questionable corporate bankruptcies. By 1931 the BOI was applying major resources to these investigations and building up a cadre of highly qualified special agents and accountants to handle these complex cases.

Hoping to stanch the troubling rise in financial crimes, Congress passed new bank fraud and bankruptcy legislation and assigned enforcement responsibility to Hoover's BOI. These cases quickly became the organization's highest priority. As the number of accountants in its field offices expanded, so did the Bureau's ability to effectively investigate fraud and political corruption. Financial crimes often involved collusion between corporate officers and bank officials, which demanded careful scrutiny of business records for evidence of forgery, false statements, and falsification of records. Tracing the route of money through a forensic examination of bank records and transactions became a routine feature of these inquiries. The increased interaction between the Bureau and the banking industry led to a greater level of cooperation and understanding, and in time, an intricate network of valuable contacts was forged between leading American bankers and the FBI.

The value of these specialized financial skills was illustrated in one of the FBI's most celebrated investigations of business fraud and political corruption during the late 1930s. Acting on a tip, New York district attorney Thomas Dewey convened a grand jury in 1938 to investigate the suspicious activities of Martin T. Manton, a prominent judge on the Second Circuit Court of Appeals. In January 1939 Dewey turned his evidence over to the federal government, and the following month Roosevelt ordered the FBI to investigate the matter. Two months later Manton was indicted on charges of obstruction of justice and conspiracy for accepting money in exchange for favorable judgments on certain cases that came before his court. At the time, Dictograph Products Corporation was engaged in a patent dispute with the Schick Dry Shaver Corporation; the original civil case, which had been decided in 1936, was significant for its wide impact on future patent cases and was being appealed in the Second Circuit Court. Through a co-conspirator, Manton secretly solicited $50,000 from the head of Dictograph, and the bribe was deposited into the account of the Forest Hills Terrace Corporation, controlled by Manton. Following a high-profile trial in New York City, Judge Manton was convicted, sentenced to two years in prison, and fined $5,000 for soliciting a bribe.[7]

With the declaration of a national emergency and the various executive orders and presidential neutrality proclamations issued in the fall of 1939, the Bureau (as directed by the president) began routinely providing information to the Department of the Treasury on the movement of foreign money through U.S. banks. The original focus was the banking activities of the Amtorg Trading Corporation and the embassy and consulate accounts of Germany, Italy, Japan, and the Soviet Union. Amtorg records at Chase Bank in New York were scrutinized for any evidence of collusion between the Soviet Union and Germany. The concern was that the Soviets were purchasing advanced technologies and products—such as molybdenum, used in the production of specialty aluminum for tanks and aircraft—and reselling them to Germany. A second concern was that the Soviets were using Amtorg as a conduit to move funds into the country from Moscow in support of the American Communist Party. In addition to paper transactions, actual money importation came under FBI scrutiny. In February 1940 a shipment of gold valued at $5.6 million arrived in San Francisco from Vladivostok, followed by a larger shipment worth twice that amount in October.[8]

This surveillance continued until May 1940, when President Roosevelt froze the U.S.-held assets of countries that had been conquered by Hitler's armies. Concerned that the Axis would try to use these funds to slow U.S. rearmament, improve its own financial situation, and accelerate economic aggression against the Western Hemisphere, Morgenthau again requested Hoover's assistance to monitor the financial reserves and suspicious transactions of such countries as France, Holland, and Belgium. FBI monitoring of the sources, routes, and destinations of money passing through U.S. banks and its coverage of Axis expenditures in the United States were both dramatically stepped up.[9]

Hoover had many confidential contacts in New York that the Bureau used in furtherance of the government's economic defense purposes. In a note sent by special messenger to the White House on May 25, 1940, Hoover informed the president that sources at New York's Marine Midland Trust Company reported that Topken and Farley, the law firm representing the German consulate in New York, had alerted the bank to expect a $9 million wire transfer from a bank in Italy. The money, according to Topken and Farley officials, was not foreign government funds but the proceeds of a private estate being transferred from Italy to an unidentified family in the United States. Marine Midland officials, the president learned, delayed the transfer to allow time to contact officials in Washington concerning a course of action. The final destination of the money was unknown, and Hoover was in the process of "having it followed." FDR approved the FBI director's actions on May 27, 1940, with a note instructing his military aide and friend, General Edwin "Pa" Watson, to "tell Edgar Hoover to use the Treasury to block any of these funds going out again."[10]

The following month Hoover reported to the White House on another investigation that was under way. This one involved a suspicious payment of $50,000 by the German consul general in New York City to the Women's Foreign Missionary Society of the Methodist Episcopal Church through the Industrial Trust Company of Philadelphia, Pennsylvania. In his report, Hoover hinted at the extent of cooperation between U.S. banks and the FBI in this tracking process. "A fund of $1,000,000 in bills of known serial numbers is carried at the Chase National Bank by prearrangement of this Bureau for withdrawals from the consulate's account," and "$46,000 of the cash surrendered for the check in the instant case is from that fund." The remaining $4,000, the report concluded, "has been identified as a part of a withdrawal of $20,000 made by the consulate general from its account at the Marine Midland Trust Company, which the institution carries on its accounts and is cooperating with the Federal Bureau of Investigation by recording the serial numbers from the cash disbursed on that account."[11]

Otto and Ruth Kuehn, naturalized U.S. citizens living in Honolulu, with connections to the Brazilian coffee industry, came to FBI attention when a confidential informant reported that for years their bank balance had averaged only $20. Equally intriguing were Mrs. Kuehn's activities. Sources reported that she regularly carried thousands of dollars from Japan to Hawaii in denominations of 500- and 1,000-dollar bills. The cash was then passed to a physician assigned to the SS *Lurline* of the Matson Shipping Lines, who took it to the West Coast of the United States, converted it into smaller denominations, and returned the money to Mrs. Kuehn. Suspecting that the Kuehns were, for unknown reasons, trying to avoid detection by transacting in smaller-denomination currency, the FBI undertook an investigation that included a careful examination of the couple's bank records. Records of the Bishop Bank in Honolulu for 1936 through 1938 revealed deposits averaging more than $23,000 a year that were cabled from the Rotterdamsche Bankvereiniging through the National City Bank in New York. At the same time, Mrs. Kuehn was regularly sending checks to relatives in Germany and Japan.[12] All this suspicious movement of money led the FBI to believe that the Kuehns might be involved in espionage.

Other intriguing information with a bearing on the Treasury Department's economic defense obligations was passed to Morgenthau by the FBI. In November 1940 Hoover reported that interesting documents belonging to the governor-general of the French colonies and the colonial administrator for the island of Martinique had been secretly copied by British authorities in Antigua. The contents included the fact that 72 percent of Martinique's commodity imports were supplied by France, that French Guiana had proposed to the French government the shipment of 244 kilograms of gold into New York City (investigation determined that another 244 kilograms had already been shipped during the first four months of 1940), and the size and strength of military forces in the Antilles islands, Martinique, and French Guiana.[13]

Funds entering the United States were not the FBI's only interest. In late October 1940 Hoover learned, probably through a wiretap, that two Italian diplomatic couriers suspected of carrying a large but undetermined amount of U.S. currency were in Mobile, Alabama, en route to New Orleans, where they were scheduled to leave the country by ship. There they were supposed to meet Gireno Roberti, a former secretary at the Italian embassy in Washington but presently assigned to Italy's embassy in Mexico City. "Kit" Carson, the assistant director of the National Defense Division, asked for Treasury Department assistance to determine the amount of money involved. His plan was for the U.S. Customs Service to examine the bags of all the ship's passengers as cover for examining the couriers' pouches. Herbert Gaston, assistant secretary of the treasury for enforcement, researched the legality of such a search and was told that it could be authorized under U.S. narcotics and smuggling laws. Gaston then sought the counsel of Adolf Berle, who fully supported the FBI's plan but warned that the Italian government would likely issue a protest to the State Department. He still urged the Customs Service to proceed with the search but cautioned that the State Department would respond to an Italian protest by denying any knowledge of the matter.[14] A search of three satchels uncovered $3,850,000 in U.S. currency destined for the Italian embassy in Rio de Janeiro, Brazil. Surveillance, however, determined that only two of the bags were placed aboard the ship. The third bag was in the hands of Roberti and Count Mario Conti, a secretary at the Italian embassy in Mexico City. Both men had boarded a train in New Orleans bound for San Antonio, Texas. The FBI requested another search of the third bag, but Sumner Welles objected. The Italians made a "vigorous protest" over the first search, and Welles characterized the incident as "bad." Although the State Department could "wiggle out of it" by claiming that it had been inadequately informed about the diplomatic status of the couriers, a similar search of two embassy officials would leave the department "with no ground to stand on and would undoubtedly provoke reprisals."[15]

By November 1940 the investigation of foreign accounts in U.S. banks was straining FBI manpower. Investigators were focusing on German, French, Italian, Japanese, and Russian funds, which were "constantly increasing at a very rapid rate." In New York City alone, FBI investigations had uncovered more than 3,700 accounts meriting careful scrutiny in connection with "subversive activities within the United States." In another U.S. city, 107 German, Italian, Russian, and Japanese accounts in twenty-four banks were being closely monitored. As manpower-intensive as this process was, it was amplified by the investigation of the "additional accounts into which funds from the above mentioned accounts may be traced."[16]

On May 16, 1940, President Roosevelt appeared before a joint session of Congress "warning of ominous days ahead" and appealing for the passage of new defense legislation that he would soon propose. "No old defense is so strong," he warned, "that it requires no further strengthening and no attack is so unlikely or impossible that it may be ignored." The president's sudden desire to energize the nation's defenses was a response to the crisis then enveloping western Europe. Hitler's dramatic military successes had forced the Roosevelt administration to reappraise U.S. military readiness. After two decades of neglect and decay, the United States now found itself with inadequate strategic stockpiles and a military establishment that had slipped to eighteenth in the world behind Spain, Sweden, and Switzerland. Compounding the president's anxieties was the growing threat to the United States' western Pacific and Asian interests. With Britain and France locked in a death struggle at home, the Japanese government began tightening its grip in Asia by demanding French closure of the Indochina border and the sealing of Chinese supply routes through Burma and Hong Kong.[17]

Forty-seven days later Congress passed the Defense Act of July 2, 1940. It authorized the president to take all measures necessary "through the appropriate agencies of the Government (1) to provide for emergencies affecting national security and defense and for each and every purpose connected therewith" and to "provide for the procurement of strategic and critical materials in accordance with the Act of June 7, 1939."[18] Then, in a shrewd bipartisan political move, Roosevelt chose Henry L. Stimson to replace Harry Woodring as secretary of war and Frank Knox, a Chicago newspaper publisher, to succeed Charles Edison as secretary of the navy. Republicans and ardent interventionists, both men were immediately empowered to begin strengthening the nation's military services and to fortify its defenses. Rapid new construction, rehabilitation of aged military facilities, and stimulation of the private manufacture of new military equipment, supplies, and munitions soon replaced the years of neglect and indifference. For the first time since World War I, research, development, and the purchase of new weapons were significantly increased through expanded contracting with the private business sector.

This pressure for a rapid military buildup soon gave rise to new concerns about U.S. corporations that were being asked to participate. Most of these companies had struggled just to stay in business during the bleak years of the Depression, and in 1940 many were still on the verge of permanently closing their doors. Corporate strategies for remaining solvent during the 1930s had been as inventive as they were numerous. One technique for obtaining new business and maintaining liquidity was the use of partnership agreements with European companies. This opened European markets to U.S. goods, spread out the risks associated with business during this period, and brought much-needed foreign investment into the United States. At the same time, however, most German industries with corporate and financial ties to U.S. businesses were contributing to Hitler's military modernization. After May 1940 the United States' corporate partners and subsidiaries in Europe suddenly found themselves under Axis control.

After a decade of ignoring these relationships, the government began questioning Axis penetration of U.S. national security through corporate chicanery. In May 1940 Thurman Arnold, the assistant attorney general who headed the Antitrust Division, revealed that for more than a year the DOJ had been investigating allegations of collusion between U.S. and foreign companies. Arnold cited the "monopolistic practices of foreign and domestic corporations" operating in the United States, which he feared could "vitally affect the adequate preparation of our national defense." Arnold gave voice to Roosevelt administration concerns, chief among them the control of vital natural resources by Axis-dominated U.S. and European companies. In one case, Arnold forced Standard Oil of New Jersey to plead no contest and accept a fine for collusion with I. G. Farbenindustrie, a large German petrochemical conglomerate. The plea acknowledged Standard Oil's deliberate failure to pursue research on artificial rubber in exchange for the German company's agreement not to compete against Standard Oil in the United States. Standard Oil's failure to research artificial rubber, Arnold argued, delayed the development of that vital technology and hurt the overall rearmament effort. Another case involved I. G. Farbenindustrie's efforts to eliminate foreign competitors by entering into agreements with U.S.

firms to stabilize prices and divide international markets. Other alarming issues included conflicting claims of patent ownership for military tech-nologies and inventions that were considered essential for rearmament, as well as thousands of applications by Axis-controlled companies for patents that could block U.S. access to military-related processes and technologies. New and intense scrutiny was focused on the legal status of Axis-controlled companies and subsidiaries operating in the United States. Equally trouble-some was Axis evasion of the U.S. government's freeze on foreign govern-ment funds deposited in U.S. banks.[19]

To bypass these restraints, Nazi-controlled industries began using their dollar assets in U.S. banks to purchase strategic resources such as magne-sium, beryllium, and chromium in the United States and elsewhere for ship-ment to Europe. Equally troublesome was the diversion of strategic materi-als to Axis nations by U.S. companies motivated by greed or indifference or because years of heavy financial dependence had exposed them to extor-tionate demands from European companies.

Solving these thorny issues became the problem of an understaffed and overstrained Treasury Department. In addition to developing remedial legislation, Morgenthau's staff was required to increase surveillance of the business activities of U.S. and foreign corporations. Having frozen the U.S. financial assets of all countries controlled by Germany and Italy, the De-partment of the Treasury began using the new defense mandate to prevent those countries from gaining further economic advantages through loop-holes in the law. Emergency regulations soon prohibited Hitler and Italian dictator Benito Mussolini from using their assets in U.S. banks and other financial institutions to purchase strategic resources. Within weeks, these measures were expanded to include all countries under Axis control. Japan was no exception. Through the summer of 1940 Morgenthau also took steps to ensure complete control of "every aspect of trade and commerce between Japan and the United States," preventing the movement of goods between "any Axis area" and the United States. Export laws were tightened, and the surveillance of foreign shipments was dramatically increased in an attempt to halt the loss of vital resources and technologies from the United States. U.S. shipping firms also came under increased federal scrutiny. Compliance examinations increased, along with the institution of rules governing the diversion of vital cargoes to third countries for later shipment to Axis-con-trolled countries. The government also began to monitor financial trans-actions connected with these questionable shipments. New Treasury Department regulations further prohibited the acquisition of property in the United States belonging to the governments of invaded countries. Included on this list were consulate and embassy buildings as well as factories, land, and any other physical property owned by the citizens of these conquered lands. Fearing that coercion and looted funds would be used by the Axis, the Treasury Department prohibited the acquisition of legal title to property in occupied territories through purchase from American owners.[20]

In early 1940 the FBI began assisting the Treasury Department in this new and enhanced regulatory effort. Two crucial factors led to this inter-agency alliance. The first was that Morgenthau's department, like most governmental agencies, was ill prepared to meet the overwhelming demands of national defense. Unlike today, the pre–World War II federal government was small and far more simplistic. Reduced tax revenues during the Depression had slowed federal hiring; retiring employees were often not replaced, leaving the Treasury Department unable to keep pace with New Deal changes in the tax laws.[21] The second factor was the reduced level of contact between Treasury Department staff and banking officials around the country.

For years, the nation had paid a high price for its inattention to the activities of the German and Soviet foreign intelligence services operating in the United States. Funds originating in Germany easily made their way to the United States. An agent posing as a legitimate businessman would deposit money in a European bank and then wire-transfer it to another bank, perhaps in Mexico or Argentina. There, another agent would wire the funds to the bank account of a sham company in the United States. The German agent controlling this company would then withdraw the money and disburse it to his local agent network.[22]

The case of German businessman Frederich Geldner is typical of the many instances of such diversion uncovered by the FBI. In September 1940, three months after Roosevelt's order freezing foreign assets, Geldner was stopped and searched on the West Coast by immigration authorities as he prepared to leave the United States for Germany. Among the items discovered in his baggage were letters from the Mexico City branch of the German South American Bank to the main office in Berlin; detailed information about the financial activities of the Banca Credito Italiana in New York City; correspondence received and sent by Topken and Farley, the law firm representing the German consulate; information regarding negotiations between Banco de Nacional of Buenos Aires, Argentina, and the Italian Shipping

Lines; and material concerning payments made to the Bosch Optical Corporation of Stuttgart, Germany, through the American Express Corporation of Zurich. Also in Geldner's possession was evidence of illegal German efforts to establish credit and sources of available funds for business in the United States.[23]

Among other cases referred to the FBI was a September 1940 attempt by a Japanese company to purchase, from a West Coast scientist, a formula for extracting high-octane aviation fuel from crude oil, in violation of the government's embargo on aviation gasoline. That same month, a New York resident attempted to smuggle blueprints of a phenol plant through South America to Germany. Another case involved confidential information reported to the Treasury Department concerning Earnest Knaack, a businessman residing in Panama. The FBI determined that Knaack represented German business interests that were attempting to establish credit and sources of funding in the United States. In early 1940 the purchasing activities of the William H. Muller Company, a New York City–based firm, came under FBI scrutiny. It was suspected of illegally buying rubber from Brazil through the Amtorg Trading Corporation and diverting it directly to Germany. On another occasion, Hoover was asked to investigate the financial transactions of a New York City–based foreign exchange firm whose Chicago representative was suspected of violating U.S. law by attempting to sell "3% Funded bonds of the German Reich" in the United States. A major concern was that such transactions would permit balances to accumulate in U.S. banks for use "in Germany after the anticipated German victory." These reports and hundreds of others like them, coupled with the increasing concentration of responsibility for civilian counterespionage in the FBI, led the Treasury Department to expand its requests for FBI investigation into suspected Axis violations of federal law. From Morgenthau's perspective, such investigations could also serve as a warning to U.S. companies about the consequences of engaging in international business activities that might be detrimental to U.S. security.[24]

Rueckwanderer

A compelling illustration of the rapidly increasing level of cooperation between the Department of the Treasury and the FBI involved the Rueckwanderer Mark Program. Started in 1936 under the direction of the German

Ministry of Economics, it remained in operation until President Roosevelt froze all German financial assets in the United States on June 14, 1941. The sophisticated scheme was originally designed to skirt the Johnson Debt Default Act and subsequent neutrality laws by quietly encouraging sympathetic Americans of German origin to make their dollars available for the use of the German government. In return, investors were offered "preferential blocked mark savings accounts" in German savings banks of their choice. Germany advertised the program on German-language radio, in German newspapers, and through local German-American Bund groups, playing on the fear of growing inflation in the United States. The allure of the program was twofold. The Nazis promised special financial compensation for those persons wishing to return to Germany and for the financial loss they would incur if they converted their dollar assets into reichsmarks at the official rate of exchange. Under the plan, any Rueckwanderer, or "returnee," who went back to Germany would receive 4.10 reichsmarks for each dollar invested instead of the official exchange rate of 2.50 reichsmarks.[25] Although this was designed to look like an ordinary foreign exchange transaction, it was actually accomplished through complex illegal currency manipulation by the German Reichsbank and government exploitation of its own Jewish citizens. To compensate for the difference between the official rate of exchange and the inflated Rueckwanderer rate, the Nazis purchased reichsmarks at depreciated rates to offset the inflated balances in the preferential savings accounts. One way they did this was through aggressive reduced-rate purchases of reichsmarks on the international market. Largely, however, the German government made up the loss by imposing draconian currency laws. These edicts prevented Jews, who were fleeing the country in droves, from transferring their property out of Germany when they departed. Thus, the refugees had no choice but to sell their assets to the government at rates far below anything they could receive on the open international market, which often left them with only the clothes on their backs. However, this tactic more than made up for the German government's losses due to the artificially inflated Rueckwanderer rate. An analysis of the program conducted by the U.S. government toward the end of the Second World War concluded that during the five-year period ending in June 1941, the German government reaped a profit of 800 percent in U.S. dollars.[26]

Investing in Rueckwanderer accounts was an intentionally complicated process. The Ministry of Economics placed certain limitations on the purchaser's use of the money invested in the program. For instance, the funds could not be used for the benefit of relatives living in Germany; nor could buyers use the funds to pay for visits to the fatherland. The funds could be tapped only when the purchaser permanently immigrated to Germany and secured the status of a legal resident under the stringent and complicated German immigration laws then in force.[27]

In addition, a potential purchaser had to meet certain German government-imposed requirements before an investment could be made. First, the would-be investor had to send a letter to the local German consulate expressing an interest in permanently returning to Germany and requesting a Rueckwanderer application. The next round of paperwork required the investor's complete biographical information, including his proposed occupation once he arrived in Germany and his current occupation and employer in the United States; a detailed listing of all the purchaser's property and assets; and any bund affiliations. The application was then returned to the consulate for review and consideration. Approval was based largely on the usefulness of the applicant's technical skills to German industry, as well as proof that the applicant and his family met the racial guidelines mandated by the Nazis. Consulate officials sent an approved applicant a Certificate of Unobjectionability, authorizing him to invest in the program. The new Rueckwanderer was then directed to a local German travel agency, where he presented his certificate and other correspondence and turned over his dollars in exchange for a receipt. Sometime later the investor received a letter from Berlin confirming that his funds had been received by the Devisenstelle, the local offices responsible for foreign exchange and export matters.[28]

The travel agent, or retailer, sent the funds to a regional wholesaler, who in turn forwarded the funds to one of five banking firms, all located in New York City, designated by the German government as processors for the Rueckwanderer transactions: Chase National Bank of the City of New York, the J. Henry Schroeder Banking Corporation, Robert C. Mayer and Company, New York Overseas Corporation, and Deutscher Handels and Wirtschaftsdienst. Each bank maintained an account for the Deutsche Golddiskontbank previously established by the Ministry of Economics for this purpose. Contrary to the letter sent to the Rueckwanderer, informing him of the existence of his new account in Germany, the funds never left the United States; they went directly into these special accounts controlled by the German government. These five banks, eager for German business, competed fiercely for the bulk of the work and the attractive fees it offered.

Each transaction resulted in a 4 percent commission—a hefty figure, considering that normal fees on such currency transactions amounted to no more than 1 or 2 percent of the total amount exchanged.[29]

President Roosevelt's declaration of a national emergency in September 1939 prompted a Treasury Department examination of the Rueckwanderer transactions. Study soon revealed that the scheme was a German government ploy to acquire U.S. dollars for its own use. The five banks involved could face federal prosecution for violating the Johnson Act, which made it unlawful for any U.S. company "to purchase or sell the bonds, securities, or obligations of any foreign government." From the Treasury Department's perspective, violation of the Johnson Act amounted to an automatic violation of the Foreign Agents Registration Act passed in 1938, the neutrality laws, and possibly the espionage law of 1917.

Germany viewed the program as a means of acquiring free U.S. dollars to support its expanding war economy. It also hoped that skilled American industrial workers would return to the German labor force and staff the factories turning out weapons of war. However, one of the real purposes of the program was far more sinister than those publicized in the United States before the war: the acquisition of vital information that could be used by Germany's intelligence services to obtain U.S. military-industrial secrets. This was the conclusion of a joint DOJ-FBI report prepared at the end of World War II. It found that the Rueckwanderer application provided the Nazis with data that could be used to assess an applicant's potential for espionage. In addition to the collection of "detailed background data, including information on all political affiliations of some ten thousand American Nazi sympathizers who purchased the mark credits," another focus was the Rueckwanderer's employment—the type of work he performed, the location of his work site, and any military projects in progress there. These were essential pieces of information that would allow the Germans to target specific U.S. companies for espionage.[30]

FBI investigation of the scheme began in the fall of 1939, when the ONI reported that a source had uncovered a German government plot involving the use of $6 million (equivalent to roughly $90 million today) for espionage in the United States. The money was destined for Hans Borchar, head of the German consulate in New York City, who then distributed the funds to other German consulates throughout the country for payment to local agents. Through the confidential assistance of Sherrill Smith, a vice president of Chase National Bank, the FBI started following the money trail by recording the serial numbers of all thousand-dollar bills withdrawn from the consulate's account at Chase. Although the original information concerning the $6 million proved to be incorrect, it exposed the Rueckwanderer program and quickly led to a nationwide examination of German intelligence and its use of the program for espionage purposes.[31]

The journey of the marked bills withdrawn from Chase soon led to Robert C. Mayer and Company of Chicago, one of the five companies authorized by the German government to operate the program. A close look at Mayer's books turned up new Rueckwanderer data, as well as interesting insights into the charitable contributions of the company's president, August T. Gauseback. Through a confidential source close to Gauseback, agents learned that he was making significant donations in small, untraceable $5 and $10 cash installments to Father Charles Coughlin, an anti-Semitic Roman Catholic priest who hosted a popular radio program at the time. From Mayer the trail led to Hautz and Company, a local Rueckwanderer wholesaler in the Chicago area. Fredrich Heinicken, a prominent German American businessman, served as the company's president, and one of his tasks was to pressure local German Americans to participate in the program. An after-hours search of his offices by FBI agents uncovered hundreds of Rueckwanderer checks made out to Chase National Bank in Manhattan. This led investigators back to the East Coast.[32]

Alarm bells soon began ringing in Washington. What was the extent of the program? How pervasive was it? What was the real purpose of the scheme? Who was behind it? And what did it mean for the larger issue of U.S. rearmament? Both the DOJ and the Treasury Department immediately sensed potential violations of federal law, in particular the recently passed neutrality laws, which prohibited loans and gifts to belligerent nations, and the Johnson Act, which prohibited gifts and loans to nations that had defaulted on loan payments to the United States. Two additional questions loomed large in the minds of IIC officials, and both involved the counterintelligence implications of the scheme. First, were the German intelligence services using the Rueckwanderer program to identify and recruit German Americans working in the defense industry? Second, and more ominously, how many had already been approached and were now supplying valuable information to the Germans?[33]

These concerns had merit. Travel agencies operated by and for German Americans were willingly cooperating with Hitler's government by handling Rueckwanderer paperwork; accepting participants' cash, checks, and money orders; and forwarding valuable personal information about applicants to foreign intelligence operators. At a time when U.S. factories were accelerating their research on advanced military technologies and introducing new weapons, the FBI, ONI, and MID had good reason to fear that the Abwehr had contrived a clever method of acquiring sensitive military and industrial secrets without showing its hand. The risk to the Germans was negligible, as no spies on the ground were needed. The completed Rueckwanderer applications contained all the necessary information and could be safely and easily scrutinized by German intelligence specialists. Attentive screening of thousands of applications could uncover previously unknown military research facilities and test sites, new production plants, and, even more critical, the nature of the work being done at a specific location. Equally troubling was the fear that perhaps thousands of German Americans, who were signaling their loyalty to the Reich by merely filling out the applications, were working on some of the nation's most sensitive military projects.

With the top echelon and midlevel framework of the scheme laid out, FBI attention now shifted toward determining the full scope of the conspiracy. The investigative emphasis became more local in nature, with the new objective of ascertaining "the functions of the travel agencies in the Nazi network throughout the United States." How many travel agencies were involved? Who was operating them? Were they willing pawns of the Nazis, serving as espionage talent spotters in the United States? Or were they merely businessmen interested in the 2 percent commission on each application?

For the first time, the criminal focus of Hoover's investigation shifted from simply convicting the offenders to identifying the participants, penetrating their organizational structure, and ultimately disrupting their activities. In a memorandum sent to the DOJ's Economic Warfare Division in August 1941, the Treasury Department laid out the history of its request for FBI assistance in the investigation of the Rueckwanderer program:

> When the Rueckwanderer investigation was first proposed, a primary consideration was that we would be enabled to investigate more precisely the functions of the travel agencies for the Nazis in the United States. The FBI has largely at our request made rather extensive investigation of the number and identities of these travel agencies. Generally speaking they present certain hypotheses. First, through the sale of Rueckwanderer Marks, food packages, etc., they enable the Nazi

organizations—consulates, Gestapo, Bunds, etc. to find who in the United States has relatives in Germany for whose well-being he is so far concerned that he will send remittances. This means that pressure can be exercised on such persons in the United States by threat of harm to relatives still in Germany. In the second place, these agencies form appropriate covering addresses for other activities. They provide, for example, ostensible employment in given communities for Gestapo agents, spies, etc., etc. In the third place they provide observation posts over communities in which no other convenient observation post exists. And finally, they have provided means for raising dollar balances for the Reich.[34]

What would become one of the largest and most extensive counterintelligence investigations in FBI history was now under way. Information secretly gleaned from the Hautz records shifted the focus back to New York City and the major banks holding the German accounts. Once again, through confidential sources in the banking community, FBI agents began to piece together individual bits of information that would eventually bring the entire operation into full view. Through the covert assistance of two Chase officials, a nationwide organizational chart of the operation, along with the identities of the wholesalers and travel agency retailers, was exposed. Leo Kelly, assistant manager of Chase's Foreign Department, and Carl Weis, his assistant, allowed agents to examine and record bank records after normal business hours without the knowledge of other Chase officials. Ledger entries, check signatures and addresses, amounts of money pledged by Rueckwanderer applicants, dates and amounts of deposits into Gold-diskontbank accounts, and thousands of other important bank records laid bare the entire conspiracy. They revealed in full detail the roles of wholesalers and retailers in the operation, including the activities of Hautz and Company, Hans Usch and Company, and another powerful retailer, Amerop Travel Services. All were operated by well-connected German American businessmen with close ties to German consulate officials in the United States and powerful bankers in Germany. German-born Hans Usch, for example, was a naturalized American citizen. His commercial credit manager was a former director of the J. Henry Schroeder Bank and the son of a director of the Dresdner bank in Germany.[35]

Preparing and signing the Rueckwanderer application was "tantamount to an oath of allegiance to the German government." So wrote the special agent in charge of the New York field office in a November 1940 memo circulated around the country to other FBI offices. Hoover shared his sub-ordinate's sentiments. "The fact that these people applied for and actually purchased Rueckwanderer marks," he said, "is in itself a very strong indica-tion of where their sympathies may lie." Having acquired the identities of and financial data on the Rueckwanderer purchasers, the next phase of the investigation was to determine the espionage threat they posed.[36]

Through the use of subpoenas and sources in the New York banking community, the FBI started producing interesting information concerning the pervasive nature of the program throughout the United States. Items of interest included transaction forms, correspondence, and the names and locations of travel agencies and foreign exchange companies engaged in the business. By November 1940, 3,500 Rueckwanderer purchase records had been uncovered dating back to 1937; by January 1941, a 281-page list con-taining the names of another 2,800 applicants had been created, based on a nightly review of Chase National Bank records. The list contained a total of 7,300 names by May 1941.[37]

An FBI investigation was opened on each applicant. Not all applicants were interviewed or exposed to lengthy scrutiny, but those affiliated with the defense industry were examined closely. After careful questioning, the security risk posed by the individual's continued employment in a defense-related industry was assessed. Not atypical was the case of Heinrich Claus. Records obtained from Hautz and Chase National Bank disclosed that Claus had purchased $5,000 worth of Rueckwanderer marks—a sizable sum at the time. Who was Claus? Did he pose an espionage threat to the nation? A separate counterintelligence investigation was opened on Claus, and agents determined that he was a machinist employed as a foreman at the Brewster Aeronautical Corporation on Long Island; at the time, Brewster was manu-facturing advanced aircraft for the U.S. Navy.[38]

Investigators learned that Chase National Bank of New York City had handled $5.8 million in Rueckwanderer transactions between September 1936 and November 1940. They also discovered that the scheme was not limited to the original five firms that had initially contracted with the Ger-mans. In a letter to Morgenthau just six months after the start of the inves-tigation, Hoover reported that the Bank of Manhattan was also handling transactions. The secretary of the treasury learned that between July 1940 and January 1941, Chase National Bank had accumulated $2.18 million in Rueckwanderer deposits; over the same period, deposits in the Bank of Manhattan were "equal to, if not greater than" those handled by Chase. By

March 1941 the FBI had successfully traced the movement of approximately $12 million worth of Rueckwanderer deposits from Germans living in the United States into the German government's U.S. bank accounts. An additional $8 million was discovered in these accounts, part of another scheme involving German American contributions for the purchase of foodstuffs for needy German citizens.[39]

The United States' entry into the war added new impetus to the FBI's program. Although it had originally obtained the identities of Rueckwanderer applicants for counterintelligence purposes, it was also maintaining a list of their names in anticipation of placing these individuals in custodial detention in the event of war with Germany. By April 1942, Percy Foxworth, assistant director of the FBI's National Defense Division (which was managing the Rueckwanderer investigation), requested and received 100 additional agents on an urgent basis to investigate between 2,000 and 3,000 Rueckwanderer cases. By the fall of 1942 the investigation determined that more than 10,000 Germans had purchased Rueckwanderer marks and that one-third of these purchasers had returned to Germany to claim their accounts. Thirty-five purchasers had their naturalized American citizenship revoked as a result of the FBI investigations growing out of the Rueckwanderer Program. Of the remaining Rueckwanderer purchasers, the FBI arrested 997 who were German aliens, and 441 of them were jailed for the duration of the war under the orders of the attorney general. Among the most famous purchasers were three of the eight Nazi saboteurs dropped off by a German submarine off the coast of Long Island in June 1942, including George Dasch, who turned himself in to the FBI and later testified at his coconspirators' trial.[40]

The phrase "follow the money" has gained popular resonance as a reference to investigating the money trail in criminal conspiracies and, more recently, in counterterrorism cases. Without the principle of following the money, the new U.S. counterintelligence apparatus would not have developed as quickly as it did. It was an important learning experience for fledgling counterintelligence investigators who were trying to understand the furtive techniques employed by foreign intelligence services trying to avoid detection. It led to the identification and careful monitoring of suspicious U.S. bank accounts and expanded FBI awareness of German, Japanese, and Soviet use of foreign banks and fraudulent companies in Europe, South America, and Asia to support their agents and intelligence operations around the world.

The close partnership between the Department of the Treasury and the FBI beginning in 1939 confirmed the acquiescence of so-called neutral governments such as those of Spain, Brazil, Argentina, Chile, and Mexico to Abwehr use of their countries as platforms for espionage against the United States. As international tensions grew more strained in the late 1930s, the emerging counterintelligence mandate began to expose the often contradictory relationships between the U.S. banking industry and the FBI. On the one hand, confidential linkages were forged between the FBI and banks in an effort to trace illegal activities and later establish undercover accounts for use by investigators in espionage cases. On the other hand, FBI agents were developing secret sources within banks to uncover evidence of questionable cooperation between U.S. banks and foreign governments that could expose these banks and their managers to criminal and civil penalties.

Another key discovery was compelling evidence that the German government was manipulating U.S. public opinion against the Roosevelt administration through secret payments to pacifist and isolationist groups. In particular, evidence was uncovered that Hitler's government was supplying the money through diplomatically protected consulate and embassy funds and accounts in U.S. banks. These new revelations and the dramatically increased flow of information resulting from this economic surveillance initiative had other effects within the government. In the end, the information obtained helped pinpoint foreign accounts in U.S. banks subject to the presidential freeze order and led to the closing of German and Italian embassies and consulates in the United States in June 1941. Last, over the coming years, the concept of following the money allowed the IIC agencies to recognize the FBI as a critical national security weapon, not only in countering espionage but also in pursuing preemptive investigations of foreign diplomatic offices and officials to pinpoint suspected intelligence activities.

CHAPTER SIX

Wires and Bugs

On May 20, 1940, Henry Morgenthau told J. Edgar Hoover that he had just spoken with General Edwin Watson and expressed the opinion that the situation facing the country demanded an emergency response. He urged Watson to appeal to President Roosevelt to immediately authorize the FBI to begin tapping the telephones of Axis diplomatic offices and suspected Nazi agents in the United States. Watson challenged this suggestion, fearing that such an order would be "illegal." To Watson's undoubted amazement, Morgenthau laconically responded, "What if it is illegal?" This pressure produced quick results. On May 21, 1940, Roosevelt instructed Attorney General Robert Jackson to direct Hoover to start tapping telephone communications to "secure information by listening devices direct to the conversation or other communications of persons suspected of subversive activities against the government of the United States, including suspected spies."[1]

Yardley

Roosevelt's order was a remarkable development, considering that Congress had outlawed the interception of any type of electronic communications six years earlier in the Comprehensive Communications Act of 1934. Likewise, any information obtained through these illegal intercepts was inadmissible as evidence in federal court. The administration's appeals to the U.S. Supreme Court for relief from this act had been rejected.

The legislation, passed overwhelmingly by Congress, was in large measure a response to the 1931 publication of *The American Black Chamber* by Herbert Yardley, a brilliant American code breaker. A midwesterner who began his government career as a young cryptographer with the State Department before the First World War, Yardley's job included responsibility for enciphering and deciphering diplomatic messages between Washington and U.S. embassies throughout the world. During a lull one evening, he used his time to decipher the personal codes used by President Woodrow Wilson. Yardley later said that he had been shocked when he broke Wilson's cipher so easily after only a few hours of effort.[2] His code-breaking skills soon caught the attention of military authorities, who were desperately in need of such talents as the United States became involved in the First World War. Under an agreement with the State Department, Yardley entered the army as a captain assigned to MI8, the War Department's code-breaking operation. By war's end, Yardley's successful solution of a number of sophisticated foreign codes and cryptosystems had earned him a reputation as the government's most skilled practitioner of the arcane science of cracking codes.[3]

Although his wartime accomplishments were impressive, they paled in comparison to his later peacetime code-breaking successes. In 1922 Secretary of State Charles Evans Hughes convened the Washington Naval Conference in the hope of settling the naval arms race that was quickly developing among the United States, Great Britain, France, and Japan, the new power emerging in Asia. After intensive negotiations, the conferees arrived at a compromise that called for a system of ratios limiting the size and number of ships that each country could construct during a certain period.

Yardley's behind-the-scenes role was pivotal to the success of American negotiators. Through years of arduous study, he and his team had learned the principal enciphering system used by the Japanese Foreign Ministry to protect its most important diplomatic communications. His new code-breaking techniques, coupled with four years of refinement, supplied U.S. policy makers with a steady stream of priceless and timely information throughout the conference. Thanks to Yardley, Hughes knew the strategy, the innermost thoughts, the confidential plans, and the intentions of the Japanese delegates sitting across the conference table. Because of Yardley, Hughes knew, without a doubt, that the Japanese needed a settlement, and he knew the point beyond which they would not settle. Skillful use of this intelligence produced an agreement that was hailed as a brilliant diplomatic success for the United States. It curtailed the construction of capital ships among the major powers for ten years; contributed to a major reduction in U.S. defense expenditures; and limited the Japanese naval buildup, thus slowing Japan's expansionist plans in Asia for a number of years.

As the United States withdrew from the international scene during the 1920s, the importance of code breaking diminished, leaving Yardley and his team with little to do. Shrinking MID budgets forced many of the army's most experienced code breakers to seek jobs in the private sector; Yardley sold real estate. MI8 funding, however, continued to be renewed annually, and with no one in Washington overseeing his activities, Yardley ran his autonomous operation for the next seven years. Yet the day was fast approaching when questions would be asked about the morality, ethics, and constitutionality of breaking foreign codes in a democratic society. These questions would mean the end of Yardley and his ten years of government code-breaking success.[4]

The Colonel

Congressional confirmation of Henry Stimson in 1929 as President Herbert Hoover's secretary of state doomed MI8. A lawyer, a former U.S. attorney for New York City, a protégé of Elihu Root (secretary of state during the Theodore Roosevelt administration), and a national leader of the Republican Party, Stimson was fiercely patriotic and held a unique distinction in American history. He served in the army as an artillery officer with the rank of colonel during the First World War, having previously served as secretary of war in the Taft administration. Shedding his uniform in 1918, citizen Stimson resumed his lucrative New York City law practice but always proudly insisted on being referred to as "Colonel" Stimson. After almost a decade in private life, Stimson was appointed to the position of governor-general of the Philippines, a post he held until he was selected to head the State Department in 1929.[5]

The new secretary of state was a nineteenth-century traditionalist who had acquired his values in a devoutly Protestant household. In his memoirs, written four years after the Second World War, he pointed to the importance of religion in his early life. Writing of his family heritage, he recalled that "both lines contained enough clergymen and deacons to keep up fairly well the moral standards of the stock." His sense of duty and morality was also instilled by his physician father, a Wall Street banker turned professor of surgery at New York University Medical School and Cornell Medical College. The elder Stimson taught his son that service to one's country was an essential calling for a citizen and that such a commitment rose to the level of a moral requirement. It was an article of faith that public service was a noble obligation pursued only by men of high moral fiber, good breeding, and strong personal background. Such men had a responsibility to behave honorably, deal truthfully, and engage in no deceit or trickery that would dishonor themselves, their families, or their government. Stimson brought the same moral paradigm that governed his personal life to his new duties. He viewed international diplomacy as a deadly serious business, and it was inconceivable to him that diplomats would ever behave less than reputably or in an ungentlemanly manner by seeking an unfair advantage over their adversaries.[6]

Intercepting and reading another nation's confidential communications for diplomatic advantage was anathema to Stimson. Privacy, a sacred right for all Americans, applied equally to nations, and for President Hoover's new cabinet secretary, any violation of that principle was an intolerable dishonor to the United States. Possessed of such an ethos, it is no wonder that the secretary of state was appalled when he first learned of MI8's existence and mission. After reading a number of deciphered translations of foreign diplomatic communications, he ordered an immediate halt to diplomatic code breaking and ended any further connection between the State Department and Yardley. From its inception, State Department contributions to MI8 had represented about 50 percent of its operating budget; Stimson's order ended this funding. War Department contributions, which accounted for the other half, were insufficient to keep the organization functioning, and MI8 effectively went out of business.[7]

The American Black Chamber

Out of work, with a wife and child to support, and in desperate need of money, Yardley decided to write a book describing the unique work he had done for the government. He titled his book *The American Black Chamber* after *Le Chamber Noire,* the highly secret cryptology center of France. Publication of the book in 1931 brought him worldwide recognition, financial success, and an international firestorm of criticism and derision. This once secret operative revealed publicly, for the first time, that the U.S. government had successfully broken codes and ciphers used by foreign nations to protect their most closely guarded diplomatic communications. He identified MI8 staff members and code-breaking techniques and methods; he recounted the theft of diplomatic mailbags, which were secretly opened to photograph their contents and then skillfully resealed to avoid detection.

The countries targeted by MI8 cryptologists, the relationship between MI8 and the British secret services as well as the Departments of War and State, scientific breakthroughs such as the British discovery of secret ink writing, and the general location of the MI8 offices in New York City were all exposed by Yardley.[8]

As destructive as these disclosures were to the image of the U.S. government, they paled in comparison to the volcanic response to his revelation with regard to the Japanese. In what was perhaps the greatest breach of U.S. government security up to that time, Yardley described MI8's remarkable successes in breaking Japanese diplomatic codes, including actual translations of coded messages from the Japanese ambassador in London to Tokyo and conversations between British officials and the Japanese ambassador in Washington—all retained by Yardley after leaving his government job. The world also learned that the State Department had heavily relied on these deciphered Japanese cables to aid negotiations during the Washington Naval Conference. To make his point, Yardley printed a verbatim transcript of a telegram dated July 13, 1921, marked "Very Confidential" from Tokyo to the Japanese ambassador in Washington. The text, which could easily be confirmed, noted that the Japanese government "wishes the subjects of discussion to be limited to the limitation of armaments questions, but in case it is necessary to discuss also the Far Eastern and Pacific problems, the discussion should be limited to questions of general principles such as territorial integrity of China, the open door, equal commercial opportunities, etc., and accomplished facts and questions concerning merely China."[9]

Domestic and international reaction was swift and predictable. The *New York Times* editorialized that Yardley's book "betrays government secrets with a detail and clarity of writing that makes one gasp." "An immoral book" was the charge of the *Japanese American*—immoral because "it boastfully narrates the pilfering, the snooping, the stealing, the spying practiced under his supervision." In Japan the exposures "ignited a firestorm" of controversy. Japanese government officials now had proof that their most secret communications had been compromised. Army officials accused the Foreign Ministry of a "serious blunder" for not paying closer attention to code security, forcing it to concede that Yardley's breakthrough "was due to the failure of the Japanese Government to effect a change in ciphers occasionally." A diplomatic protest was immediately filed, charging the United States with a gross breach of diplomatic etiquette. Armed now with a powerful propaganda tool, right-wing groups used Yardley's revelations to whip up anti-

American sentiment in Japan. The controversy helped the Japanese government justify its withdrawal from the League of Nations and rationalize its increasing military aggression in the Far East. W. Cameron Forbes, the U.S. ambassador to Japan, was forced to report to Washington in November 1931 that "the Black Chamber evidently made a great impression in Japan. I often hear references made to it in conversation with various classes of Japanese. According to the publishers of the Japanese edition, more than 40,000 copies have been sold. It remains a best seller at the present time." In fact, 33,119 copies were sold in Japan; on a per capita basis, that was nearly four times better than sales in the United States.[10]

Reaction

An outraged Congress took up the matter. The Democratic leadership charged that irresponsible government action and careless disregard for the security of confidential government information characterized twelve years of Republican control of the White House. Bewildered by the absence of any federal statute prohibiting the public disclosure of code information, both the House and the Senate quickly voted on the necessary legislation. On June 10, 1933, an act providing for the protection of government records, which became known as the Yardley Act, was passed; it was soon signed into law by President Roosevelt. The new law prohibited anyone who had access to codes and ciphers through their employment with the U.S. government from publishing such codes or any information "obtained while in the process of transmission between any foreign government and its diplomatic mission in the United States." Violators of the Yardley Act faced a $10,000 fine, a ten-year prison sentence, or both if convicted.[11]

Passage of the Yardley Act closed a loophole in the government's ability to protect national secrets. Yet at the same time, it fueled the debate over the emerging technology of wire and wireless communications. Throughout the 1920s and 1930s the number of radios in American households exploded, and with their popularity came increased controversy among radio station owners who were eager to enter this new business. Recognizing the seriousness of the problem, Congress again weighed in and imposed rules governing the entire communications industry.

The result was the passage on June 10, 1934, of the Comprehensive Communications Act (CCA). This landmark legislation, signed into law by Franklin Roosevelt fifteen months into his first term, imposed federal regulatory standards on the new field of wire and wireless communications. For the first time, it gave legal definitions to a number of technical terms, including *wire communication, radio communication, interstate communication, foreign communication,* and *radio station.* The centerpiece of the sixty-four-page law was the creation of the Federal Communications Commission (FCC), which was given a broad mandate to monitor and regulate all aspects of "interstate and foreign commerce in communication by wire and radio." It could assign radio frequencies, handle complaints concerning misuse, bring criminal charges for fraudulent activity involving commercial radio stations, and generally subject all communications matters to its regulatory authority.[12]

The Yardley Act had been on the books for only a year when the CCA was passed. With MI8 abuses still fresh in everyone's mind, Congress began to recognize the vulnerability of wire and wireless communications and their susceptibility to intrusion. At the same time, the balance between law enforcement needs and privacy was poorly understood; cases of criminal misuse of the telephone were rare, due to the small number of telephones then in existence. Compounding the problem was the scarcity of investigations of criminal activity involving telephone usage, which meant a paucity of meaningful precedents and case law. The lack of such data severely hampered efforts to frame sensible legislation that balanced the constitutional right to privacy with the legitimate need of law enforcement to intercept the telephone conversations of criminals. As a result, Congress inserted language into the CCA that would cripple the federal government's ability to investigate criminal activity using this new technology. The CCA required that:

> no person not authorized by the sender shall intercept any communication and divulge or publish the existence, contents, substance, purport, effect, or meaning of such intercepted communication to any person; and no persons not being entitled thereto shall receive or assist in receiving any interstate or foreign communications by wire or radio and use the same or any information therein contained for his own benefit or for the benefit of another not entitled thereto; and no person having received such intercepted communication or having become acquainted with the contents, substance, purport, effect, or meaning of the same or any part thereof, knowing that such information was so obtained, shall divulge or publish the existence, contents, substance, purport, effect, or

meaning of the same or any information therein contained for his own benefit or for the benefit of another not entitled thereto.[13]

This clause placed a total ban on any interception of telephone and wireless communications under any circumstances. In effect, interception of any communication would require the permission of both parties to the conversation, rendering legitimate law enforcement interception virtually impossible. This legal standard prevailed throughout the remainder of the decade. As the popularity of the telephone grew, so too did criminal use of this technology. Under increasing pressure to stem the growing tide of violence and lawlessness during the 1930s, law enforcement authorities and prosecutors around the country began appealing to the courts to allow the interception of telephone conversations for evidentiary purposes. In all cases they were rebuffed. Case after case saw wiretap evidence either fail to be admitted at a defendant's trial or be successfully challenged at the appellate level, resulting in an overturned conviction.

Nardone

The case that made this point involved a criminal named Frank Carmine Nardone. A Philadelphia native, Nardone was charged by the federal government in 1937 with liquor smuggling and conspiracy to conceal illegal liquor. The government's evidence was based on telephone conversations between Nardone and a coconspirator intercepted by the Treasury Department. Nardone was convicted, and his attorneys appealed to the U.S. Supreme Court, which heard arguments in 1937 and again in the fall of 1939. The attorneys claimed that the federal wiretap evidence used to convict Nardone had been illegally obtained because the CCA barred the admission of such evidence in federal court. Government attorneys challenged this claim, arguing that since passage of the CCA, bills had been introduced in Congress to specifically prohibit government wiretapping, and each attempt had failed. The Supreme Court overturned Nardone's conviction, with the majority of justices concluding as follows:

For years controversy has raged with respect to the morality of the practice of wire-tapping by officers to obtain evidence. It has been the view of many that the practice involves grave wrong. In the light of these circumstances we think another well recognized principle leads to the application of the statute as it is written so as to include within its sweep federal officers as well as others. That principle is that the sovereign is embraced by general words of a statute intended to prevent injury and wrong.[14]

After losing the first round, prosecutors retried Nardone. This time, they relied not on the original conversations intercepted by federal agents but rather on telephone conversations recorded by private detectives and uncovered during the search of an office. Confronted with the evidence against him, the other party to these conversations pleaded guilty and agreed to cooperate with federal investigators and testify at Nardone's trial. The recordings were entered into evidence, the witness corroborated the conversations between Nardone and himself, and for a second time the government won a conviction. Once again, Nardone appealed. This time, the appeal was based on the claim that any wiretap evidence, regardless of how it was obtained, was inadmissible in federal court. Government attorneys countered that the conversations were admissible—even though, admittedly, they had been illegally recorded by the private detectives—because the detectives had not been acting as agents of the government.

In December 1939 the Supreme Court issued its second Nardone ruling. In the minority opinion, two justices argued that criminals were becoming better organized and were employing every technological advantage available to them. Mindful of the advances made in the communications field and the growing number of telephones in use, they argued that wire interception of communications by police authorities was necessary to slow the growing lawlessness in the country. They reasoned that Congress, in its original consideration of the CCA five years earlier, had been creating legislation in previously uncharted waters, forcing it to be particularly sensitive to the potential for private and governmental misuse of this new technology. In the minority's view, the framers of the legislation had certainly understood that telephones would eventually be used by criminal elements for illegal purposes and did not intend for the law to ban the legitimate pursuits of law enforcement agencies. Their arguments failed to sway their colleagues, however. A majority of the justices agreed with Nardone's argument and once again overturned his conviction. Writing for the majority, Justice Felix Frankfurter noted that "the decision was not the product of a merely meticulous reading of technical language. It was translation into practicality of broad consideration of morality and public well-being." In accepting

Nardone's argument, the Court permanently barred governmental use of the seized recordings as evidence. Frankfurter concluded that "the essence of a provision forbidding acquisition of evidence in a certain way is that not merely evidence so acquired shall not be used before the court, but that it shall not be used at all." As a result of this ruling, wiretap evidence could not be used in federal criminal proceedings and, in effect, federal wiretapping of any sort was prohibited.[15]

Six months later the Federal Circuit Court of Appeals in New York tightened wiretapping rules even further when it threw out evidence derived from a telephone conversation in which one of the parties had authorized the eavesdropping. This case involved a businessman who had given his secretary permission to listen to his telephone conversations for the purpose of taking notes. Writing for the court's majority, Judge Learned Hand supported the ban on wiretapping but suggested that he did not entirely accept the Supreme Court's logic in the Nardone case. Hand believed that the Supreme Court had strayed too far in its protection of privacy rights and had given criminals a major weapon against law enforcement authorities. In a separate opinion he endorsed the reasoning of Supreme Court Justice Charles Clark, who had sided with the government in both Nardone cases. "From the public standpoint," Clark argued, "it means that if criminals take the precaution of communicating with each other by wire or radio they obtain a new kind of partial privilege for themselves, and lessen the risk that one of their number can effectively betray them to the police."[16]

Side Step

Civil libertarians claimed a major victory in the struggle between privacy rights and law enforcement needs. Newspaper editorials around the country hailed the Nardone decision. A blow "struck for liberty," registered the *Boston Globe*. Calling the Court's decision a "death blow" to government wiretapping, the *Washington Post* predicted that it "may bring about the complete abolition of this particular form of espionage by State, local, as well as Federal law enforcement officials." The *New York Times* noted that citizens' protection from unreasonable searches "is advanced" and even invoked the words of venerable Supreme Court Justice Oliver Wendell Holmes: "We have to choose, and for my part I think it a less evil that some criminals should escape than that the Government should play an ignoble part." On the West Coast, the *Los Angeles Times* echoed its eastern brethren, calling it "the best public policy."[17]

Hoover was undoubtedly disappointed over the Supreme Court's decision. It meant the loss of an important investigative tool just as allegations of German espionage and sabotage were on the rise following the president's recent declaration of a national emergency. In December 1939 the FBI began focusing attention on Japanese propaganda activities in the United States. Investigations were started on the Japan Institute, the Japanese Foreign Trade Federation, the Domei News Agency, Japanese consulates and consulates general, and eleven other Japanese establishments in the United States suspected of disseminating propaganda. In addition, in early January 1940 Karl Schleuter, posing as a seaman aboard a transatlantic ship, was arrested as he entered New York City at Ellis Island. Schleuter had fled the United States in the spring of 1938 following his indictment in the Rumrich espionage case. On January 14, 1940, eighteen German-American Bund activists were arrested in New York, and large caches of weapons were found. All were charged with seditious conspiracy for attempting to violently overthrow the U.S. government.[18]

Hoover's growing reputation came with a price. Critics charged that the Roosevelt administration was transforming the FBI into a political police force. Senator George Norris, an isolationist and administration critic, accused the FBI of becoming the equivalent of the Russians' Unified State Political Directorate (OGPU) and German Gestapo. Calling Hoover the "greatest publicity hound on the American Continent," Norris clamed that there was no justification "for some things which to him appeared to have been done by the FBI in violation of civil rights." Supporting Norris was Senator Burton Wheeler, the powerful chairman of the Interstate Commerce Committee, who pushed through a Senate resolution calling for the appropriation of $25,000 to investigate illegal government wiretapping. Fearing a "resurgence of a spy system conducted by government police," Wheeler wrote to Attorney General Robert Jackson urging an investigation of Hoover to determine "whether the legitimate rights and liberties of any of our people have been frustrated and denied." The American Civil Liberties Union (ACLU) added its voice to the controversy in April 1940. Based on an examination of a dozen recent criminal cases prosecuted on the state and federal levels, the ACLU claimed that it had uncovered evidence that charges against the accused were overblown and that criminal statutes may have been used for "ulterior political purposes." In the case of eighteen

Christian Front members arrested on weapons charges in January 1940, the ACLU specifically criticized the imposition of bail before an indictment had been issued and characterized the $50,000 bail as "outrageous." The ACLU then pointed an accusing finger at President Roosevelt himself; charging that he had seriously erred by authorizing the Bureau to investigate "subversive activities."[19] Critics even claimed that the criminal charges against the eighteen German-American Bund members were grossly inflated and deliberately timed to impress Congress with the need for additional FBI funding. In an internal memorandum, Hoover revealed his concern about these public attacks. He warned his staff that the bund case was "vitally important to the Bureau, not only because of the character of the case, but because of the forces which are very definitely trying to embarrass the Bureau in their contention that the case was not properly handled or should not have been initiated in the first place."[20]

An angry Hoover wasted no time responding to these attacks. He called the OGPU charge absurd and stated that the personal attacks against him were nothing more than Communist Party tactics designed to "cover their own Trojan horse activities." During a press interview in March 1940, Hoover bristled at the OGPU charge. He emphatically denied that the FBI had any interest in serving as a "national police force" while characterizing U.S. law enforcement as essentially a "local problem."[21]

Shortly after becoming attorney general, Jackson took substantive steps to rebut the administration's critics and ensure that all investigative organs of the government complied with the provisions of the Nardone ruling. On March 18, 1940, he issued instructions prohibiting FBI wiretapping under any circumstances. Next, he effectively compelled all other federal investigative agencies to conform to the same order. Although violations of income tax laws, narcotics laws, mail fraud, and alcohol tax laws were investigated by agencies of the Treasury Department and, as such, were not bound by Jackson's ruling, they were required to present their cases to the Justice Department for prosecution. Since all federal prosecutions fell under his jurisdiction, all "cases, wherever originating, must, under this rule, be free of illegality on the part of the government if they are to be presented to courts under the sponsorship of the Department of Justice." Thus, the government's investigative agencies had no choice but to comply with Jackson's sweeping order. Not doing so meant risking DOJ refusal to prosecute a case.[22]

Jackson then set up a new unit in the DOJ designed to strengthen his control over the FBI in politically sensitive cases and to weaken the power of local U.S. attorneys. Until then, the FBI had presented cases for prosecution directly to the U.S. attorney in the locale where the crime was committed. U.S. attorneys, appointed by the president, were generally long-standing residents of their districts and subject to the political realities of the areas where they served. For the previous two years, the FBI had been investigating a large number of neutrality law violations involving the foreign recruitment of Americans who had volunteered to fight in the Spanish civil war. In February Jackson dismissed the indictment of sixteen persons who had enlisted in the Spanish war in violation of a law passed in 1818. "The United States Attorney," Jackson noted, "is subject to no criticism in this connection, for he has acted strictly in accordance with his instructions from Washington." Citing the need for better coordination and control of prosecutions, Jackson ordered the new Neutrality Unit to review all FBI investigations of violations of neutrality, treason, sedition, espionage, and foreign enlistment laws. Only the Neutrality Unit could authorize prosecution by a local U.S. attorney.[23]

Although Hoover wanted wiretap authority to pursue counterespionage matters, Jackson's order left the FBI director no choice but to publicly condemn the practice. Speaking at a National Police Academy graduation ceremony in the spring of 1940, the attorney general reassured the American public that "nothing in the American police picture warrants fears that 'it is permeating our country like an OGPU or a Gestapo.'" At the same ceremony, Hoover described wiretapping as a "thoroughly unethical practice" that should be used only in an "extreme emergency," such as "the protection of human life or the apprehension of the vilest criminal."[24]

Privately, however, Hoover told Jackson that he was "greatly concerned" over the wiretapping restrictions imposed on the DOJ by the Supreme Court, insisting that the technique was an essential weapon in the battle against foreign espionage and sabotage. Cases that could be solved through wiretapping would now be stopped in their tracks. Investigations would arise, he feared, "particularly in kidnapping and espionage, in which successful investigation will be impossible without the use of telephone taps." Hoover also claimed that the elimination of wiretapping as a legitimate law enforcement tool had "curtailed the Bureau's activity in espionage cases." The FBI director then issued a warning to Jackson: "A repetition of disastrous catastrophes like the Black Tom explosion must be anticipated if every care is not exercised to prevent such occurrences." Laying the problem on the line, he insisted that "the Bureau cannot cope without wiretaps." Jackson took the opposite position, calling wiretapping a source of "real danger" if allowed to proceed unsupervised. The attorney general and future Supreme Court justice believed that it should be employed sparingly and only within the confines of existing statutes. Otherwise, he concluded, wiretapping should be considered a criminal offense.[25]

Less than a month later, German forces moved against France and the Low Countries, and within days of the invasion, Morgenthau began pressuring the president to ease the wiretapping restrictions on the FBI. Henry Stimson, the new secretary of war, backed Morgenthau, fearing that industrial unrest, strikes, Communist labor agitation, and saboteurs could lead to industrial slowdowns or, worse, the shutdown of factories engaged in military production. He hoped that wiretapping would be useful in identifying leaders and instigators. Faced with these new international realities, Roosevelt had no qualms about his decision and promptly issued his fateful order to the FBI.[26]

Years later, Jackson recorded his view of the president's decision to ignore the Supreme Court's ruling in an unfinished memoir that he wrote shortly before his death in 1954. As the attorney general and chief law enforcement officer of the United States, Jackson was compelled to obey the decisions of the Court. President Roosevelt, a Columbia University Law School graduate, often viewed issues crossing his desk in a markedly different way from conventional lawyers. Jackson believed that Roosevelt respected the law and considered himself and his office as subordinate to the Constitution. But to Roosevelt, presidential decision making was less a matter of "legal or illegal" and more a matter of "right or wrong." As a man who had "no patience with treason," he would have "employed ruthless methods to suppress it." Without strong feelings concerning civil liberties, it followed that President Roosevelt saw "no legal limitations on his decisions" during a national emergency. In the president's defense, however, Jackson noted that during Roosevelt's twelve years in office, the wiretapping decision was the only time he ignored the Supreme Court.[27]

By September 1940 the FBI director reported to the White House that his agents were eavesdropping on "all telephone conversations into and out of the following embassies: German, Italian, French, Russian, and Japanese." Electronic eavesdropping was a force multiplier that offered investigators vital information and new insights into foreign intelligence that went well beyond mere evidence collection. In twenty-four hours, trained linguists eavesdropping on telephone calls could answer questions that would have consumed hundreds of hours of investigative time and effort. A diplomat's personal and business behavior, as well as the identities of friends and business colleagues, could be quickly ascertained. The nature of such relationships and the tracking of daily, weekly, and monthly schedules could be essential elements in determining whether surveillance should be started and, if so, when and where to institute it. Interception of conversations through microphone and telephone monitoring allowed an assessment of the personalities of embassy personnel, a ranking of the staff hierarchy, and the identification of persons in contact with the embassy who might be recruited as human sources of information.[28]

CHAPTER SEVEN

Opportunities Missed

Hoover's new counterintelligence role did not end the FBI's friction with the State Department and other federal agencies. This emerged in the case of the United States' first significant breakthrough into the workings of the Soviet intelligence services.

Krivitsky

Walter Krivitsky was born Schmelka Ginsburg in Podvolchiskia, Poland, in 1899. In his youth he joined the Communist Party and later the Soviet army after the overthrow of the Russian czar. In the early 1920s he was inducted into the Fourth Department of the Soviet General Staff, which was responsible for foreign intelligence collection. The Fourth Department would later become the Soviet Military Intelligence Agency (Glavnoye Razvedyvatelnoye Upravlenie, or GRU), by which title it is still known today. It was responsible for the collection of foreign military, industrial, and political intelligence, and it accomplished this mission primarily by secretly dispatching intelligence officers throughout the world. Some of these officers posed as representatives of Soviet trading organizations such as Amtorg in New York City, Arcos in London, and Westorg in Berlin. These corporations had been established by Joseph Stalin during the mid-1920s after the opening of foreign markets to exports of Soviet wheat and raw materials. Posing as official representatives of the Soviet government legitimized the presence of these intelligence officers, and their cover duties provided direct access to foreign businessmen, bankers, and government officials who could be assessed and targeted for possible espionage recruitment.[1]

A second type of intelligence agent was the "illegal" officer. Unlike those assigned to Soviet establishments in foreign capitals, the illegals operated alone, shrouded in anonymity. They normally posed as European businessmen, journalists, or academicians and carried false identification documents.

During the 1930s these illegal officers were far more numerous than the so-called legal ones due to the limited number of official platforms available to the Soviet government. The illegal officer would slip into a country anonymously and establish an innocuous business as a cover for his intelligence activities. The business often had nothing to do with the officer's intelligence assignment, yet its nature was an important consideration when the GRU prepared an officer for duty in the West. The business had to be completely plausible and verifiable, but at the same time, it had to offer a logical reason for the officer's frequent absence from home and office for long periods. Sudden and unexpected travel was a routine feature of an intelligence officer's life, and success in the espionage business depended on avoiding suspicion. Although his cover business was situated in a particular country, his espionage work often took him to other countries whose national secrets were frequently the real targets of Soviet espionage. Detection by the local counterintelligence service was avoided by the use of a separate channel of communication between the intelligence officer in the field and his headquarters in Moscow. He communicated primarily by couriers who carried messages and secret intelligence. Clandestine radio communications, though more vulnerable to discovery, were also used to send short, coded administrative messages.

Despite differences in their cover assignments, the mission of legal and illegal officers was the same: the recruitment and handling of agents with access to an adversary's critical political, industrial, and military information.

Krivitsky was an illegal officer. In 1934 he switched from the GRU to the NKVD (People's Commissariat for Internal Affairs), a reassignment necessitated by the increased need for experienced intelligence officers to expand NKVD activities abroad. A field officer his entire career, Krivitsky served in Europe during the 1930s using many different identities. By 1937 he was the senior illegal NKVD officer in Holland, where he posed as Dr. Martin Lessner, an Austrian rare book collector and art dealer. He was responsible for directing the activities of other intelligence officers, planning operations, and recruiting and handling agents in Holland and, even more importantly, inside Hitler's government.[2]

While Krivitsky was loyally conducting espionage activities for his NKVD masters throughout Europe, Stalin secretly began accelerating the blood purges of his perceived enemies and rivals. Having already dispatched many of Lenin's old associates and colleagues during the mid-1930s, he turned his attention to silencing those who could testify to the brutality that characterized his ascension to the top of the Soviet empire. For Stalin, this meant turning on his principal instruments of terror and suppression—the NKVD and the GRU.

In March 1937 Nikolai Yezhov, head of the NKVD and Stalin's principal toady, commenced a purge of the organization by eliminating its leadership. Over the next few months, loyal GRU and NKVD officers were arrested at all hours of the day and night and ordered to confess to crimes they had not committed. Most quietly met their fate at the executioner's hand; others took their own lives rather than face Stalin's justice. During 1937 at least 3,000 NKVD officers who were loyal to Genreik Yagoda, the first head of the NKVD and Yezhov's predecessor, were executed. About 20,000 NKVD men had fallen victim to the purge by the beginning of World War II.[3]

Krivitsky was keenly aware of the slaughter of his friends and colleagues. Through the couriers he used to transport information, he began receiving ominous warnings about life in Moscow and the reception that awaited intelligence officers who returned there. As a seasoned twenty-year veteran, he understood the brutality of the Soviet system and the atmosphere of suspicion and betrayal that characterized Stalin's leadership. He had no illusions that his life would be spared. Krivitsky knew that it was only a matter of time before an old rival or one of Stalin's victims, desperate to save himself, discredited him, forcing his return to Moscow to face charges of disloyalty.

Krivitsky's moment of truth occurred in December 1937 following the death of Ignace Reiss. Reiss had been Krivitsky's close boyhood friend. Both had entered the GRU together as young men, had transferred to the NKVD at the same time, and had worked together as senior illegals in Europe throughout the 1930s.[4] Reiss, an exceptional recruiter, had brought many communist sympathizers into the NKVD, including a young Communist Party member named Hede Massing, the former wife of well-known German Communist Gerhard Eisler. She was later credited with recruiting a number of high-level Americans for Soviet espionage.[5]

In mid-1937 Reiss was unexpectedly summoned to Moscow. Well aware of the fate that awaited him, he abandoned the party, announced his defection in an open letter to Stalin, and went into hiding in Europe.[6] Given his prestige in the NKVD, this daring and public rebuke of Stalin incensed the Kremlin and prompted other lesser-known intelligence officers to make a similar decision to defect to the West.[7]

Krivitsky, along with many other officers in Europe, was ordered to assist the NKVD in locating and executing Reiss. Krivitsky undoubtedly feigned cooperation in the hunt while beginning his own cathartic reexamination of the political loyalties that had brought him to this point. Despite Reiss's considerable skills and years of experience as an intelligence officer, he was no match for NKVD fugitive hunters. Three months after his defection, a passerby found his body with five bullet holes in the head and seven more in the torso on a roadside near Laussanne, Switzerland. Stunned by the gruesome discovery, Krivitsky had no doubt that the NKVD had finally caught up with his friend. At the same time, he was chillingly aware that their close personal and professional relationship over two decades made him the next logical target for Stalin's vengeance. For the next three months, Krivitsky carefully planned his defection while carrying on his daily routine so as not to arouse the suspicions of his superiors. He began exploring the range of options available to an experienced Soviet intelligence officer with years of military and NKVD secrets stored in his memory. Finally, in December 1937, he made contact with representatives of the French Security Service and was offered protection by Premier Leon Blum. Over the next year, he provided the French with a treasure trove of details concerning his espionage activities in Europe. He cataloged the complete history of his twenty-year involvement in Soviet espionage, including the full scope of Soviet intelligence penetration of the key defense, industrial, and political organizations of the western European powers. The new defector remained in seclusion in France with his wife and child until the end of 1938, participating in an exhaustive series of interviews with French counterintelligence officials. With the assistance of William Bullitt, the U.S. ambassador to France, Krivitsky and his family quietly left Europe and arrived in the United States on November 15, 1938, for what he hoped would be a new life free of Stalin's terror.[8]

Facilitating Krivitsky's journey to the United States was Isaac Don Levine of the *Saturday Evening Post*. A frequent traveler with European roots, Levine was a keen observer of the international scene. Politically conservative and an ardent anti-Nazi and anti-Stalinist, he used his writing to expose the evils awash in Europe in the late 1930s. He often met in Paris with Ambassador Bullitt, and it was during one such encounter that Bullitt told him about Krivitsky's break with Stalin. Levine recognized the potential story value of the former NKVD agent's revelations and urged the ambassador to issue the necessary visas for Krivitsky and his family to travel to the United

States. Levine agreed to assist with his relocation and introduce him to key officials in the Roosevelt administration.[9] Upon his arrival in New York, Krivitsky became one of the highest-ranking NKVD defectors ever to set foot in the United States. He soon established contact with other American journalists in an effort to publish his story and obtain the financial means to start a new life. One of the first Americans he met was journalist Paul Wohl, who obtained lodging for Krivitsky and put him in contact with influential Americans who could assist him.

Collaborating with Levine, Krivitsky authored a number of articles that appeared in the *Saturday Evening Post* in the spring of 1939. The revelations were electrifying. For the first time, the American public learned of the extent of Stalin's purges of his political rivals, his military leadership (including Marshal Mikhail Tukhachevsky), and the Soviet secret police apparatus. He outlined in stark detail the true goal of Stalin's foreign policy toward Hitler while revealing a side of the Soviet leader that had been dismissed by Western political leaders. He described Stalin as fearful of Hitler's power and desperate to pursue accommodation with the Nazi leadership. Stalin's policy, he wrote, was to silently watch the Nazis extend their tentacles throughout the world while wooing Hitler with assurances of important concessions and a free hand in exchange for peace toward the Soviet Union. Stalin's policy toward Hitler was one of "appeasement," Krivitsky wrote, and he acknowledged that both the secret and public records he had seen convinced him that the more aggressive Hitler became, the more Stalin "pressed his courtship."[10]

Krivitsky's sensational revelations created a national furor. The propaganda apparatus of the Communist Party of the United States instantly went into action after publication of the first article. The party loudly denounced Krivitsky as an imposter and a liar, characterizing his assertions about Stalin and Soviet spying as fabrications. Not content with simply rebuking him, the party pressured the Department of Labor to deport Krivitsky as an illegal alien. At the same time, however, his claims caused serious political problems for the Department of State, which was deluged with letters from citizens and politicians alike demanding that his disclosures be investigated. The views of Congressman John McCormick of Massachusetts typified those of many Americans who read the defector's revelations. He described it as an "amazing article" that should receive "the attention, consideration, and investigation of the State Department." Loy Henderson, the State Department's Soviet desk officer, met with Krivitsky in March 1939. Henderson, who had previously served in Moscow, believed Krivitsky and found his allegations compelling. In a memorandum for his bosses, he characterized Krivitsky's articles as containing "certain very important information." He reasoned that it would be unconscionable to gain Krivitsky's confidence, extract the information he had about the Soviet Union, and then "stand aside and permit him to be deported." Henderson's dilemma—and that of the Department of State in general—was being unable to intervene on Krivitsky's behalf if the Department of Labor decided to act against him.[11]

Ignoring Krivitsky's broader revelations concerning the inner thoughts of the Soviet leadership, State Department officials chose instead to focus narrowly on his knowledge of the illegal use of U.S. passports. In Krivitsky's first article he had described the NKVD's confiscation of hundreds of valid U.S. passports from American volunteers when they arrived in Spain to fight in the International Brigades. They were never returned to their American owners. Passports were also taken from the bodies and personal effects of Americans killed in action in Spain. Thousands of American passports acquired in this fashion ended up in NKVD laboratories for later use by Soviet illegals. The State Department was very sensitive about its investigative prerogatives in passport matters and was anxious to avoid any public embarrassment for failure to act on Krivitsky's allegations. Fletcher Warren, Messersmith's deputy, prepared a memorandum outlining the department's concerns. He expressed fear of the political repercussions of pursuing Krivitsky's information but warned of an equally explosive reaction for failure to investigate the charges of passport irregularities. Warren warned his bosses of "tremendous criticism of the Department if it failed to get as much information as possible from Krivitsky before his departure." To guarantee that Krivitsky's testimony would never become public, he suggested that the defector be questioned before a federal grand jury, "without this Department having to take any responsibility for his being held over."[12]

The confusion about how to proceed did not end with Messersmith. The communist press attack, together with the Soviet government's demand that Krivitsky be expelled from the United States, forced the Department of Labor to reexamine his visa status and consider deportation proceedings against him as an undesirable alien.[13] Krivitsky was stunned at the accusations of insincerity and communicated his anger to the State Department through Levine. To demonstrate his truthfulness, he then offered to provide "to the United States government information concerning a number of GPU agents alleged to be in Washington."[14]

On June 28, 1939, Krivitsky met in New York with Ruth Shipley, chief of the Passport Office of the Department of State, and provided detailed information previously unknown to the U.S. government. The defector explained the importance of U.S. passports for NKVD operations and described how laboratory technicians manufactured fraudulent passports in Moscow—disassembling genuine passports, washing the pages, and then creating forged ones to suit their particular needs, including altering the photographs. He then identified a Soviet illegal agent who had entered the United States in the 1930s with the task of obtaining as many genuine U.S. passports as possible for use by agents. The NKVD and GRU used multiple passports, according to Krivitsky, to confuse opposing counterintelligence services, making it hard for them to ascertain whether a particular person was or ever had been in a certain country. False U.S. passports permitted agents unfettered movement when traveling. An agent would enter a country on one passport and depart using another passport under a different name and nationality and with a forged entrance visa attached. An agent might use as many as ten different passports while moving from country to country, creating the impression of being ten different persons.[15] Krivitsky provided the true identities of at least two Russian agents in the United States who had obtained false passports, and he estimated that one particular agent had fraudulently obtained approximately 100 to 150 passports while in the United States. Then, in terrifying detail, he outlined how the NKVD would extract a confession from a person suspected of disloyalty, saying, "they always did talk; if you hurt them continuously for ten days there was usually nothing left to get further information from—in other words, two or three days of torture would bring forth a confession and a torture as long as ten days would result either in death or insanity."[16]

Finally, Shipley questioned Krivitsky about the organization of the Soviet espionage apparatus in the New York City area. He explained that there were approximately fifteen persons who constituted the inner circle; each operated twenty agents, and each individual network was responsible for a particular type of secret work, which he did not specify. Krivitsky estimated that there were between 250 and 300 agents in the New York City area.[17]

The FBI had also been reading Krivitsky's sensational articles in the *Saturday Evening Post*. Hoover was keenly aware of the defector's problems with the Department of Labor. By the summer of 1939 the Bureau had developed some insight into Krivitsky's past activities and associates but remained mistrustful of him.[18] These suspicions stemmed from a number of sources. One was Krivitsky's first article entitled "Stalin's Hand in Spain," which described his role in the secret arming of communist forces through a series of sophisticated European front companies and his establishment of an espionage apparatus in Spain. His credibility, in Hoover's view, was worthless. He based this conclusion on an editor's note accompanying the article that described Krivitsky as a "refugee having determined to give up all political activities though he is still a believer in the true Communism of Lenin." Another factor was Krivitsky's legal representation by New York City attorney Louis Waldman, who had successfully defended accused Soviet spy Robert Osman during his court-martial in the Panama Canal Zone in the early 1930s. At the same time, Levine was blackballed by Hoover simply because of his association with Krivitsky.[19]

The key piece of evidence against Krivitsky, however, was an assertion he made that conflicted with information contained in Hoover's files. At an interview conducted by the FBI on July 27, 1939, in Waldman's office, Krivitsky named Emil Kleber as the "head of the International Brigades" and a "general of the Comintern." Kleber had received worldwide notoriety as an Austrian soldier of fortune and naturalized Canadian who had joined the White Guards and, while fighting the Bolsheviks, been converted to communism. Krivitsky claimed that Kleber's true name was Moishe Stern. He described their friendship during the 1920s and charged that Kleber's swashbuckling persona was a creation of the NKVD. Stern had served in the military section of the Comintern in the late 1920s and later traveled to China on a confidential mission. He explained that Stern, who had died in 1937 during the purges, had never conducted espionage in the United States. FBI records contradicted Krivitsky's claims. Hoover's investigators had never confronted a defecting Soviet intelligence officer and had no experience interviewing such a unique source of information. Krivitsky, despite his experience, undoubtedly approached his first interrogation by the U.S. counterintelligence service with a certain degree of anxiety and caution, which was apparently interpreted by the FBI as evasion. Without further investigation to clarify the discrepancy between Krivitsky's information and the Bureau's files, the defector was deemed untrustworthy, and his revelations were dismissed.[20]

Nine days later, Krivitsky dropped his biggest bombshell in the final installment for the *Saturday Evening Post*. The article entitled "My Flight from Stalin" offered rich details about his handling of American espionage agents. He identified the leadership of the NKVD's foreign intelligence organization and provided insights into its worldwide methods of operation. He described the use of "tiny rolls of photographic film" to transmit large volumes of secret reports and a sophisticated film laboratory in Moscow to process this film using the "finest American photographic apparatus." He identified Margaret Browder as an NKVD agent who had worked for him in Europe. She was the sister of Earl Browder, the head of the Communist Party of the United States and a presidential candidate in the 1936 election. Margaret, posing as Jean Montgomery, had been trained in subversion and clandestine radio operations at a special school in Moscow. Later, in the guise of a student, she had worked with Krivitsky performing espionage duties and establishing clandestine radio stations in central Europe. The article also outlined the espionage activities of Katherine Harris, Earl Browder's wife. She too had served as Krivitsky's agent for many years and had been particularly valuable as a courier in Europe because she held a U.S. passport, making travel across international borders easy. Krivitsky identified another prominent American and his wife as agents and members of the Communist Party, revealing that they had been recruited as spies and ordered to go "underground," posing as owners of a Soviet-financed film export company in Romania. Finally, he identified the senior Soviet military intelligence officer in the United States as Colonel Boris Bykov.[21]

Questions about Krivitsky's credibility only complicated the problems of counterintelligence responsibility and coordination among governmental agencies. With Krivitsky's revelations now public, the FBI again attempted to question him on October 6, 1939. A month later Hoover informed Warren that the interview had concerned matters "separate and distinct from passport frauds." During the interview, Krivitsky related that he had been in "communication with representatives of Department of Labor concerning immigration matters and with representatives of the Department of State regarding passport matters." Hoover noted that when his agents learned of these contacts they had discontinued the interview, deciding that it would not be "discreet to intrude upon those matters already under investigation by other departments of the government." Hoover concluded by asking whether Messersmith wanted his agents to interview Krivitsky about the passport fraud issue. Four days later Messersmith informed Hoover that no further interviews would be necessary, and Krivitsky was never again contacted by FBI investigators.[22]

In August 1948, nine years after Krivitsky's FBI interviews, Whittaker Chambers became a household name when he testified before a congressional committee investigating high-level espionage in the Roosevelt administration. Chambers admitted membership in the Communist Party and his recruitment into the GRU in the late 1920s, and he described his duties as a courier of secret information. Then he dropped a bombshell that would make him an ideological icon for the next half a century. Alger Hiss, he told a startled committee, had been a spy for the Soviet Union before the Second World War. Hiss—of Johns Hopkins University and Harvard Law School, clerk to Supreme Court Justice Oliver Wendell Holmes, senior World War II State Department official and leader in the creation of the United Nations, and friend and confidant of future Secretary of State Dean Acheson—had routinely passed large volumes of sensitive information to the Soviet government through Chambers. Hiss emphatically denied the charges, and Chambers was initially vilified for his accusations. Yet seventeen months later, Hiss stood convicted of perjury, and in January 1949 he began serving a six-year sentence at Lewisburg Federal Penitentiary.

There is an old saying that if "'ifs' and 'buts' were candy and nuts what a wonderful world this would be." This saying is applicable to historians trying to examine this period in U.S. counterintelligence history. How can we make sense of the FBI's failure to recognize a unique and extraordinarily valuable source of information that could have broken open Soviet intelligence activities in the Western Hemisphere like an egg? Krivitsky was a senior Soviet intelligence officer with a large storehouse of information; his entire career in the GRU and NKVD had been a regular routine of treachery, deceit, fear, and betrayal. He understood Stalin's twisted mind and knew that his vengeance did not recognize oceans, national borders, or foreign laws. Even in the United States, Krivitsky was racked with anxiety and feared for his life. Given his state of mind, it is understandable that he was less than forthcoming with Hoover's investigators. With sensitive handling and a professional long-term approach, the Bureau could have guaranteed his security, facilitated his resettlement in the United States, and possibly won his confidence and trust. In return, Hoover would have had a vital key to the entire Soviet espionage apparatus in the United States. With some patience, Krivitsky might have told Hoover's investigators that he had talked with Chambers for ten hours, discussing the latter's relationship with the GRU, only two months before Krivitsky's interview with the FBI. This could have led to the early discovery of Hiss, State Department officer Lawrence Duggan, Assistant Secretary of the Treasury Harry Dexter White, Special Assistant to the President Lauchlin Currie, and numerous other highly placed Soviet agents.[23]

Tragically, the United States' emerging counterintelligence service, at this critical period in the nation's history, lacked the sensitivity and professional skills to recognize Krivitsky's unique value and chose to ignore him. Yet within a year, the Bureau would intensify its efforts to uncover Soviet intelligence activities, without ever tapping into the one man who knew all there was to know about the enormous challenge facing Hoover's fledgling counterspies.[24]

Orlov

Alexander Orlov's sad thirty-five-year odyssey in the United States began on August 13, 1938, when the train carrying him, his wife, Vera, and their only child, Maria, crossed the border from Canada at Rouses Point, New York. Orlov, an NKVD senior officer under Soviet diplomatic cover, was running for his life. Only a month earlier, while serving as the Politburo's adviser to the Spanish Republican government and Stalin's personal representative in Spain, he had received an ominous cable from NKVD head Nikolai Yezhov, ordering him to travel to Amsterdam to meet an unnamed official who would be arriving in the next few days. Orlov's keen instincts, honed through years of European espionage in Stalin's service, warned him of a trap designed to lure him back to Moscow to face a farce of a trial and execution by firing squad.[25]

Since his assignment to Spain in 1936, Orlov had been watching with concern the increasing paranoia of Stalin and his henchmen toward their old revolutionary allies as well as their political enemies. Rumors of wild accusations of treason, forced confessions, loyal party men making absurd public pleas for forgiveness, and the recall of NKVD friends and colleagues from assignments in western Europe to face a similar fate had reached Orlov at his Barcelona headquarters. So when he received Yezhov's instructions, General Orlov, one of Stalin's most senior NKVD officers, finalized a decision that had been months in the making.[26]

He cabled Yezhov, agreeing to make the meeting as ordered, and behaved as if nothing was out of the ordinary. Then he gathered up his wife and daughter and proceeded to Paris, where he first sought the assistance of Ambassador William Bullitt in the hope of acquiring U.S. travel visas for himself and his family. Failing this, he next turned to the Canadian embassy, where he was more successful. On the night he was scheduled to meet the mysterious visitor in Amsterdam, Orlov was still in France, boarding a ship at Cherbourg that would take him to Quebec, Canada, the first stop in his new life.

Orlov knew that his failure to make the meeting in Amsterdam would set in motion a worldwide manhunt to find and kill him. Under no false illusions about the skill and tenacity of the Soviet intelligence services, Orlov made a deliberately bold move designed to acknowledge that skill but warn Stalin that pursuing him could be a very dangerous undertaking. Upon his arrival in Quebec, Orlov sent letters to both Yezhov and Stalin announcing his intention to disappear and break off relations with the NKVD. To protect his family and Vera's relatives still living in the Soviet Union, he offered the two men a deal: if they agreed not to harm his family and not to send assassination squads to find him, the vast amounts of knowledge he had accumulated about Stalin's crimes and NKVD espionage activities would forever remain a secret. To further ensure his security, he entrusted the letters to a distant family member living in New York City, who traveled to Europe and mailed the letters from a Paris post office. To authenticate the letters, Orlov affixed his thumb print, for easy NKVD verification.[27]

The U.S. embassy in Quebec was Orlov's next stop. There he was personally received by the ambassador, who welcomed him into his office and engaged him in a lengthy and friendly discussion. When Orlov explained that he and his family were on an extended vacation to Canada and the United States, the ambassador arranged U.S. entry visas for them with a liberal time limit of one year. Orlov was stunned at this turn of events; years later he told his FBI handler that he had been so excited when he left the embassy that he "didn't even think his feet were touching the ground." Soon after arriving in the United States, Mr. and Mrs. Alexander Orlov became Mr. and Mrs. Alexander Berg and disappeared into American society.[28]

Although it is questionable whether the FBI would have realized Orlov's extraordinary value in its efforts to penetrate Soviet intelligence activities in the United States, a number of events prevented such an encounter from taking place. The first occurred when Orlov arranged to have a New York City lawyer named John Finerty handle his immigration case. Finerty was a good choice; he had a good reputation as a civil rights attorney and had previously served as counsel for Nicola Sacco and Bartolomeo Vanzetti, two

Italian-born anarchists from Massachusetts who had been convicted and sentenced to death for armed robbery and murder following a controversial trial that received worldwide publicity. Later, Finerty was a member of a commission established by Professor John Dewey that concluded that Stalin's charges against Leon Trotsky at the show trials in Moscow had been baseless.[29]

Orlov informed Finerty that he wanted to defect and revealed his status as a Soviet diplomat, but he omitted the sordid details about his escapades in Spain. Wasting no time, Finerty took Orlov to Washington, D.C., where they discussed his situation personally with James L. Houghteling, the commissioner of immigration and naturalization. After hearing his story, and learning that the family had accumulated $22,800 and had American relatives willing to sponsor them, all agreed that Orlov was at risk and that the best course of action was "to avoid publicity and keep his arrival secret." No record of Orlov's importance as a source or his decision to reside in the United States was ever made by immigration officials. As one historian described it, "the way had now been cleared for the Orlov family to go underground, which they did early in 1939 by heading for the West Coast."[30]

A second missed chance occurred in December 1940. During the summer of 1940 Congress had passed the Alien Registration Act, which required all aliens residing in the United States to register with the federal government. With Finerty's help, the Orlovs sought a way to comply with the law but not divulge their whereabouts. Doing so, however, required Finerty to ask for the assistance of an old friend, Francis Biddle, who was then serving as attorney general of the United States. Biddle, recognizing the gravity of the situation, put Finerty in touch with Earl G. Harrison, the director of alien registration, who would handle the matter personally. Orlov explained the circumstances of his defection from the NKVD, and Harrison escorted the Orlov family to the offices of Richard Eggleston, postal inspector in charge, who expedited the process. After giving his address as care of John F. Finerty, 120 Broadway, New York City, New York, Orlov was properly registered and once again disappeared.[31]

During August 1941 the Orlovs, living quietly in Massachusetts, appeared at the Pilgrim Trust Bank in downtown Boston to retrieve the contents of a safe-deposit box they had rented earlier. Their efforts were stymied by President Roosevelt's executive order issued in May 1941 that restricted the banking activities of aliens who could not provide evidence of naturalization. Under the watchful eye of a suspicious bank official, they removed their passports and a Canadian bank book but were stopped when they tried to remove a quantity of undeveloped roll and flat-pack film. Bank officials waited until January 1942, more than a month after the Pearl Harbor attack, before notifying the FBI's Boston office of the Orlovs' visit.[32]

An FBI investigation was initiated on Alexander and Marie Berg (aka Orlov) under the administrative category "Internal Security–G," which stood for the wartime enemy Germany. Although the Bergs described themselves as Russian, the Pilgrim Trust official found them to be "people of some breeding," leaving him with the definite impression that they were German. An exhaustive investigation to identify and locate the Bergs was unsuccessful, even though a monthly money order appeared at the bank for the safe-deposit box rental fee. Suspicion grew that the Bergs were continuing to pay the fee to protect the box's contents, but with insufficient evidence to support a search warrant, the FBI never had the opportunity to discover what it contained. At the war's end, the FBI was no closer to finding the Bergs, and the case was closed. On May 9, 1950, more than ten years after last visiting Pilgrim Trust Bank, Orlov reappeared, reclaimed the film, and closed the account.[33] It was not until the spring of 1953, after the publication of Orlov's reminiscences in *Life* magazine, that the FBI realized he had been living quietly and anonymously in the United States for more than fifteen years.

What did the United States lose because of the delay in getting to Orlov? With the hindsight of almost seventy years, the loss could be considered enormous. However, given the absence of any U.S. counterintelligence structure and the inexperience and mind-set of the FBI, it is doubtful that the significance and extraordinary value of his information would have been appreciated. Another unknown factor is the extent of Orlov's cooperation with U.S. officials had they known that he was living right under their noses. He had made a pact of silence with Stalin in exchange for his life and the lives of his relatives in the Soviet Union. Today, questions still linger about Orlov's cooperation, even after decades of protection by and collaboration with the FBI. Edward Gazur, the retired special agent who served as Orlov's FBI handler, wrote that one evening they had a lengthy conversation about Kim Philby, a leading member of the British establishment, senior MI6 officer, KGB spy, and one of the so-called Cambridge Five, who defected to Moscow in the early 1960s. The topic of Philby arose during a conversation about the famous British intelligence officer Sydney Reilly, who had been executed by the new Soviet government shortly after the October Revolution of 1917. Orlov described Reilly as a courageous officer, a true hero in the British tradition, who was willing to take extraordinary risks in furtherance of an assignment. Philby was the opposite of Reilly because, in Orlov's view, he was probably the most important source the KGB ever had against the Western intelligence services. In the final chapter of his book, entitled "Mystery," Gazur concludes that Orlov "knew what he was talking about based on his probable knowledge of Philby's recruitment."[34]

Whether or not Orlov knew about the Cambridge Five, had he been interviewed in 1938, he could have provided U.S. intelligence with a full and complete history of his central role in Soviet intelligence for the previous eighteen years. Orlov fought for the Red Army at the age of twenty-three and later conducted guerrilla operations, dynamiting bridges and rail lines, and secured intelligence during the Russo-Polish War in 1920. His daring and courageous exploits soon led to his acceptance into the Cheka, the Extraordinary Commission for Combating Counterrevolution and Subversion, which was established under the leadership of Felix Dzerzhinsky to root out and destroy opposition to the new Soviet government. Orlov was posted to France under the alias Leon Nikolayev; his cover was assignment as an economic official with the Soviet trade delegation. From Paris he was sent to Berlin, posing as the control chief for the Soviet trade delegation, an assignment that involved the pursuit of industrial espionage on a grand scale. In 1933 his vast experience led to a transfer to the NKVD, and he soon found himself traveling around Europe posing as an American businessman named William Goldin. Finally, in September 1936 Orlov arrived in Spain with the express purpose of bringing that government into the Soviet orbit. He oversaw all Soviet intelligence operations, ran the NKVD's spy school, and recruited agents, including idealistic Americans who had traveled to Spain to fight in the civil war on the Republican side. Included in this group was Morris Cohen, who fled the United States in 1949 with his wife, Lona; they reappeared as illegals in England in the 1960s, posing as obscure book dealers named Peter and Helen Kroger. Based on a request from the French counterintelligence service, the CIA questioned Orlov extensively in 1965. His debriefing was very informative and included detailed explanations of a vast array of sophisticated Soviet tradecraft.[35]

More than five decades after Orlov's 1938 defection, historians John Costello and Oleg Tsarev established his importance when they were allowed brief access to NKVD files following the collapse of the Soviet Union in 1989. Mikhail Spiegelglas confessed, shortly before his execution, that

Yezhov had issued an order not to pursue Orlov when he learned that the "non-returner" had threatened to "expose compromising material as soon as he detected the slightest hint of surveillance." Orlov's NKVD colleague Pavel Sudaplatov, along with Orlov's own dossier, substantiated his "knowledge of the major operations involving agents in most of the underground networks in Europe, Britain and the United States."[36]

(Above) Group photo of Rumrich's unit at Fort Clayton, Panama Canal Zone. Rumrich is at the extreme left in the front row. The date is unknown, but the caption at the bottom— "Wishing you holiday greetings"— suggests December. (Library of Congress)

(Left) Guenther Rumrich's arrest photograph, February 1938. (FBI)

Left to right: Guenther Rumrich, Otto Voss, and Erich Glaser during their trial in the fall 1938. (Library of Congress)

Special agent Leon Turrou, lead investigator in the Rumrich espionage case, at the time of the Rumrich trial. (Library of Congress)

Attorney General Homer Cummings was ordered by President Roosevelt in October 1938 to prepare recommendations for the reform of counterespionage policy. (Library of Congress)

Stewart T. Wood, commissioner of the Royal Canadian Mounted Police, secretly exchanged intelligence and other information with Hoover. (Royal Canadian Mounted Police)

Beginning in early 1939, special agent Stanley J. Tracy, senior administrative assistant to Hoover, chaired a secret committee of the FBI, ONI, and MID that oversaw the coordination of ongoing investigations. (J. Edgar Hoover Center for Law Enforcement)

Special agent W. Richard Glavin, senior administrative assistant to Hoover, chaired a secret committee of the FBI, ONI, and MID in early 1939 to plan policy for counterespionage investigations. (J. Edgar Hoover Center for Law Enforcement)

Brigadier General Sherman Miles, assistant chief of staff of the War Department's Military Intelligence Division, was a member of the Interdepartmental Intelligence Conference and one of Hoover's rivals. (Library of Congress)

J. Edgar Hoover, FBI director and chairman of the Interdepartmental Intelligence Conference, circa 1940. (J. Edgar Hoover Center for Law Enforcement)

Admiral Walter S. Anderson, director of the Office of Naval Intelligence and the first naval representative of the Interdepartmental Intelligence Conference. (U.S. Navy)

(Left) Special agent Louis C. Beck was sent by Hoover to the U.S. embassy in Moscow in July 1940, where he posed as a State Department employee. His reports regarding embassy security were forwarded to the White House. (FBI) (Right) Percy Foxworth, assistant director of the New York field office and the first head of the Special Intelligence Service. (University of Mississippi)

Percy Foxworth, close confidant of Hoover and the first head of the FBI's ultrasecret Special Intelligence Service, shown here with General Manuel Bonitez y Valdes, head of the Cuban National Police Force. Date unknown. (University of Mississippi)

(Left) Hugh Clegg, an FBI assistant director and head of training, was dispatched to London in November 1940 to conduct a survey of British wartime police, counterintelligence, and foreign intelligence methods. (J. Edgar Hoover Center for Law Enforcement) (Right) Earl J. Connelley, who led the investigation in many of the FBI's most sensitive cases, was sent to New York to oversee the Sebold case. (FBI)

Cartoon from the April 1941 *Investigator*, the FBI's in-house journal, humorously depicting Hugh Clegg and Lawrence Hince's secret trip to London. (J. Edgar Hoover Center for Law Enforcement)

House located at 28 Hillside Drive (now Bankside Drive North) in Centerport, New York, where for seventeen months special agent Morris Price exchanged radio messages with the Abwehr in Hamburg, Germany. (FBI)

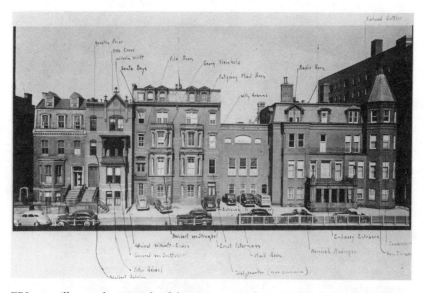

FBI surveillance photograph of the German embassy in Washington, D.C., circa 1941. Note the location of the mailroom and the radio room, as well as the names written on the photo, which correspond to the location of each person's office. (FBI)

CHAPTER EIGHT

Special Overseas Assignments

Astor

On May 4, 1940, six days before Hitler invaded Holland and France, Percy Foxworth, the special agent in charge of the FBI's New York Office, received a telephone call from Vincent Astor (son of business tycoon Colonel John Jacob Astor IV, who went down with the Titanic in 1912), who claimed to have urgent information from President Franklin Roosevelt. Both Roosevelt and Astor were Dutchess County, New York, natives, men of privilege and inherited wealth with roots extending back to the original Dutch settlers of the colony. Astor's vast estate was situated in Rhinebeck, only a few miles north of Roosevelt's famous Springwood home at Hyde Park. Both men shared a keen interest in politics, and Astor had been one of Roosevelt's earliest political supporters, campaigning for him in 1928 when he ran for the governorship of New York. Years later, when he was looking for rest and recreation, Roosevelt would board Astor's yacht, the Nourmabal, for long, lazy cruises in the company of old friends and cronies.[1]

Astor was also a leading member of a mysterious group called the "Room." This secret society, which had been founded in 1927 by Astor, Kermit Roosevelt, and Theodore Roosevelt Jr. (sons of President Theodore Roosevelt), met regularly in the front parlor of Astor's New York town house. Made up of an odd and informal conglomerate of prominent East Coast socialites, bankers, businessmen, journalists, world explorers, and amateur intelligence buffs, its purpose was to keep members current on world developments. Although he was never a member, President Roosevelt was on intimate terms with most of the members, whom he knew from his college days at Harvard and from New York political, social, and financial circles. Astor, like Roosevelt, had a keen interest in intelligence gathering and espionage. Early in Roosevelt's presidency, Astor offered him the

159

use of the Room as a private source of intelligence not otherwise available through normal government channels. Roosevelt eagerly accepted and used Astor throughout the 1930s to collect military and political information throughout the world. Private wealth and an enthusiasm for yachting allowed Astor to travel the oceans posing as what he really was—a fabulously wealthy yachtsman. But while he was making these port calls and acting the celebrity, he was quietly acquiring and recording useful data on docks, naval storage facilities, ship movements, and a host of other intelligence tidbits. As managing director of the Western Union Telegraph Company, Astor also ordered the interception of European and Latin American communications in and out of the United States, in violation of the Comprehensive Communications Act, which prohibited the U.S. government's involvement in any electronic eavesdropping. Throughout the early and mid-1930s, the president often turned to Astor and his coterie of amateur spies for a steady supply of timely intelligence on critical world developments.[2]

The outbreak of war in Europe in September 1939 only increased Roosevelt's need for Astor's services. Information-gathering methods of dubious legality had to be employed to obtain the data required to make timely strategic judgments. Astor quickly responded to the demands of the chief executive. Within a month of German forces crossing the Polish border, Astor mobilized the Room to meet the administration's pressing need for information, and by October 1939 he was reporting to Roosevelt that he had assigned two of his Western Union employees to monitor, on a full-time basis, all radio broadcasts emanating from Cuban, Mexican, and Swiss radio stations. From other Room members with ties to the New York banking establishment, Astor acquired sensitive financial information on individuals and companies, assuring the president, "Tomorrow, I am starting to work on the banks, using Chase as the Guinea Pig," because "espionage and sabotage need money, and that has to pass through the banks at one stage or another."[3]

During that May 4 telephone call, Astor told Foxworth that he was with President Roosevelt at Hyde Park and had just learned that Carl Norden was scheduled to depart at noon that day for Zurich, Switzerland, aboard the SS *George Washington*. He had learned of Norden's last-minute travel plans from Admiral Harold Stark, the chief of naval operations; Stark, in turn, had just received a telephone call from Norden, who was in New York awaiting the ship's departure. The president, Astor insisted, wanted a special agent to accompany Norden to Europe. The agent's duties were vague and, in Foxworth's mind, seemed to be limited to acting as "a chaperon" and serving as "protection." If Norden experienced difficulties and was "taken from the boat at Gibraltar by the British, of which there was apparently some fear," then the agent was not to interfere in any way but should contact the nearest U.S. consul and radio FBI headquarters for further instructions.[4]

Norden

Carl Norden, born in Semarang, Java, in 1880, was a Dutch citizen who immigrated to the United States after the First World War. He soon obtained employment with the Sperry Gyroscope Corporation in the New York City area. Educated as an engineer, this brilliant technician possessed an inventive mind that he applied to the development of new mechanical devices for the U.S. military. Among his early inventions was an airplane arresting gear for aircraft carriers. After leaving Sperry he formed the Norden Company, which soon rivaled his old employer in the development of new and improved high-altitude bombsights, capable of pinpoint accuracy, to be used in naval aircraft flying horizontally over moving enemy ships. Throughout the Depression years, Norden continued improving his device for the navy, believing that it was the only U.S. military service capable of protecting his invention from foreign predators. His disdain for the War Department stemmed from the army's firm adherence to competitive military contracting laws of the late 1920s. Instead of contracting exclusively with the Norden Company, as the navy did, the army issued multiple bids for contracts to the industrial community, and the Norden Company often lost the bidding war.[5] Eventually his resentment became so intense that when the army decided to purchase his device, Norden refused to sell it. He was so stubborn on this point that the navy was forced to buy a number of the devices from Norden's company and then turn them over to the Army Air Corps without Norden's knowledge.[6]

"Old man dynamite," as the navy brass referred to Norden, was an eccentric genius. He was also self-centered, driven, impatient, and abrasive, and he had little tolerance for anyone unfortunate enough to possess a lesser mind. Norden hated bureaucracies and was indifferent to the mundane daily requirements of running a major corporation. His disdain for collective approaches to the solution of technical problems made it impossible for him to collaborate on projects with other technicians. He preferred to work alone with pencil and paper, drafting ideas and blueprints either in his New York office or at his family residence in Zurich. Though a devoted family man, he kept his wife and children in Switzerland, viewing them as a distraction from his scientific work. Norden routinely visited his family, but his habit of abruptly leaving for Switzerland without notifying the U.S. military leadership was a problem. Norden's mercurial behavior and his indifference toward his own safety and the security of his top-secret bombsight were constant sources of irritation to military officials. Navy fears about losing this critical weapon were intensified when copies of the bombsight plans were found in the offices of the Sperry Corporation—a discovery that forced navy officials to issue a specific order concerning its security: "All correspondence and conversation relating thereto" should be considered secret, and every precaution should be taken "to prevent information regarding this development from becoming available to any person who may utilize it in any manner contrary to the best interests of the United States."[7]

On November 16, 1939, General Henry H. "Hap" Arnold, chief of the U.S. Army Air Corps, vented his frustration over Norden's behavior in a letter to the navy's Bureau of Aeronautics, complaining, "it seems to me that it brings up what may prove to be a very serious situation. If Mr. Norden does consider himself at liberty to go to a foreign country and build equipment some of our secret projects undoubtedly will be compromised." Arnold also expressed concern over Norden's recent sale of a portion of his company to his business partner. Freed from the daily administrative burdens of running a company, Norden now considered himself "a free will agent as regards the disposition of any brain children," noting "that he could work for anyone."[8]

Struggling to keep Norden and the new bombsight technology safe and secure, the army and navy went to great lengths to accommodate him. Ever sensitive to Norden's personal vulnerability due to his erratic travel habits and his value to unscrupulous European powers, the navy tried with little success to convince him of the danger he exposed himself to by visiting Europe. As the war clouds over Europe darkened, the navy attempted to impose some level of security, including using the State Department's diplomatic pouch to ship his notes and drawings to the United States.[9]

The British government also had an interest in Norden's bombsight technology. In fact, the decision to dispatch an FBI agent to accompany Norden may have been precipitated by the navy's interception of a British wire that characterized him as a "dangerous individual, destitute, and friendly with the Nazi Government in Germany."[10] Growing increasingly concerned about the imminent possibility of a hot war in western Europe, Stark was vigorously increasing the navy's readiness to fight a two-ocean war if necessary. Mindful of Hitler's aggressive behavior in western Europe, and fearful that Norden could be taken by the British at Gibraltar or by German or Italian agents in Europe, the admiral moved to intensify security for the United States' most important military inventor.[11]

Special agent M. Clair Spear, a mild-mannered, soft-spoken man assigned to the FBI's New York office, was selected for the assignment. Astor arranged a thirty-minute delay of the scheduled noon departure of the SS *Washington* so that Spear could obtain a passport, receive the necessary radio codes for secure communication with Hoover, and meet with Norden and get him to agree to allow Spear to accompany him on the trip. Time was so critical that Spear's fellow FBI agents rushed to his apartment to pack his bags.[12]

Norden greeted Spear cordially, expressed concern about the potential danger facing them both, and indicated his appreciation for Spear's companionship and service as a bodyguard. Norden even entrusted personal letters to his wife, keys to his safe-deposit box in New York City, currency, and two technical sketches to Spear for safekeeping. Like Stark, Hoover was worried about the welfare of the two men. Aside from their personal safety, he feared that their lack of diplomatic status left them vulnerable to an intrusive British customs search at Gibraltar and an Italian search at Genoa, which might compromise Norden's material and Spear's identity, codebooks, and FBI connection. That fear intensified when he learned that Norden's property was in Spear's possession and that Norden feared detention by European authorities. Particularly troublesome to Hoover was the safe-deposit key, because the only existing plans to the bombsight were in Norden's safe-deposit box in the vault of the Bank of Manhattan. Fearing that unauthorized persons could obtain Norden's blueprints, Hoover pressed Foxworth for the identities of those with access to Norden's box. Foxworth assured his boss that the only persons with keys were the officer of the bank, the president of the Norden Company, and Norden, but he noted that "anyone getting the keys could enter the safety deposit box." Hoover's bewilderment was amplified when Foxworth related that he "was not sure that the keys which Spear has are for this particular safe deposit box" and that neither the navy nor the army possessed any designs of the bombsight "which would be worth anything at all."[13]

Hoover might have forced the cancellation of Norden's voyage had he been in possession of a critical piece of information that he obtained about two months later. In July 1940, through the double-agent penetration of the Duquesne espionage ring (see chapter 11), FBI agents learned that the German government had a spy assigned to the SS *Washington*. Adolf Henry August Walischeweski, a German citizen, was serving as a steward aboard the ship and acting as a courier between the United States and Europe.[14]

British interference was also a major concern for Hoover. There is "very possibly a British Intelligence Officer on the boat . . . will take Norden and the Agent off at Gibraltar for search." If the letters to Mrs. Norden in Spear's possession were discovered by the British authorities, Spear could be held as a prisoner of war, which could pose a huge political problem for the Roosevelt administration. To avoid such a possibility, Hoover ordered Spear to put all the incriminating items, including his codebook, in a sealed envelope and place it in the captain's safe. In this way, the material would remain secure until the ship returned to New York, at which time Spear could recover the package from the safe. Hoover then suggested that any messages between Spear and Washington should be communicated through the diplomatic code of the U.S. consul wherever he happened to be located.[15]

On May 10, 1940, while the SS *Washington* was still at sea and the German army was smashing into the Low Countries and France, Spear received further coded instructions from Hoover ordering him to destroy the two bombsight sketches that Norden had brought to work on while vacationing. Only hours before entering Gibraltar, he tore them up and tossed them over the side of the ship in the presence of Harry Manning, the ship's captain. The previous day Manning had received coded instructions from U.S. naval authorities ordering him to cooperate fully with Spear. The FBI agent then placed Norden's U.S. and Swiss currency in Manning's safe for security and, at Norden's request, returned three personal letters and a New York bank statement that dealt with his late mother-in-law's estate. Spear radioed Hoover that Norden had in his possession a letter from the secretary of the navy to be "used in emergency." Hoover warned Spear that any use of the letter would be Norden's decision alone but advised Spear to "memorize number keys and keep same in your possession." He then ordered Spear to destroy his coded instructions.[16]

As the ship neared Gibraltar, Spear reported to Hoover that Norden was growing "increasingly upset and worried" that he would be forcibly removed from the ship and imprisoned at Gibraltar or in England. He confided to

Spear that the British were "treacherous"; he said that they suspected him of being a Nazi agent and believed that he was using his significant influence with U.S. naval and military authorities to engender anti-British feelings among them. Norden was also worried that the British knew about his bombsight and fire control inventions and wanted access to them—either by seizing him and forcing him to share his knowledge or by holding him hostage in an attempt to maneuver the United States into negotiating for his release, which would allow the British to demand his inventions.[17]

The SS *Washington* arrived at Gibraltar at noon on May 10, 1940, six days after leaving New York. Upon docking, Spear and Norden proceeded to Norden's cabin to discuss his anticipated confrontation with the British customs authorities. As they entered, both were surprised to find it occupied by "two British Naval Officers and a Marine." Spear offered an impromptu fabrication to the British officers and quickly backed out of the room. Norden also withdrew, but after receiving instructions from Nathan Hawley, the American consul at Gibraltar, Norden reentered his cabin and submitted to an interview.[18]

Spear later learned that the British authorities were indeed looking for a "Mr. Norden," but after being informed by Hawley that the U.S. government desired Norden's safe passage, the British officers claimed that they had made an error in identity and that the "Mr. C. L. Norden then present was not the man they were looking for." Norden told Spear that the British officers had been surprised to learn that he was traveling on a Netherlands passport and warned Norden that "they know all about him and his work in the United States." Spear later reported hearing the officers apologize a number of times to Norden and Hawley and assure Norden of "unmolested passage" through the port of Gibraltar at any time.[19]

When the SS *Washington* eventually arrived in Genoa, Italy, the German invasion had been raging for four days, and there was serious concern that Italy would enter the war on the side of Germany.[20] Fearing the worst, the U.S. Navy issued secret orders to Captain Manning to stop all cargo loading and immediately return the ship to New York. In accordance with Astor's suggestion, Foxworth wired Spear that an "invitation has been extended to you, the friend, and the wife to live aboard the 'Washington.' Suggest you accept." Based on these communications, Spear informed Norden that he should cancel his vacation in Europe and return to the United States as soon as possible. Norden agreed and telephoned his wife in Zurich, instructing her to proceed immediately to Genoa with the family. Days later Mrs.

Norden arrived alone in Genoa and explained that the other family members were unwilling or unable to return to the United States. With Spear and the Nordens safely aboard, the SS *Washington* departed Genoa on May 19, 1940, passed through Gibraltar without incident, and arrived in New York City on May 28.[21]

Kent

Tyler Gatewood Kent was born to Captain William Patton Kent and Ann Herndon Kent on March 24, 1911, at the mission hospital in Newchang, Manchuria. Captain Kent, who was fifty-four years old at the time of Tyler's birth, was serving as the U.S. consul there. Following Captain Kent's death, young Tyler and his mother, a Virginia native, returned to the United States and settled in Washington, D.C. Tyler attended the Kent School in Kent, Connecticut, and the St. Albans School in Washington; in 1929 he entered Princeton University, where he studied modern languages.[22]

After three semesters Kent suddenly left Princeton and sailed for Europe, where he began studying Russian at the Sorbonne in Paris. He spent the following summer in Madrid studying Spanish. In the fall of 1933 Kent returned to the United States and enrolled as a special student at George Washington University, where he studied history and economics. Given the close ties between the university and the State Department, it appears that his new status as a special student was designed to prepare him to follow in his father's footsteps and springboard him into the diplomatic service.[23]

After sixteen years of nonrecognition, President Roosevelt restored relations between the Soviet Union and the United States on November 17, 1933. Plans were soon under way for the exchange of ambassadors and the establishment of diplomatic representation at Washington and Moscow. Learning that the new ambassador-designate, William C. Bullitt, was looking for qualified staff members for the new embassy, Kent applied for a position. His Russian-language skills and family connections led to Kent's appointment as a State Department clerk on February 12, 1934. Two days later he took the oath of office, and within weeks the twenty-three-year-old linguist boarded the SS *Washington* for the trip to Europe. He would remain in Moscow for the next five and a half years.[24]

In 1934 the State Department was a relatively small federal department consisting of only two categories of employees: foreign service and civil service. Despite its small size, the gap between the two categories was a wide one. Foreign service officers were generally better educated, had better social and financial connections, and considered themselves the privileged international representatives of the national interest. At least two-thirds of the senior officers had attended Groton Preparatory School and Harvard University, and membership in an old, established family with roots to prominent early Americans greatly added to a foreign service officer's credentials. Sumner Welles, who would later serve as Roosevelt's undersecretary of state, was a direct descendant of Charles Sumner, the abolitionist senator from Massachusetts. William Phillips, an assistant secretary of state, was descended from abolitionist leader Wendall Phillips and John Jay; Ambassador Joseph Grew's son-in-law, Jay Pierpont Moffatt, who held many senior positions in the department, could also count John Jay as an ancestor. It was an elitist group of white males that formulated its own rules specifically to weed out candidates who did not fit its collective perception of the type of person qualified to be an American diplomat. Emphasis was placed on poise, grace, family connections, and lineage. As one noted historian later explained, "the standards were similar to those of a fashionable Washington club," and only the right kind of person was permitted to join. Alger Hiss, who was responsible for preparing the foreign service entrance examination in the late 1930s, told an interviewer years later that "if a black slipped through the net he would be sent to Liberia until he resigned. Women were sent to the jungles of South America." Those who made the cut were welcomed as members of an exclusive circle akin to a close-knit professional club.[25]

Kent's life in Russia was light-years away from his life in the United States. Since the overthrow of the czar, Stalin's efforts to modernize the nation using the Soviet model had resulted in total failure. Both the industrial and agricultural sectors of the economy were hopelessly behind the rest of the industrialized world and were increasingly characterized by ballooning bureaucracies, numbing inertia, declining production, and a general malaise and indifference that was only worsened by the worldwide economic depression of 1929. By 1932 the system of forced collectivization, along with drought, dangerously low crop yields, and escalating state procurements, had produced the worst famine in the history of twentieth-century Europe. Some estimates put the Soviet death toll from starvation at 7 million.[26] The constant adulation of the system by the Soviet leadership in the face of this reality increased the hostility and suspicion of Soviet bureaucrats toward

Westerners. Stalin's terrifying purges during the second half of the decade only added to the tension among citizens and foreigners, and nowhere was this coalition of terror and national atrophy more visible than in the capital city of Moscow. The cold, gray, forbidding atmosphere of this lifeless city held little enjoyment for any diplomat unfortunate enough to be assigned there. Charles Bohlen, a Soviet expert who accompanied Bullitt to his new post in 1934, complained that the shortage of consumer goods in Moscow "was striking" and that exorbitant official rates forced diplomatic missions to turn to the "black market" for rubles in order to maintain the embassy at an affordable level.[27] Similar sentiments were voiced by George Kennan, a young Russian specialist assigned to Moscow. Even before the first members of the new embassy staff arrived, he keenly felt the isolation and loneliness that were a diplomat's constant companions in Moscow during this period. "We regarded ourselves," he wrote years later, "as a lonely and exposed bastion of governmental life, surrounded by a veritable ocean of official Soviet ill will."[28]

Living conditions in Moscow in 1934, particularly for a young American bachelor serving as a diplomatic clerk, were difficult. Housing for clerical support staff was woefully inadequate and often unavailable; even when living quarters could be secured, the clerical staff was frequently forced to uproot in order to make room for professional foreign service officers. In Kent's case, he lived in the Hotel Moscow for a full year. The personal isolation, meager salary, absence of any social life not controlled by the local counterintelligence service, embassy rules prohibiting fraternization with the local population, and boring surveillance of daily activities made diplomatic life in Moscow almost unbearable. Another factor that irritated Kent was the gulf between the clerical staff and the professional foreign service personnel. It was a dangerous environment for a man like Kent, whose keen interest in money was matched only by an "irrepressible passion for womanizing and sexual adventuring."[29]

Kent's youth and reckless personal behavior made him an easy target for the local NKVD counterintelligence service, which was undoubtedly monitoring his every move. Recognizing his extraordinary value as a potential source of high-grade intelligence information, and accurately assessing his penchant for womanizing, the NKVD sent in a beautiful female agent. Tatiana "Tanya" Alexandrovnaya Ilovaiskaya was an engineering student in Moscow when she and Kent first met; they quickly became lovers and continued their romantic relationship throughout his tour of duty in Moscow. Kent probably knew that he was being targeted by the NKVD and undoubtedly understood that Tanya was in its service. Nevertheless, Kent ignored these harsh realities and the possible criminal consequences, as well as the potentially damaging effect on U.S. security.[30]

Soviet surveillance of most of the embassies in Moscow during the 1930s was total and complete, and the U.S. embassy was no exception. In addition to the thirty-five Americans assigned as foreign service personnel, there were thirty-three Russians working there as stenographers, telephone operators, cooks, maids, and secretaries. They were also required to report to the NKVD on the daily activities of the American diplomatic personnel. They supplied information about the Americans' personalities and foibles that could be used to recruit them as Soviet intelligence sources. Russian housekeepers had the complete run of the embassy, which allowed them to place listening devices to capture sensitive conversations. Documents and cipher material stolen by the Russian staff members could easily be compared with the ciphered telegrams sent from the embassy, simplifying code breaking. This counterintelligence penetration of the embassy was not a secret; it was generally accepted by the ambassador and his staff as an unavoidable part of doing business in Moscow. Bullitt naively believed that the embassy should convey an impression of openness and that honesty at all levels should characterize relations with the Soviet government. Soviet eavesdropping eventually became so pervasive, however, that senior embassy staff members were forced to write out their confidential reports in long hand rather than risk a microphone picking up their dictation to a stenographer.[31]

State Department couriers traveling alone and carrying diplomatic pouches in the Soviet Union were even more vulnerable than embassy staff. Entrusted with the U.S. government's most carefully guarded secrets, their every move was monitored from the moment they entered Soviet territory. The goal of the surveillance was to isolate the courier, separate him from his bags, and then open and search them without his knowledge. A courier traveling by train would be assigned to a particular railway car, and while he was asleep his bag would be removed and opened and the contents photographed in a special laboratory aboard the train. The bag would then be resealed and returned, and the courier never even knew that it had left his custody. NKVD creativity at separating a courier from his bags rose to an art form that included the use of prostitutes or drug-laced food to distract or incapacitate the courier while the technicians did their work.[32]

The NKVD intensified its efforts to obtain signal intelligence information, with the hope of placing the code-cracking process on a real-time basis. In the early 1930s a combined unit comprising specialists from the NKVD and the Fourth Department of the GRU was formed to obtain foreign cipher material to aid Soviet code breakers. It became the NKVD's most secret agency and was housed in the Lubyanka, headquarters of the NKVD. Unlike its Western counterparts, it grew into the largest and best-resourced signals intelligence agency in the world, making the acquisition of cipher materials through espionage a major priority during the 1930s.[33]

Both Bullitt and his successor, Joseph C. Davies, were woefully ignorant of the extent of the Soviet government's access to the embassy's secrets. In an attempt to improve relations with Stalin, they encouraged contacts with Russians at all levels, opening up valuable opportunities for counterintelligence penetration. Ivan Teaton, the assistant military attaché, was shocked when he first arrived in Moscow in 1934 and observed the poor security conditions. The marine guards, who had been requested for security duty by Ambassador Bullitt, were supplied with female Russian-language instructors who offered sexual favors in addition to language training. Teaton complained about open homosexual liaisons among the staff, romantic liaisons with Russian women, and the open-house atmosphere of the embassy, where "there were usually two or three ballerinas running around."[34]

There is little doubt that Kent did enormous damage to U.S. national security while he was stationed in Moscow as a clerk-translator and a communicator in the embassy's code room. Years later he admitted to British interrogators that he had removed "substantial quantities" of confidential information, including internal correspondence and diplomatic messages that he encoded and decoded, and stored it at his residence. There is also little doubt that Tanya was an informer. In a closed society like Moscow, where Russian citizens were forbidden to have contact with foreigners, the mere fact that she was permitted to have a relationship with Kent meant that she was providing details of his activities. Tanya's access to his quarters also meant that the NKVD could easily copy anything Kent kept there.[35]

Also assigned to the U.S. embassy staff in February 1934 was a twenty-two-year-old navy code clerk named Henry W. Antheil Jr. Bothered by ill health and desperate to get out of Moscow, Antheil obtained a brief leave back to the United States in the spring of 1939, followed by reassignment in Europe. His new duties entailed extensive travel throughout northern and central Europe delivering codebooks for embassy communicators. He also worked for a short time at the American legation in Berlin, reorganizing the code room; shortly afterward he was reassigned to Helsinki, where he performed the same function for U.S. diplomatic posts in the Baltic region. On

June 15, 1940, while returning to Helsinki, Antheil's Estonian airliner was attacked by Soviet aircraft in connection with Stalin's moves against Latvia, Estonia, and Lithuania. The plane crashed into the sea, killing everyone on board.[36]

Upon learning the circumstances of Antheil's death, the State Department publicly hailed him as a hero, and he was personally eulogized by Secretary of State Cordell Hull. Five days later, in accordance with foreign service regulations, Robert McClintock, the U.S. consul in Helsinki, conducted an inventory of Antheil's personal property. Among the items found were confidential State Department telegrams decoded by Antheil but never given to the U.S. minister to Finland or any member of his staff; messages sent from the minister in Helsinki to the State Department regarding Antheil's imminent transfer to Stockholm, Sweden, which Antheil had falsified; and another message characterizing him as "one of the Department's three highly trained and experienced code men," which he had forged. Based on this evidence, McClintock concluded that Antheil had desperately wanted to stay in Helsinki. Further investigation revealed that the young navy man had a Finnish girlfriend and that during his Moscow assignment he had continually tried to arrange a permanent transfer to Finland. McClintock concluded that Antheil's personal files reflected "a preoccupation amounting to almost an obsession with regard to a transfer from Moscow and particularly to Helsinki or one of the Scandinavian capitals."[37]

Also found in Antheil's footlocker were the encoded messages and work sheets of a personal communication from Alexander Kirk, the chargé d'affaires at the U.S. embassy in Moscow, to the U.S. ambassador in Berlin; numerous coded messages with accompanying plain text; twenty copies of paraphrases of telegrams sent by the U.S. embassy in Moscow during 1937 and 1938 describing the political situation in the Soviet Union; and a copy of a translated letter sent to Antheil dated November 30, 1938, from an individual identifying himself as Alexander Ivanovich Fomin. The Fomin letter discussed "my intended purpose that is, to become a spy, as it is usually put, of a progressive country such as the USA." McClintock's examination uncovered additional evidence that in the months before Antheil's death he had been corresponding with his brother George, who was conducting research for a book on the situation in Europe. Antheil had been assisting his brother's efforts by supplying him with information from confidential diplomatic cables, using a special code the two of them had devised. In the end, McClintock's gravest concern was the "dangerous disregard, which this supposedly experienced and expert code clerk showed of the first principle of preserving the secrecy of the codes." To emphasize this point, McClintock noted that two copies of the combination to the code-room vault, neatly typed on cards, were found lying on a shelf in Antheil's wardrobe, along with miscellaneous clothing.[38]

As the assistant secretary of state responsible for diplomatic facilities and foreign service personnel overseas, it fell to Breckinridge Long to address the security problems posed by the Kent and Antheil affairs and their impact on the U.S. government's ability to respond to events in war-ravaged Europe. Long confided to his diary the profound political and security implications of these scandals:

> The clerk who was killed in an airplane flying from Tallin to Helsinki as courier seems to have been somewhat indiscreet. . . . Examination of his effects after his death disclosed copies of some code messages in his room and a confidential letter he was not supposed to have which apparently had been opened and addressed to Kirk in Berlin. . . . The disturbing part is that this clerk from Helsinki and the one from London served together in Moscow. The one in London had a Russian woman he associated with and the one in Tallin seems to have had a Finnish lady friend. But we do not know that she was in Moscow. Both of them spoke Russian and both of them were indiscreet.[39]

In September 1939 Kent was reassigned to the U.S. embassy in London as a code clerk, where he quickly fell into his old habit of filching sensitive communications from the embassy code room and storing them at his apartment. He simply "took copies which were surplus and were to be discarded, burned in an incinerator," he later told an interviewer. Another unwitting source was Ambassador Joseph P. Kennedy, who was having important political documents copied for his own private collection. According to Kent, "Part of my function was to make these copies. And it was quite easy to slip in an extra carbon."[40]

The first hint of a serious leakage of information from the London embassy occurred in February 1940, when Guy Liddell requested a meeting with Herschel Johnson of the U.S. embassy to discuss information "which may be of interest to the State Department." Johnson learned that a trustworthy MI5 informant with access to the German secret service had reported that since the start of the European war in September 1939, the Germans had been receiving information from the U.S. embassy in Berlin, including "practically everything from Ambassador Kennedy's dispatches to President Roosevelt including reports of his interviews with British statesmen and officials." German leaders were often receiving these reports at a rate of two a day from a source referred to as the "Doctor."[41]

The State Department began an investigation to identify the source of the leak, but with no further information available and few resources, it was forced to limit the investigation to auditing its security and cable-handling practices and tightening up some procedures. Even with these steps, no suspect was identified. Senior department officials nevertheless harbored nagging fears about a hemorrhage of confidential information that could seriously impair their ability to function.[42] Long confided his growing anxiety to his diary on April 4, 1940:

> It has developed that certain information has been leaking. Just where the leak is nobody knows. How recently there has been leakage is not known. We do not know that there has been any leakage since the actual outbreak of the war. The reason we know there was any leakage prior to that time is that we have now been confidentially informed from British sources that certain American news is known in Berlin. It must have got to Berlin out of London through some form of secret communication. How it was obtained in the first instance for transmission to Germany is not known.[43]

On May 18, 1940, MI5's Captain Maxwell Knight met with Ambassador Kennedy, Johnson, and other key members of the embassy staff to inform them about an ongoing MI5 investigation of British fascist groups operating in England. Knight identified Kent as being closely associated with members of the Right Club, a leading fascist organization described by Knight as "a Fifth Column organization which, under the cloak of anti-Jewish propaganda, conducts pro-German activities." It was headed by Captain Archibald Henry Maule Ramsey, a prominent Conservative Party member, scion of one of Britain's most prominent aristocratic families, and member of the House of Commons. The Right Club's tactics included the pursuit of embassy employees in London, the cultivation of their friendship, and an assessment of their ideological leanings in the hope of acquiring from them confidential information that could be useful to Germany and Italy. Kennedy and Johnson learned that Ramsey's principal espionage contact was Anna Wolkoff, the daughter of a former admiral of the Russian Imperial Navy.[44]

Knight revealed that British authorities had been investigating Kent's activities for the past eight months, unbeknownst to the Americans. He first became a target of British investigation in October 1939, following a tip from the Stockholm police that a suspected Nazi agent named Ludwig Ernst Mathias would be entering the British Isles. Surveillance was placed on Mathias from the moment he entered British territory, and on October 8, 1939, he was observed entering the Cumberland Hotel in London and meeting with Kent. The two men spent the remainder of the evening together, and when he left Kent's room, Mathias "was seen to be carrying a bulky envelope, approximately 10" by 6".'"[45]

Knight told Kennedy that Scotland Yard had warrants for Kent's arrest and a search of his residence. Despite his anger over MI5's dilatory disclosure of the investigation, Kennedy authorized the search of Kent's flat on May 20, 1940. Meanwhile, Johnson contacted Sir Alexander Cadogan, the permanent undersecretary of the Foreign Office, to discuss Kent's diplomatic status. With Ambassador Kennedy's authorization, Johnson informed Cadogan that the ambassador waived Kent's diplomatic immunity, subjecting him to prosecution in Great Britain.[46]

Recovered the next morning during the search of Kent's flat were approximately 1,500 confidential cables that had passed through the U.S. embassy to and from Washington, sensitive internal embassy documents, and the raw "strip cipher" used to encode messages from the embassy. Kennedy later told Washington that "it was not until the search of his premises had been made that we had any idea of the extent to which he had abstracted copies of the Embassy's highly confidential material." The Special Branch detectives found documents that "filled a suitcase," including copies of telegrams filed in folders with penciled titles such as "Turkey," "Germany," "British Cabinet," and "Churchill." Analysis revealed that these were true readings of telegrams to the State Department in the embassy's "most confidential codes and about the most secret subjects," many of which had been coded and copied by Kent himself. Johnson reported that Kent's position in the embassy gave him the opportunity to make additional copies of documents and that the evidence indicated he had been collecting this information over a long period. Equally ominous was the discovery of Kent's correspondence with Ramsey, a heavy brown leather volume containing the entire membership list of the Right Club and "brand-new" duplicates of the keys to the embassy's index bureau and code room.[47]

A copy of a message from Prime Minister Winston Churchill to President Roosevelt that had been delivered to the U.S. embassy during the early-morning hours of May 20, 1940, was also found. It described the air war in France, the continued existence of the current British government in the wake of the collapse of British and French forces in Europe, and Britain's desperate need for U.S.-manufactured Curtiss P-40 fighter aircraft awaiting delivery to the U.S. Army Air Force. Although Johnson expressed concern over Kent's theft of this message, he was convinced that it had not been compromised. Kent had been under continuous surveillance since the previous day, rendering him incapable of delivering it to his conspirators.[48] Johnson was less confident, however, when Special Branch investigators found photographic plates measuring approximately 3¼ by 4¼ inches containing a top-secret message from Churchill to FDR, dated February 28, 1940, which addressed the passage of U.S. ships through the combat zone surrounding the British Isles and the special provisions that were being considered to allow them free movement without inspection.[49] Also disturbing was the absence of any photographic equipment in the apartment capable of making the plates.[50]

The impact of Kent's arrest on Hull and his staff was immediate and devastating. "On my return," Long wrote on the evening of May 20, 1940, "Sumner [Undersecretary of State Sumner Welles] sent for me, and told me about the unfortunate occurrence in London which involved one of our code clerks in work of espionage and his arrest by the British authorities." He then recorded the State Department's deepest fear to his diary, noting that Kent's treachery "may mean that our communication system is no longer secret."[51]

Before the State Department could even react to the Kent arrest, it was hit with another crisis related to the security of its communications with its embassies in Europe. Long confided to his diary:

> I am enormously concerned about the situation developed in London and about the further fact that Bullitt when he burned his own codes burned some secret devices which were intended for communication and directed to three or four other of our Missions in southern and southeastern Europe and Ankara. I am now considering the possibility of sending a courier on the first Clipper to Portugal and having one of the naval ships there go to Ireland with the devices to get to London to supplant the one which is now gone and to have another naval ship take

the others to Rome for transmission to points east to replace the ones Bullitt destroyed. Bullitt must have had a real holiday when he destroyed those codes.[52]

The magnitude of the security breach confronting the State Department was becoming very clear. On May 22, 1940, Long was informed about the compromise of the highly secret Roosevelt-Churchill communications. Learning of Kent's prior assignment in Moscow, he speculated that the young clerk "apparently came under the lure of some monetary consideration, and made a connection which when he was transferred to London (which was done on the recommendation of [U.S. ambassador to Moscow Laurence] Steinhardt) he found profitable to continue."[53]

Even more traumatizing for Kennedy and Long was the stark revelation that Kent had removed from the embassy, without discovery, a series of communications so sensitive that their publication could conceivably destroy the Roosevelt administration and imperil future U.S. assistance to the increasingly isolated Great Britain. These top-secret personal messages between Churchill and Roosevelt had begun on Christmas Day 1939, while Churchill was still first lord of the Admiralty. In the wake of a U.S. policy of strict neutrality, and faced with fierce isolationist opposition, the president's candid dialogue with a member of the British cabinet made him dangerously vulnerable to charges of illegally assisting the British and French governments.[54] Fear of an even larger security breach within the State Department deepened as a steady stream of reports about Kent's confessions began arriving in Washington. Among the details provided to British interrogators was Kent's admission that he had used a camera belonging to another embassy code clerk to photograph the documents found in his room and that this clerk had since been transferred to the U.S. embassy in Madrid, Spain.[55]

This presented Long with a serious dilemma. Should he send a message to Madrid "to check up on the man" and verify Kent's story? If the code clerk in Madrid was involved in an espionage conspiracy, the State Department had no way of communicating with Madrid without warning the suspect. "We could not telegraph the Embassy in Madrid on this subject," he feared, "without the expectation that the very man who was the subject of the telegram would decode the message." Even worse was the possibility that the suspect in Madrid "might have answered it without the knowledge of the Chargé d'Affaires."[56]

Long was stymied. For years, the State Department had ignored security difficulties at its own headquarters—a gross inattention that included disregard for the confidentiality and safe management of documents that moved through its own bureaucracy, as well as large-scale duplication of and unaccountability for documents marked "strictly confidential." Sensitive documents were easily accessible to hundreds of employees, along with extra copies of these documents that often sat unguarded in a code room that was locked only at night. Years later a State Department employee testified that hundreds of cables had sat around for days or even weeks where any "charwoman" or "messengers" could get at them.[57] Now, Kent's arrest in England, a possible accomplice in Madrid, the appalling discoveries among Antheil's personal effects in Helsinki, and the sporadic rumors about information leaks in other European capitals forced Long to concede the possibility that there might be "other cells of an aggressive diplomacy of another Government representing their interests in our own offices abroad."[58]

The FBI Undercover in Europe

On June 4, 1940, a meeting was held in the office of Secretary of State Cordell Hull that included Sumner Welles, Breckinridge Long, and General Sherman Miles, the newly appointed head of the War Department's MID. Their discussion focused on the spy crisis and the possibility of conducting undercover inspections of American diplomatic personnel and buildings overseas. They quickly concluded that State Department investigators were limited in number and too well known to foreign service officers and consular staff members. Long was ordered to reach out beyond the State Department for qualified investigators who could be sent abroad "in capacities that will permit them to have very close and rather intimate contacts with the personnel of our various offices." Posing as State Department couriers, they could visit U.S. diplomatic establishments while carefully observing and recording the ongoing activities. Financing for this unique undercover operation was supplied by the State Department's emergency fund; monies were transferred into the department's public funds and paid from those accounts, however, to avoid any suspicion. The candidates for this assignment would be specially chosen and vetted, and Miles offered to select half a dozen men for posting to London, Rome, Berlin, and Moscow. From these cities they would travel throughout Europe to carry out their cover assignment.[59]

Two days later Miles reported that he could not deliver six men due to a lack of qualified personnel, so Long turned to Hoover for help. Throughout the month of June 1940, Hoover's staff combed through personnel files looking for experienced investigators with the requisite language skills for this particular assignment. With an increasing number of foreign assignments for special agents, the sudden critical need for personnel with language skills, and the new foreign counterintelligence challenges, some long-standing institutional weaknesses within the FBI hiring system were exposed. Special agents who had claimed a language aptitude on their employment applications "almost invariably . . . disclaim ability to speak the language with the fluency that had been recorded in the evocation record." Some blamed the lapse of time since they had last used their language skills, and others were simply "liberal in their estimates of their ability."[60]

By month's end, however, FBI officials had selected Louis Beck, Raymond Leddy, Horton Telford, William Doyle, and Peter Hoehl. Each was told to report to Washington within twenty-four hours for an unspecified assignment. Leddy and Doyle spoke Spanish and were assigned to Madrid and Lisbon. Hoehl, who spoke German, was assigned to Berlin; Telford went to Rome; and Beck went to Moscow.[61]

Telford was typical of the five agents selected for this assignment. Born into a Mormon farm family in 1909 in Idaho Falls, Idaho, he graduated from high school in 1929. After two and a half years of missionary work in France, where he developed a proficiency in the language, he returned to the United States and enrolled at Chafee College in Ontario, California. A year later he moved to Washington, D.C., where he attended the Georgetown School of Foreign Service. In 1935 he entered Georgetown School of Law while working as an FBI clerical employee. After graduating with a law degree in 1939 he was hired as a special agent of the FBI. Following training, he was briefly assigned to a three-man office in Aberdeen, South Dakota, and then went to the FBI's Detroit office, where he was working at the time of his selection for the overseas mission.[62]

The five agents were met in Washington by Edward Tamm, who was then serving as the assistant director in charge of the National Defense Division. He introduced them to Hoover, who offered a pep talk and some details concerning the disruption of the State Department's communication system caused by the outbreak of war in Europe. Without mentioning the Kent espionage matter, he told them that the FBI had been requested to provide agents to carry the diplomatic mail throughout Europe. Next,

Tamm escorted them to Long's office for additional briefings. A day or so later they traveled to New York City, where they received a one-week crash course on the workings of the State Department and the particulars of their assignments. Although each agent knew that he had been selected because of his language skills, none of them (with the possible exceptions of Beck and Hoehl) were told anything about Kent's arrest. Nor were they informed of Antheil's death and the possible compromise of secret information in Berlin. They had no idea when they would return to the United States and (again with the possible exceptions of Beck and Hoehl) were given no specific instructions regarding their real missions. At least two of the agents had no contact with any FBI official during their entire service in Europe.[63]

The five agents sailed from New York for Lisbon on July 4, 1940, aboard the SS *Manhattan*. They were the only passengers aboard the ship, which was returning to Europe under State Department orders to pick up Americans stranded by the surprise German invasion of Holland and France. Hoover gave them strict orders not to identify themselves as FBI agents; they could, however, acknowledge that they were diplomatic couriers working for the State Department. Avoidance of all contact with the ship's crew and officers was mandatory—and with good reason. One of the crew members was Richard Herman Hartwig Kleiss, a cook who was being investigated by the FBI as a key member of a major German espionage ring. Hoover knew the danger facing his agents if the German and Italian intelligence services found out their true identities and mission.[64]

While en route to his Moscow assignment, Beck stopped at the U.S. embassy in Berlin, where he was introduced to State Department inspectors Avery M. Farran and Lawrence C. Frank. They informed Beck that Long had advised them of Beck's assignment in Europe, including all the details of the arrangement, and that they had been instructed to cooperate fully with him. Beck learned then that confidential information had been leaking out of the U.S. embassy in Moscow, making the British reluctant to reveal certain confidential information to U.S. authorities. Beck also learned that Frank and Farran had no suspects in this matter and did not know how the information was being supplied to the Soviet government.[65]

When Beck arrived in Moscow on August 8, 1940, he was thirty-two years old. From Milwaukee, Wisconsin, his family eventually settled in California, where Beck received a law degree from the University of Southern California and worked in the Bank of America's Trust Department in Pasadena before joining the FBI in February 1939. Beck was fluent in German (which he probably learned from his German mother) and Spanish, as well as "passable" in Russian.[66]

His real identity was unknown to any member of the embassy staff, including Ambassador Steinhardt. Identified merely as a new courier, Beck was assigned as an internal embassy messenger; a role that offered him access to all offices and sections of the embassy building at frequent intervals throughout the day, allowing his independent assessment of the day-to-day operating conditions and the personal behavior of the staff. His detailed observations, which were reported to the president, revealed the ease with which the Soviet intelligence services could recruit American diplomatic personnel to commit espionage. He witnessed mind-boggling laxness and an absence of even the most rudimentary security procedures, as well as compromising behavior on the part of embassy personnel. Beck's findings included flagrant violations of the rules regarding fraternization—sexual relationships between embassy officers and Soviet women, and open homosexual relations between embassy staff members and foreigners—as well as illegal money and gold transfers.[67]

Beck's report described the general plan of the embassy and its complement of approximately thirty-five American employees and another thirty-three Soviet employees working in key positions as translators, librarians, typists, economic advisers, telephone operators, and messengers. All the American staff members, excluding the ambassador and four clerks, resided in the embassy building, composed of twenty-five apartments with "at least one Soviet servant for each." Code room security procedures were poor. Code clerks behaved indifferently; they took lengthy breaks from the code room and left confidential cables out unattended. Unauthorized persons also entered the code room, chatting at length with the code clerks.[68]

Beck also examined the procedures for destroying confidential material, which revealed the egregious practice of combining the original drafts of confidential messages with the original drafts of the coded telegrams for burning in the basement. In the hands of NKVD experts, he warned, these two items could simplify efforts to break into and read all confidential communications transmitted to and from the embassy. Just as troubling was the practice of burning confidential papers in bundles, with no security oversight to ensure that the documents had been completely destroyed. In fact, Beck reported to Hoover that he had in his possession the original messages, written by Ambassador Steinhardt, concerning the Kent and Antheil cases, which he had "secured surreptitiously from the fire." Soon after arriving at the embassy, Beck took over the job of "personally" disposing of such messages.[69]

After a few months, Beck concluded that it was "practically impossible for a single man to live a normal life while attached to the American Embassy at Moscow." State Department policy at the time was to send single men to Moscow and to house them, two to an apartment, above the embassy offices. They had difficulty finding friends outside the embassy because the Soviets refused to associate with foreigners. Soviet citizens caught fraternizing with foreigners "generally disappear and it is understood they are exiled to Siberia." Lacking any sort of normal female companionship, they turned to a group of Soviet prostitutes who operated out of a specific hotel in Moscow and concentrated "only" on embassy staff members. When a new man arrived in Moscow, he began receiving telephone calls from these women. Beck theorized that the NKVD's goal was to arrange for a prostitute girlfriend for each embassy staff member interested in such pursuits. He characterized these women's knowledge of the goings-on in Moscow diplomatic circles as "amazing" and no doubt very useful to the local NKVD counterintelligence service. NKVD guards kept a constant watch on the front of the embassy building, and when a woman from the "regular group" was seen in the company of an attaché, no effort was made to follow her. In contrast, any "unauthorized" woman was followed until she left the company of her American escort; then she was promptly taken into custody and questioned.[70]

Prostitutes could easily obtain information from embassy staff members, even though many of the men neither understood nor spoke Russian and the women allegedly spoke no English. The absence of newspapers and magazines from the United States made life in Moscow so dull and isolating for the men that they eventually began gossiping about embassy matters. Beck strongly suspected that the women actually understood English and reported these conversations to their NKVD controllers. Embassy staff also talked among themselves. During a conversation with Beck, embassy employee Edwin Smith told him that Charles Bohlen, a senior embassy officer, had just arrived in Moscow carrying new confidential codes and that Beck himself was about to be sent to Persia to secure Russian currency "on the Black Bourse."[71]

Next came revelations about "sexual perversion among staff members." It was common knowledge that code clerk Robert Hall and the ambassador's secretary, George Filton, were involved in a romantic relationship. They met secretly in the embassy's code room until a distraught Hall eventually resigned his position at the embassy. Filton, who had been active in Moscow's underground gay community for a number of years, contemplated suicide because his requests to transfer to another post had been repeatedly rejected by Washington. Beck had no doubt that the NKVD was fully aware of such indiscretions and routinely used these and other security violations "as a lever to pry confidential information from them, this observation being particularly pertinent to the ambassador's secretary." Assigning only single men to such an environment for three or more years had terrible consequences. Beck's suggested remedy was the British procedure of sending married couples to Moscow for shorter periods.[72]

Another security breach involved the behavior of code clerk James Lewis, who was living with a Soviet woman. Although desperate to marry her and get her out of Russia, Lewis knew that discovery of their relationship would mean his automatic transfer without her. Vice-consul Donald Nichols, who had been assigned to the embassy for two years when Beck arrived, was romantically involved with Tanya Ilovaiskaya, Tyler Kent's former girlfriend. During the summer of 1940 Nichols lived with her in a country home that he leased at a cost of 4,000 rubles. Beck described Ilovaiskaya as a well-dressed woman who held a special driver's license issued by the NKVD and traveled extensively throughout Europe—a distinction that Beck found "unusual among Soviet citizens." Nichols's country home often served as a gathering place for embassy staff members and Russian women, and "since there was a certain amount of drinking it appears probable that on occasions confidential matters would unavoidably be discussed."[73]

Endgame

On October 23, 1940, three months after Beck's arrival in Moscow, Kent went on trial for espionage at the Old Bailey Courthouse in London. He was prosecuted on seven counts of espionage in a five-day trial that was closed to the public. Count one of the indictment charged him with possessing a letter dated October 19, 1939, containing information about a woman, later identified by the FBI as Evelyn Strand, and another person identified as Terence Edward Stephens. Strand was described as a Soviet agent who had been trained in Moscow as a radio operator between 1932 and 1935 and was, at the time, working at Communist Party headquarters in New York City. Stephens, the letter noted, had served in the International Brigade during the Spanish civil war and later moved to the United States. Count two focused on a letter dated November 7, 1939, that was directed to the FBI from MI5 requesting an investigation of Armand Labis Feldman and Willie Brandes. The FBI considered Feldman to be a known "Soviet espionage agent" operating under the instruction of Gaik B. Ovakimian, the head of Soviet espionage in the United States and director of Amtorg Trading Corporation in New York City. British intelligence authorities viewed Feldman as the "Soviet Agent in Charge of an English espionage organization," and Brandes was suspected of serving as an "important link in the Soviet espionage organization."[74]

Counts three and four dealt with Churchill's messages to Roosevelt dated January 29 and February 28, 1940, both of which had been found in Kent's flat. Count five charged him with revealing the contents of the messages to Anna Wolkoff, a codefendant and suspected agent of the German and Italian governments. The final two counts were larceny charges and of little consequence.[75] Years later Max Knight wrote a summary of the Kent case for a secret MI5 history of the period. What Kent had stolen from the embassy, Knight concluded, "would be of the greatest value to the enemy," with the potential for "incalculable harm to the Allies." In the end, Kent was convicted on all counts and sentenced to seven years in a British jail.[76]

The IIC was kept completely in the dark about the facts of Kent's treachery. FBI efforts to obtain a copy of the trial transcript proved futile. In March 1941, nearly six months after Kent's conviction, an FBI agent was permitted to examine and take notes from one of the two copies of the trial transcript in existence. It was held by the Department of State, and the other was buried in the archives of the British Foreign Ministry. The department's document security may have been poor in other regards, but it was rock solid concerning the transcript, because neither the British nor the U.S. government could afford a revelation of the secret communications between Roosevelt and Churchill. Special agent Robert Wall, who reviewed the trial transcript for Hoover, related the "hopes" of senior State Department officials that "this information will be kept in the utmost secrecy in view of the circumstances and the embarrassment which would come to the State Department if the facts were ever disclosed in any manner."[77]

Lessons Learned

Norden and Kent served as important lessons for Hoover and the FBI. Norden exposed fundamental weaknesses in the military-industrial security relationship, which was becoming increasingly problematic as the nation began rearming. Norden was under no obligation to discuss his travel plans with his military customers, despite the fact that he knew the secret of the United States' most advanced military technology. With the focus of counterespionage perceptibly shifting from internal security and loyalty issues to the protection of important military, political, and economic information, Hoover began asking tough questions of his IIC colleagues. How could effective counterintelligence be achieved without paying serious security attention to key scientists and engineers, as well as blueprints, diagrams, and other related documents?

From an institutional perspective, the Norden incident also demonstrated Hoover's confidence in his counterintelligence leadership role. He was leading the FBI down a new path, one that diverged from its traditional law enforcement responsibilities. The head of the IIC was willing to undertake risky missions outside U.S. borders, where failure could mean potential embarrassment to the Roosevelt administration or the FBI or, worse, serious harm to the special agents carrying out the assignments.

The Kent case contained a multitude of lessons. Hoover learned the consequences of ignoring security in foreign countries. The NKVD's easy exploitation of Kent in Moscow and the vast array of secrets it reaped undoubtedly made an indelible impression on Hoover. Another vital lesson was that U.S. counterintelligence efforts would be worthless if Americans working abroad were not adequately shielded from the local counterintelligence services. In effect, the NKVD successes reported by Beck served as an effective primer for the FBI, offering fresh lessons on how to investigate foreign intelligence activities in the United States, where to concentrate its efforts for maximum advantage, and the value of human sources, particularly those inside embassies and consulates, who could supply useful information for national policy making.

Both cases strengthened Hoover's position as a leader in this new field. This was particularly so with the Kent case. The State Department's failure over the years to take adequate precautions against the predatory behavior of the German and Soviet intelligence services caused President Roosevelt to lose confidence in it. The revelation of the theft of the highly sensitive Roosevelt-Churchill communications was a serious embarrassment to the State Department, forcing it to reexamine and revise its own secret communications system, and causing the president to switch to military communications for his most sensitive messages. As a result, the State Department's grip on counterintelligence policy slipped even further, with a consequent strengthening of the roles of the FBI and the military.

CHAPTER NINE

British Security Coordination

A major obstacle to the FBI's development of a robust counterintelligence service was the absence of liaison with the British services. Until the cataclysmic events in western Europe during the spring of 1940 materially altered American and British needs, only the RCMP had any direct interaction with FBI authorities. Both Canada and the United States believed that their 3,000-mile border and expanding economic relations demanded closer cooperation between their respective national police agencies. During the mid-1930s RCMP officers began attending the newly created FBI National Police Academy. From these humble beginnings came the recognition that discussion and cooperation would significantly benefit both services. In 1937 FBI officials began routinely meeting with their Canadian counterparts on a wide range of mutually relevant investigative issues.

This cooperation was limited, however, to criminal investigations. All security and counterintelligence investigations requiring the assistance of foreign security services had to be passed through State Department and military channels. This awkward situation hindered direct contact and discussion between the FBI and the counterintelligence experts of other nations. The reasons for this prohibition were twofold. First, from a bureaucratic standpoint, the State Department viewed security and counterintelligence as a function of diplomacy, requiring that control of such matters be in the hands of foreign policy professionals. Second, the Roosevelt administration, ever sensitive to its foreign policy critics, hoped to avoid accusations of neutrality law violations stemming from increased FBI and military contact with foreign security services.[1]

This policy was abruptly halted in June 1940. Following the collapse of France and the evacuation of British and French forces from Dunkirk, Great Britain suddenly found itself in a dangerously vulnerable position. Across the English Channel the German army was poised for an invasion of the British Isles; simultaneously, the German navy was engaged in a vicious submarine campaign along the Atlantic sea-lanes. Despite the plucky British spirit—as personified in the new prime minister, Winston Churchill—and a commitment to fight on alone, many thoughtful observers believed that Great Britain's destruction was imminent. Among them was President Roosevelt's own ambassador in London, Joseph Kennedy. Faced with such pessimistic reports, Roosevelt sent William Donovan, a World War I Medal of Honor winner, successful Wall Street lawyer, and future head of the Office of Strategic Services, to London for an independent assessment of the British staying power. Donovan's report helped reassure the president of Britain's fighting capacity, as well as the immediate need for accelerated security and intelligence exchanges between the two governments.

Political reality in the United States also came into play. The series of neutrality laws passed by Congress to keep the country out of war forced England and France to pay cash for military supplies manufactured in the United States, as well as to ship them through the submarine-infested Atlantic in their own vessels. Staving off disaster meant ensuring that the 20 million tons of essential provisions shipped yearly from East Coast ports to Great Britain experienced no disruption from either sabotage or the fickleness of U.S. politics. To ensure a continual flow of material, Sir Stewart Menzies, head of MI6, hastily dispatched William Stephenson to New York City in June 1940.

Prime Minister Churchill had, in the words of one prominent British intelligence historian, "a fascination with cloaks and daggers and [his] exaggerated expectations of what they could achieve."[2] Upon becoming prime minister in May 1940, Churchill wasted no time putting his own stamp on the British intelligence and counterintelligence establishments. He immediately sacked his old friend Sir Vernon Kell, the longtime head of MI5. Believing that fifth-column groups were rampant in Great Britain, Churchill thought that Kell had shown a marked lack of zeal in dealing with them. Next he ordered the hasty improvisation of a secret underground movement headed by Hugh Dalton, the minister of economic warfare. The Special Operations Executive, as it came to be known, was conceived by the prime minister as a means to "set Europe ablaze" through sabotage, assassination, and a general program of indigenous mayhem and harassment of the enemy. Churchill was also enraptured by the British code-breaking successes against German military and naval ciphers. The Royal Air Force victory in the Battle of Britain later that summer was due, in large part, to the ability to read the minds of the Luftwaffe leadership through the unraveling of their encoded communications. It was no surprise, then, that

Churchill's orders to Stephenson were clear, precise, and direct: "assure aid for Britain, to counter the enemy's subversive plans throughout the Western Hemisphere . . . and eventually bring the United States into the war."[3]

Stephenson's official role was to administer passport matters as the new British passport control officer. His real purpose, however, was to expand the British intelligence presence in the United States and the Western Hemisphere. Stephenson possessed all the personal and professional qualities that Menzies deemed essential for such a delicate assignment. He also had a wide range of experiences that were not common among intelligence officers in government service. The ruggedly handsome Stephenson was born in Iceland in 1896. He was commissioned as a second lieutenant in the Royal Canadian Engineer Corps and in 1915 was fighting in the trenches of France. Later that year, while convalescing in England after a gas attack, he developed an interest in flying and soon volunteered for the Royal Flying Corps. He was captured and imprisoned by the Germans after being shot down during an aerial combat mission five months before the war ended. As a private citizen, Stephenson exhibited a flair for business, and some shrewd financial moves led to a number of lucrative acquisitions, including a large stake in the Pressed Steel Corporation, a major supplier for auto assemblers such as Morris, Humber, Hillman, and Austin. As his fortune and international stature matured, so did his relations with MI6. He traveled widely during the 1930s, meeting important business and political figures throughout Europe and North America. Information gleaned from these encounters was routinely passed to British intelligence officials for analysis by the Industrial Intelligence Control Center in London, a clearinghouse for strategic commodity information. These qualifications—his extensive business interests, strong organizational skills, and familiarity with many U.S. political and business leaders—trumped Stephenson's lack of professional intelligence experience, making him an excellent choice for his new role.[4]

Stephenson replaced Sir James Paget, a retired naval officer, and quickly relocated the passport control offices to Rockefeller Center Plaza in Midtown Manhattan. Having been briefed on U.S. intelligence coordination and control problems, Stephenson was under strict orders from Whitehall to move cautiously and avoid any flap that could enflame anti-British sentiment in the United States. New and untested approaches to intelligence liaison were needed if Britain was to survive, and Stephenson quickly set about forming a partnership with Hoover and the FBI. In April 1940, two months before being named to his new position, Stephenson had made a courtesy visit to Hoover during a nationwide tour of U.S. firms handling British contracts. The idea for this introductory meeting had been concocted by Menzies, who hoped to establish relations "on the highest level possible between British SIS and the U.S. Federal Bureau of Investigation." Hoover was eager for closer cooperation but warned Stephenson that the State Department was sensitive to public criticism of the exchange of intelligence between the two countries. Stephenson learned that the FBI was under orders to refrain from any direct collaboration with British intelligence officials, and he got the impression that only presidential intervention could alter this situation.

As Hoover expected, British sources soon began lobbying the White House about the potential benefits of such a relationship. Information was essential to an effective intelligence service, and good relations with the FBI would offer British intelligence access to rich data on issues that were critical to Stephenson's mission. Good relations would also help ensure the amicable settlement of conflicts arising from inadequate coordination, while minimizing the political risks to President Roosevelt associated with the exposure of a foreign intelligence service and a counterintelligence service operating at cross-purposes on U.S. soil. Roosevelt endorsed the British proposal for closer intelligence cooperation without hesitation. "There should be the closest possible marriage," the president said, "between the FBI and British Intelligence," and instructions were issued for the FBI to establish relations with the British as soon as possible.[5] Hoover moved quickly to cement a liaison with the British secret services. The FBI's New York office was ordered to do everything possible to garner the maximum benefit from this new relationship. The FBI director, in the words of the official historian of the British Security Coordination, "could hardly have been more cooperative." He was "more than its licensor. He was, in a very real sense, its patron." The benefits of this relationship would far outlast the crisis of the Second World War.[6]

With Menzies's blessing, Stephenson proposed the formation of a security organization composed of specialized departments that would devise strategies for the physical protection of British property. These new units served in an advisory capacity, briefing U.S. government agencies on security measures and antisabotage precautions for factories, railroads, shipyards, and docks, as well as investigating and reporting on sabotage and subversion. This organization also vetted the reliability of manufacturers working on British contracts and applicants for jobs in British missions in the United States. At a minimum, this organization needed to establish "the closest possible liaison with the American and Canadian departments concerned with these activities—FBI, the RCMP, the U.S. and Canadian intelligence organizations, the Customs and Immigration, and the local police and port authorities." Seven months later, an agreement was quietly reached between the two governments, and the British Security Coordination came into existence.[7]

Hoover was in lockstep with the new passport control officer. He quickly ordered the creation of guidelines governing the swift and steady flow of information between the BSC and the FBI. He reassigned Percy Foxworth, his newly appointed chief of the Special Intelligence Service (SIS), to serve as the principal liaison officer. Foxworth, with his keen grasp of counterintelligence, recognized the benefits of a close FBI-British relationship. As Hoover's point man with Stephenson, he played a central role in working out the early details of the information exchange and created the code name "Stott" to camouflage BSC as the source of information in internal FBI-BSC correspondence. His charm, openness, and willingness to share information soon won over his British partners. When Stephenson learned of Foxworth's SIS role and his related travel throughout Latin America between September and December 1940, he ordered all MI6 stations along the route to cooperate fully with Foxworth. In March 1941 Foxworth was promoted to assistant director of the National Defense Division, replacing Hoover's close confidant Hugh Clegg. A year later Stephenson suggested to William Donovan, the new director of the Office of Strategic Services, that he recruit Foxworth to head the organization's counterintelligence staff.[8]

Hoover's introduction to the British was a watershed event in the formation of the FBI's counterintelligence program. During the first eighteen months of this extraordinary collaboration, unprecedented initiatives were started that would have positive implications for the United States' ability to prosecute the war after Pearl Harbor. At the same time, it laid the foundation for U.S. counterintelligence for the remainder of the century.

Among the most important of these collaborations was the joint initiative against illegal German wireless transmissions. The British had originally addressed this issue a year earlier, shortly after they declared war on Germany. In September 1939 MI5 and the Special Branch of Scotland Yard launched a primitive effort to detect illegal wireless transmissions to German agents in Great Britain. As they scanned the atmosphere over the next year, they gradually uncovered signals beamed between newly conquered

German territories throughout Europe. The Radio Signals Service (RSS) captured these signals and sent them to the British Government Codes and Cypher School (GC&CS) for decoding. Through deciphered messages, advanced radio direction-finding techniques, and analysis, the GC&CS-RSS began to unravel the bewildering complexities of these thousands of signals. Sophisticated British signal tracking systems soon mapped a fairly clear picture of the routes used by the Germans' clandestine wireless networks in Europe, Asia, Africa, and, most significantly for the FBI, Latin America. By early 1940 GC&CS-RSS specialists discovered that the wireless transmitter-receiver was a favored form of communication not only for the Abwehr but also for the Gestapo and the Sicherheitsdienst. Collaboration with the Americans in this new field soon became a high priority for the BSC. The volume of illegal messages was increasing at an alarming rate, severely straining British capabilities. Sitting astride the radio lanes between South America, Japan, and Germany, the United States was well suited for safe and uninterrupted interception. Its unique geographic features, together with an abundance of technology and personnel, offered Menzies an excellent means of easing England's burden and expanding British-American coverage of the Western Hemisphere.[9]

Hoover quickly endorsed a joint wireless intercept project, which led to the systematic collection and analysis of clandestine signals in the Western Hemisphere. Autumn 1940 marked the beginning of a coordinated approach among the RSS, FBI, FCC, and U.S. Coast Guard for monitoring shortwave wireless broadcasts from South America. Supporting this collection effort was an MI6 monitoring station based in Rio de Janeiro, Brazil, with messages decoded in Canada by the National Research Council and in Washington by the FBI and ONI. Over the next eighteen months this effort paid large dividends to all the partners in the enterprise, uncovering and sorting illegal transmissions in increasing numbers. This collaborative approach also unearthed espionage networks and illegal transmitters in South America that were targeting the United States, making FBI investigations in the Western Hemisphere considerably easier.[10]

FBI Education Begins

Stephenson's mandate was clear. He arranged for the Canadian government to invite the FBI to inspect its defenses and manufacturing plants and to confer with police and intelligence personnel on issues of mutual interest. Hoover's selection of special agent Edward Coffey as his representative was particularly instructive. As head of the FBI Laboratory Section, Coffey was responsible for all scientific and technical aspects of the FBI's growing counterintelligence mission. Among the briefings he received in Canada was a review of the operations and functions of MI6's new secret training site, known as "Camp X," located along Lake Ontario sixty miles from Toronto. In November 1940 another invitation was extended for the FBI to examine counterintelligence and intelligence operations in England. Hoover ordered the delegation to "proceed immediately upon this mission," choosing Hugh Clegg and his assistant for training, special agent Larry Hince. Clegg was ordered to study all aspects of the British procedures, in the hope of incorporating their techniques "in our training schools now being held and to be held."[11]

Clegg and Hince departed New York by ship in early December 1940, bound for Lisbon and then on to London by plane. A fellow passenger on the London flight was Ernie Pyle, the American journalist who became legendary for his frontline combat reporting during the Second World War. Clegg's first taste of the war in Europe occurred during that flight when the plane was forced to fly close to the water to evade German radar and the ever-present scout planes. Then, on his first night in London, a German bombing attack shocked Clegg out of bed and into a basement air-raid shelter at the Claridge Hotel. During his two months in England, he witnessed firsthand a number of such attacks—experiences that offered real context for the reports he later provided to Hoover.[12]

The visit was an unprecedented event in the FBI's law enforcement and counterintelligence education. For the first time a government allowed another nation's counterintelligence leadership to inspect its most secret wartime police, counterintelligence, and counterespionage techniques and procedures. Every aspect of policing was thrown open for Clegg's examination, beginning with a briefing on the importance of the police officer in wartime by Sir George Abiss, the assistant commissioner of the Metropolitan Police Force of London. He explained the officer's symbolic role and his actual functions—both of equal importance to the population. He described the police officer as a calming figure who represented "normal peace time law and order" by serving as a "bulwark for the maintenance of morale of the civilian population" amidst the horror and chaos of nightly bombings. The police officer, unlike the soldier, was always present, reminding civilians of what constitutes normalcy, "standing at his post in the midst of air raid confusion," directing the movements of air-raid personnel, "giving advice calmly," and serving "as a steadying influence" that "prevents the growth of any tendency toward panic." When the police officer "keeps cool . . . the population follows," and because of this discipline and professionalism, "there had been absolutely no panic in London, in spite of the devastating air raids."[13]

The permanence of police stations was paramount, because their loss meant a potential breakdown in civil order and the ability to respond promptly to the effects of German bombing. At first the stations were secured with sandbags, which were subject to rapid deterioration from the weather and rats, which frequently burrowed into the bags. Later these stations were structurally strengthened with additional bricks and mortar, intended to allow them to withstand a bombing attack or to be quickly reoccupied if hit directly. Clegg also learned about the British police philosophy of the redundancy of police records and communications, so that all police stations, all levels of the police hierarchy, all emergency services, and all levels of government could maintain constant communication. This was particularly important because of the air-raid precaution duties of the police, which involved the management of bombing scenes—what the British called "incidents." The police might be called on to apprehend German aircrews, separating them according to rank following their arrest; manage air-raid scenes, which were often many square miles in size; provide emergency communications; identify casualties; facilitate the rapid movement of emergency equipment in blackout conditions; maintain traffic movement, both civilian and military convoys; man war, traffic, and air-raid centers; evacuate endangered areas; and enforce blackout restrictions.[14]

Clegg's survey was not confined to London. He traveled throughout England and visited police authorities in Liverpool, Bristol, Coventry, Stratford on Avon, and Oxford, where he studied urban and rural policing techniques. He saw first-aid posts, hospitals, and first-aid crews and ambulance parties in action. Police departments of all sizes were examined to determine how they utilized resources, employed volunteer assistance, and modified their functions to adapt to constantly changing wartime exigencies. Even British spiritual life and police morale caught Clegg's attention. Officers on patrol throughout the night were particularly mindful that blackout enforcement severely restricted the German pilots' ability to find their targets. During blackout periods and air-raid warnings, all windows had to be covered completely. Lighting in churches, however, was "restricted to the minimum necessary to enable the minister to read the service," yet sufficient "to enable the congregation to move to and from their places." At the police headquarters in Oxford, his escorts showed Clegg a recreation room with a "most unusual feature." Along with the standard pool tables and dartboards was a "regular bar with full-time day and night service." The thinking, according to the chief constable, was that force readiness and response were so critical that officers were encouraged to drink in the station rather than at local taverns or public houses. Clegg later reported to Hoover that "if an officer desired a drink, and the majority did, either on or off duty, they could do it in the police department where moderation would be more likely."[15]

The Special Branch of the Metropolitan Police Force of London also received Clegg's attention. He learned about the unique relationship between this division of police and the government's security service (MI5) in matters dealing with intelligence and national defense. The police worked in close liaison with MI5, reporting national defense violations and conducting investigations. Such a relationship was essential because MI5 was not a law enforcement organization, could not investigate criminal violations, and could not bring charges against individuals. Larger police departments throughout the country had their own special branches; smaller departments used war duty officers whose only job was to handle national defense work. In general, the Special Branch investigated espionage, sabotage, subversion, and Irish Republican Army (IRA) bombings, as well as provided security for the royal family, foreign dignitaries, the prime minister, and other cabinet members.[16]

Clegg later reported that in one year the Special Branch in London investigated 83 IRA bombings and cooperated with other police departments on another 93 bombings. In 1939, at the request of MI5, it made nearly 1,500 inquiries, investigated more than 500 members of the British Nazi Party, made another 5,600 inquiries into subversive and other issues, investigated over 1,100 naturalization cases at the request of the Home Office, and searched almost 25,000 passport office records, along with another 34,000 records in connection with "alien tribunals." Special Branch officers in undercover roles attended more than 1,000 fascist, antifascist, and IRA organizational meetings to collect intelligence. Among the 19 groups under close surveillance were Cypriotus, Aid for Spain Campaign, the Nordic League, the British Council for Christian Settlement in Europe, and the

Communist Party of Great Britain. Clegg found these figures impressive, considering that London's Special Branch had a total of 187 officers.[17]

Both Clegg and Hince were afforded unprecedented access to the most secret MI5 and MI6 techniques. MI5 officials explained that they viewed key government departments and ministries as customers, and as information was developed, it was circulated among the relevant clients. MI5 answered only to the cabinet, out of concern that control by the military services might lead to preferential treatment. Although MI5 was committed to providing its customers with the best service possible, it still doggedly maintained its independence, believing strongly that "no customer should control the Security Service." The American observers also learned about MI5 procedures concerning plant protection and port control and the maintenance of "nationalistic tendency and suspect lists," consisting of aliens or citizens whose "words, interests, or deeds are believed to be inimical to the welfare of the realm." Tactics of the British Watcher and Enquirer Service were also demonstrated. This service employed several hundred full-time MI5 workers engaged in conducting surveillances of diplomats and espionage agents, manning observation posts, and making pretext inquiries concerning suspects and suspicious activities. Clegg and Hince studied the role of the MI5 "undercover agent," whose mission was to obtain employment in "subversive and suspect groups in order to keep closer watch on their activities." The two men witnessed firsthand how MI5 inserted undercover agents in foreign embassies, consulates, and front companies; conducted telephone surveillance; examined mail; and intercepted diplomatic pouches. Clegg later described for Hoover a demonstration of the taking of "photographs with concealed cameras in lighting fixtures near the fronts of embassies and surveillances of individuals arriving at or departing from foreign embassies or consular offices."[18]

The exposure of the FBI delegation to the workings of Britain's Secret Intelligence Service (MI6) was just as thorough. Clegg visited MI5 and MI6 installations throughout Great Britain, including those in Scotland and the Lord Gorhambury estate in St. Albans, which housed the V Section of MI6. Like MI5, MI6 was directly responsible to the prime minister and the cabinet; its $14 million budget was concealed as a Foreign Office appropriation. Menzies's staff briefed the Americans on an MI6 structural setup that had no official existence and explained how professional "intelligence officers" assigned to "stations" around the world hunted for secret information.

Station makeup, MI6 wireless communication techniques, methods for establishing business and diplomatic cover for intelligence officers, and the filing system were demonstrated, as were the cooperation and coordination arrangements among MI6, the postal authorities, RSS, GC&CS, and all civil, military, and naval attachés around the world. A key lesson picked up by Hoover's two representatives was that MI6 maintained "an extensive counterespionage service . . . operated separately . . . in each country." Clegg told Hoover:

> The methods of counterespionage operations in foreign countries include surveillances, watching diplomatic representatives and controlling hotels, restaurants, taxicab establishments, railroads, shipping and air line services to the extent that information is obtainable from some employee who is either a British Agent or has been overreached so as to serve in this capacity. They further make investigations, intercept mail, telegrams, and telephone calls, and make use of microphones. They seek to provoke diplomatic representatives to pay or ask for information, in order that they may be denounced, and they further seek to penetrate the enemy secret intelligence organization and to sabotage the enemy's organization wherever possible.[19]

FBI-BSC Sharing

Hoover was equally helpful to the British by undertaking steps to protect priceless cargoes destined for the British Isles. A key initiative in this cooperative effort was the establishment of the "port observer" position in all major U.S. shipping centers. The port observer's mission was to ensure an uninterrupted flow to England of vital Lend-Lease provisions through coordination with the ONI, Coast Guard, MID, and FBI. Information was exchanged concerning suspicious activities and persons around the ports, and sources were developed in a relentless effort to prevent sabotage and labor disruptions before they occurred. Control of travelers' movements in and out of the Western Hemisphere was another essential feature of this security arrangement. It required the port observer to record the age, nationality, occupation, and destination of all travelers entering and departing U.S. ports and then index these data for use in identifying suspicious persons and exposing unusual travel patterns. In April 1941 the FBI began passing to the BSC the passenger lists of all Japanese ships entering and leaving West Coast ports. Three months later the BSC was receiving, examining, and indexing the names and destinations of 20,000 travelers a month.[20]

BSC-FBI surveillance of U.S. ports, plant protection, and control of the movement of international travelers were all elements of an overall plan to detect Axis espionage and seal off the Western Hemisphere from German sabotage. Censorship of mail passing between North and South America and Europe was also important to this effort. In late August and September 1939, MI5 and specialists from Imperial Postal and Telegraphic Censorship began monitoring mail moving in and out of Great Britain. After the fall of France, coverage was expanded to include Ireland and Caribbean island nations that came under Germany's control with its European victories. The British routinely monitored all mail moving in and out of the Western Hemisphere by ship or by plane through the British-controlled islands of Bermuda, in the middle of the Atlantic Ocean, and Jamaica and Trinidad in the British West Indies. Ships and aircraft making the long trip between Europe and the Americas were forced to stop for refueling at Bermuda. During these stopovers, letters and packages were removed and taken to the Imperial Postal and Telegraphic Censorship station in the capital city of Hamilton. There, specially trained technicians scrutinized addressees, return addresses, unique markings, handwriting, and other external features and recorded the results for future reference. If suspicions surfaced about a letter or package, an experienced technician would use more intrusive techniques. Envelopes and packages would be opened, the contents would be examined and recorded, and the item would be resealed, leaving no hint that any tampering had occurred. Examiners studied the plain text messages in letters, conducted chemical tests to uncover secret writing, noted watermarks to establish the paper manufacturer, and studied inks. Microphotographs—so small that multiple messages could be hidden behind the stamp on an envelope—passing through the international mail posed a serious challenge to British censors. By 1940, however, sophisticated equipment began scanning letters and packages for them.[21]

A highly secret exchange of mail intercept information began between MI6 and the FBI. Within months, any suspicious mail passing through Bermuda to or from the United States was being discussed with the BSC representative in Hamilton, who then forwarded it to the BSC's New York station, where it would be provided to an FBI representative for investigation. Years later, following the creation of the SIS, Bermuda censorship leads were forwarded to undercover agents in Central and South America for investigation. This combination of increased British knowledge of German espionage tactics and the FBI's growing understanding of German espionage communications contributed to improved British censorship techniques. Examining mail for telltale signs of espionage is the equivalent of looking for a needle in a haystack. Knowing the enemy's methods made sorting, sifting, and examining mail quicker and more efficient. Over the next five years, thousands of valuable leads in the United States and South America were uncovered in this manner, resulting in the arrest and prosecution of hundreds of German and Japanese agents operating in the Western Hemisphere. So useful was this FBI-BSC relationship that an FBI agent was assigned to the Bermuda censorship station by November 1941.[22]

"Joe K" and "Fred Lewis"

A brief examination of two cases illustrates the importance of the FBI-BSC counterintelligence relationship. The investigation of "Joe K" began within months of the BSC's establishment. Between January and March 1941, Bermuda censors began intercepting letters to addresses in Germany, Spain, and Portugal signed simply "Joe" or "Joe K." Couched in bland language suggesting friendship or a family relationship, the letters casually discussed the production, construction, and performance of U.S. companies. Microscopic examination using chemical analysis revealed messages "written in secret ink on the backs of the letters" concerning the "strength and activities of United States troops throughout the country, the production of planes and the number of ships taking supplies from United States ports to Britain, together with information concerning the nature of their cargoes." One secret ink message that must have particularly rattled the censors reported that "the British have 70,000 men on Iceland." It went on to note that "the SS Ville de Liege was sunk about April 14—many thanks," and "13 B-17C were at McCord Field, Wash. with British markings—later some B-17C were seen at Vancouver, B.C. enroute to Gandar Lake, N.F.—arrived in England some weeks ago." Unaware of the author's identity but desperate to locate this spy ring, Bermuda censors remained alert for additional correspondence to these European addresses and additional "Joe" or Joe K" correspondence.

A break in the case occurred in March 1941 when a "Joe K" letter with another secret ink message reported that "Lido" had been struck and killed in New York City by a taxi on March 18, 1941, while in Joe K's company.

Using the accident as a starting point, investigators soon identified "Lido" as Jose Lopez Lido, a visitor traveling on a Spanish passport who had arrived by ship in San Francisco three weeks before his death. Spain's complicity in German espionage was confirmed when Lido was identified as Ulrich von der Osten, a German army major. The BSC then determined that he had served as a senior Abwehr official in Madrid, and his burial arrangements had been handled through the Spanish consulate in New York City. FBI investigation of the financial arrangements for Lido's burial led to the identification of Joe K: he was an American citizen named Kurt Frederick Ludwig.[23]

Born in Freemont, Ohio, Ludwig was thirty-eight years old. At the age of six he had immigrated with his parents to Germany, where he remained until 1925. He then returned to the United States and stayed until 1933, when he went back to Germany. In March 1940 Ludwig again entered the United States and quietly settled in New York City. Well trained in Germany and Spain, it took Ludwig only a couple of months to assemble a highly effective eight-member network that soon began supplying Germany with a steady stream of military information. His ring comprised the following: Helen Pauline Mayer, a Long Island housewife; Rene Froehlich, a former army private who sold defense magazines and gathered ship information; Paul Borchardt, a former German army major who taught at Seton Hall University (he analyzed the data collected by the ring); Carl Victor Mueller, a machinist who collected industrial production figures; Lucy Boehmler, Ludwig's eighteen-year-old secretary, who acquired military information through casual conversations with soldiers on leave; Carl Herman Schroetter, a Miami boat captain; and two teenagers, Hans Pagel and Frederick Schlosser, who studied ship movements on the New York waterfront. Two months after sending the critical "Lido" message, Ludwig and Boehmler left New York and began traveling throughout the southeastern United States. Watched continuously by the FBI, both were observed mailing letters at different locations along the way. These messages were intercepted, examined by the FBI, and retained as evidence because they contained information concerning "United States military establishments throughout that area."[24]

Ludwig panicked when he read the sensational headlines reporting the arrest of the Duquesne espionage ring in June 1941. In a desperate effort to hide, he abruptly altered his travel plans and spent the next month at a summer resort in Pennsylvania operated by a German-American Bund society, where he planned his next move. Coverage of his mail by the FBI and

British censors unearthed reports about other conspirators and Ludwig's growing fear of arrest. A surreptitious FBI search of his room at the resort uncovered extensive evidence of espionage, including secret inks disguised as white pills, small bundles of toothpicks used as secret writing instruments, paraphernalia used to encode messages, detailed data on U.S. aircraft production and military forces, and leads to a shortwave radio that was later recovered during a search of his Long Island residence.[25]

The endgame for Ludwig began on August 2, 1941, when he left the resort and began driving toward the West Coast. He was under constant surveillance by FBI agents, who saw him burning papers one evening at a tourist camp near Yellowstone National Park. Ludwig abandoned his car in Butte, Montana, and continued his westward journey by bus. His increasingly erratic behavior led Hoover to conclude that Ludwig was destroying evidence that could implicate him in espionage and provoked the concern that "he would possibly leave the United States at the first opportunity." Mindful of his first misstep in 1938, when his inexperience had allowed so many spies to flee the country and evade prosecution, Hoover took immediate action to ensure Ludwig's arrest The evidence gathered by the FBI and BSC, coupled with Ludwig's apparent attempt to flee the country, convinced the U.S. attorney for the Southern District of New York to issue an arrest warrant.

There are two noteworthy points about the Ludwig case. First, by the eve of the Pearl Harbor attack, new investigative and prosecutorial mechanisms had been developed to conceal the FBI's relationship with the Bermuda censorship operation. Second, evidence secretly uncovered in Bermuda and passed to the FBI through BSC channels could be used in U.S. courts without exposing the relationship. Illustrative of these points is the technique employed when Ludwig was originally identified. After examination, the "Joe K" letters were allowed to proceed through the normal postal process. Letters to "Joe K" entering the United States were tracked by the FBI and the U.S. Postal Service until they arrived in New York City, where they were "accumulated by the Postmaster." This procedure permitted the Department of Justice to hide the role of British censorship at Bermuda. At the same time, Ludwig could be arrested and charged with using the "United States mails in forwarding to a foreign country material relating to national defense." The U.S. attorney for New York obtained a search warrant for the incoming letters and seven additional letters mailed by Ludwig during his travels to various mail drops in Europe. The BSC was referred to as a "confidential source," and the censorship technician who first discovered the Joe K letters testified before a grand jury but never appeared publicly in open court. He "testified for the Bermuda censors and was thanked; but the part played by Bermuda censorship was deliberately understated for reasons of policy."[26]

The second case, involving "Fred Lewis," started shortly after the Japanese attack on Pearl Harbor. While Bermuda technicians were conducting a routine scan of letters, they discovered an envelope postmarked from New York City containing a fictitious return address, the name "Fred Lewis," and an address in Spain known to British censors as an Abwehr mail drop. Analysis revealed a secret message describing ship movements through New York Harbor. Subsequent letters described U.S. troop assignments and the destination of war materials. With Britain losing ships and sailors to German U-boats at a horrific rate, anything affecting its Atlantic lifeline was given the highest priority. The BSC immediately passed the letters to the FBI, and an investigation was launched.

Complicating matters after the U.S. declaration of war was the expanded role played by the military services in the FBI's relationship with the BSC. Before Pearl Harbor, suspicious letters with secret writing were allowed to pass to the intended recipient after analysis by the British censors. With American troops now at risk, the U.S. military services objected to those letters reaching their destination and falling into the hands of the enemy and its agents. Most secret messages contained both accurate and erroneous information that was usually based on the author's speculation. This blend of intelligence enabled the Bermuda censors to meet the demands of the military while maintaining the viability of the counterespionage investigation. With the use of newly developed techniques that mimicked the original author's handwriting, intercepted secret messages could be rewritten using identical paper and ink chemicals. The letter would then be forwarded to its destination without jeopardizing Allied military secrets. Accurate information could be sent too late to have any military value.

The attempt to identify Lewis was hampered by the paucity of letters and the author's stinginess in revealing anything about himself. BSC analysis disclosed only that he was an air-raid warden, had a garden, had lost his house at one time through foreclosure, and had been nursed by his wife at home during a lengthy illness. The only other items of value to the BSC were two obscure references to "realizing his button-patent" and a "camouflaged royalty settlement from South America." Despite a close watch, no additional "Fred Lewis" letters were discovered passing through Bermuda between April and November 1942. With the investigation stymied, the BSC and FBI theorized that this particular German agent had ended his spying activities when the United States entered the war, had nothing to report to or receive from Germany, or had already repatriated. A fourth and more worrisome possibility was that the agent was aware of BSC-FBI interest in him and had continued his Abwehr correspondence using new intermediaries, cover names, or mail drops.[27]

To find "Fred Lewis," Hoover's investigators began a futile canvass of all button patent applications, the handwriting of all recent repatriates to Germany, home foreclosures, and air-raid wardens in the New York area. At the same time, Bermuda censors reexamined the correspondence and discovered that two previously examined letters contained references to a trip to Portugal "about a year ago." This revelation prompted an FBI inspection of all baggage declarations for travelers bound to Europe—approximately 50,000 of them—in the hope of matching the Fred Lewis handwriting with the handwriting on a declaration. This painstaking search eventually produced a match to a person identifying himself as Ernst Fritz Detlev Heinrich Lehmitz. A closer look at Lehmitz revealed that he was a naturalized U.S. citizen of German origin. Evidence continued to accumulate, and eighteen months after the discovery of the first Fred Lewis letter, Lehmitz was arrested for espionage on June 28, 1943. A search of his house uncovered additional information that led to the arrest of Erwin Harry De Spretter, a Uruguayan-German engineer residing in the United States.[28]

Wiedemann

Hoover energetically embraced his new British intelligence partners, but not without some suspicions about their commitment to complete disclosure. Like many government officials with memories of the First World War, he still recalled the widely publicized postwar allegations that Whitehall had maneuvered the Wilson administration into the war. Suspicions still lingered twenty years later. Adolf Berle, an army intelligence officer during World War I, remained wary of the British and urged close scrutiny of their behavior to prevent something similar from happening to President Roosevelt. As assistant secretary of state with responsibility for intelligence coordination, he counseled "caution" in U.S. dealings with the British, fear-

ing secret negotiations "by which the United States was ultimately committed to enter the World War almost without the knowledge of the State
Department."[29]

Hoover was equally wary of the BSC when it refused his offer to use the
FBI's communication system to send messages from New York to London.
Evidence of Hoover's uncertainties during this period are highlighted in an
examination of the FBI investigation of Frederick Wiedemann, head of the
German consulate in San Francisco. Wiedemann was born in Bavaria and
served as a German military officer during the First World War (reportedly,
he was Hitler's commanding officer). After joining the Nazi movement in
the early 1920s, he vigorously supported Hitler's march to power and eventually moved up through the ranks of the party. His loyalty and dedication
eventually led to a promotion to the coveted position of personal aide to
the new chancellor of Germany. As the 1930s wore on, he became increasingly disillusioned with the Nazis, hoping instead for a return of the Hohen-
zollerns to the German throne. During postwar interrogations, Wiedemann
claimed that he was a "German rather than a Nazi."[30]

Hoover first learned about Wiedemann in January 1939 when he received a letter from Thomas Dewey, the district attorney for New York City.
Dewey's note was accompanied by an anonymous letter identifying Wiedemann as a spy and claiming that the German consulate was the "headquarters of the Japanese espionage." The letter writer explained that Wiedemann had been chosen for the assignment because Hitler trusted him and
his ability to conduct espionage and also because the Japanese government
"feels more than uneasy" that its diplomats in the United States were being
watched. Both the German and Japanese governments hoped that Wiedemann would "enable them to dupe the American authorities and to develop
espionage on a large scale."[31]

In February 1939 Hoover brought these anonymous allegations to the
attention of the State Department and indicated that the FBI would not
investigate Wiedemann's activities without the department's prior authorization. George Messersmith, then serving as the State Department's intelligence coordinator, acknowledged Wiedemann's new position as consul
general but instructed Hoover to take "no immediate action in investigating" his activities. Over the next month, two dispatches from the U.S. embassy in Brussels describing Wiedemann's close relationship with Hitler
moved Messersmith to reconsider his decision. However, hoping to avoid

the actual authorization of an official investigation, Messersmith requested that Hoover check on Wiedemann informally by obtaining "all information they could" but "in such a manner so there would be no indication that we are looking into his activities." Digging in his bureaucratic heels, the FBI director refused to conduct any investigation without the specific authority of the State Department and asked for the latitude "to conduct a discreet investigation" of the new consul general. State Department authorization was refused, and nothing was done for another year.[32]

In May 1940 Hoover again requested permission to look into Wiedemann's activities, based on information obtained from a conversation between an FBI double-agent source and a major espionage player. Hoover's source reported that Wiedemann was actively involved in espionage in the United States and was using the diplomatically protected consulate to distribute messages and packages between German agents in the United States and elsewhere. Despite these new and compelling charges against Wiedemann, the State Department turned down Hoover's request for the third time in eighteen months.[33]

The growing influence of the IIC and the White House's encouragement of a close relationship between the BSC and the FBI gradually loosened the State Department's grip on FBI counterintelligence investigations of foreign diplomats. Since February 1940 the Duquesne case (see chapter 11) had been producing a steady stream of evidence that German diplomatic establishments were involved in espionage. White House–authorized telephone coverage of Spanish, Soviet, Japanese, and Vichy French embassies and consulates in June and July of that year likewise exposed a broad pattern of illegal activities by Axis diplomats.

In the fall of 1940 the BSC approached Hoover with a plan to contact Wiedemann. Apparently, MI6 had received information suggesting that the consul general was dissatisfied with his current situation and was willing to chat with British representatives. Stephenson recommended Sir William Wiseman—a Cambridge University graduate and British aristocrat—to handle the contact. Wiseman's military career had ended abruptly in early 1915 after he was gassed at the Battle of Ypres. Declared unfit for further military service, he was reassigned, at the age of thirty, to head Britain's newly opened MI6 station in New York City. Wiseman left MI6 after the war but remained in New York, taking an executive position with the investment banking firm of Kuhn Loeb. He later served on the board of directors of the U.S. Rubber Company and the Kansas City Southern Railroad.

Throughout this time, Wiseman maintained his contacts with British intelligence officials.[34]

Hoover accepted Stephenson's idea and authorized the contact. On October 3, 1940, Wiseman and Wiedemann met in a San Francisco hotel room for three hours. Their conversation was a wide-ranging exploration of the Munich accords, Hitler's character, and Wiedemann's motivation for agreeing to the meeting. Wiedemann explained that although Hitler was good for Germany, National Socialism would be the ruination of the country. "I am a German officer of the old tradition," he told Wiseman. About Hitler he said, "Today he believes himself to be a superior to Napoleon, and is convinced he can conquer the world." Wiedemann feared that "peace between England and Germany is impossible. The Nazis are interested only in a dictated peace designed to give them the necessary time to make additional unspecified plans." He warned Wiseman that the strategy of the German General Staff was to defeat England after the fall of France. General Ludwig Beck, head of the General Staff, had formulated a plan to invade England back in 1914 and had been updating it as late as the summer of 1940. Included in the original plan was a ploy to prevent British shipping from using the Mediterranean Sea through close cooperation with the Balkan states and closer ties with Spain's leadership. For reasons unknown to Wiedemann, the idea had been scrapped, but he speculated that Field Marshal Hermann Göring had interfered with an amateurish plan of his own that was rejected by both the army and navy.[35]

Hitler and his henchmen, in Wiedemann's opinion, were ignorant of the United States. They viewed it as a nation of "gangsters" with little political influence or military importance. The Nazis' disdain for Roosevelt and the United States was so deeply etched in their minds that accurate and objective reports from consulates and embassies were regularly dismissed. These reports often served as excuses to recall their authors back to Berlin. As a result, German diplomatic reporting from the United States and elsewhere was, in Wiedemann's view, routinely slanted to conform to the preexisting beliefs of the Nazi leadership.[36]

Wiseman prepared a report summarizing the meeting, which the BSC provided to the FBI. He believed that Wiedemann's motivation for agreeing to the secret meeting was genuine. Wiseman assessed the consul general as a patriotic German and disillusioned anti-Nazi who believed that Hitler and his associates were leading the German people toward complete destruction. Wiedemann's doubts about Germany's future, however, were in conflict with his national loyalty, as evidenced by his refusal to discuss any details of his assignment at the consulate. For this reason, no British follow-up was attempted.[37]

Although Hoover accepted the British version of the meeting, he had no real need for it. To ensure that the White House and the Department of State received a complete accounting of the meeting, Hoover had ordered that microphones be installed to capture a permanent record of the entire discussion. In what was to become standard FBI procedure, a complete transcript was prepared, and individual items of importance were summarized and sent to policy makers. Emerging from the Wiseman-Wiedemann meeting were eleven separate reports with such titles as "The Peace Plan," "German Campaign against England," "Adolf Hitler," and "German Analysis of Italy."[38]

In spite of the growing bitterness that developed between Stephenson and Hoover after the United States entered World War II, there is little question that the FBI-BSC relationship opened the floodgates of progress for Hoover's new counterintelligence service. Among the most important but little-known benefits was the British decision to open all its counterintelligence and most of its foreign intelligence secrets to the FBI. Hugh Clegg's trip to London in November 1940 served as perhaps the best training experience in the Bureau's counterintelligence history.

Another important benefit of this new relationship was that Hoover could decide what information would be shared with the British without its passing through the State Department filtering system. The FBI and BSC now had the luxury of direct exchange. This sharing of leads and ideas led to increased understanding and mutual trust. It is noteworthy that this mechanism was in place and fully functional before U.S. entry into the Second World War.

Finally, the relationship also contributed to the development of the FBI's Special Intelligence Service, which is the topic of the next chapter.

CHAPTER TEN

Special Intelligence Service

As important as the Interdepartmental Intelligence Conference was in establishing the jurisdictional boundaries for each member agency, it left many critical questions unanswered. How would the IIC counter foreign espionage against U.S. interests outside its borders? What steps should be taken to more aggressively gather intelligence about the intentions of Central and South American countries that continued to maintain cordial relations with Axis nations?

Evidence was rapidly mounting that the German intelligence services were using South American countries to aid their espionage operations against the United States. Funds originating in Germany for the payment of agents in the United States were passed through South American banks to avoid FBI and Treasury Department scrutiny. German ship crew members moving in and out of South American ports regularly carried secret material, money, and messages. FBI investigations were uncovering secret wireless transmitters in Mexico and mail drops in Brazil for Abwehr agents in the United States.

With German forces on the move in western Europe and Scandinavia in early May 1940, J. Edgar Hoover and Adolf Berle began informal conversations about German subversion in Central and South America and the cozy relationships between the Nazis and these Latin American governments. Berle urged the director to send special agents to certain countries to investigate these activities. Further discussion among the IIC members led to the decision to establish a formal foreign intelligence structure under the direction of the FBI.[1] On May 29, 1940, the same day that the IIC signed its first formal delimitation agreement, Hoover "confidentially" informed General Miles and Admiral Anderson that "upon the instructions of the President," arrangements were under way to send FBI agents to Mexico and Cuba in a limited effort to begin monitoring German activities. Both Miles and Anderson complained about their own ability to collect intelligence in foreign

207

countries. The military and naval attachés handled intelligence collection in South American countries at the time, but as diplomatic officials, their pursuit of critical information through espionage was severely restricted. Anderson, undoubtedly speaking for the MID as well as the ONI, explained that military attachés were handicapped in their intelligence-gathering efforts because they were forbidden to recruit paid informants.[2]

Five days later, Hoover convened another meeting of the IIC in his office, with Berle present. The topic this time was the formation of a Special Intelligence Service (SIS) to conduct overseas espionage and counterintelligence activities. General Miles endorsed the idea in principle, explaining that it was essential to monitor trends in South America, particularly in Colombia and Venezuela. He cautioned the committee, however, against any setup that would interfere with the functions and duties of the military attachés. Hoover then reminded the others that in November 1938 the Brazilian government had requested FBI counterintelligence training for its police forces, and in January 1939 special agent Edward K. Thompson had been sent to Brazil for that purpose. Hoover crowed about the mission's success in establishing important police contacts while also gathering "a great deal of most interesting information." Berle, whose opinion was pivotal to any decision about the formation of an intelligence organization, quickly approved the idea and suggested that a committee be formed to examine the issue and offer recommendations.[3]

Until U.S. entry into the Second World War, most Americans paid little attention to the idea of the government engaging in foreign spying. From the time of George Washington's presidency, it had been an article of faith that the nation would stand alone, avoiding "entangling alliances" and relying instead on the vast ocean expanses for protection from foreign wars. Over the century and a half of the nation's existence, major organized intelligence-gathering systems had been employed only by Union and Confederate forces during the Civil War and, more than fifty years later, during the First World War, when the U.S. military reconstituted a special intelligence branch for the collection of information in support of European operations. In both instances these apparatuses were terminated at war's end. Before the Second World War, the U.S. economy and American ideals merged to create a lofty and unrealistic standard that held intelligence gathering against foreign countries to be inherently immoral and un-American. Such beliefs were not confined to the average man in the street; many in the government shared this view. One official wrote that the United States "by tradition has been a no snooping nation whereas every other great power has for centuries maintained elaborate and expensive organizations." John Riheldaffer, an ONI official charged with setting up a secret intelligence-gathering section, observed that "espionage is by its very nature not to be considered as 'honorable' or 'clean' or 'fair' or 'decent.'" Describing the type of person who would cooperate with American operatives, Riheldaffer characterized paid informants as individuals who would accept appeals to patriotism and at the same time "to the lowest nature of individuals—greed, lust for power, revenge, etc."[4]

Fletcher Warren of the State Department, Edward A. Tamm of the FBI, Colonel James Lester of the War Department, Captain H. D. Bode of the Navy Department, and Seldon Chapin of the Department of State made up the committee suggested by Berle. On June 6, 1940, they concluded that the formation of a Special Intelligence Service "is not only desirable but essential at the present time" and recommended an immediate decision "as to whether this program will be placed in operation." They then offered their vision of the function, structure, and operating procedures of the proposed organization. Sensitive to the political risks of public knowledge of this new undertaking, the group strongly advised that the exposure of one clandestine operative in South America should never jeopardize the larger network of operatives, nor should any operative possess knowledge of others' identities or locations. The committee recommended that the organization's chief of service be a prominent American businessman based in a large metropolitan industrial center—preferably New York City. Strict avoidance of any connection with the U.S. government was essential; rather, the chief should be engaged in "a business which would justify the use of persons to work in a foreign country." The proposed system required that the field operatives collecting intelligence be kept in the dark about which governmental agencies were on the chief's report distribution list. Likewise, the chief would forward the reports to the interested governmental agencies without revealing the source. The receiving agencies would then send these reports to their accredited representatives in the particular country for comment. Their analyses would be returned to the agency, forwarded through liaison to the chief of service, and sent back to the operative with notations concerning the report's accuracy or the continued interest in the particular subject. The creation of a Technical Committee was also suggested to assist the Special Intelligence Service in two important ways. First, the committee could routinely provide the SIS with special items of current information developed by the individual governmental departments. This would keep the service fully informed about other intelligence that might have an impact on its operations. Second, the Technical Committee could serve in an "advisory manner" with regard to SIS administration, functions, and the ongoing evaluation of the flow of information. In this way, the service could also be kept up-to-date about current issues of interest. Warren and his four colleagues had no illusions about the implementation time required for such an undertaking. Nevertheless, they warned their superiors that regardless of how long it took, it was "essential that such an organization be established in time of peace if it is to function at all adequately in any possible future crisis."[5]

Five days later, the IIC (again with Berle in attendance) reconvened to discuss the committee's findings. Each member agreed with the proposals and pledged his support for the formation of such a service, with Admiral Anderson urging that President Roosevelt's approval be obtained before taking any further action. With General Miles present in his office, Berle telephoned the president on June 24, 1940, to ask for his guidance. Berle informed the president that the choice of agency to administer the new service lay with the FBI, ONI, or MID. In classic Roosevelt style, the president told Berle that he "wished that the field of foreign intelligence should be divided." He ordered the FBI to take responsibility for "foreign intelligence work" in the Western Hemisphere "on the request of the State Department," with the understanding that the department could request help from the FBI for "special assignments" elsewhere. The MID and ONI "should cover the rest of the world, as and when necessity arises." Adding to the vagueness of the president's order was a proviso concerning the work of the proposed Special Intelligence Service. Roosevelt insisted to Berle that the new SIS "not supersede any existing work now being done."[6]

The order provoked an immediate controversy over the duties of the SIS. In a letter to Hoover captioned "Scope of the SIS," Miles described conversations with FBI officials that led him to conclude that Hoover's interpretation of his intelligence-gathering mandate might be "encyclopedic in scope." Fearing FBI encroachment on military intelligence responsibilities, Miles suggested "definite limits" on the categories of information collected by the new service. Rather than taking the lead over other governmental agencies involved in foreign intelligence collection, in his view, the SIS should "primarily . . . supplement by undercover information the data which our accredited agents in foreign countries could obtain." In an attempt to further limit the SIS mandate, he urged that it concentrate on "subversive activities" in foreign countries, including such groups as "disaffected nationals, and . . . foreign agents of the Nazis, Fascists, and Communists . . . with particular emphasis on those activities which are hostile to the United States or which are conducted by organizations having direct leads in to the United States."[7]

Hoover's own puzzlement over the president's broad order led him to refer Miles's letter to his own internal National Defense Conference (NDC) for its views. Composed of associate FBI director Clyde Tolson, inspector Earl Connelley, Clegg, Foxworth, and Tamm, the NDC began studying the president's briefly worded order and looking at the whole question of the Bureau's new SIS responsibilities. The simply worded directive, in their interpretation, imposed no limitations on what the SIS could collect. Disagreeing with Miles's contentions, the conference members also questioned his motives. Tamm, writing to Hoover on behalf of the full committee, suggested that the head of the MID was concerned about the potential success of the SIS and the "probability that the Bureau will discover and report intelligence information that his operatives are unable to secure." Hoover raised the issue at the next IIC meeting on July 28, 1940. He agreed with Miles that SIS activities should not conflict with the intelligence-gathering efforts of the military services. At the same time, however, he emphasized that the president's order imposed no limitations on the type of information the SIS could pursue. Miles's position was severely weakened when Anderson sided with Hoover. After carefully studying the issue, the admiral had concluded that, in addition to counterintelligence information, the SIS could gather political, economic, and military information through the active pursuit of espionage in foreign countries. In his view, there should be no limit on what it could collect, and its mandate "should be as liberal as possible." Assistant Secretary of the Treasury Herbert Gaston, also in attendance at the meeting, supported Hoover as well. A month later, Berle and the State Department lined up behind the ONI and Treasury endorsement.[8]

Each governmental agency with an interest in Latin America became a customer of the SIS, providing it with a broad mandate to secretly acquire foreign intelligence. Provisions were also made for other governmental agencies to request special FBI-SIS investigations, and it was understood that any information collected that was deemed of "urgent and vital interest would be provided to the President as he desired."[9] The specific intelligence of interest to the various agencies was as follows:

1. State Department—All material pertaining to Latin America.

2. Navy Department—All material relating to the activities of foreign naval departments, maritime information concerning espionage agents and their activities.

3. War Department—All material pertaining to the movement of troops in Latin America, espionage agents and their activities which pertain to military interests.

4. Office of the Coordinator of Inter-American Affairs—All material pertaining to subversive political activities, enemy propaganda, data regarding commerce and individuals dealing commercially with sympathizers or subjects of Axis nations.

5. Office of Coordinator of Information—All matters pertaining to Latin America which are related to enemy subjects and activities in Europe.

6. Treasury Department—Information regarding the movement of questionable or enemy funds and the individuals responsible therefor.

7. Maritime Commission—Maritime matters involving shipping and port commerce.

8. Board of Economic Warfare—Matters concerning strategic materials and commercial data.[10]

Foxworth

Hoover wasted no time filling the new SIS leadership job. On July 2, 1940, he appointed one of his most trusted agents, thirty-three-year-old Percy "Sam" Foxworth. A native of Purvis, Mississippi, Foxworth was a graduate of the University of Mississippi and a lieutenant in the U.S. Naval Reserve (1937–1941). At the time of his appointment, he was serving as the special agent in charge of the FBI's New York office, where he managed many of the Bureau's most sensitive counterintelligence and espionage cases. He had earned Hoover's trust during his eight years in the Bureau, proving himself to be a strong leader capable of deftly handling a variety of investigative matters, as well as the politically sensitive issues that frequently landed on Hoover's desk.[11]

Foxworth's skills and discretion were occasionally used to resolve sensitive personal matters concerning the Roosevelt family, including an awkward business entanglement involving Elliott Roosevelt, the president's son. During the late 1930s Elliott managed a number of radio stations in Texas that were owned and operated by the Hearst Corporation. After forming

the Texas State Network, with himself as the corporation's president, Elliott gradually began acquiring stations in Texas and throughout the Mid-
west, eventually owning a total of twenty-three local stations. At the time,
the Mutual, Columbia, and National networks produced high-quality programs that were broadcast nationwide and picked up by local radio stations
for their own audiences. Elliott envisioned capitalizing on the popularity
of those shows by selling a minute or two of airtime before and after each
program to local businesses for advertising purposes. At the president's request, G. Hall Roosevelt, Eleanor's brother, stepped in and suggested that
his nephew recruit John Kantor, a skilled advertising man, who could aggressively recruit potential customers.[12]

Based on Hall's recommendation and his own assessment, Elliot hired
Kantor at an annual salary of $10,000, plus $50 a week for expenses. What
the president's son did not know was that Kantor was a con artist. In 1932
he had been jailed for stock fraud; since then he had been arrested multiple
times for larceny, false pretenses, and conspiracy and had been linked to a
federal investigation of McKesson and Robbins, which was suspected of trying to sell 3,000 nonexistent Enfield rifles to foreign customers, in violation
of President Roosevelt's arms embargo. Puffing up his own background,
Kantor claimed that his wife was a second cousin of President William
McKinley and that his son was MacKinlay Kantor, the prominent newspa-
perman (and future Pulitzer Prize winner for *Andersonville,* a novel about
the famous Confederate prisoner of war camp). Further complicating matters was the fact that when Elliott hired him, Kantor was under indictment
for mail fraud and was free on bail.[13]

Upon learning of Kantor's murky background and fearing the potential
political embarrassment for his father, Elliott approached Attorney General
Frank Murphy for advice. Murphy urged him to end his relationship with
Kantor in the presence of witnesses and recommended that Foxworth be
one of those witnesses. Foxworth—identified only as "Mr. Ellsworth"—was
present at Elliott's New York City office on June 22, 1939, and watched quietly as Roosevelt terminated his business relationship with Kantor and had
him sign a previously prepared letter on Texas State Network stationery.
Attached to it was a check to Kantor for $583.33 "in final payment for all
services which you have rendered the Texas State Network and/or Elliott
Roosevelt, President of the company personally or as an official of the company." The letter was signed by Kantor and Roosevelt, with Frank Fenton, a
Roosevelt assistant, serving as a witness. Kantor was provided with a copy

of the letter, Elliott kept the other copy, and the original was given to Fox-worth, who passed it on to Murphy.[14]

The SIS Begins

With the SIS's commission established and Foxworth firmly in place, work proceeded throughout the summer and fall of 1940 to build a foreign intelligence organization. On July 2, 1940, the president issued secret instructions to the Treasury Department for the disbursement of $400,000 for the creation of the FBI's Special Intelligence Service; another $400,000 was authorized from the fund fifteen months later on October 4, 1941; and three months later, another $100,000 was authorized, bringing the total to $900,000.[15]

Because Congress was never informed of the SIS initiative, the initial funding was facilitated through unconventional means. It was drawn from a special White House discretionary fund, referred to as the Emergency Fund of the President, hidden deep within the Military Appropriation Act, signed by the president on June 13, 1940. The Emergency Fund, which had been established "to meet unforeseen emergencies of a confidential character in connection with the national security and defense," required no congressional disclosure and no detailed accounting of expenditures. In the case of the initial funding of the SIS, the attorney general supervised expenditures, which required him to prepare a "certificate of the amount of such expenditure . . . [which] shall be deemed a sufficient voucher for the sum therein expressed."[16]

The dispatch of FBI agents to South America soon followed. Agents drawn from offices around the country were brought to Washington, where they received a brief training session before their assignment. The course of instruction consisted of familiarization with the country of assignment, a rundown of the type of work expected of them, and a review of useful ONI, MID, and State and Treasury Department files. The training of these SIS undercover agents was seriously hampered by the absence of any meaningful data on the extent and nature of fascist and communist penetration in Central and South America, except for whatever evidence had been acquired through espionage cases and economic surveillance up to that point in the United States. After World War II, a classified five-volume history of the SIS prepared for internal FBI use emphasized that when the program started, there was a "complete absence of any accurate data or details concerning the true extent of or nature of subversive activities, current or potential, in Latin America."[17] After a number of false starts, Foxworth was eventually introduced to Lawrence Duggan, chief of the American Republics Division, and his staff, who regularly provided helpful background material.[18]

At the request of the U.S. minister to Haiti, one special agent was sent to Port-au-Prince to survey the extent of Axis penetration there and in Santo Domingo. In September 1940 FBI undercover agents were sent to Peru, Chile, Brazil, Uruguay, Argentina, and Venezuela. Gus Jones, the special agent in charge of the FBI's San Antonio office, had been in Mexico since September 1939 conducting criminal and counterintelligence investigations with Mexican police authorities. With the support of Josephus Daniels, the U.S. ambassador to Mexico, Jones was given office space at the embassy, although he was not technically assigned to the embassy and carried no official title. Special agent Edward Thompson continued to provide counterintelligence training to the Colombian and Brazilian military and law enforcement organizations as the accredited FBI representative in those countries. From that position, Thompson was able to provide a steady stream of intelligence reports back to Washington. According to the FBI's own history of the period, the SIS had fourteen undercover FBI agents either stationed permanently in or traveling through South America by January 1, 1941.[19]

SIS Headquarters

In August 1940 the FBI's New York office, through the assistance of Nelson Rockefeller, hastily set up the Importers and Exporters Service Company in room 4332 of the RCA Building at 30 Rockefeller Plaza. The new FBI front company was ostensibly engaged in the business of providing information to nonexistent client companies interested in developing opportunities for international trade. Its real purpose was to provide cover for the activities of FBI agents posing as businessmen operating in Latin America. The site of the office was chosen because of increasing concerns about Nazi and Comintern surveillance of the FBI's New York office and agents during their daily activities. Special agent Jerry Doyle, an experienced investigator with many years in the New York office, was the first person assigned to this office; he posed as a businessman handling normal commercial activities, but in fact, he was managing the undercover agents' day-to-day activities. Doyle

and later his replacement, special agent Robert Guerin, were also responsible for liaison with the MID, ONI, and BSC in New York City, but they
maintained no public contact with the FBI's Manhattan office.[20]

Importers and Exporters Service Company soon proved to be impracti-
cal. It did no real business, had no genuine clients, and posed serious credibility problems for the undercover FBI agents who were in contact with
South American companies interested in doing business with the fictitious
firm and its nonexistent U.S. clients. It continued as a front for the New York
office but was no longer the cover company for undercover agents. In June
1941 it was finally shut down completely when a steady stream of adver-
tisers, business investigators, and solicitors created unacceptable security
concerns. Although the company was disbanded, the Rockefeller Center
office remained in place until November 1945, when it was finally discontinued.[21]

Gradually the duties of this office expanded, taking on a vital support
function for the SIS. As the demand for agents in South America increased,
so did the need for plausible and effective business covers. Doyle and Guerin
became responsible for contacting corporate officials in the New York City
area and soliciting their cooperation for the FBI's new program. In his role
as assistant director of the New York office and head of the SIS, Foxworth
tried to meet all of New York's social, political, and business elites, and he
came close to succeeding. Among his many friends and acquaintances were
Morris Ernst; Louis De Rochmont; Comtesse Guy Du Bourg De Bozas;
Vincent Astor; Cornelius Vanderbilt Jr.; S. Oakley Vanderpoehl; Harold
"Hap" Flanigan, chairman of the board of Manufacturers Trust Company;
U.S. District Court judge Grover M. Moscowitz; Lieutenant General Hugh
Drum; Father Robert Lloyd, rector of Georgetown University; Bob Shaplen,
a reporter for the *New York Herald Tribune*; *New York Daily News* sports-
writer Jack Miley; New York City mayor Fiorello La Guardia; New York
stage actor Harry Silve, and Billy Rose, the legendary New York showman
and husband of comedienne Fanny Brice.[22]

Hoover also made personal contacts and encouraged Foxworth to cultivate influential businessmen of potential value to the SIS. Vincent Astor
assisted in this effort. His wealth and wide-ranging business, social, and political connections opened many doors for Hoover and the SIS. Winthrop Al-
drich, the chairman of Chase Bank and grandson of John D. Rockefeller Sr.,
was also helpful. Like scores of other well-placed business executives, they
performed a vital role by providing cover assignments and introductions to

others who were willing to offer assistance. Companies such as American Telephone and Telegraph, United Fruit Company, U.S. Steel, Armour Meat Corporation, and *Newsweek* magazine (owned by Vincent Astor) provided cover positions for agents. In general, cover assignments with large corporations were preferable because of their size, their influence, and, most important, their vast business and commercial interests throughout Central and South America. During the war, business leaders also dispatched selected employees (referred to as special employees) to South America to assist SIS agents in their intelligence-gathering activities.[23]

Jurisdictional boundaries for the SIS were formally approved by the IIC in February 1941. All agreed that the SIS would have exclusive jurisdiction for the collection of "economic, industrial, financial, [and] political" intelligence in the Western Hemisphere, as well as "subversive activities information." Accomplishing this task also required the IIC to agree to the FBI's "exclusive jurisdiction" for contacting and developing relationships with "American companies having personnel, facilities and interests" in Latin America. In both cases, the Republic of Panama and the Panama Canal Zone were excluded; they remained under the jurisdiction of the MID.[24]

Communication and Administration

With the FBI's new "businessmen" arriving steadily in Latin American capitals and making contacts in the local community, they gradually began to procure information that required action in Washington. However, with poor fluency in the language, limited contacts in the local American community, and no capability of verifying information, they could supply policy makers in the United States only with rumors and hearsay picked up through casual conversations and other informal means. A major problem for Hoover's men was getting the fresh data back to FBI headquarters in a manner that was both quick and secure from the prying eyes of local censors. Before leaving the United States, the undercover agents had been supplied with a post office box address in New York City to send their correspondence, a code system referred to as the "X-code," and special inks for secret writing. The X-code had been designed by the FBI laboratory to conceal messages sent through the international cable system and occasionally through the mail. Government censorship of all outgoing and incoming cables and the enforcement of laws requiring the registration of codes increased dramatically as international tensions rose. With the British on a war footing, scrutiny of mail passing through Bermuda, Jamaica, and other international postal choke points often delayed letter deliveries from the undercover agents to Washington by many weeks. These concerns made repeated use of the simple X-code increasingly risky. To ensure the security of the SIS operation, the X-code had to be replaced with a stronger encryption system called the XY-code; this system still had weaknesses, but it was more secure and less detectable. However, because the XY-Code was useful only for very short messages hidden in innocuous letters sent through the international mail, much of the information was slow in arriving or never made it to the United States at all.[25]

With the goals and problems of the new service outlined, Foxworth pressed Hoover on the tactical changes that he envisioned. It was "impossible," in his opinion, for an SIS operative to enter a large South American city "unknown and alone" and expect him to "develop within a reasonable time reliable information of value." In addition, the current method of having operatives communicate with Washington by mail, using code and secret writing, was too slow and inefficient. Foxworth told Hoover that large amounts of valuable, time-sensitive information were available, but it was too dangerous and too time-consuming for the agent to keep the data at his home, analyze it, and then commit it to code and secret writing. Routine mail was not an option because of the concern about local censorship. International telephone communications, still very primitive, were out of the question because of the ease with which the local counterintelligence service could intercept messages. To remedy this problem, Hoover was urged to ask for State Department assistance. Foxworth suggested that one U.S. embassy official in each Central and South American country be told the identity of the local SIS operative for the purpose of providing discreet assistance and facilitating SIS transmission of data back to Washington through the State Department's diplomatically protected mail and couriers. The embassy official could also provide other invaluable assistance, such as passing on important leads about the activities of various fascist and communists groups, supplying information on key businessmen willing to assist the SIS, providing the identities of disgruntled or disaffected local bureaucrats who might be willing to serve as informants, and advising about changes in local politics and police tactics that could have an impact on the operative's continued effectiveness. All this could make the undercover agent's task easier and more secure.[26]

The situation soon became so difficult that in a conference with Berle on April 17, 1941, Foxworth sought his help in getting an FBI agent assigned to each embassy in Central and South America to assist the undercover agents operating there. Berle was frank with Foxworth and admitted that there was intense resistance to the idea of FBI personnel being assigned to embassies. Through Berle's efforts, however, the impasse was broken. That same month, Spruille Braden, the U.S. ambassador to Colombia, requested the assignment of an FBI agent to the embassy in Bogota. With the precedent established, FBI agents were soon posted to embassies in Caracas, Venezuela; Rio de Janeiro, Brazil; and Santiago, Chile.[27]

In October 1940 Hoover approved a series of SIS-related administrative recommendations from his NDC. Chief among them was the creation of a special "running card index" designed for SIS use only. The index contained the identities of any "pro-Nazi, pro-Communist, pro-Japanese, or pro-Fascist" person coming to the attention of SIS operatives. The system listed the names, aliases, addresses, telephone numbers, and so forth contained in correspondence sent to FBI headquarters from SIS operatives in Central and South America. Actual reports from field operatives would be maintained in the Bureau's general file system. Duplicate index cards were prepared, with one card filed alphabetically and the other according to geographic region.[28]

Foxworth's Epiphany

In the summer of 1940, Nelson Rockefeller was appointed assistant secretary of state; his specific title was coordinator of commercial and cultural relations between the American republics. Prompted by growing concern over the commercial and financial ties between the Axis and the right-wing governments of Central and South America, President Roosevelt hoped to use the Rockefeller family's vast business interests in those regions as a weapon in an economic war against the Axis. One of Rockefeller's first acts was to arrange for a delegation to visit all the nations of Central and South America, survey conditions there, and develop plans for U.S. government action. Ambassadors in each country on the delegation's itinerary were instructed to identify key representatives of U.S. companies who were "considered anti-U.S. or pro-Nazi in their sympathies" and those "considered undesirable from the standpoint of the national interest of the United

States." They were also asked to identify local persons, preferably Americans, whose loyalty to the United States was unquestioned and who could replace the foreign managers whose loyalties were questionable. Upon returning to the United States, the delegation would attempt to persuade the companies to make the replacements.[29]

In August 1940 Foxworth briefed Rockefeller on the SIS and sought his support for the fledgling service. Arrangements were made for the new SIS chief to join the delegation during its two-month tour. Although his cover story is not known, Foxworth insisted that his FBI affiliation not be divulged to anyone. This avoided awkward questions about why an FBI official would be accompanying a business delegation, and it allowed candid discussions without inhibiting the group from achieving its goals.[30]

After two months of travel, personal observations, and intensive discussions, Foxworth returned to the United States with a different understanding of the problems facing SIS agents. Before his trip, he had believed that undercover agents should operate alone for their own safety and that their identities and locations should be known only by a select group of officials in Washington, D.C. Foxworth was quickly dispelled of these notions, and scrapping these ideas became the centerpiece of his post-trip briefing to Hoover on December 4, 1940. The goals of SIS operations in Latin America, Foxworth explained, should be the development of informants capable of supplying a steady stream of useful information that could be obtained only through espionage. American officials in the countries he had visited told him that volunteers often approached the local U.S. embassy and consulate offering valuable information, but because of their diplomatic status, embassy personnel were prevented from taking any action; as a result, this information was generally filed away and ignored.[31]

Foxworth then related a conversation he had had with a representative of Pan-American Airways in Rio de Janeiro to illustrate another necessary change. According to the airline representative, a Spanish aviation company was trying to secure a concession to operate a transatlantic line between Brazil and Spain. Three weeks earlier, however, Lufthansa, the German airline, had been denied a similar concession by the Brazilian government. It was the opinion of the Pan-American representative that the Spanish company was negotiating on behalf of the Germans. This anecdote had been offered to Foxworth in confidence, and only because someone had vouched for him. Such informants, he was told, "will not talk openly to just any person who comes along." Thus, Foxworth believed that it was vital to make the identity of the local SIS operative known to one or two specially selected businessmen "if any results are to be accomplished."[32]

The next topic on Foxworth's list was the need for a special analytical component at FBI headquarters that was capable of producing accurate and timely assessments for SIS customers based on incoming intelligence reports. His recommendation was predicated on numerous conversations with State Department officials, who often criticized SIS reports as being "completely and totally inaccurate so far as the political information is concerned." To remedy these complaints, he urged a simple change in the FBI's reporting of information, with an emphasis on whether the intelligence being reported had been verified. For example, he recommended attaching an addendum indicating that the information was "unconfirmed" or a "rumor" or that the FBI could not "vouch for its authenticity."[33]

Finally, Foxworth touched on the human dimension of sending men to strange environments to conduct dangerous work. He told Hoover that as part of his fact-gathering trip he had solicited comments and observations from FBI agents stationed in South America. His report emphasized that all the men currently serving in those assignments were married, and he expressed concern about their morale. Foxworth stressed the need to reunite these men with their wives and families at the earliest possible date. He reminded Hoover that all other governmental agencies with representatives abroad routinely bore this expense, and he suggested two possible solutions. First, a ruling from the attorney general could be obtained to determine whether SIS appropriation funds could be used for the relocation of families. Second, if this initiative violated the law, a congressional amendment to the original FBI appropriation could be sought, allowing for the transportation of agents' families.[34]

Hoover's Response

Given his conservative cast of mind and complete lack of practical knowledge of foreign intelligence practices, Hoover attempted at least twice over the next eighteen months to unload responsibility for the SIS onto another IIC service. His first choice was the navy. In July 1941 Tamm discussed with Hoover a proposal by ONI officials to move their undercover agents into Mexico to answer questions concerning West Coast defenses. Hoover was in full agreement with his deputy's suggestion that the entire SIS program in Mexico be reassigned to Captain Alan Kirk, Admiral Anderson's successor as ONI director. "If he does this," Tamm wrote, "the services of at least a half dozen [FBI] Agents . . . can be well used on other work, and possibly by this means we may over a period of time get rid of most of the work in the SIS field."[35]

It is little wonder that five days after receiving Foxworth's recommendations, Hoover responded with less than wholehearted enthusiasm. Hoover was obsessed with ensuring the secrecy of the SIS and was intent on avoiding any number of potentially serious problems that could result from its public exposure. First, there was the overriding concern for the physical safety of the undercover agents if South American counterintelligence services learned of their presence. Second, Hoover feared the political repercussions for the president if his congressional, media, and other isolationist enemies became aware of the SIS's existence. These concerns led him to approve, "most reluctantly," Foxworth's suggestions for briefing businessmen and embassy officials on the SIS mission. But as he told Tamm, he was still concerned that these steps would "inevitably result in uncovering the whole SIS structure." He also endorsed a separate NDC proposal for a broad-based training program for Latin American police agencies to assist them in establishing their own intelligence organizations; this would lead to new FBI relationships that could materially contribute to the SIS intelligence and counterintelligence mission in Latin America. Berle threw his full support behind these changes and began taking steps to canvass all ambassadors for the names of candidates who could help in this effort.[36]

It is not surprising that the FBI director's fixation on security forced him to reject Foxworth's proposal for the relocation of undercover agents' families to Latin America. Hoover believed that wives and children could be exposed to danger and posed a potentially serious security risk to the agent and his mission. In explaining his decision, however, he hid behind the potential legal obstacles, insisting that there was "absolutely no legal authority" for the government's authorization of expenses for family relocation. Instead, he decided that the SIS should assign "as far as possible, unmarried men" to its Latin American operations.[37]

Assigning only unmarried men to the SIS severely limited the pool of candidates for this sensitive FBI assignment. Seasoned veterans with years of investigative experience and skills at spotting, assessing, and dealing with informants were now barred. Thus, SIS applicants were generally young agents only a year or two out of training school. Age and experience were trumped by the need to get agents out in the field quickly, where, it was hoped, they could familiarize themselves with the local language and customs and develop their skills and talents. The relative youth of these undercover agents posed additional problems that had not been anticipated by the FBI leadership. For one, they stood out noticeably in the communities where they were required to operate; this often raised embarrassing questions for them and, even worse, jeopardized their security. Years later, the FBI criticized this practice, noting that even after the United States entered the war, the typical undercover agents were largely young, "healthy, intelligent, personable Americans of draft age and obvious military potentiality operating under weak and frequently illogical covers . . . despite the fact that their country was at war."[38]

Crosby and Papich

Typical of the men who served in the SIS was Kenneth M. Crosby. Born in Greeneville, Tennessee, in 1916, Crosby graduated from the University of Mississippi in 1937 and received a law degree two years later. After a brief stint with a law firm in Atlanta, he joined the FBI as a special agent in the fall of 1939. After training, he was assigned to Huntington, West Virginia. Following a transfer to Boston, he was assigned to a Worcester, Massachusetts, "road trip" handling new plant protection duties at major industrial facilities. In May 1941 he was reassigned to the New York office, where he investigated the Amtorg Trading Corporation and the Duquesne espionage case. Following the Japanese attack on Pearl Harbor, this tall, lanky, good-humored bachelor was approached by Foxworth and asked whether he was interested in a foreign assignment. With little idea what he was getting into, Crosby immediately accepted and was sent to Washington, D.C., where he and other special agents from around the country attended a six-week training program designed to prepare them for their Latin American duties. The course of study included lectures on informant development, local culture and history, secret writing techniques, and coded communications. When the SIS first started in July 1940, strong language skills had been a requirement for undercover assignments. It was only as the program expanded and required more personnel that language skills became scarce and classes in Spanish and Portuguese became necessary. In May 1941 two Spanish-language courses, one elementary and one advanced, were inaugurated at the

FBI's Washington field office. Spanish classes were held six evenings a week after normal training hours. By November 1941, increased demand for undercover candidates necessitated the development of a four-week course, twelve hours daily, geared to the candidates' preexisting language skills. Special agents who were destined for Brazil attended the Berlitz Language School to learn Portuguese.[39]

Crosby was kept in the dark about his future assignment until the end of training. Then he learned that he was being sent to Buenos Aires, Argentina, where he would pose as a stockbroker for the New York brokerage firm of Merrill Lynch Pierce Fenner and Beane. Having no brokerage experience, he was sent to New York City and, through the highly confidential cooperation of Charles Merrill, was enrolled in the company's training course. He became a registered broker after passing the New York Stock Exchange Institute examination. His undercover training in Washington, his affiliation with his cover company, and his assignment in Argentina were confidential; he was not permitted to discuss his activities or whereabouts with any family members or friends.[40]

With his brokerage license in hand, the twenty-four-year-old Crosby left New Orleans for Buenos Aires in April 1942 aboard the SS *del Brazil*. His cover assignment was to establish the firm's first brokerage office in Argentina's capital city. Assisting him initially was the manager of the Buenos Aires branch of the National City Bank. Crosby presented a letter to the manager, prepared by Merrill, introducing him as an employee and requesting his help. As the two men became friendly, Crosby revealed the actual nature of his assignment. The bank manager offered his unqualified cooperation in the young stockbroker's true SIS mission. This provided Crosby logical and even plausible reasons for extensive travel throughout the country, meeting and cultivating its most prominent financial, business, social, and political leaders.[41]

Another SIS recruit was Sam J. Papich, a Montana native of Yugoslav heritage. He attended Northwestern University, where he excelled at football, and graduated with a degree in civil engineering. After employment with the U.S. Steel Corporation, he joined the FBI at age twenty-three in March 1941. After training school in Washington, D.C., and a brief assignment in Philadelphia, he was assigned to the FBI's New York City office. Immediately after the Japanese attack on Pearl Harbor, Papich was dispatched to Ellis Island to direct the processing of dangerous aliens and Americans who had been arrested. In late December, through the office grapevine, Papich learned about the SIS and volunteered his services to Foxworth. With less than a year of FBI service, no wife, and no special obligations preventing his assignment abroad, Papich was quickly accepted and sent for training and an eight-week course in Portuguese. His post was Rio de Janeiro, where he would be posing as a representative of the Dun and Bradstreet Corporation. Like Crosby, Papich underwent an indoctrination course at his cover company's corporate offices in New York City. This particular cover gave Papich ample opportunity to travel around Brazil without arousing suspicion, developing a wide range of sources and meeting a wide variety of people while assessing companies and their management under the guise of inclusion in Dun and Bradstreet records. Papich remained in Brazil for five years and eventually closed the SIS operation in 1947, when responsibility for foreign intelligence was turned over to the newly created Central Intelligence Agency.[42]

During the summer of 1941 the FBI established a goal of 250 undercover agents operating in South America by November 1942. By December 1941, eighteen months after its creation, the SIS had 78 undercover agents and special employees in every country of Central and South America. By June 1942, this figure had almost doubled; four months later, as more trained agents and cover companies became available, this figure jumped to 196, including 156 special agents in all kinds of undercover SIS roles. Finally, by December 1942, there were 209 special agents and special employees operating in Latin America and serving in liaison roles in Havana, Cuba; Ottawa, Canada; Port of Spain, Trinidad; Kingston, Jamaica; and Hamilton, Bermuda. Within a few months of U.S. entry into the war, arrangements were made for the assignment of a small number of special agents to serve in the new role of legal attaché or civil attaché at U.S. embassies in selected countries.[43]

CHAPTER ELEVEN

Ducase

On February 8, 1940, the SS *Washington* tied up at a New York pier and began unloading passengers and baggage. At the gate, special agents of the FBI and representatives of the State Department awaited the arrival of one passenger who had sailed from Genoa, Italy: William G. Sebold. After the necessary introductions, the agents escorted him to an interview room at the FBI's Manhattan office, where, over the next few days, he told a story that his rapt audience found difficult to grasp. In rich detail, Sebold recounted his 1939 European sojourn, focusing on his recruitment by the German military intelligence service for espionage in the United States, the circumstances leading up to his decision to cooperate, and his training at a secret espionage school in Hamburg, Germany. Then, upon his return to the United States, he had been instructed to purchase a shortwave radio and, after waiting a sufficient time to ensure his security, to start broadcasting to Germany on a prearranged frequency using a specially designed code.[1]

Not surprising to his listeners was the fact that secret messages and sensitive documents were being smuggled out of the United States. The Rumrich case had identified couriers operating aboard ships who routinely carried instructions, money, letters, and documents to and from their Abwehr superiors. What was shocking was Sebold's fascinating description of German technical advancements in microphotography, including the ability to shrink a standard sheet of paper to a size smaller than a human fingernail. Sebold claimed that he had studied the equipment and been instructed on techniques for reducing and concealing multiple sheets of paper using this new process. If true, the implications of his story were stunning. Such a breakthrough meant that uncovering incriminating messages and documents during routine customs searches of individuals and luggage would be practically impossible. As if reading his interrogators' minds, Sebold removed his watch from his wrist, opened the back, and withdrew five microphotographs hidden in the mechanism—safely carried off the ship and undetected during a customs inspection at the pier earlier that day. Three of

226

the microphotographs contained instructions for three key German espionage agents in the New York City area. The other two were codes for these agents to use when transmitting and receiving messages.[2]

Before leaving Germany, Sebold had been instructed to make contact with a New York City resident named Herman Lang. He knew little about Lang except that he was a member of a German espionage network who would recognize the phrase "Hamburg Berlin greeting from Rantzau." These words signaled that Abwehr wanted Lang to return to Germany, for reasons unknown to Sebold. Three days after his arrival, he was supposed to send a telegram to "Hugo Sebold," using his true name and a fictitious address, verifying his arrival in the United States. Over the next fourteen days, he was to establish a permanent address in the New York City area using the alias "Harry Sawyer" and to do nothing that might create suspicion. If he suspected that he was under FBI observation, he was to send a warning to the Abwehr using the phrase "am in doctor's care." Finally, if hostilities between the United States and Germany appeared imminent, Sebold was to immediately send a cryptic warning to Germany through the following addresses: C. S. Wang, C. S. Wang Travel Service, Szechuan Road, Schanchei; L. E. Moeller, ESDU, c/o Mrs. Guilermo Moeller, Sao Paolo, Rua Docarmo 9; and Dr. Bernado Ge Rua, De Albuquerque, Coimbra Port.[3]

Sebold's Tale

The central figure in this investigation was a naturalized American citizen named William Gottlieb Sebold. Born in Mulheim Ruhr, Germany, in 1899, Sebold had served in the German army during the First World War and was discharged in 1919. A year later, he entered the merchant marine, leading a nomadic life sailing between Europe and North and South America, frequently changing jobs, and eventually settling in California. Following a brief visit to Germany in 1934, he returned to the United States, married an American woman, and got a permanent job at the Consolidated Aircraft Company in San Diego, California. Six months later an illness forced a move to the East Coast, where he became a U.S. citizen in 1936 and lived in New York City until he departed for Germany in early 1939 aboard the SS *Deutschland*.[4]

Soon after his arrival in Germany, Sebold was telephoned by a person named "Dr. Gassner," who expressed an interest in discussing conditions in the United States. After twice ignoring his requests, Sebold received a letter from Gassner informing him that he "must cooperate" or risk bringing "the pressure of the state" on himself if he did not cooperate.[5] Soon after receiving Gassner's letter, Sebold discovered that his identification papers, including his U.S. passport, had mysteriously disappeared, leaving him with no way to prove his real identity. The loss of the documents was no accident. Facing increasing pressure from German intelligence authorities and without identification, Sebold saw no option but to meet with Dr. Gassner. Their initial conversations focused on his life in the United States and his future plans. He answered questions about his family in Germany, his employment with the Consolidated Aircraft Company, his German American friends in the States and their employment, and the chance of him securing a future job in the U.S. aircraft and defense industries. After a number of meetings, Gassner insisted that Sebold meet a person named Dr. Hugo Rankin—probably an Abwehr officer—who continued the questioning. During one session, Sebold mustered the courage to mention his missing identification papers. Rankin suggested that, as an American citizen, he could apply for a new U.S. passport, but he warned Sebold not to mention their meetings to consulate officials. Then he offered the chilly reminder that Sebold was also a German and subject to German law. A frightened Sebold desperately tried to leave Germany but was repeatedly stymied at the French, Belgian, Dutch, and Luxembourgian borders because he lacked proof of U.S. citizenship. He returned to his hometown of Mulheim Ruhr, where Gassner began appearing to badger him with questions about "bombing planes, coast patrol boats, the equipment used, bomb sights, bombing racks, and similar matters." After fielding questions that he could not answer, a frustrated Sebold suggested that Gassner send someone to the United States to obtain the information he wanted. Gassner proposed that Sebold accept this assignment, and when Sebold demurred, Gassner threatened him with arrest and potentially serious consequences to his family. Trapped and with no way out, Sebold reluctantly agreed to cooperate with German authorities. A few days later he received a package containing money and instructions to proceed to Hamburg, where he would begin his espionage training.[6]

Over the next few months, the Abwehr's newest trainee underwent an intensive course of instruction designed to prepare him to function safely in the world of foreign espionage. Lessons included microphotography, Morse code, radio-transmitting techniques, encoding and decoding of messages, personal security, and disguises. Finally, he was ordered to establish a clandestine radio station for communication with Germany following his return to the United States.[7]

Sebold completed his espionage training and obtained a new U.S. passport on January 30, 1940. Before leaving Germany he was contacted by an Abwehr operative who identified himself as Hugo Sebold, an obvious alias. He gave Sebold $500 in cash and ordered him to deliver it to Everett Roeder, who resided in a Long Island suburb of New York City. Sebold was also given the five microphotographs. The three German agents for whom those instructions were intended were Colonel Frederick Duquesne, c/o Air Terminals, 17 East 42nd Street, New York City; Lilly Stein, 127 East 54th Street, New York City, and Roeder. Sebold was also ordered to supply the Abwehr with a steady stream of information concerning shipping activities in New York Harbor and to serve as a communicator between Germany and its American agents through shortwave radio transmissions.[8]

The "Ducase" Begins

Sebold's story electrified the FBI, but the agents found it implausible. The FBI had been duped before by people with wild imaginations. The war in Europe and the increasing popularity of spy stories contributed to a burgeoning number of unfounded allegations about Nazi espionage and sabotage. Suddenly, in the midst of this mania, a hapless, unemployed, German American aircraft worker with no access to secret information and no immediate prospects for obtaining such data comes forward with a fantastic tale of foreign intrigue, extortion, radio transmitters, and espionage on a scale previously unimagined. Why would the vaunted Abwehr select such an unlikely candidate for such an important intelligence assignment? Were the Germans capable of making so fundamental a mistake, or was Sebold a provocateur sent to sow confusion among the U.S. counterintelligence services? Although the FBI clearly questioned Sebold's credibility, his remarkable story could not be ignored. Most important, there was no question about the five microphotographs hidden inside his wristwatch.

Doubt soon dissolved when Sebold named Stein, Roeder, and Duquesne as the intended recipients of the microphotographed instructions. At first, the FBI suspected that Stein was the alias of a woman who had entered the United States in the early 1930s and been arrested in New York City for making a speech on behalf of the communist movement, but this turned out to be erroneous. Roeder was employed as an engineer with the Sperry Gyroscope Company in Brooklyn, New York; he had previously worked at the Airplane and Marine Direction Finder Corporation and the Arma Engineering Company, both of which manufactured sophisticated instrumentation for navy ships. The FBI also learned that Roeder had borrowed money from a local bank in anticipation of the receipt of "royalties" for unspecified work performed for Germany. The identification of Sebold's other contact, Herman Lang, was even more distressing; Lang was a senior inspector for the Norden Corporation, manufacturer of the top-secret Norden bombsight—the most important U.S. military secret at the time.[9]

The identification of Duquesne solidified the FBI's belief in Sebold's truthfulness. Born in South Africa, Frederick Joubert "Fritz" Duquesne had fought against British forces during the Boer War, been captured and imprisoned on the island of Bermuda, escaped on a sailboat bound for the United States, and disappeared overboard in the Chesapeake Bay. After settling in New York City, he reinvented himself as a journalist, man of mystery, big-game hunter, and world traveler, earning his living by writing and lecturing about his genuine and fictional adventures. A decade later he was arrested for trying to sabotage ships carrying supplies to Britain and France during the First World War. Having convinced a judge that he was mentally incompetent, Duquesne was moved from his jail cell to the psychiatric ward at Bellevue Hospital, from which he escaped a month later. Fourteen years later Duquesne made headlines again when he was arrested on a British extradition warrant, which a U.S. court later dismissed, allowing him to remain free in the United States.

The "Ducase," as it became known within the FBI, rapidly transformed the manner in which the nation's first civilian counterintelligence service conducted espionage investigations with a worldwide scope. Procedures routinely used by police investigators now had to be blended with new techniques. With Sebold's arrival, the FBI suddenly found itself investigating a combination of intelligence activities that included diplomatic officials on U.S. soil, double agents, anonymous German agents hidden within the fabric of American society, clandestine radio communications, mail drops in neutral countries, and foreign funds in U.S. banks used to pay foreign agents. Advanced technical procedures were developed, involving shortwave radio communications, large-scale telephone surveillance, and new photographic techniques. FBI agents had previously been dispatched to Cuba and Mexico to conduct criminal investigations in conjunction with local law enforcement authorities. Now they would be sent to Asia and Europe in undercover roles to investigate Ducase leads. The goal of these efforts was twofold: to build prosecutable espionage cases against foreign agents, and to lift the veil of secrecy shrouding Germany's intelligence collection in the Western Hemisphere and neutralize the foreign intelligence services by controlling all their activities in the United States.

Hoover's skills as a counterintelligence investigator and manager were limited. For his first seven years with the Department of Justice, his work in the Alien Section had been largely administrative, having nothing to do with counterespionage and counterintelligence. He never took any specialized counterintelligence courses, and during the first sixteen years that he led the Bureau, very few cases of that type were investigated. During his entire career in law enforcement, Hoover made only one arrest; a fact that became a source of controversy in 1936 when he was verbally attacked by Tennessee senator Kenneth McKeller during an appearance before the Senate Appropriations Committee. McKeller, the committee chairman, was apparently angry because of Hoover's refusal to appoint McKeller's cronies to special agent positions. In an attempt to embarrass the FBI director, he blistered him with questions about his qualifications for leading the FBI, particularly the fact that he had never made an arrest. Hoover tenaciously defended himself, but he was forced to concede McKeller's point (Congress had authorized the FBI to make arrests only in 1934). Mortified by his treatment, and with his vanity severely bruised, an outraged Hoover vowed to put this issue to rest by arresting a major fugitive. He ordered his staff to inform him immediately when Alvin "Creepy" Karpis, the nation's most well-publicized fugitive, was located. When Karpis was discovered three weeks later hiding in a New Orleans rooming house, Hoover flew there and arrested him personally.[10]

Hoover's only genuine foray into counterintelligence management was the calamitous investigation of the Rumrich espionage ring less than two years earlier. In spite of his poor record in this area, he instinctively recognized the Ducase's unprecedented potential to penetrate German espionage activities in the United States. As the new counterintelligence coordinator for the U.S. government, he recognized that the traditional criminal investigative approaches, which had so muddled the Rumrich case, had to be replaced with new and innovative ideas. The issuance of subpoenas, grand jury appearances, and direct interviews of witnesses and subjects of the case were no longer applicable. Success in the Ducase demanded the covert

acquisition of evidence over the longest possible period to thoroughly corroborate Sebold's assertions, control the activities of the principal subjects,
and determine the exact role of each conspirator. Ideally, a ring member's
first hint of FBI scrutiny would occur at the time of his or her arrest.

The initial concern was that the ring was larger than the four persons
identified by Sebold. Cautious and patient investigation of Stein, Roeder,
Lang, and Duquesne over a long period might reveal other important espionage connections in the government, the rapidly expanding war industries,
and the U.S. armed forces, and it might determine exactly what secrets these
German agents had already acquired. Hoping to avoid another Rumrich fiasco, Hoover insisted on absolute secrecy; knowledge of the case outside the
FBI was restricted to only a few key government officials. Within the Bureau
the same rule applied. FBI leadership placed the highest priority on the Ducase both at headquarters, where a special unit was established to manage
it, and in the New York City office, where a special squad was established to
handle the investigation.

Hoover's selection of the FBI agent to lead the investigation only reinforced the national importance of this case. Inspector Earl Connelley was
personally dispatched by Hoover from Washington, D.C., to New York to
assume overall management of the case. Connelley was a legend in the organization. Following army service during the First World War, this Cin-
cinnati, Ohio, native joined the original Bureau of Investigation in 1920,
four years before Hoover was appointed the acting director. A thin, wiry
man with a prickly personality, Connelley was a thorough, no-nonsense
investigator with a keen mind and a quiet, thoughtful approach to his work.
Over the years he rose through the ranks and eventually became a special
agent in charge in various FBI offices around the country. In the early 1930s
Hoover designated him the Bureau's first assistant director for field operations. Connelley traveled around the country, personally supervising many
of the FBI's most celebrated cases, including the Lindbergh kidnapping, the
Kansas City Massacre, the arrest of Karpis in Louisiana, the Weyerhauser
kidnapping case in the Pacific Northwest, the arrest of the Barker family in
Florida, and the arrest of members of the John Dillinger gang in 1934. Connelley would later supervise many sensitive espionage cases during the Second World War, the Smith Act trials of American Communist Party leaders
in 1947, the Alger Hiss perjury investigation, and the Brinks robbery in
Boston, Massachusetts.[11]

Sebold was central to the success of the case. By the middle of February 1940, he had told his complete story and, after some initial reluctance, agreed to act as a double agent against the Germans. In fact, he was the first double agent ever operated by the FBI. Sebold was the FBI's gateway into the operation; he was the only person who could paint a complete picture of the scope and size of German espionage in the United States and, in the end, bring it down like a house of cards. Special agent Richard Millen, assigned to the Laboratory Section of the Identification Division, was sent from Washington to question Sebold regarding the construction of the radio transmitter. During the interview, Millen also counted the money that Sebold had smuggled into the country taped to his back.[12]

Hoover took special care in selecting the special agent who would have day-to-day responsibility for Sebold. James C. Ellsworth was chosen for this delicate assignment. Born into a ranching family on the Idaho-Washington border in 1909, Ellsworth was raised in the Mormon Church, graduated from the University of Kansas and Kansas City Law School, and served as a missionary in France and Germany as part of his religious obligation. Language courses in college and two years of daily use in Germany made him fluent in German. Following a brief business career, he joined the FBI in 1935. A number of field assignments followed before his promotion to management and eventually the position of assistant special agent in charge of the Los Angeles field office. Investigative and management experience combined with German-language proficiency made Ellsworth ideally suited to work with Sebold.[13]

Ellsworth was conducting an interview in Laguna Beach, California, when he received a message from his boss, Richard Hood, informing him that Hoover wanted him in New York City for reasons not specified. Ellsworth left immediately, assuming that his testimony was needed at a trial involving a fraud case he had investigated while assigned to the Newark, New Jersey, office. As it turned out, Ellsworth remained in New York working the Ducase for the next two years.[14]

Because of their early suspicions about Sebold, the FBI was concerned about divulging Ellsworth's true identity to the new double agent. Sending bogus agents to a counterintelligence service was a well-known ploy used to determine how knowledgeable a counterintelligence service was about the activities of espionage operatives in a particular country. The bogus agent initially feeds the counterintelligence service information of significant value to build trust; later, the agent is able to pass false information without raising suspicions. The initial verifiable information makes the later false data more believable. In this way, an intelligence service could misdirect a security service by inserting elements of truth into fabricated information. At worst, the information derived from such sources could mislead national policy makers—a possibility that raised FBI suspicions about Sebold's true loyalties.[15]

Two special agents from the New York field office met Ellsworth upon his arrival in New York. With little explanation, they took away his FBI credentials and his personal documentation and provided him with false identification to use in his dealings with Sebold. After initial introductions, Sebold and Ellsworth began living together, constantly moving from place to place to avoid detection but generally residing in various New York City hotels. Hoover ordered both men placed under twenty-four-hour observation for their protection, as well as to determine whether Sebold was under observation by the Germans or was secretly contacting the Abwehr. Following weeks of checking and verification, Ellsworth finally established Sebold's honesty. Given his new full-time role as an FBI double agent, Sebold was reunited with his wife, and arrangements were made to pay him $50 a week.[16]

Within two months of his arrival in New York, Sebold contacted Duquesne, Stein, and Roeder according to the prearranged instructions, and he attempted to meet with Lang. After some initial skepticism, Duquesne accepted Sebold's story and agreed to work with him. It was only then that Duquesne acknowledged receiving "a letter from China" signaling Sebold's expected arrival. Duquesne encouraged Sebold to obtain a job at the Grumman Aircraft Corporation but warned him to avoid the German American community in New York. To divert suspicion, Sebold was urged to criticize Hitler and speak out against the Nazis at every opportunity. "Tramp," as he was code-named by the Abwehr, was warned that no mistakes would be tolerated, and the security of the ring made it essential that he protect his identity.[17]

The FBI then received another startling lesson in intelligence tradecraft when Duquesne acknowledged that he did not know any other ring members—nor did he want to know the identities of the other persons contacted by Sebold. Duquesne hinted at his value to the Germans, explaining that he owned a legitimate business that offered easy access to information about ship movements in and out of the port of New York. He described how his messages were sent to Germany through the mail using a sophisticated coding scheme to escape detection by the authorities. Sebold then told Duquesne that he was under orders to construct a radio transmitter to improve the timeliness of information moving between Germany and the U.S. network.[18]

During his first series of interviews with the FBI, Sebold explained that he had been given $500 to cover his travel expenses and to make some purchases when he arrived in the United States. The Abwehr had instructed him to buy a Leica camera to photograph documents, as well as the equipment needed for the construction of a portable transmitter and receiver. Transatlantic radio communications would allow vital, time-sensitive information to be sent quickly and securely to Germany, guaranteeing an uninterrupted flow of intelligence if diplomatic relations between the United States and Germany were broken. When the radio was ready for use, Sebold was to notify his Abwehr superiors by mail; they would then dispatch a courier to New York with the necessary broadcast frequencies.

Construction of a small, inexpensive shortwave radio capable of transmitting a strong signal across the Atlantic Ocean presented the FBI with one of its most complex counterintelligence challenges to date. Over the next three months, technically trained special agents from the FBI Laboratory Section feverishly began constructing a low-powered Morse code radio transmitter and receiver capable of reaching Hamburg, Germany. With so little money available, the challenge was to build a compact radio capable of spanning thousands of miles of ocean under all atmospheric conditions while not arousing the suspicions of ring members. After canvassing dozens of secondhand shops in New York City, FBI technicians found a sufficient quantity of cheap radio components. A tiny out-of-the-way bungalow overlooking a remote stretch of Long Island Sound in Centerport, New York, was selected as the radio site. Mindful that successful construction of a radio too quickly might arouse suspicions, plausible reasons for delay had to be provided to Abwehr officials, who were growing impatient. Shortly after his arrival, Sebold started receiving messages through couriers requesting military information, undoubtedly in anticipation of the invasion of France, which was only weeks away. In April 1940 he was ordered to supply the quantity and schedule of "delivery of planes to England . . . the construction of airplane carriers," and, most importantly, additional data regarding "the mobilization plans in the United States." Fearing the disruption of normal courier and mail communications, the Abwehr expressed concern about

Sebold's progress on the radio and pressured him to begin transmitting as early as May 15, 1940. By the beginning of May, the Centerport radio was ready for operation. A test, however, revealed a problem—the radio lacked sufficient power to send a signal to Europe. After some trial and error, a large antenna and a 500-watt amplifier were installed on the roof of the FBI offices in New York City, which captured the radio signal and boosted it to Hamburg without raising Abwehr suspicions.[19]

A unique feature of the art of radio deception is that the person transmitting the message can be identified by his or her style of tapping out a message—known among shortwave radio operators as "fisting." To a skilled operator who routinely receives transmissions, each sender's fisting style is as identifiable as a fingerprint. This presented a problem, because Sebold's Abwehr instructors were familiar with his impressive fisting style. Hearing a Morse code transmission tapped out with a different fist would signal to the Germans that Sebold was not the person sending the message, triggering suspicions that the FBI was controlling the case.[20]

The problem was solved when it was decided to assign an FBI agent to handle all communications at the Centerport site—after he perfected Sebold's fisting style. Both Connelley and Ellsworth still had some doubts about Sebold's motives and were worried that he might send unauthorized messages or even signal the Germans that he was under the FBI's control. More banal and practical reasons were also considered. As the scope of the case expanded, Sebold would be busy with other aspects of the investigation, such as meeting ring members, identifying new suspects, and meeting frequently with his FBI handlers. In addition, Connelley envisioned this case ending with the indictment and trial of ring members, and, as an experienced law enforcement officer, he knew that the Centerport radio operation would be the centerpiece of the prosecution's case. If Sebold sent the messages, he would be required to appear in court to provide complex testimony about shortwave radio transmissions, which might be difficult for a jury to comprehend. And if a nervous Sebold became flustered and confused under hostile cross-examination from a skilled defense attorney, his credibility with the jury might be undermined, doing serious damage to the government's case. Assigning an FBI agent to transmit the messages solved all these problems. An agent would be trained in the rules of evidence and experienced in giving trial testimony, making him an authoritative and compelling witness for the jury.[21]

Special agent Morris H. Price was selected as the FBI's Centerport communicator. Price was reassigned from the Milwaukee field office to New York in May 1940 to handle these duties for the duration of the case. A gifted investigator with years of practical experience, Price was also a skilled radio operator qualified to send and receive international Morse code. To help Price convince Abwehr technicians that he was Sebold, recordings were made of Sebold tapping out a lengthy series of practice messages; Price listened to those recordings for hours and repeatedly practiced his technique so that he could mimic Sebold's fisting style. Once Price was confident in his ability to impersonate Sebold, the Centerport station started broadcasting on the evening of May 19, 1940. After repeated test messages and hours of nervous waiting, the Centerport radio suddenly came alive with the German response. For the next sixteen months, until September 1941, Hamburg maintained a radio relationship with Price. The security of this communications link was of paramount importance to the Abwehr. In only its second message, sent on May 27, 1940, "Sebold" was cautioned to transmit only "two times per week" but be prepared to "receive and send daily." For his own safety, he was also told to transmit "at other times" using frequencies "outside the amateur band." By July, Sebold was instructed to confine his messages to "pure military and technical inquiries. However, listen to us daily."[22]

With Price's fist now accepted as Sebold's, the Centerport-Hamburg transatlantic radio link settled into a routine. Price would write the coded number groups received from "AOR," as the Hamburg station was known, on a piece of paper and turn them over to Ellsworth. He and Sebold would then decode the number groups using an Abwehr system based on the pages of the English novel entitled *All This and Heaven Too* by Rachel Young. Once decoded, the message was translated from German into English. For messages broadcast from Centerport, the process was reversed. Written messages were translated into German and then encoded into the number groups. Price then took the list of numbers and transmitted them to Hamburg. If a ring member offered a handwritten message to Sebold for transmission, he would insist that it be typed, supposedly to ensure accurate encoding. In fact, this procedure was used to guarantee the presence of latent fingerprints on the letter for future comparison with those of the letter writer, as well as to link the author's typewriter to the key markings on the letters.

As the months passed, insights emerged concerning the Abwehr's capacity to quickly alter its methods of communication with far-flung agents. Changing political environments often forced the ring to use mail drops in different countries. In late April 1940, for instance, Sebold received a letter from his superiors delivered by Erwin Siegler, the chief butcher aboard the SS *Manhattan*. Siegler was a courier for the Abwehr and, until then, had been unknown to the FBI. The letter responded to a message Sebold had sent the previous month. To ensure delivery, he had mailed copies of the letter through mail-drop addresses in China, Brazil, and Portugal. The German response pressed him for news on the progress of his shortwave radio project. Then, perhaps in anticipation of the German invasion of France, scheduled to begin two weeks later, the Abwehr advised him to change the mailing address of future letters to avoid the scrutiny of British censors. This took the guise of a casual letter: "Since I don't expect conditions to remain friendly, I shall try to leave Italy at the beginning of next month and if you want to write to me please write to Dr. Shmid-Gyula, Irany utca 25, Budapest, Hungary." A year later, he was ordered to discontinue using a mail drop in China because of the changed political conditions there.[23]

Twelve days after radio contact was established with Hamburg, the IIC began sending a steady flow of reports to the White House listing the Abwehr's intelligence demands. They expressed an urgent need for "monthly production of airplane factories. Export to all countries especially to England and France. Number, type, date of delivery. By steamer or air. Armature and armament. Payment cash and carry or credit." Observations and reports on the movements of the French ship *Normandie* and the "number of Allison [aircraft] motors made in series in Indianapolis [that] have been delivered up to now," as well as the number that "were manufactured in General Motors works before Autumn 1939," were also demanded.

During the life of the Centerport radio station, the vast majority of communications continued to focus on German intelligence requirements and administrative matters such as frequency changes, meeting times, and payments to agents. In August 1940 the Abwehr inquired about the status of the aircraft carrier *Saratoga*, which it suspected was ferrying planes to Halifax, Nova Scotia, for shipment to England. A month later it wanted the "newest data concerning hydraulic fuel pumps," as well as information concerning the United States' "newest bombsight," as reported in an article that appeared in the *New York Herald Tribune* on June 16, 1940. Typical of the confusion arising out of this type of communication was Sebold's reply days later that no such article about new bombsights had appeared in the newspaper.[24]

Industrial information and manufacturing data were also a high priority. For example, in November 1940 the Germans asked about the number of workers and the type of products manufactured at the Fairchild Aircraft Corporation in Jamaica, New York. Similar inquiries were posed about the Grumman Aircraft Corporation in Bethpage, New York. Questions included "orders for sky rockets? How many? From whom? What deliveries to England? Armament. Details and deliveries of Gruman Fighter F Four F. Republican Aircr. Farmingdale. How many planes ordered by Sweden. How many of this order goes to England?" As late as June 1941, shortly before the ring was arrested, the Germans were still telling Sebold that they urgently needed aircraft information. Even after the arrests, Centerport received demands for updated reports on the "condition of the American airforce industry, detailed accounts about falling off of production in various factories (including machine tool factories) through strike agitation."[25]

The regularity and reliability of Sebold's reporting steadily solidified German confidence in his performance. This resulted in more important assignments of value to the FBI. Leads to other spies, unavailable to Hoover's investigators through any other means, suddenly surfaced. In November 1940 Sebold was ordered to have Duquesne recruit "Baroness Renee Bucovich." The message described her as "divorced from Von Friesen now married to Italian of Jugoslavian birth, care of Miss Harcourt, British, Fifty-seventh and First Avenue East." Also on the list were "Baron Von Esenhardt, former German air officer, and Paul Kreutzenstein, German Brazilian, known sportsman. Latter two in New York telephone book. Expect early report." Another Hamburg message suggested that someone in the ring had attempted to approach Edward Von Gontard, described as a vice president of the Anheuser Busch Company and "very pro-German."[26]

Compelling evidence of Sebold's importance to the Germans surfaced in late 1940 when Centerport received an urgent message requesting assistance for another German shortwave operation in Mexico. Hamburg was having difficulty receiving the station's signal due to the inadequate power of the transmitter, the long distances involved, and frequent signal disruptions caused by unpredictable atmospheric changes. Connelley and Ellsworth, seeing an opportunity to identify additional German espionage networks in South and Central America, radioed their agreement to help. Couriers delivered the necessary frequencies and transmission times to Sebold. On

January 1, 1941, Price received his first message from the Mexican station, using the call letters "GBO," for relay to Hamburg. The Abwehr's egregious security failure proved to be a counterintelligence bonanza. Within days of GBO's first transmission, Connelley ordered special agent Saylor Irwin to travel to Mexico and locate the German radio site. Irwin, a former navy radio technician, visited Centerport for a few days to familiarize himself with the fisting characteristics of the German communicator in Mexico. With FBI-supplied radio direction-finding equipment hidden in a backpack, Irwin traveled to the Southwest and quietly slipped across the Mexican border. Over a period of weeks, he patiently took radio bearings until he located the transmitter in Veracruz, Mexico.[27]

Without the necessary codes, however, the FBI could not decipher the messages concealed in the series of random number groups that Price was relaying back and forth between Germany and Mexico. With time, however, the growing volume of transmissions helped FBI cryptanalysts peel away the code, exposing the clear text messages. German agent networks and objectives in Mexico and South America, as well as insights into intelligence activities in these regions, were soon laid bare. FBI investigators in Mexico identified the radio operator as Carlos Retelsdorf, an agent assigned to a German espionage network led by George Nicolaus. Nicolaus, a German, had entered Mexico in March 1940 after his expulsion from Colombia for "directing German espionage activities in that country." Using the code name "Max," he took over the leadership of the Sicherheitsdienst's political section, directing a collection of German espionage agents throughout Mexico and Latin America.[28]

Through radio contact with Hamburg, the FBI learned that a person named Paul Fehse, a German immigrant and U.S. citizen residing in New York City, was serving as head of the "Marine Division of the German espionage system in the United States." Investigation of Fehse proved to be a windfall for FBI investigators. Fehse arranged meetings between Sebold and other unknown agents, directed ring activities, correlated information, and ensured that material was relayed to Sebold for transmittal to Germany through the Centerport station. Fehse introduced Sebold to Carl Reuper, a naturalized American citizen who had emigrated from Germany in 1929. Reuper had worked for a number of electronics corporations and was currently an inspector for the Westinghouse Electric Corporation in New Jersey, where he had access to sensitive photographs, plans, and technical diagrams for a wide variety of state-of-the-art inventions with military applications. Probably for reasons of security, Reuper and Fehse decided not to use Sebold's communication link to Germany. Surveillance, however, soon tied Reuper to Felix Jahnke, Axel Wheeler-Hill, and Joseph Klein. All three were American citizens who had arrived in the United States in the 1920s. Jahnke and Klein came from Germany, and Wheeler-Hill had been born in czarist Russia. Ever fixated on the security of its networks, the Abwehr had ordered Jahnke and Wheeler-Hill to recruit Klein, a radio technician. Like Sebold, he was instructed to build a shortwave radio capable of sending and receiving signals between the United States, South America, and Germany. With Hoover's agents watching closely, Klein built the radio and installed it in Wheeler-Hill's Bronx, New York, apartment. Until the arrest of the entire group in June 1941, Jahnke operated the radio and the FBI intercepted its signal, broke the code, and exploited the contents of messages transmitted and received. Gleaned from this traffic was critical defense-related information supplied by Reuper that later served as evidence against him at his espionage trial.[29]

Something not anticipated by Connelley was the need to continually demonstrate that Sebold was not under FBI control. It called for a delicate balance between boosting Sebold's credibility by transmitting high-quality information, which could place American and British lives in danger, and denying the Abwehr other valuable information. The IIC had to weigh the risks and benefits of giving up important scientific and military data to German planners versus the chance of compromising the case. This concern applied not only to American secrets but to British secrets as well. In May 1941 an overworked Sebold was asked for "all reports that could be of interest with respect to aviation," as well as the latest data concerning "Canadian aviation, number and model of front line airplanes: how many, the number and locations of squadrons." He was then instructed to ascertain the "aviation training plan now in progress in Canada," including the "type, location, and capacity of the individual schools" and "their number."[30]

Often there was no way to avoid giving the Germans valuable information that was potentially harmful to the United States' military buildup. In some cases, however, decisions were made not to pass on certain information because of its extreme sensitivity or to alter the text of the transmissions by eliminating certain parts. Less than a month after the start of the German advance into Holland and France, for example, Sebold received a letter from Duquesne requesting him to tell Hamburg that the "U.S. has 303 war ships 2665 planes and an army of 227,000." Startled by the accuracy of this information, the IIC voted not to send it. In July 1940 Duquesne dictated the following message to Sebold and ordered him to transmit it as soon as possible:

> The *Cambria* and *Seinilia* brought over children and unlisted passengers of British Commission to the U.S.A. Rothschilds are staying as guests of Morgans. Confidential report to the White House that America will be able to produce 12,000 planes a year. Two 14-inch guns removed from Sandy Hook to San Francisco and from there to the Philippines Islands.

Available records indicate only that a portion of this message was sent on July 15, 1940.[31]

Duquesne was a pivotal member of the espionage ring. Unlike Fehse, whose job required him to be at a specific place on a daily basis, Duquesne's lengthy absences did not attract attention. On a monthly basis he sent a wide variety of U.S. Army reports on new weapons and military technologies, including the specifications for a silencer attachment for a pistol, airplane wing designs, a gas mask containing a mustard gas neutralizer, and an experimental device to help direct a plane toward its target. Other items included material used in manufacturing life jackets, a Chemical Warfare Service field manual, and a copy of a U.S. patent entitled "methods and means for reproducing infra-red images."[32]

Duquesne supplied Sebold with copies of publicly available technical magazines such as *Aero Digest, Canadian Aviation,* and *Aviation* so that he could microphotograph key pages containing articles of importance and send them to Germany through couriers. As an energetic spy committed to acquiring as much information as possible, Duquesne often criticized Abwehr's timidity, complaining on one occasion that he could not travel to Georgia to observe army maneuvers scheduled for the summer of 1940 because of a shortage of funds. Despite these frustrations, his collection record was impressive, as illustrated by a portion of a message Duquesne sent at the end of May 1940 through the Centerport station:

> Rolls Royce have engine designed to go in the wings flat like meat in a sandwich. Lycoming have one also. I sent blueprints by China. Allies ordered additional 10,000 machine guns, motorcycles, side cars. U.S. Intelligence getting news through Myron Taylor in Vatican. Priest working for Catholic information. Canadians adopted hand-thrown shell which I wrote of. Going into immediate production.

He then told the Abwehr:

> SS *Champlain* taking munition cargo in day or two. She is large passenger cargo liner armed anti-submarine anti-aircraft. May carry members of French Purchasing Commission. Sails in two days. Will be picked up by convoy off Bermuda. She is going to Cherbourg. Did you receive Army Mask and mustard gas canister on the *Conte Savoia* and the *Rex*?[33]

Sebold frequently ascertained future espionage plans in conversations with the indiscreet Duquesne. Targeted for theft were the schematics for the U.S. Army's new Garand rifle, a new telescopic gun sight, and steel plate from foundries in Pennsylvania. The steel, manufactured for a variety of military purposes, including weapons and ship hulls, would be sent to Germany for metallurgical examination. The two men met sixteen times during the sixteen-month life of the case and frequently corresponded by letter to reduce the risk of accidental discovery. The letters, however, routinely contained valuable secrets for passage to Germany, such as U.S. patent information for a bombsight, airplanes, and photographic technologies, and blueprints and schematics reduced to microphotograph size and given to couriers crossing the Atlantic Ocean.

Of the three persons initially identified by Sebold when he arrived in New York, Lilly Stein seemed least likely to be a German spy. Living quietly in a ground-floor apartment on East 54th Street in Manhattan and operating a women's apparel shop, Lilly Barbara Carola Stein was an attractive Austrian native and a former artist's model. However, she had been trained in Hamburg at the same intelligence school where Sebold studied, and she arrived in New York in early 1939 to assume her espionage duties. An earlier romantic relationship with Ogden Hammond Jr., vice-consul in Vienna and son of the U.S. ambassador to Spain, may have been the original impetus for the Abwehr's interest in her. Despite her ordinary and rather prosaic lifestyle, FBI investigation of her daily activities quickly revealed some important information about her. Analysis of her mail showed regular payments from Dutch and South American banks, and her apartment mailbox served as a mail drop for the network. She often met Duquesne and passed money to him. Another intriguing fact was her friendship with Else Weustenfeld, an employee of Topken and Farley—the law firm that represented the German consulate in New York City. Weustenfeld immigrated to the United States from Europe in 1927 and became a U.S. citizen ten years later. She first came to the FBI's attention in April 1940 when a still suspicious Everett

Roeder told Sebold that he would send a letter concerning their meeting to Germany through a woman named "Else" who worked for the law firm representing the German consulate. Closer examination of her background revealed that she had once lived with Hans Ritter, the brother of senior Abwehr officer Nicolaus Ritter, who formed the original Duquesne ring. As an employee of Topken and Farley, Weustenfeld secretly distributed money received by the consulate for German agents in the United States. Her role in this espionage network convinced the Roosevelt administration that diplomatically protected Germans assigned to embassies and consulates were engaging in espionage in the United States.[34]

By midsummer 1940, ring members were becoming more comfortable with Sebold and also became more forthcoming with their secrets. On Sebold's second visit to Stein's apartment in June 1940 she handed him a letter dated June 5, 1940, postmarked "Detroit, Michigan," containing the typewritten signature "Heinrich." Between June and August 15, 1940, she gave him thirteen "Heinrich" letters for passage to Hamburg through couriers. For reasons that are still unclear, Hamburg ordered Sebold to discontinue his contact with Stein after that date.

Unfortunately for the Abwehr, the break between Sebold and Stein came too late. FBI examination of the letters identified "Heinrich" as Edmund C. Heine. Born in 1891 in the village of Zeulen Roda, in Germany, Heine attended eight years of public school and three years of commercial training before entering the German army. After an accident shortened his military career, he entered the hardware business and later became a traveling salesman. Heine arrived in the United States in 1914 and became a citizen in March 1920. In 1918 he began working for the Ford Motor Company, traveling throughout South America and Europe representing the company's tractor division. He was named assistant manager in Spain in 1923, and two years later he was promoted to manager of Ford operations in Germany and transferred to Berlin. For the next nine years he was responsible for hiring and firing, financing, and vehicle sales, as well as the construction of a manufacturing plant for a new German shareholding company called Ford Motor Company A.G. He later claimed that he resigned in 1935 rather than submit to company demands that he renounce his U.S. citizenship and become a German national. After leaving Ford, Heine took a sales position with the Chrysler Corporation in Spain but was forced to flee the country with his family when the Spanish civil war broke out. Unemployed, with no job prospects, Heine returned to Germany and settled in a small town near the Bavarian Alps.[35]

Heine arrived in the United States on May 13, 1940, aboard the SS *Manhattan*. Why he returned to the United States is unclear. At first, he claimed that the outbreak of war in Europe forced his return. In later interviews, he accused U.S. consulate officials in Munich of forcing him to return to the States or risk losing his citizenship. Recruited by the Abwehr in Germany, Heine purchased a small company in Detroit to use as a base in his pursuit of aviation information for the Germans. He was completely ill suited for this assignment. He had no aviation experience or training, and his company did no legitimate business. He was forced to study aviation magazines and hire an aeronautical engineer to provide him with a basic education in aviation so that he could even marginally fulfill Abwehr requirements. Heine was understandably vague in his statement to the FBI concerning his recruitment by the Abwehr. He said that after returning to Germany in 1936, he contracted his services to companies trying to settle affairs with U.S. businesses. While working for the Volks Wagen Verke, he had been introduced to a "Dr. Wirtz who asked me whether I would not keep my eyes open and inform him through certain mailing addresses made available to me about the aviation development in general." Wirtz gave him a list of twenty-five categories to monitor and a number of mailing addresses where he was to send the information. Heine memorized everything and destroyed the list while on the voyage to the United States. Heine rationalized his espionage by explaining that this "not very important personage [Dr. Wirtz] still belongs to the group Volks Wagen Verke or some group associated with this enterprise, and . . . he was interested enough in aviation development to request of me anything that might be of interest."[36]

The Japanese Connection

The Centerport station had been in operation for less than five months when an unexpected message was received that would add a new dimension to Hoover's counterintelligence education. Sebold was ordered on October 19, 1940, to instruct Roeder to visit the "Nippon Club at one six one West Ninety-third Street" and give a letter to "Mr. E. Satoz" containing irrelevant information and with the written salutation "Will." Upon handing him the letter, Roeder was to utter the phrase "Kind regards from the Steamer." Roeder followed the instructions. Later, he reported to Sebold that he had passed the letter to an elderly Japanese man, who had questioned him about the fictitious information but offered no further comment. Sebold reported these events to Hamburg and awaited further instructions.

Seven months later Sebold received another message concerning this matter. On May 18, 1941, the Abwehr ordered Roeder to meet Satoz at a different restaurant. On the night and time designated by Hamburg, both Sebold and Roeder visited the restaurant and asked for Satoz. A moment later a Japanese man appeared and identified himself as "Mr. Kato." After introducing himself with the prearranged code name "Steamer," Sebold produced one of his own business cards with the phrase "Sato from Steamer" written on the reverse side. After a few minutes of idle conversation, Kato invited Roeder and Sebold to another location where they could continue their conversation privately and without interruption. They took a taxi to a private house in Lower Manhattan, where a young Japanese woman greeted them at the door. Sebold later described her as an American because she "spoke fluent English with a New York accent." A few minutes later, in a private room, Kato identified himself as "Mr. Ezima" and gave Sebold his telephone number. Ezima then insisted that all future meetings with Sebold take place at this residence. Some fast talking by Sebold convinced Ezima that meetings in Sebold's business office in Midtown Manhattan would be far more secure, and much easier to explain. Sebold and Roeder supplied Ezima with the information they had brought and then departed. Before leaving, Sebold and Roeder were informed that it would take a month for the material to reach Germany.[37]

Mr. Kato and Mr. Ezima were soon identified as the same person—Takeo Ezima. Born in Japan in 1904, he had entered the United States in August 1938 and was employed in the "engineer inspecting business at New York, and other places in the United States." Records of the Bureau of Immigration revealed that Ezima was a lieutenant commander in the service of the Imperial Japanese Navy and that he had limited diplomatic immunity. The identification of a Japanese navy officer participating in the German espionage ring was a watershed event for U.S. counterintelligence. It provided the Roosevelt administration with concrete evidence of the close collaboration between the Abwehr and Japanese intelligence in their efforts to steal U.S. military secrets. Ezima's exposure led to extensive surveillance of his activities to determine what steps he took to pass the Sebold information on to Germany. Surveillance and telephone eavesdropping led investigators to meetings between Ezima and Kanegoro Koike, an official assigned to the Japanese consulate in New York City and "paymaster of the Imperial Japanese Navy."[38]

Gathering Evidence

Another unique feature of the Ducase was the use of hidden cameras to record meetings between Sebold and other ring members. The rare opportunity to use photography in this fashion presented itself in late October 1940, when Abwehr officials ordered Sebold to establish "a large deposit with a New York bank." Evidently interested in arranging a faster and more secure payment process for their agents, they asked him for his suggestions.[39] Ellsworth and Connelley realized that if Sebold were responsible for the network's funds, he could, in effect, control the entire ring. By monitoring a single bank account, investigators could follow the disbursement of funds to known and as yet unknown ring members. They knew, however, that surveillance was a risky undertaking. Lengthy surveillance of a naturally suspicious money courier could lead to discovery, which could corrupt the case and prompt the Abwehr to halt the entire operation. This was not an idle fear. Less than a month after the operation had started, Connelley got his first scare when Sebold received a cryptic letter from Duquesne, who suspected that he was being followed and warned that the ring might have been compromised.[40]

Uppermost in Connelley's mind, however, was that concentrated, secure surveillance offered an opportunity to strengthen the case against the espionage ring. Until now, all meetings between Sebold and the others had taken place on the street or in out-of-the-way restaurants. Duquesne and the other conspirators went to great lengths to avoid eavesdropping on their conversations. They were always conducted in secret, with no one else present. Even if they were observed by the FBI, no one could testify about what had been said except the participants. This could become a crucial issue at any future trial. In addition, although Sebold had volunteered to assist the FBI, how could they prove that it was actually the German intelligence service sending and receiving shortwave signals back and forth across the Atlantic Ocean? Defense attorneys would question Sebold's motives. They would suggest that he was working with the FBI because he had been caught spying and was trying to avoid punishment. Or they could claim that he suffered from mental instability and had fabricated the whole story. Or he could be accused of concocting a fantastic hoax simply to remain on the FBI's payroll, casting the government as dupes. They would question why thirty-three average persons, most of them American citizens with no record of disloyalty, would betray the United States. In the end, however, they would charge that there was no way to corroborate Sebold's claims that this odd assortment of people had passed him damaging national defense information. It would be his word against their clients'.

Hoover and Connelley had no doubt about their course of action. Seizing the initiative, Sebold and Ellsworth sent a message with significant implications for the Abwehr and the FBI. They radioed, "I have good connections in Diesel Line. I recommend opening a small research office as licenced businessman a suitable space present no difficulties. As research offices continually need money you can send me a large amount." They added that this large sum could then be withdrawn and deposited "in smaller sums in various banks making any size of payments to agents easier" and "without suspicion." Three days later Hamburg signaled Centerport that "we are in agreement open office immediately advise when and where you want remittance sent and the highest amount possible for you to handle without suspicion."[41]

So, with the Abwehr's blessing, Connelley and his staff secretly established the Diesel Research Corporation in early December 1940. Sebold opened the firm's business account at Chase National Bank in New York City. Arrangements were made through Vincent Astor to locate the business on the sixth floor of the Newsweek building at 152 West 42nd Street. To enhance the FBI's technical coverage, Sebold's offices, occupying rooms 627 and 628, were brightly painted and equipped with special lighting to facilitate high-quality still and moving pictures that would secretly document Sebold's meetings with ring members. The office was also equipped with hidden microphones. The conversations were recorded next door, in room 629, and transcripts were made. Each meeting was also observed by special agents William G. Friedman and John G. Fellner. Both men were fluent in German and took contemporaneous notes of the conversations for later use at trial.

Once everything was in place, Sebold encouraged his coconspirators to meet at his new office, claiming that it reduced the risk of being seen together in public. By the spring of 1941, dozens of meetings had taken place at the Manhattan office, and evidence against the ring members was piling up. Money regularly arrived in the Diesel Research Corporation's bank account, usually in amounts of $5,000 from banks in Mexico. As the funds accrued, Sebold received instructions from Hamburg to begin distribution. With Sebold now serving as both paymaster and chief communicator with Hamburg, ring members began visiting his office to turn over their information and receive financial reimbursement. Payments were usually made in amounts ranging from $300 to $500. At the same time, lengthy conversations between Sebold and the ring members were recorded in complete detail. Although such recordings were still barred from being used as evidence in federal courts (under the *Nardone* ruling), they documented the history of the network's operation in the United States and provided a clear picture of German espionage activities. Hoover's investigators carefully analyzed the tapes and coached Sebold on what questions to raise at future meetings.

If the records of U.S. attorney Harold M. Kennedy, who later prosecuted the case, are any indication, the Diesel Research Corporation was an unqualified success in cementing the case against the ring. Eighty-one meetings were recorded on still and moving pictures and by live monitoring between December 10, 1940, and June 25, 1941—the equivalent of one meeting every two days. As an example of the importance of the Diesel Research operation, at Duquesne's trial, Sebold testified that he and Duquesne had met at his office, where the suspicious Duquesne had given Sebold stolen documents in exchange for $500. Duquesne's attorneys challenged Sebold's account, denying that such a meeting ever took place. Kennedy called special agent Friedman to the stand, and his testimony included a moving picture that documented the meeting between the two men, leaving Duquesne's credibility with the jury in shambles.[42]

Some of the questions raised by Sebold's conversations with ring members could not be resolved by further inquiries and had to be investigated. This was particularly true of the role of conspirators residing in Europe, Mexico, Latin America, and Asia. As more names and addresses outside U.S. borders began to surface, Hoover launched efforts to identify them. Without informing the political leadership of the countries involved, but with IIC concurrence, special agents were sent abroad to conduct these investigations. Within months, discreet inquiries were under way in Havana, Shanghai, Sao Paolo, Rio de Janeiro, and Lima. These were dangerous undertakings for investigators and a potential political embarrassment for the Roosevelt administration if the FBI presence in these countries was discovered. Yet despite these uncertainties, the information uncovered significantly broadened the FBI's understanding of the skill, tenacity, and techniques of the German intelligence services.

Endgame

In the spring of 1941, Fehse began complaining to Sebold about the pressures of his life as a spy. Adding to his anxiety was the arrest of Rene Mezenen, a courier who served as a steward aboard the Pan-Am Clipper flying between New York and Portugal. On April 5, 1941, Mezenen was arrested at LaGuardia Airport while boarding a flight for Lisbon. He was charged with violating the recently passed Act to Expedite the Strengthening of the National Defense when he was discovered carrying 158 ounces of "pure platinum," a rare mineral used in the manufacture of specialized machine tools. Days later, Mezenen quietly pleaded guilty and was sentenced to a federal prison term. The unhappy Fehse asked Sebold to obtain Hamburg's permission for him to return to Germany to visit his family. Fehse was authorized to travel to Lisbon, where arrangements would be made for his passage into Germany. However, Hoover was adamant about not allowing such an important espionage figure to get away. Ever mindful of his agency's stumble three years earlier in the Rumrich case, Hoover would not countenance a second public humiliation of himself or the FBI.[43]

By March 1941, enough evidence had been developed against Fehse to arrest him on espionage charges. To do so, however, would alert the rest of ring, causing them to flee before the FBI and prosecutors were ready to conclude the case. Even worse would be the exposure of Sebold as a government source. Fortunately, it had been determined that Fehse's involvement in espionage had begun years before the Ducase investigation. Fehse had been sending letters to his German superiors containing the identities, cargoes, and destinations of ships departing from New York City. One of his letters had ended up in the post office's "dead-letter office" for lack of adequate postage. Years later, close scrutiny of outgoing and incoming international mail, including undelivered mail, became a routine feature of FBI counterintelligence activities, and Fehse's incriminating letter was discovered. At first it could not be linked to him because it contained no identifying notations. Later, when Fehse began corresponding with Sebold, the handwriting on the letters was matched. Moving quickly, federal prosecutors in New

York indicted Fehse for violating the Foreign Agents Registration Act, and before his ship could depart, he was arrested by the FBI. On April 1, 1941, he pleaded guilty to the charge and was sentenced to a year in federal prison. Shock and panic undoubtedly gripped ring members, but on the surface, there was no connection between his arrest and their activities. With no immediate fallout on the rest of the group, Fehse's arrest was attributed to his own carelessness years earlier, which allayed some of their anxiety.[44]

The ring members' worries continued to grow, however, during the spring of 1941 as the Roosevelt administration steadily increased political and economic pressures on Germany and Italy. In April the Treasury Department ordered the Coast Guard to prevent the departure of thirty Axis ships berthed in U.S. ports, instructing that they be placed in "protective custody." The 850 German and Italian crewmen were arrested and charged with suspicion of sabotaging the vessels and the cargoes. When the German embassy formally protested the action, the Roosevelt administration responded by seizing these ships, along with another thirty-nine that belonged to Germany, Italy, and Denmark. A second shock came on May 16, 1941, when Congress authorized the president to transfer any ships lying idle in U.S. ports to Great Britain. At the same time, the Department of State declared Admiral Alberto Lais, the Italian naval attaché in Washington, persona non grata and ordered his expulsion from the United States for his involvement in these sabotage efforts.[45]

As the Duquesne group stood by helplessly, wondering about their own fate, an Amtorg Trading Corporation official named Gaik Ovakimian was arrested. Amtorg had been incorporated in the United States in the 1920s to serve the business needs of the new Marxist government of the Soviet Union and any U.S. companies wanting to do business with Moscow. Headquartered in New York City, it also served as a principal base for NKVD and GRU industrial espionage. In 1933 Ovakimian—a short, stocky, dark-skinned Armenian—arrived in the United States and assumed the duties of an obscure Amtorg official. In fact, this thirty-five-year-old engineer was the NKVD's key intelligence officer in North America, specializing in industrial espionage. According to an FBI report prepared in 1942, Ovakimian received a "scholarship" from the Soviet government to serve as a research fellow at the Rockefeller Institute in New York from January 1937 to January 1940. His duties as a chemical researcher offered him direct access to many of the United States' leading scientific theoreticians and industrial technologies. His skills as an intelligence officer and his tireless efforts were handsomely rewarded in 1938 with his recruitment of Julius and Ethel Rosenberg as Soviet spies. Another indicator of Ovakimian's importance to Moscow was his assignment in 1939 to assist Ramon Mercader, the young Spanish Communist who later murdered Leon Trotsky at his fortified compound in Mexico.[46]

In mid-April 1941 Hoover learned that, after eight years at Amtorg, Ovakimian was making arrangements to return to the Soviet Union with his wife and daughter. Within days, federal warrants were authorized charging him with violating the Foreign Agents Registration Act, and on May 5, 1941, he was arrested. The Soviet government's claim of diplomatic immunity for Ovakimian was denied, but he was released on $25,000 bail and placed in the custody of Victor Feduishine, the Soviet consul general in New York. Two months later, while Ovakimian was awaiting trial in New York City, German forces invaded the Soviet Union. To Hoover's great frustration, the State Department pressured the Department of Justice into dropping the charges against Ovakimian as a gesture of friendship to the Soviet government. He and his family departed the United States for the Soviet Union on July 23, 1941.[47]

The passage of German espionage messages to Hamburg had already been hampered by the seizure of Axis ships in U.S. ports. The president dealt the German spies another blow on June 14, 1941, with an executive order freezing all Axis financial assets in the United States and closing all Axis consulates. Suddenly the ring was cut off from its source of funds, and panicky ring members began making hasty arrangements to return to Germany. As a result, the Department of Justice decided to end the Ducase and make arrests at the end of the month.

Meanwhile, on the morning of June 10, 1941, Sebold received an unexpected visit from Franz Stigler and Erwin Siegler, seamen who acted as couriers for the network. They warned Sebold that the Abwehr believed that the United States was drawing close to war with Germany, and both men were worried about being stranded in the United States if hostilities began. Sebold learned that they had signed on as crew members of ships scheduled to sail from New York that very day. One would depart at four that afternoon, and the other at midnight. Both men planned to jump ship in Portugal and return to Germany. Sebold's information was immediately passed to Francis Biddle, who was serving as acting attorney general in the absence of Robert Jackson. Even though the government's arrest and prosecution preparations were incomplete, Biddle authorized the immediate arrest of Siegler and Stigler, who were taken into custody as they boarded their ships that afternoon.[48]

Although the arrest authorization had come from the highest level of government, the actual charges against the men posed a problem. The U.S. attorney for New York had not finished drafting the complex espionage indictments against Stigler, Siegler, and the other conspirators. Prematurely arresting them for espionage could compromise the prosecution of the entire ring and would certainly open the case to public exposure. To keep the two seamen in the country without jeopardizing the espionage case, the Department of Justice charged them with attempting to leave the United States without notifying their draft boards. Then, in a move whose legality was questionable at best, both were isolated in a cell in the New York field office of the FBI for ten days without appearing before a federal magistrate to hear the charges against them. This shaky legal subterfuge provided the U.S. attorney and the FBI with the necessary time to finalize plans for the arrest of the entire ring two weeks later. After returning to Washington, Jackson was briefed on Biddle's actions, and the attorney general expressed his misgivings about the government's behavior and the legality of the peculiar arrangements in a memorandum to President Roosevelt. In it he noted that "Biddle never informed me about his decision until after the arrests were made. I think I would have been more courtish."[49]

As Siegler and Stigler sat in an FBI jail cell, Undersecretary of State Sumner Welles announced that German diplomatic establishments in the United States had engaged in activities "of an improper and unwarranted character." Such behavior, he warned, was "inimical to the welfare of [the United States]" and would not be tolerated. Within days all twenty-four German consulates around the country were closed, as well as the German Library of Information, the German Railroad Information Office, and the Transocean News Service.[50]

Over the next two weeks, feverish efforts were made to craft proper indictments and secure a federal judge's signature on the thirty-three arrest warrants. Once the paperwork was finished, a team of ninety-four FBI agents led by Connelley began arresting ring members on the evening of June 29, 1941. By the next day, nineteen were in custody in New York City, four in New Jersey, and another six in various parts of the country. Over the next few days, the last four were arrested. The fact that Sebold was not among them raised no immediate suspicions. Ironically, Hamburg was pleased that U.S. counterintelligence had not discovered his activities and continued to communicate with the Centerport station for another two months. Only when Sebold began testifying in court against the Duquesne conspirators did the Abwehr realize that he had been working against them from the beginning.[51]

A primary goal of counterintelligence is to disrupt the activities of the opposition's service. The Sebold double-agent operation clearly achieved that objective. Between September and December 1941, the trials of the principal ring members were trumpeted daily in the leading newspapers. Americans, like the Abwehr, were introduced to the new photographic techniques employed by the FBI to capture the discussions in Sebold's office. Detailed testimony from Ellsworth and Price about the arcane role of the Centerport station, together with other equally damaging evidence, caused some of the conspirators to give up any hope of a successful defense. A number of them simply pleaded guilty in the hope of receiving a lighter sentence.

The centerpiece of the trials was William G. Sebold. In a simple and straightforward manner, he told his compelling story to the world from the witness stand in a federal courtroom in Brooklyn, New York. He described his forced recruitment by the Abwehr while visiting Germany in 1939 and the dire consequences for him and his family if he refused to cooperate. Under careful questioning by the prosecutor, Sebold corroborated the trial testimony of Ellsworth, Price, and dozens of other FBI agents and witnesses. Despite withering cross-examination, Sebold held his ground, kept his poise, never wavered, and walked off the witness stand with his story solidly intact.

German Reaction

The Nazi leadership in Germany was dumbfounded. For years the Abwehr and the German Foreign Ministry had worked at cross-purposes concerning the collection of foreign intelligence against the United States. Joachim von Ribbentrop, Hitler's foreign minister, deemed it essential that the United States remain neutral and keep out of the British and French orbit. Toward this end, he pursued a vigorous effort of underwriting and otherwise financially supporting American groups opposed to foreign intervention. Wishing to do nothing to provoke a confrontation with the United States, he had extracted a promise from Abwehr chief Wilhelm Canaris in April 1940 that his organization was engaged in no espionage in the United States and had no agents there. For his part, Canaris fundamentally disagreed with Ribbentrop. He spoke fluent English and, during his early years in the German navy, had met many Americans. Having served in the Western Hemisphere, he understood the U.S. war-making potential and had a healthy respect for it. Furthermore, Canaris appreciated the United States' huge industrial capacity and firmly believed that Americans would not stand idly by and watch war from the sidelines. As head of the Abwehr, he was aligned with no particular German service but was responsible for meeting the intelligence needs of all three arms of the German military establishment.[52]

In May 1940 Hans Thomsen, the German ambassador to the United States, explained to Berlin that his chief task was to "prevent by all means at my disposal the entry of the United States into the war and to cultivate the few valuable contacts we still have here." He also complained that his efforts were being "sabotaged by the activities of agents of the Wehrmacht." In his view, these spying activities were "the surest way of bringing America into action on the side of our enemies and of destroying the last vestiges of sympathy for Germany."[53]

With such opposing bureaucratic views, the recriminations and finger-pointing over this espionage catastrophe were swift and inevitable. Thomsen questioned the competence and professionalism of Canaris and his intelligence staff while warning of the effect that this calamity would have on German-American relations. In a sharply worded telegram to Ribbentrop, he warned that "various counterintelligence agencies have trained totally unqualified persons, and then sent them over here on missions." Those operations, according to the ambassador, were characterized by "naivete and irresponsible carelessness," lacked "any kind of coordination" with his staff, and conveyed the impression that the agencies involved were in competition with one another. "These poorly organized operations by irresponsible and incompetent agents," he noted, "may cost us the last remnants of sympathy which we can still muster here in circles, where political opposition is of interest to us."[54]

Six days later, from his special train in Rastenburg, East Prussia, where Hitler was directing the invasion of the Soviet Union, Ribbentrop demanded explanations from the Abwehr and the Sicherheitsdienst. Two months later, in a memorandum entitled "Germans Arrested in the U.S.A. under Suspicion of Espionage," he received his answer. Ernst Eisen Lohr, the minister attached to the office of Ambassador Karl Ritter, reported that the delay in responding to the foreign minister's order was due in large part to the Ober Kommando der Wehrmacht (high command of the German army), which objected "to the criticism of the Abwehr in the U.S.A. made by Thomsen." He went on to note:

> Of the 17 people arrested whose names became known from reports of the Embassy in Washington and also from press reports four worked for the Abwehr. Only one of those arrested is known to the SD [Sicherheitsdienst] and that person did not have instructions nor did he submit reports on his own. The substantive work of the four who had been active on the instructions of the Abwehr has produced militarily valuable results and cannot be criticized.[55]

With the conviction of the last Duquesne ring member in December 1941, the hero of this story, William Sebold, was secretly moved by the FBI to the San Francisco area for his own protection. There, employment was arranged for him in the burgeoning wartime aircraft industry. He and his wife, Marie, slipped into anonymity, carving out a new life as faceless California suburbanites. They were never heard from again.

The startling success of the Duquesne case solidified the FBI's role at the center of U.S. counterintelligence and gave birth to the popular cultural belief that the Bureau was the nation's first line of defense against foreign and domestic espionage. It launched the popular myth of Hoover as the guardian of the "American way of life." His warnings to the American public in support of the war effort and the need for vigilance carried a moral force that few other prominent Americans could muster. Five years later, with the new worldwide threat from the Soviet Union, Hoover became a leading anticommunist icon and, years later, a lightning rod for critics condemning cold war excesses.

Aside from the impact of the case on its two principal protagonists, it also had important short-term consequences. The exposure of the ring essentially broke the back of German military espionage in the United States on the eve of the nation's entry into the Second World War. Just when it needed large quantities of high-grade information about industrial production, military force status, senior-level plans and intentions, and scores of other issues, the German military high command was denied the intelligence essential for its successful prosecution of the war.

CONCLUSION

This story began with the observations of a curious postal worker in Aberdeen, Scotland. In this quiet city nestled between the Grampian Hills and the rugged coastline of the North Sea, this obscure Scotsman traveled the same route every day, bags brimming, delivering mail to the same houses. Like the mailman, most of the residents along his route were Scottish, most born and raised in Aberdeen, with few friends outside the country. So it was not surprising that the unusual mailing habits of Mrs. Jessie Jordan caught his attention. She regularly received letters and packages from foreign cities and incurred considerable expense mailing her own letters and packages to addresses in Europe and elsewhere around the globe.

From the simple inquisitiveness of a simple postal employee emerged one of the most pivotal espionage cases in U.S. history. It exploded on the national scene, catching the imagination of the American public with tales of cunning spies, stolen secrets, and governmental blunders and ineffectiveness. The relentless press exposure forced a gradual shift in Americans' perception of the gravity of the espionage threat, and the public was soon demanding that the government take action to counter this new and frightening menace.

Looking back over more than six decades, one is struck by the momentous decisions made by the Roosevelt administration in addressing the espionage crisis. Within six months of the Rumrich ring convictions, control of counterespionage policy was shifted away from the State Department and consolidated in a committee of specialized agencies, marking a significant departure from historical precedent. Others actions included the formulation of cooperative approaches between the FBI and the military services to establish unprecedented security procedures for factories and industries producing war-related products and materials. The move of the Immigration Bureau from the Department of Labor to the Department of Justice also contributed to the counterintelligence process by implementing new procedures and creating a law enforcement orientation for the new service.

257

The passage of the Alien Registration Act in 1940, which led to the registration of millions of aliens living and working in the United States, along with the massive job of fingerprinting Americans working in military-related factories and plants and the millions of young men eligible for the draft, resulted in the explosive growth of the FBI's Identification Division.

One cannot ignore the seemingly mundane decisions that, in retrospect, contributed to the development of this new government function. For example, Henry Morgenthau recognized the need to cooperate with J. Edgar Hoover because the treasury secretary lacked the resources to monitor the movement of international money through U.S. banks. Hoover had the necessary resources and skills, developed over a period of fifteen years. His intricate network of bankers, businessmen, and commercial contacts made him well positioned to collect sensitive financial information and observe suspicious transactions; this ability uncovered espionage and aided in the formulation of U.S. counterintelligence policy.

When examining the development of the counterintelligence system during this period, two decisions stand out: President Roosevelt's May 1940 order to begin electronic surveillance of foreign agents, embassies, consulates, and other establishments in the United States; and his order a month later that had the IIC initiate a foreign espionage apparatus, leading to the creation of the Special Intelligence Service.

Wiretapping and the use of microphones immediately altered the landscape. With the stroke of a pen, the United States moved into the era of modern counterintelligence. With Roosevelt's wiretapping order, the FBI was free to eavesdrop on foreign activities, which broadened the opportunities to detect and prevent espionage in the United States. It moved the Bureau away from its strictly law enforcement style of problem solving and toward the broader and more nuanced world of the counterintelligence discipline. The birth of the Special Intelligence Service signaled the beginning of the United States' recognition of foreign espionage as a legitimate function of government.

Hoover's role in this process was central. When Rumrich was arrested in February 1938, the FBI director was the head of a small federal law enforcement agency with shared responsibility for investigating violations of the espionage laws. Fourteen months later he acquired exclusive jurisdiction to investigate such cases. Twenty-seven months later he was the head of the nation's first modern, albeit inexperienced, counterintelligence service, as well as chief of its first foreign intelligence service. In February 1938 his freedom of action in the counterespionage field was tightly limited. By July 1940, however, he was one of the most powerful figures in the national security world.

Two years after Hoover first learned about Rumrich, William Sebold entered the FBI director's life. Over the next twenty-two months, this simple aircraft worker's heroic role in the complex investigation of the Duquesne espionage ring led the Bureau to its greatest counterespionage triumph in its twenty-six-year history under Hoover's direction. With his flair for publicity and promotion, Hoover exploited this case in ways that benefited both the security of the nation and his own career. By July 1941, the myth of the FBI as the powerful guardian of the nation's freedoms had become deeply entrenched and would be perpetuated for decades to come. At the same time, Hoover's reputation as the United States' number-one spy fighter was fostered.

The initiatives taken by the Roosevelt administration during this period are remarkable. Within a short period, and in complete secrecy, a formidable U.S. security structure was conceived and established. Equally notable was the fact that these initiatives took place in the politically charged pre–World War II atmosphere, which often kept the president on the defensive against those who accused him of moving the country toward intervention in the European war. Policies were implemented with no congressional discussions and, occasionally, in violation of U.S. law. Wiretapping was a case in point. The Supreme Court had outlawed the practice, but the president, as chief foreign policy officer of the United States, insisted that its use was a necessary weapon in support of the common defense. Likewise, by December 1940, FBI agents assigned to the SIS were working in South and Central America in a variety of undercover guises, violating the laws of these sovereign nations by stealing political, military, and economic secrets for use by U.S. policy makers. Again, Congress was kept in the dark, with no opportunity to offer legislative advice, consent, or discussion. After the Pearl Harbor attack, secrecy became the watchword, and doing everything necessary to defeat the enemy was the only thing that mattered.

Compelling arguments can be made for these actions taken shortly before the war and continued during the conflict. But why weren't these decisions reexamined after the war? With the Truman administration, facing the new worldwide menace of communism, and a powerful new Soviet Union posing a major threat to world peace, no thought was given to altering the nation's counterintelligence posture. Instead of trying to reconcile sensitive and controversial counterintelligence practices with existing federal law, the government chose to nurture the seeds of abuse sown by President Roosevelt's prewar decisions. Over the next thirty years, counterintelligence tactics improved, its leadership matured, memories of the early days faded, and the technology for countering foreign intelligence advanced considerably. The law, however, remained stuck in the late 1930s. It was only after the scandal spawned by the Watergate break-in, and President Richard Nixon's efforts to shield his crime by invoking national security, that Congress began reexamining these decisions—decisions made to meet the challenges of the early 1940s and adhered to as the standard for counterintelligence practice for the next thirty-five years.

APPENDIX A

Sebold's List of Abwehr Requirements

The following list was contained in the microphotographs that William Sebold turned over to the FBI upon his arrival in the United States on February 8, 1940, as set forth in a memorandum from Hoover to President Roosevelt on February 12, 1940.

1. To ascertain if the International Telephone and Telegraph Company had offered the French and English Governments a new procedure of bombing which works as follows:

> The airplane is directed by a ray against the target, crossing a second ray shortly before reaching the target by which the bomb could be released. Particulars pertaining to the construction of the device and how it had worked out in tests were requested, as well as information concerning any negotiations in the French and English Governments with a view of selling it to them.

2. Information was requested concerning a branch factory of the French plant of "Potez" in Montreal.

3. Information was requested concerning Professor Bullard of the Hober or Rober College, who is said to be an expert in chemical warfare. Information was asked as to his status with the Army and details requested concerning a new means of protection against mustard gas with which cloth uniforms are impregnated.

4. Information was requested concerning new developments in the line of anti-aircraft guns.

5. Information was requested concerning anti-aircraft shell with so-called "electric eye."

6. Instructions were issued to get a copy of "Hartour Espionage Law."

7. Instructions were given to "keep us up to date on all developments in the aircraft industry" with further particulars as to the instructions.

8. Information was requested concerning a cable for high frequency service said to have been recently developed.

9. Information was requested concerning anti-fog devices.

10. Request information concerning bacteriological warfare from airplanes.

No number 11

12. Request for information concerning new gas mask development.

13. Ask for information about the trench crusher.

14. Request for catalogues of sending and receiving tubes and radio receivers and radio senders.

15. What became of new gun turret designed for Sunderland flying boats which Captain Luncstedt was ordered to develop?

16. Request for information concerning Sperry range finder.

17. Ask for information as to whether any personnel of the U.S. Army and Navy were going to Europe as camouflage volunteer corps and also ask to be immediately advised of any signs of mobilization in this country.

18. Ask for information concerning a new metal cleaning compound.

APPENDIX B

Duquesne Ring Conspirators

The following individuals were named in Indictment #CR–38425, dated July 1, 1941, U.S. District Court, Eastern District of New York.

Name	Residence	Country of Birth	Citizenship	Profession
Paul Bante	New York, NY	Germany	U.S.	Tool and dye maker
Max Blank	New York, NY	Germany	German	Employee of German Library of Information
Alfred Brockhoff	New York, NY	Germany	U.S.	Mechanic
Heinrich Clausing	New York, NY	Germany	U.S.	Ship's cook
Conradin Dold	?	Germany	U.S.	Shipping clerk
Frederick Duquesne	New York, NY	South Africa	U.S.	Businessman
Rudolf Eberling	New York, NY	Germany	U.S.	Shipping clerk
Richard Eichenlaub	New York, NY	Germany	U.S.	Casino owner
Heinrich Eilers	?	Germany	U.S.	Ship steward
Paul Fehse	?	Germany	U.S.	Ship's cook
Edmund Heine	Detroit, MI	Germany	U.S.	Businessman
Felix Jahnke	New York, NY	Germany	U.S.	Fountain clerk
Gustave Kaercher	New York, NY	Germany	U.S.	Mechanical engineer
Joseph Klein	?	Germany	German	Photographer
Hartwig Kleiss	?	Germany	U.S.	Ship's cook
Herman Lang	New York, NY	Germany	U.S.	Inspector, Norden Corp.
Evelyn Lewis	New York, NY	U.S.	U.S.	?
Rene Mezenen	New York, NY	France	U.S.	Flight attendant
Carl Reuper	Newark, NJ	Germany	U.S.	Inspector
Everett Roeder	New York, NY	Germany	U.S.	Draftsman
Paul Scholz	New York, NY	Germany	U.S.	Bookstore clerk
George Shuh	New York, NY	Germany	U.S.	Carpenter
Erwin Siegler	New York, NY	Germany	U.S.	Seaman/butcher
Oscar Stabler	New York, NY	Germany	U.S.	Seaman

Name	Residence	Country of Birth	Citizenship	Profession
Heinrich Stade	New York, NY	Germany	U.S.	Musician/waiter
Lilly Stein	New York, NY	Austria	Austrian	Shop owner
Franz Stigler	?	Germany	U.S.	Seaman
Erich Strunck	?	Germany	U.S.	Seaman
Leo Whalen	?	Germany	German	Boat owner
Adolf Walischewski	?	Germany	U.S.	Seaman
Else Weustenfeld	New York, NY	Germany	U.S.	Legal secretary
Axel Wheeler-Hill	New York, NY	Russia	U.S.	Truck driver
Bertram Zenzinger	Santa Monica, CA	South Africa	South African	Mechanical dentistry

APPENDIX C

Unindicted Duquesne Ring Coconspirators

The following individuals were unindicted coconspirators of those listed in appendix B.

Name	Aliases	Residence
I. A. Alberti		Coimbra, Portugal
Alberto E. Beau	Albert Eduard Beau	Coimbra, Portugal
	Al Eduard Beau	
	Eduard Beau	
	Alberto Eduard Beau	
C. H. Breezing		Rio de Janeiro, Brazil
"Hans" Bremer		?
Nelly Cately		Rome, Italy
Herbert Dobler	H. Dobler	Lisbon, Portugal
	H. Duarte	
"Toni" Doe		Milan, Italy
Ernesto Eilers		Lima, Peru
"Hans" Fisher		?
Dr. "Otto" Gassner	Adolf Gerhoff	Hamburg, Germany
	Anzieger	
	Anzinger, Gerhoff	
	A. Gerhoff, G. Hoff	
	Giehle, G. R. Hoff	
	G. E. R. Hof, Giese	
"Hans" Gieber	Giesler "Hans" Gieser	?
Pedro Gonzales	Pedro Gonzales	?
Albert Herzog		Bremen, Germany
"Wilhelm" Hethey		?
"Ernst" Hintz		Hamburg, Germany
"Heinrich" Holms		Stockholm, Sweden
"Adolf" Meier	Schneider	?
K. O. Merkel		Lisbon, Portugal
L. E. Moeller		Sao Paulo, Brazil
Otto Muehlberger		?
S. T. Neeland		Bremen, Germany
"Fritz" Palm		Hamburg, Germany

Name	Aliases	Residence
"Hans" Peters	Admiral Peters	?
Pablo Phillips		Madrid, Spain
Carlos Pitzuck	Carlos Pietzuck	Genoa, Italy
Nikolas A. F. Ritter	Nikolaus Adolf Fritz von Ritter	Hamburg, Germany
	Nicolaus Adolf von Ritter	
	Nicolaus Fritz Ritter	
	Frank Harris	
	Fred Harris	
	Dr. Leonhardt	
	Nikolaus	
	Nikki	
	Rantzau	
	Dr. Renken	
"Max" Schott		Lisbon, Portugal
George Sessler	George, George Sessler	?
	George Sinclair	
	Zeller	
Dr. Shmid Gyula		Budapest, Hungary
Heinrich Sorau	Heinrich Kurz	Hamburg, Germany
	Rhinehardt	
	Sandell	
	Sanden	
	Sander	
	Hugo Sebol	
	Henry Sorau	
	Dr. Hu Stein	
	Heinrich Kunz	
Peter Straaten		?
"Adolph" Thiele		?
C. S. Wang	C. S. Wong	Shanghai, China
"Heinrich" Westphal		?
Bertram Wolfgang Zenzinger	Wandter, B. Zenzinger	?
"Frederick" Zimmdar		Santos, Brazil

APPENDIX D

Sentences of the Duquesne Ring Conspirators

Name	Sentences
Paul Bante	18 months (FARA) $1,000 fine (FARA)
Max Black	18 months (FARA) $1,000 fine (FARA)
Alfred Brockhoff	5 years (espionage) 2 years (FARA)*
Heinrich Clausing	8 years (espionage) 2 years (FARA)*
Conradin Dold	10 years (espionage) 2 years (FARA)* $1,000 fine (FARA)
Frederick Duquesne	18 years (espionage) 2 years (FARA)* $1,000 fine (FARA)
Rudolf Eberling	5 years (espionage) 2 years (FARA)* $1,000 fine (FARA)
Richard Eichenlaub	18 months (FARA) $1,000 fine (FARA)
Heinrich Eilers	5 years (espionage) 2 years (FARA)*
Paul Fehse	15 years (espionage) 2 years (FARA)*
Edmund Heine	2 years (FARA) $5,000 fine (FARA)
Felix Jahnke	20 months (FARA) $1,000 fine (FARA)
Gustave Kaercher	22 months (FARA) $2,000 fine (FARA)

Name	Sentences
Joseph Klein	5 years (espionage) 2 years (FARA)*
Hartwig Kleiss	8 years (espionage)
Herman Lang	18 years (espionage) 2 years (FARA)*
Evelyn Lewis	1 year (espionage)
Rene Mezenen	8 years (espionage) 2 years (FARA)*
Carl Reuper	15 years (espionage) 2 years (FARA)*
Everett Roeder	16 years (espionage)
Paul Scholz	16 years (espionage) 2 years (FARA)*
George Shuh	18 months (FARA) $1,000 fine (FARA)
Erwin Siegler	10 years (espionage) 2 years (FARA)*
Oscar Stabler	5 years (espionage) 2 years (FARA)*
Heinrich Stade	15 months (espionage) $1,000 fine (FARA)
Lilly Stein	10 years (espionage) 2 years (FARA)*
Franz Stigler	16 years (espionage) 2 years (FARA)*
Erich Strunck	10 years (espionage) 2 years (FARA)*
Leo Whalen	12 years (espionage) 2 years (FARA)
Adolf Walischewski	5 years (espionage) 2 years (FARA)*
Else Weustenfeld	5 years (espionage) 2 years (FARA)*
Axel Wheeler-Hill	15 years (espionage) 2 years (FARA)*
Bertram Zenzinger	8 years (espionage)

* Prison terms for espionage and FARA violations served concurrently.

FARA, Foreign Agents Registration Act.

APPENDIX E

Expenditures for Special Intelligence Service Operations, July 2, 1940–June 30, 1947

Fiscal Year	Funds Available	Total Expenditures
1941	$400,000	$144,430.61
1942		
Carried forward from 1941	$225,569.39	$755,569.39
Additional appropriations	$500,000.00	$769,596.10
1943		
Appropriations	$2,900,000.00	$2,895,973.29
Less 1942 deficit	$14,026.17	$2,810,568.18
1944		
Carried forward from 1943	$75,305.11	$5,525,305.11
Additional appropriations	$5,450,000.00	$3,525,000.00
1945		
Carried forward from 1943	$75,305.11	
Carried forward from 1944	$1,925,000.00	$3,000,305.11
Additional appropriations	$1,175,000.00	$3,175,305.11
1946		
Carried forward from 1945	$175,000.00	
Additional appropriations	$2,771,357.00	$2,946,357.00
1947		
Appropriations	$3,000,000.00	
Expenditures to June 30, 1947		$1,989,172.89
Total	$15,185,529.89	

From *History of the SIS,* vol. 1, p. 35.

NOTES

ABBREVIATIONS

FRC   Federal Records Center
LOC   Library of Congress
NARA   National Archives and Records Administration
POF   President's Official File
PRO   Public Records Office
PSF   President's Safe File
RG   Record Group
USNA U.S. Naval Academy

CHAPTER ONE: RUMRICH

1. Hoover memorandum, to Charles Malcolmson, October 4, 1943, FBI file "Guenther Gustave Maria Rumrich, with aliases, et al.," 65-748, FBI Reading Room, Washington, D.C. (hereafter, Malcolmson memo).

2. Ibid.; Tamm memorandum to Hoover, "Contemplated Prosecution in Connection with the Guenther Gustave Rumrich Espionage Case on October 14, 1938," 10/10/1938, Box 2, Folder 18, J. Edward Lawler Papers, James Branch Cabell Library, Special Collections and Archives, Virginia Commonwealth University, Richmond, Va. (hereafter, Rumrich prosecution memo).

3. Rumrich FBI file; Ladislaw Farago, *The Game of the Foxes* (New York: David McKay, 1971), 56.

4. Stanley Hirshorn, *General Patton: A Soldier's Life* (New York: HarperCollins, 2004), 56.

5. Edward M. Coffman, *The Regulars* (Cambridge, Mass.: Belknap Press of Harvard University Press, 2004), 318. Coffman offers an often humorous, often sad, but always interesting look at the remarkable transformation of the U.S. Army between 1898 and 1941. Those forty-three years saw the army grow from a small garrison force keeping peace on the country's western frontier into the force of millions that led the nation through the Second World War.

6. Malcolmson memo; Rumrich prosecution memo; Farago, *The Game of the Foxes,* 58.

7. In the 1930s a major source of U.S. passports for the Soviet intelligence services was the Spanish civil war. "Most volunteers with passports were asked to surrender them

on arrival in Spain; they were then forwarded to Moscow Center by diplomatic bag. The NKVD was particularly pleased with a haul of two thousand United States passports later used by its illegals." Christopher Andrew and Oleg Gordievsky, *KGB: The Inside Story* (New York: HarperCollins, 1990), 159. Rumrich was told that the "German Government needed some blank U.S. passports for use in sending agents into Russia." FBI Seattle report, September 25, 1943, Rumrich FBI file (hereafter, Seattle report).

8. Seattle report; Rumrich prosecution memo; Guy Liddell, "German Espionage Case in the United States," undated, Robert J. Vansitart Papers, Churchill College, Cambridge University, England.

9. Liddell, "German Espionage Case"; Nigel West, ed., *The Guy Liddell Diaries*, vol. 1, *1939–1942* (London: Routledge, Taylor and Francis Group, 2005), 2 (hereafter, *Liddell Diaries*).

10. Farago, *The Game of the Foxes*, 60–61.

11. "Woman Convicted as Spy in Scotland," *New York Times*, May 17, 1938, 2; Farago, *The Game of the Foxes*, 60; Liddell, "German Espionage Case."

12. *Liddell Diaries*; Katherine A. S. Sibley, *Red Spies in America* (Lawrence: University Press of Kansas, 2004), 73; Andrew and Gordievsky, *KGB: The Inside Story*, 223–224.

13. Farago, *The Game of the Foxes*, 61.

14. "Crown" letter, January 17, 1938, Vansitart Papers.

15. Liddell, "German Espionage Case."

16. Ibid.

17. "Nazi Spy Ring Cracked by Va. Major," *Washington Post*, June 22, 1938, 1; Rumrich prosecution memo.

18. Memorandum, "Guenther Gustave Rumrich, et al., Impersonation, Espionage," February 27, 1938, Rumrich FBI File; Telephone Logs of the Director, vol. 1, serial 114X, FBI Reading Room.

19. Leon Turrou, *Where My Shadow Falls* (Garden City, N.Y.: Doubleday, 1949), 57, 63, 83, 147.

20. Farago, *The Game of the Foxes*, 59.

21. Rumrich prosecution memo.

22. Ibid.

23. "2 Nazi Officials Indicted as U.S. Spy Ring Heads," *Washington Post*, June 21, 1938, 1; "Germans Here Ask Place in Politics," *New York Times*, October 7, 1934, 26; Rumrich prosecution memo.

24. Farago, *The Game of the Foxes*, 32–37; Interrogation of Erich Pfeiffer, RG 319, Intelligence Research Report (IIR) XE 002935, Box 174A, NARA, College Park, Md.

25. Farago, *The Game of the Foxes*, 37.

26. Ibid., 17.

27. Ibid., 18.

28. Rumrich prosecution memo.

29. Ibid.

30. Ibid.

31. Ibid.

32. Ibid.

33. Ibid.

34. Eitel left the *Bremen* and Abwehr service in the spring of 1936 but was eventually picked up again by the Abwehr for espionage duties. MI5 tracked his movements until early 1944, when he offered his services to U.S. intelligence representatives in Lisbon. Eitel was "ready to betray his masters of ten years' standing while admitting only to five, to reinsure his European future through American favour." After the Americans accepted his offer, he began supplying regular information on "the Abwehr in general and its Lisbon personalities in particular; and was used by his new contacts to 'feed' false information, directly or indirectly to his full-time masters." Camp 020 Report on the Case of Karl Eitel, RG 220, Entry 190A, Box 9, Folder 21, NARA.

35. Ibid.

36. Hoover memorandum to Frank Murphy, May 2, 1939, Box 23, Frank Murphy Papers, Bentley Historical Library, University of Michigan, Ann Arbor; Rumrich prosecution memo; J. Edward Lawler, handwritten notes, undated, Lawler Papers.

37. Greibl was unaware that the FBI was recording his conversations with Dreschel. Later, when he discussed the meeting with Turrou, he omitted anything that implicated him. The report notes that the recording "showed quite clearly that he and Dreschel had for a long time been co-operating and that both of them were equally involved." Upon determining that Scheutz left the ship in Havana, Hoover dispatched an FBI agent to Cuba to arrange his detention and extradition to the United States. With the assistance of the Cuban police, Scheutz was found living at the Plaza Hotel in Havana. His hotel expenses were billed to a "local agent of the German intelligence service named Louis Clausig." History of the Federal Bureau of Investigation, FBI Crime Records Statistics, RG 65, Box 4, NARA.

38. United States v. Carl Schleuter, Box 840, RG 21, FRC, New York, N.Y.

39. "2 Nazi Captains in N.Y. Spy Case Skip Bail, Sail," *Washington Post,* June 4, 1938, 1.

40. Rumrich prosecution memo; "Key Man Vanishes in Spy Hunt," *New York Times,* May 19, 1938, 1. Liddell, "German Espionage Case." In May 1938 material witness warrants were issued for Wilhelm Boehnke, Walter Otto, Lutz Leiswitz, Johann Hart, and Johann Kleiber. All were crew members aboard the SS *Bremen.* On June 30, 1938, Udo von Bonin, Herman Menzel, Ernst Mueller, Erich Pfeiffer, Herbert Jaenichen, Carl Eitel, Karl Schleuter, Theodore Scheutz, "Fritz" Schmidt, William Lonkowski, Werner Gudenberg, First Name Unknown (FNU) Schmidt, FNU Sanders, Johanna Hoffmann, Ignatz Greibl, Otto Voss, Erich Glaser, Guenther Rumrich, and Jessie Jordan were charged with conspiracy to commit espionage and failure to appear before a grand jury "to address charges going back to January 2, 1935." United States v. Udo von Bonin, C 102/462, July 30, 1938, Box 849, RG 21, FRC, N.Y. Charges against the remaining fourteen defendants were dismissed on March 4, 1950.

41. Lawler memorandum to Tamm, May 12,1938, Lawler Papers.

42. New York letter to FBI HQ, July 25, 1938, Lawler Papers.

43. Annie Hoover died on February 22, 1938. John Fox, FBI historian.

44. "Hoover Writes, Why Can't I? Turrou Pleads," *Washington Post,* June 24, 1938, 1. "Last Friday morning, June 24, 1938, I was shown a copy of a signed statement, bearing my signature in which I had promised to write nothing and give out no information about the activities of the FBI while I was in the service and after my resignation. The date of this sworn statement was November 1935. I have no recollection of having

signed this statement. Nor can I recall the circumstances." U.S. v. Schleuter, RG 21, Box 849, FRC, N.Y.

45. U.S. v. Schleuter, RG 21, Box 849, FRC, N.Y.; Diaries of Homer Cummings, June 21, 1938, Special Collections and Archives, University of Virginia, Charlottesville.

46. "4 High-Ranking Nazis Named as Spy 'Brains,'" *Washington Post,* June 23, 1938, 4; Stern letter to Roosevelt, June 23, 1938, PSF, Box 10, Franklin D. Roosevelt Library, Hyde Park, N.Y.

47. Roosevelt Presidential Conferences, June 24, 1938, in *Complete Press Conferences of President Franklin D. Roosevelt,* vol. 11, no. 469 (New York: DeCapo Press, 1972), 1050. Turrou published his self-adulatory version of the case entitled *Nazi Spies in America* (New York: Random House, 1939).

48. "2 Nazi Captains."

49. "Mrs. Greibl Seized as She Plans Flight," *New York Times,* June 10, 1938, 1.

50. "Editor Posts Bail for 'Spy' Witness," *Washington Post,* June 12, 1938, 1.

51. Indictment 102-460, June 20, 1938, Box 840, RG 21, FRC, N.Y.

52. "Reich Plot to Get U.S. Defense Plans Outlined by Hardy," *New York Times,* October 18, 1938, 1.

53. "Witness Story Hits at Turrou, Russian Asserts that Ex-Agent was Patient in Psychiatric Ward," *New York Times,* November 16, 1938, 1.

54. "Third Spy Guilty; Jury Urges Mercy," *New York Times,* December 2, 1938, 1; U.S. v. Erich Glaser, Box 840, RG 21, FRC, N.Y.; "4 Nazi Spies Given 2 to 6 Years in Jail," *Washington Post,* December 3, 1938, 1.

CHAPTER TWO: A LOOK BACK

1. Coffman, *The Regulars,* 205; Ralph H. Van Deman (USA Ret.), *The Final Memorandum,* ed. Ralph E. Weber (Wilmington, Del.: Scholarly Resources, 1988), xi–xii.

2. Van Deman, *The Final Memorandum,* xiii.

3. Ibid., xv.

4. Ibid., xviii.

5. Ibid., xix.

6. Bruce W. Bidwell, *History of the Military Intelligence Division, Department of the Army General Staff: 1775–1941* (Frederick, Md.: University Publications of America, 1986), 258; John P. Finegan, *Military Intelligence* (Washington, D.C.: Center for Military History, United States Army, 1998), 44.

7. Finegan, *Military Intelligence,* 44.

8. Jeffrey M. Dorwart, *Conflict of Duty* (Annapolis, Md.: Naval Institute Press, 1983), 5–6.

9. Ibid., 8.

10. Ibid., 9.

11. Ibid., 14–15, 55.

12. Ibid., 23; Luke McNamee, "Keeping Our Navy Strong," in *Proceedings of the Naval Institute* (Annapolis, Md.: U.S. Naval Institute Press, May 1923), 505–508.

13. Dudley Knox, "Public Indoctrination," in *Proceedings of the Naval Institute* (Annapolis, Md.: U.S. Naval Institute Press, June 1929), 485–489.

14. Dorwart, *Conflict of Duty,* 53.

15. Ibid., 40–44.

16. Ibid., 66.

17. Ibid., 66–68.

18. "Charges of Illegal Practices of the Department of Justice," in *Hearings before the Committee on Rules, House of Representatives,* 66th Cong., 2nd sess., pt. I (Washington, D.C.: Government Printing Office, 1920).

19. Ibid.

20. Ibid.

21. Richard Gid Power, *Not without Honor* (New York: Free Press, 1995), 22–23.

22. Memorandum, General Intelligence Division—Department of Justice, October 5, 1920, FBI Reading Room.

23. Ibid.

24. Alpheus Thomas Mason, *Harlan Fiske Stone: Pillar of the Law* (New York: Viking Press, 1956), 138.

25. Ibid.

26. Ibid., 113.

27. Ibid., 114.

28. Don Whitehead, *The FBI Story* (New York: Random House, 1956), 55–65.

29. Ibid., 64.

30. Stone memorandum, FBI Reading Room.

31. Ibid.; Colonel James H. Reeves, USA, Assistant Chief of Staff for Intelligence, letter to Hoover, September 29, 1925, FBI Reading Room.

32. Hoover memorandum to Assistant Attorney General William Stanley, October 24, 1933, FBI Reading Room. The BOI was renamed the U.S. Bureau of Investigations in 1932, the Division of Investigation (which included the Bureau of Prohibition) in 1933, and finally the Federal Bureau of Investigation on July 1, 1935.

33. T. N. Stapleton memorandum to Hoover, November 20, 1933, FBI Reading Room.

34. "Address of John Edgar Hoover, Federal Bureau of Investigation, Department of Justice before the International World Police at Montreal, Canada on October 26, 1937," RG 65, Box 4, NARA; Hoover memorandum to Acting Attorney General Stanley Reed, October 9, 1935, FBI Reading Room.

35. For information concerning Samuel Dickstein's espionage relationship with the NKVD, see Allen Weinstein and Alexander Vassiliev, "Crook: A Soviet Agent in Congress," in *The Haunted Wood* (New York: Random House, 1999); memorandum, October 27, 1933, FBI Reading Room.

36. Hoover memorandum to Sam Cowley, May 10, 1934, FBI Reading Room.

37. Hoover memorandum to Cowley, May 17, 1934, FBI Reading Room.

38. Hoover memorandum to Cummings, June 11, 1936, Box 10, POF, OF10b, FDR Library; Joseph B. Keenan letter to Hoover, January 30, 1934, FBI Reading Room; Cummings note to Roosevelt, April 19, 1937, with attached "Memorandum for the Attorney

General," April 12, 1937, Box 57, Departmental File, Justice, Hoover, J. Edgar 1937–1940, PSF, FDR Library; Cummings letter to Roosevelt, May 25, 1938, with attached memorandum entitled "Silver Shirts, May 17, 1938," Box 57, Departmental File: Hoover, J. Edgar 1937–1940, PSF; Hoover letter to Roosevelt, October 15, 1938, POF, OF10b, Box 10, FDR Library; Hoover letter to Marvin McIntyre, November 2, 1938, Box 57, Departmental File: Hoover, J. Edgar 1937–1940, PSF, FDR Library.

39. Hoover confidential memoranda, August 24, 1936, August 25, 1936, FBI Reading Room.

40. Ibid.

41. Hoover memorandum to Tamm, "Strictly Confidential," September 10, 1936, FBI Reading Room.

42. FBI Bulletin No. 17, May 15, 1939, Box 2, Folder 18, Lawler Papers.

43. Hoover letter to all SACs, October 1, 1938, Box 2, Folder 18, Lawler Papers.

44. R. J. Brandt memorandum to Tamm, July 18, 1938, "Supervision of the Bank Robbery Desk and Other Matters which are Handled by the Bank Robbery Supervisor," Box 2, Folder 38, Internal Memoranda, Lawler Papers.

45. Tamm memorandum to Hoover, August 29, 1936, FBI Reading Room.

46. Turrou, *Where My Shadow Falls*, 157.

CHAPTER THREE: CONTROVERSY AND CONFUSION

1. "Spies," *New York Times*, December 2, 1938; "Over the Coffee," *Washington Post*, January 17, 1938, sec. III, 3; "No Cause for Hysteria," *Washington Post*, June 22, 1938.

2. "Four Spy Suspects in Cristobel Jail," *New York Times*, October 18, 1938.

3. Gorin was tried and found guilty of espionage on March 19, 1939. He was sentenced to six years in prison and a $10,000 fine. The Supreme Court later upheld the conviction. On June 22, 1941, the sentence was suspended at the request of the State Department. Gorin's probation was conditioned on the payment of the $10,000 fine and court costs and his permanent departure from the United States within forty-eight hours. That same day, he paid the fine and immediately sailed from Los Angeles for Vladivostok, Russia. House Committee on Un-American Activities, *The Shameful Years: Thirty Years of Soviet Espionage in the United States*, 82nd Cong., 2nd sess., January 6, 1952; "Coast Air Plant Worker Convicted as Spy," *New York Times*, December 23, 1938; Hoover memorandum to Murphy, March 22, 1939, Box 89, Murphy Papers.

4. *Press Conferences of President Franklin D. Roosevelt, 1933–1945*, vol. 12 (New York: DaCapo Press, 1972), 145–146, 150–151: "These trials demonstrated how unprepared we are to cope with this business of 'spying' which goes on in our country. The disclosures in the spy investigation, however, lead the Government to believe that only by reinforcement of our intelligence services can we successfully combat the activities of foreign agents in our country." Undated memorandum setting forth Roosevelt's response to the question, "What about the spy question?" President's Secretary File, FDR Library.

5. Cummings Diaries, October 24, 1938; Hoover memorandum to Murphy, March 16, 1939, Murphy Papers.

6. "The Work, Functions, Organization of the Federal Bureau of Investigation in Time of War," October 14, 1938, RG 65, Box 4, NARA; Hoover memorandum to Mur-

phy, March 16, 1939, with attached Cummings letter to President Roosevelt, October 20, 1938, Murphy Papers.

7. Hoover memorandum to Murphy, March 16, 1949, with attached Cummings letter to Roosevelt.

8. Ibid.

9. Ibid.

10. Ibid.

11. Ibid.

12. Ibid.

13. Ibid.

14. Ibid.

15. Ibid.

16. Hoover memorandum to Murphy, May 4, 1939, Harold Smith Papers, Diary Entry May 9, 1939, Box 1, Folder "Daily Memoranda April–June 1939," FDR Library.

17. Hoover memorandum to Murphy, January 19, 1939, Murphy Papers; February 7, 1939, letter from SAC to selected SACs ordering them to begin liaison with G2 representatives in their areas; Joseph B. Keenan letter to Frank J. Wilson, Chief of the U.S. Secret Service, et al., February 7, 1939, reproduced in its entirety in Hoover memorandum to Murphy, March 16, 1939, Box 89, Murphy Papers.

18. "The present German Government is not friendly toward us. They consider that we are one of the obstacles in their way toward their objectives. They have no desire to clash with us but their objectives in South America and in Central America and Mexico are so definite that they realize to reach them they must be faced with a weaker instead of stronger United States." Messersmith memorandum, July 22, 1937, Inventory No. 947, George Messersmith Papers, University of Delaware, Newark.

19. "Messersmith Memorandum for the Record" marked "Strictly Confidential," February 21, 1938, Inventory No. 951, Messersmith Papers.

20. Messersmith to Raymond Geist, May 19, 1938, Inventory No. 994, Messersmith Papers.

21. Messersmith to Cordell Hull, February 17, 1938, Inventory No. 947, Messersmith Papers.

22. *Liddell Diaries,* 1.

23. Ibid., 2.

24. "Liaison with the United States Government Intelligence organizations arising out of the German Espionage Case," undated, Vansitart Papers.

25. Ibid.; J. E. Lawler memorandum to Edward Tamm, July 1, 1939, Lawler Papers.

26. "Liaison with the United States Government Intelligence organizations," Vansitart Papers.

27. Ibid.

28. Tamm memorandum for the file, February 28, 1939, FBI file 66-5424, 113.

29. The Brazilian government's growing concern about subversion in 1937 and 1938 forced a clampdown that included regulating the activities of Nazi organizations and arresting communists who distributed subversive propaganda. Acknowledging their lack of the skills needed to investigate these activities, Brazilian officials requested the State Department to send "as soon as possible three or four trained Secret Service operators to organize and direct a proper Service here." Sumner Welles issued a memo requesting

the dispatch of special agent Edward Thompson to Brazil to instruct local police agencies on counterintelligence methods and to assist in the construction of such a service. On Welles's December 10, 1938, memo, Roosevelt scrawled, "S. W. Yes—it should be done. Very important." Six days later the issue was discussed in some detail at a White House cabinet meeting. Homer Cummings later recorded that Welles, representing Secretary Hull at the meeting, spoke of the "extent of the activity of German Agents in South America, especially in Brazil where evidence in the hands of the State Department indicated an attempt to foment revolution" (Cummings Diary, December 16, 1938). With White House approval of the highly confidential assignment, Welles instructed Thompson "to assist the Brazilian Government for the purpose of giving technical advice in the training of Brazilian special agents and police operatives. The exact nature of your duties will, of course, depend upon the needs and desires of the Brazilian Government, which will be made known to you upon your arrival. You should not, however, engage in any actual investigation on behalf of the Brazilian Government." Thompson left from New York City aboard the USS *Uruguay* on January 13, 1939, and arrived in Rio de Janeiro on January 26. R. M. Stotten letter to Welles, November 4, 1938, RG 59, Decimal File 832.105/21; Welles letter to President Roosevelt, December 10, 1938, Decimal File 832.105/25; Welles letter to Thompson, January 12, 1939, RG 59, Decimal File 832.105/25; Frank Murphy letter to Hull, January 18, 1939; Stotten telegram to Hull, January 27, 1939, RG 59, Decimal File 832.105/27, NARA; Hoover memorandum to Murphy, March 20, 1939, Murphy Papers.

30. Hoover memorandum to Murphy, March 20, 1939, Murphy Papers.

31. Hoover memorandum to Murphy, May 2, 1939, Murphy Papers.

32. Welles letter to Roosevelt, May 29, 1939, POF 313, Box 1, Folder "Colombia, Gov't of," FDR Library.

33. Murphy letter to Roosevelt, June 17, 1939, PSF, Box 9, Folder "State Department 1939–1940," FDR Library.

34. *Final Report of the Committee to Study Government Operations with Respect to Intelligence Activities: Intelligence Activities and the Rights of Americans,* U.S. Senate, 77th Cong., 2nd sess., book II, 26–27.

35. Messersmith letter to President Roosevelt, "Memorandum of the Proposed Consolidation of the Departments of Commerce and Agriculture into the Foreign Service of the Department of State," November 19, 1938, Box 299, Folder "Hopkins Papers, Book 2, Reorganization of State Department," Harry Hopkins Papers, FDR Library.

36. Roosevelt memorandum to Hull, June 26, 1939, PSF/Confidential File, Box 9, Folder "State Department 1939–1940," FDR Library.

CHAPTER FOUR: INTERDEPARTMENTAL INTELLIGENCE CONFERENCE

1. Dr. John Fox, FBI historian, Washington, D.C., April 4, 2005.

2. "Investigator," January 1952, 4–5, J. Edgar Hoover Center for Enforcement, Washington, D.C.

3. War Department memorandum, "Subjects to Be Discussed by Colonel Churchill at FBI Conference, Tuesday, May 14, 1940; memorandum, "Meeting with Mr. Tamm,

Federal Bureau of Investigation—April 9, 1940, courtesy of Dennis DeBrandt; Hoover letter to Watson, June 3, 1940, OF10b, FDR Library.

4. War Department memorandum, "Coordination between the War Department and the FBI," prepared by Major Cyrus H. Searcy, January 28, 1939, U.S. Army Military Historical Institute, Carlisle, Pa.

5. Bidwell, *History of the Military Intelligence Division*, 284.

6. "Miles Heads Army Intelligence," *New York Times*, May 1, 1940, 8; Major General U. S. Grant III letter to Miles, October 32, 1940; Lady Nancy Astor letter to Miles, undated; Douglas Fairbanks Jr. letters to Miles, undated; Box 7, Nelson A. Miles Family Papers, Manuscript Division, LOC; *General Patton: A Soldier's Life*, 198; Coffman, *The Regulars*, 156.

7. Major Sherman Miles, "Notes on the Dardanelles Campaign of 1915" (West Point, N.Y.: U.S. Military Academy, 1924); Siegfried Beer, "Target Central Europe: American Intelligence Efforts Regarding Nazi and Early Postwar Austria," Working Paper 97-1 (Karl-Franzens Univesitat Graz, Austria, August 1997); R. Manning Ancell with Christine M. Miller, *The Biographical Dictionary of World War II Generals and Flag Officers* (Westport, Conn.: Greenwood Press, 1996), 226.

8. Miles letter to Lieutenant Colonel Hoover, director, FBI, January 4, 1941, and Hoover letter to Miles, February 10, 1941, RG 65, Box 4, NARA.

9. *Henry L. Stimson Diaries*, Yale University Library (microfilm by Yale University Photographic Services), copyright by Stimson Trust and Yale University Library, Reel 6, diary entries October 11, 1940, 53; February 13, 1941, 23; May 20, 1941, 84; October 23, 1939, 26. "Hoover and Miles did not get along." Adolf Berle Diaries and Adolf Berle Papers, October 17, 1940, FDR Library.

10. Robert Jackson, *That Man* (New York: Oxford University Press, 2003), 68.

11. Hoover memorandum to Jackson, April 26, 1941; McCloy letter to Jackson, May 6, 1941, Box 94, Robert Jackson Papers, LOC; Jackson, *That Man*, 69.

12. McCloy letter to Jackson, May 6, 1941, Box 94, Jackson Papers; Jackson memorandum to Roosevelt, April 29, 1941, Box 94, Jackson Papers (emphasis in original); Jackson, *That Man*, 69.

13. Memorandum, "U.S.S. Rainbow, Kobe, Japan," June 17, 1908; draft, "Light Cruisers—Our Navy's Needs," Walter S. Anderson Papers, Naval Historical Foundation, Washington Navy Yard, Washington, D.C.

14. Ancell and Miller, *Biographical Dictionary*, 491.

15. Walter S. Anderson Diary, April 18, 1940, and September 26, 1940, Anderson Papers; Arthur J. R. Smith, "The Development of the Conference Board of Canada," *Canadian Business Economics*, Winter–Spring 1997, 104.

16. Hoover letter to Knox, January 11, 1941, Anderson Papers; Dorwart, *Conflict of Duty*, 116; Robert B. Stinnett, *Day of Deceit* (New York: Free Press, 2000), 35; interview of Admiral Walter Anderson, March 9, 1962, p. 220, Oral History Research Project, Columbia University, New York, N.Y.

17. Adolf Berle and Beatrice Bishop Berle, *Navigating the Rapids, 1918–1971*, ed. Travis Beal Jacobs (New York: Harcourt, Brace, Jovanovich, 1973), 94.

18. Berle Diary, March 12 and 13, 1940.

19. "It has been necessary for the Federal Bureau of Investigation to open offices at Juneau, Alaska, Honolulu, Hawaii, and the Panama Canal Zone, as well as in a number

of more strategically located cities within the continental United States in order to more effectively and expeditiously handle the investigation of national defense matters as well as their regular duties." Frank Murphy memorandum to Roosevelt, January 10, 1940, OF10, FDR Library.

20. Lawler memorandum to Tamm, July 1, 1939, Lawler Papers; S. T. Wood letter to Hoover, November 21, 1939, POF, FDR Library.

21. Cyril Mills letter to Liddell, March 3, 1943, PRO, Kew, England; Liddell Diaries, September 13, 1939, 20.

22. "The Identification Division of the FBI," U.S. Department of Justice, 1967, 1.

23. "Digested History of the Federal Bureau of Investigation," October 15, 1938, RG 65, Box 15, NARA.

24. Ibid.

25. Ibid.; interview of George Bonebrake, February 4, 2000. Bonebrake was an FBI fingerprint examiner until his retirement in 1976. During his more than thirty-year FBI career, he served as a member of the FBI "Disaster Squad," a team of forensic experts routinely dispatched to airplane crashes, explosions, and other incidents involving a large loss of life to identify the human remains through fingerprints and footprints. It was Bonebrake who identified the latent print found on the rifle used to murder Dr. Martin Luther King as belonging to James Earl Ray.

26. Hoover memorandum to Jackson, December 2, 1940, Jackson Papers.

27. Rumrich FBI file.

28. "Identification Division of the FBI."

29. Hoover memoranda to Jackson, October 18, 1940, and November 9, 1940, Box 90, Jackson Papers; Hoover letter to Watson, October 25, 1940, with attached memorandum, "Present Status of Espionage and Counterespionage Operations of the Federal Bureau of Investigation," October 24, 1940, OF10b, Box 4, FDR Library. In a radio broadcast, attorney general Robert Jackson touted the success of the registration and fingerprinting of aliens. He noted that during the four months ending December 21, 1940, the government had registered 4.2 million aliens, even though it had originally estimated a total alien population of 3.6 million. Jackson Papers, Box 40, Folder "Alien Registration and Democracy," Columbia Broadcasting System, Station WJSV, Washington, D.C., December 21, 1940, LOC.

30. "Investigator," January 1952, 3, J. Edgar Hoover Center for Law Enforcement, Washington, D.C.; Liddell Diaries, December 11, 1940, 116; Bryan Burrough, Public Enemies (New York: Penguin Press, 2004), 341.

31. H. H. Clegg memorandum to Hoover, November 3, 1939, Earl J. Connelley Personnel File, 67-2162-463, FBI Reading Room.

32. "German Espionage," Vansitart Papers; Edward A. Tamm Personnel File, 67-1585, FBI Reading Room.

33. FBI Organizational Chart, February 18, 1941, J. Edgar Hoover Center for Law Enforcement, Washington, D.C.

34. Ibid.; Anderson Diary, April 14, 1940, and September 26, 1940, Anderson Papers.

35. Hoover letter to Watson, June 3, 1940, OF10b, FDR Library.

36. Hoover letter to Lt. Col. J. M. Churchill, acting chief of staff, MID, March 26, 1940,

with attached report of special agent A. R. Miller, "North American Aviation, Inc., Ingleside California," January 18, 1940, RG 165, Box 2615, MID Correspondence 1917–1941, NARA; "A Brief of FBI Plant Survey of North American Aviation, Inc., Los Angeles, California," RG 165, Box 2615, MID Correspondence 1917–1941, NARA.

37. *Suggestions for Protection of Industrial Facilities*, FBI, December 1941, RG 165, Box 2615, MID Correspondence 1917–1941, NARA.

38. Sibley, *Red Spies in America*, 61–62.

39. *Suggestions for Protection of Industrial Facilities*; Hoover letter to Edwin Watson, June 3, 1940, OF10b, FDR Library.

40. Hoover letter to Col. Warren McCabe, October 2, 1940; FBI Report of special agent (SA) J. W. Savage, February 2, 1940, "Raymond Charles Simpson"; FBI Report of SA John J. Horan, October 8, 1940, "Dr. Arthur Schramm"; FBI Report of SA W. J. Taylor, May 29, 1940, "Charles Negata," RG 165, Box 2617, NARA. In the case of Negata, FCC records revealed that he was a legitimate amateur radio operator.

41. FBI report, "Jones Orin York, aka, Espionage–R," 65-2223, June 6, 1939. York lied to the FBI during his interview. He was a Soviet espionage agent until well after the Second World War. In 1950 the FBI reinterviewed him with additional information at hand. He confessed to espionage and identified William Wolfe Weisband as his prewar contact. Weisband would provide him with money and instructions, and York would supply classified information to be passed along to Soviet intelligence officers operating in the United States. Weisband was one of three known Soviet agents who informed the KGB that the Army Security Agency had decrypted the Soviet's communication system that was later known by the code name Venona.

42. Ladd memorandum to Hoover, November 12, 1948, "Amadeo Sabatini, Internal Security–R."

43. *Liddell Diaries*, April 26, 1942, 247–248.

44. State Department letter to Colonel Churchill, February 14, 1940; British Security Coordination, *The Secret History of British Security Coordination in the Americas, 1940–1945* (New York: Fromm International, 1999), 365. Borchardt was arrested on December 8, 1941, and charged with espionage. He was later convicted and sentenced to a forty years in prison. "'Refugee' Linked to Spy Ring; Others Named in Indictment," *New York Times*, March 3, 1942, 13; Margaret Bovari, *Treason in the Twentieth Century* (New York: G. P. Putnam and Sons, 1963), 34–35.

45. Fletcher Warren letter to Hoover, July 11, 1940; FBI file 65-13888, "Itaru Tachibana with Aliases," courtesy of Kenneth Ringle (hereafter, Tachibana FBI file).

46. Tachibana FBI file.

47. Memorandum, March 22, 1944, Tachibana FBI file.

48. Tachibana FBI file.

49. Ibid.

50. Ibid. The DNI believed that the limited arrest authority of naval investigators was detrimental to the ONI. "The effective operation of naval intelligence in connection with espionage in the United States is handicapped by the fact that a Naval agent has no legal authority to make an arrest outside of strictly Naval jurisdiction no matter how vitally the Naval interest may be involved, nor how urgent it may be that the arrest be made." Dorwart, *Conflict of Duty*, 116.

51. Tachibana FBI file.

52. Dorwart, *Conflict of Duty,* 116.

53. Ibid.

54. Desmond Young, *Rutland of Jutland* (London: Cassell, 1963), 4–8.

55. He remained in Brixton Prison until June 1942, was transferred to the Isle of Man and then back and forth between Brixton and Man during 1943, and was quietly released from custody in the fall of 1943. He died of self-induced asphyxiation in January 1949. *Liddell Diaries,* November 14, 1941, 192; December 8, 1941, 200; Young, *Rutland of Jutland,* 176, 179–180.

56. George Martin, *Madame Secretary* (Boston: Houghton Mifflin, 1976), 440.

57. Welles memorandum to Roosevelt, May 18, 1940, Box 90, Jackson Papers. Coverage of the movement of suspected spies is a fundamental component of counterintelligence. As the FBI increasingly turned its attention to the surveillance of foreign officials and visitors, the laxity of U.S. immigration regulations began to affect Bureau efforts. Hoover informed Jackson that Europeans could purchase citizenship for $5,000 in countries such as Honduras, the Dominican Republic, Cuba, Colombia, and Bolivia with no background inquiries or residency requirements. These purchases made them residents of the Western Hemisphere, allowing them entry into the United States without any documents. Hoover memorandum to Jackson, May 14, 1940, Box 92, Jackson Papers.

58. Francis Biddle, who served as solicitor general, was placed in charge of overseeing the smooth transfer of the Immigration Bureau into the Department of Justice. He later wrote in his memoirs that Perkins never "relished its supervision" and had been neglecting immigration matters for some time. He recalled that the immediate cause of the president's decision was the secretary's failure to furnish urgently needed information to the White House concerning the number of deportable aliens in the country. Roosevelt then decided that immigration "should be tightened." Francis Biddle, *In Brief Authority* (Garden City, N.Y.: Doubleday, 1962), 106. Further evidence of how ill prepared the government was on the issue of alien control can be seen in a coded teletype sent by Hoover to all FBI special agents in charge, ordering them to "furnish Bureau as soon as possible by airmail special delivery letter a list of names and present addresses of those persons in your district who should be considered for custodial detention pending investigation in the event of a national emergency. Indicate in furnishing information whether the individual according to best available data is or is not a citizen of the United States. Information should be furnished indicating whether these persons possess communistic, fascist, Nazi, or other nationalistic backgrounds. Sample information with source should be furnished to justify consideration in this group including specific acts or statements." FBI HQ teletype to all SACs, June 15, 1940, Official and Confidential Files. Even the State Department plotted behind the scenes for the transfer of the Immigration Bureau to the Department of Justice. On May 27, 1940, Adolf Berle recorded in his diary that he had conducted "a little confidential work with Hoover and Tamm. Since thanks for a swift little meeting of Welles and myself, the Immigration Bureau is now being turned over to the Department of Justice. (This because we simply cannot trust the administration of the Department of Labor.) Justice is having its problem." Berle memorandum, May 29, 1940, Berle Diaries, Roll 2, FDR Library.

59. Biddle, *In Brief Authority,* 107. Berle's thinking reflected that of the president and many other administration officials concerning the need to balance alien controls with constitutional guarantees. Berle confided this dilemma to his diary: "the object is to prevent 'fifth column' who are really foreign agents or who are trying to commit crimes, at the same time to prevent this machinery from being used hysterically, in violation of civil liberties and every decent idea of progress." Berle memorandum, April 25, 1940, Berle Diaries, Roll 2, FDR Library.

60. Joint Agreement of the Secretary of War and the Attorney General Respecting Internment of Alien Enemies, July 18, 1941, RG 338-2-7, 014.31 Enemy Aliens File, Commission on Wartime Relocation and Internment of Civilians, NARA.

61. Michelle Malkin, *In Defense of Internment* (Washington, D.C.: Regnery, 2004), 54.

62. Ibid., 53.

63. "Memorandum on Division of Duties between Military Intelligence Division, Office of Naval Intelligence and the Federal Bureau of Investigation," signed by Hoover, Miles, and Anderson, June 5, 1940, RG 65, Box 1, Special Intelligence Service Administrative File, NARA; memorandum, "Measures for Cooperation and Control of Counter-Intelligence Matters Affecting Plant Protection," Adjutant General letter to All Corps Area Commanders, July 1, 1940, SIS Administrative File.

64. Ibid.

65. "Memorandum Outlining the Investigative Jurisdiction and Responsibilities of the Federal Bureau of Investigation of the Department of Justice, the Military Intelligence Division of the War Department and Office of Naval Intelligence of the Navy Department, February 7, 1941, RG 65, Box 1, NARA.

66. Ibid.

67. "Memorandum on Division of Duties."

CHAPTER FIVE: FOLLOWING THE MONEY

1. Henry Morgenthau III, *Mostly Morgenthau* (New York: Ticknor and Fields, 1991), 286.

2. Jules Witcover, *Sabotage on Black Tom Island* (Chapel Hill, N.C.: Algonquin Books of Chapel Hill, 1989), 13–25; Kai Bird, *The Chairman* (New York: Simon and Schuster, 1992), 80–89.

3. Morgenthau's attitude toward Germany only hardened when he learned that the investigation had uncovered evidence that Hitler's vice-chancellor, Franz von Papen, had played a key role in the plot while serving as the German military attaché in Washington, D.C., from 1914 to 1917. Solid proof was obtained when a cable dated January 26, 1915, to von Papen from Arthur Zimmerman, Germany's undersecretary of state, was discovered in the German Foreign Ministry archives. Zimmerman told von Papen that "sabotage can be carried out in every kind of factory for supplying munitions of war" in the United States. Bird, *The Chairman,* 80.

4. McCloy interviewed James Larkin, an Irish nationalist, in December 1933. Larkin provided a written affidavit acknowledging his participation in the Black Tom Island and

Kingsland sabotage. He admitted that Captain Karl Boy-Ed, Germany's naval attaché in Washington, had offered him "$200 per week" to organize a group of non-German men to work along the waterfront because "the Germans were under strict surveillance." The Germans also gave Larkin a demonstration of an incendiary device composed of a white phosphorus chemical compound. Bird, *The Chairman*, 88.

5. Morgenthau letter to Vice President John Nance Garner, October 8, 1941, Report of the Subcommittee to Investigate the Administration of Internal Security and Other Internal Security Laws of the Committee on the Judiciary, United States Senate, Morgenthau Diaries, vol. 1, 1967, 149, Henry J. Morgenthau Papers, FDR Library.

6. "You can see by the accompanying memorandum that the Boss wants you to read this and send it back to me to put in our secret files." Watson's letter contains a typewritten footnote referring to a January 6, 1940, Hoover memorandum to Watson and Roosevelt's instructions to "show this to Henry Morgenthau, Jr. in confidence and file? F.D.R." Following Roosevelt's instructions is an abstract of Hoover's letter (original not contained in the file) that reads in part: "transmitting photostatic copy of memo showing withdrawals made from Amtorg Corp. at Chase Nat'l Bank during week ending Dec. 22, 1939. This company is trading and commercial agency of the Soviet Gov't." Watson letter to Morgenthau, January 11, 1940, OF10b, FDR Library.

7. In 1939 the New York office of the FBI had a total complement of approximately 100 special agents. Twenty-five were assigned exclusively to financial and bank fraud matters. The Manton case was the most important investigation in the New York office at that time. Interview of Eugene Rinta, November 12, 1998; "Manton Praises Referees," *New York Times*, August 25, 1938, 13; "Dewey Says Judge Manton Got $400,000 for Litigants, Sends Charges to Congress," *New York Times*, January 30, 1939, 1; "Manton Sentenced to Two Years after Futile Plea," *New York Times*, June 21, 1939, 1.

8. In her 2004 study of Soviet espionage in the United States, Katherine Sibley writes that Raymond E. Rockefeller, an analyst for the Dies committee, produced a report entitled "Preliminary Report on Examination of Bank Statements of Russian Banks." His report suggests that the Soviet Union was indeed engaging in such activities. Sibley, *Red Spies in America*, 72.

9. Morgenthau acknowledged Hoover's request for suggestions about how FBI representatives could obtain data on foreign funds in general and French funds in particular. He told Hoover that the Treasury Department "is anxious to cooperate" and offered him access to department files and Federal Reserve Bank records for additional useful information. Morgenthau letter to Hoover, December 3, 1940, Morgenthau Papers.

10. Hoover letters to Watson, May 25, 1940, and June 4, 1940, and Hoover letter to Watson, "Present Status of Espionage and Counterespionage Operations of the Federal Bureau of Investigation," OF10b, FDR Library; Foxworth wire to Hoover, May 24, 1940, Hoover letter to Roosevelt, May 25, 1940, Roosevelt note to Watson, May 27, 1940, OF10b, Box 11, Folder "Justice Department, FBI Reports, 1940," 55–99, FDR Library.

11. At a cabinet meeting on the day after the German invasion of Holland and Belgium, Roosevelt personally ordered Morgenthau to freeze Dutch and Belgian funds in U.S. banks. Doris Kearns Goodwin, *No Ordinary Time* (New York: Simon and Schuster, 1994), 35. Morgenthau thanked Hoover for a series of reports on German and Italian funds in a letter to Hoover, December 9, 1940, Morgenthau Papers.

12. FBI Report of SA A. I. Means, "Otto K. Kuehn, with aliases, Friedel Kuehn, with aliases," Espionage–G, October 30, 1940, RG 165, Box 4082, Report 419, NARA. Note copies of Means's report were sent via IIC liaison to the MID and ONI.

13. Gaston memorandum to Morgenthau, November 11, 1940, Box 222, Morgenthau Papers.

14. Ibid.

15. Ibid.

16. Hoover letter to Morgenthau, November 29, 1940, Box 224, Morgenthau Papers.

17. Goodwin, *No Ordinary Time,* 44; Mark M. Lowenthal, "Searching for National Intelligence: U.S. Intelligence and Policy before the Second World War," *Intelligence and National Security* 6, no. 4 (1991): 737–739; Robert Dallek, *Franklin D. Roosevelt and American Foreign Policy, 1932–1945* (New York: Oxford University Press, 1979), 239–240.

18. *U.S. Statutes at Large* 54 (1939): 712.

19. John Morton Blum, *V Was for Victory* (New York: Harcourt, Brace, Jovanovich, 1976), 132–133. For an informed study of how German companies used front corporations in the United States to avoid British economic blockade, see "The Campaign against German Business," in *The Secret History of British Intelligence in the Americas, 1940–1945* (New York: Fromm International, 1999); Arnold letter to John L. Sullivan, May 16, 1940, RG 56, NARA; A. V. Sullivan, Treasury Department clerk, letter to Brennan, August 14, 1940, with attachment entitled "History of National Defense Bills in Numerical Order," RG 56, NARA.

20. Morgenthau letter to Vice President Garner, October 21, 1941, Morgenthau Diaries, vol. 1, 147–148.

21. David Brinkley, *Washington Goes to War* (New York: Ballantine Books, 1988), 62.

22. Sophisticated strategies for the movement of large sums of money were routinely used by foreign intelligence services. Soon after the British Security Coordination (BSC) was established in New York City in July 1940, U.S. banks were regularly used to move funds abroad covertly to pay for weapons and supplies. Illustrating this was a transaction involving the BSC and the Office of Strategic Services (OSS) under General William Donovan. After consultation with the Treasury Department and the Bankers Trust Company, the BSC paid the dollar equivalent of nearly 2 million Portuguese esquedos. "This money was required by agents of SOE [Special Operations Executive] and OSS and was made available to them through the Lisbon office of Bensuade & Co." *Secret History of British Intelligence in the Americas,* 428.

23. Morgenthau letter to Hoover, September 19, 1940, Morgenthau Papers.

24. Hoover letter to Watson, September 28, 1940, Report 329, and Hoover letter to Watson, September 3, 1940, Report 293, OF10b, FDR Library; memorandum, "FBI Letters Turned over to Mr. Gaston," September 19, 1940, Morgenthau Papers.

25. "Confidential Report Re Sale of Preferential Blocked German Marks in the United States," Department of Justice, War Division, Economic Warfare Section, May 30, 1945, RG 60, NARA; George Jaffin memorandum to Howard F. Corcoran, March 4, 1943, RG 60, Entry 258B, Box 82, NARA (hereafter, Jaffin memo).

26. Jaffin memo.

27. Ibid.

28. Rueckwanderer Application, RG 60, Entry 258B, Box 821, NARA; "Confidential Report Re Sale of German Marks."

29. Norman J. Goda, "Banking on Hitler: Chase National Bank and the Rueckwanderer Mark Scheme, 1936–1941," U.S. Intelligence and the Nazis, National Archives Trust Board for the Nazi War Crimes and Japanese Imperial Government Records, Interagency Working Group, Washington, D.C.

30. Jaffin memo.

31. Goda, "Banking on Hitler." As soon as the FBI became aware of the scheme, the New York office opened an espionage investigation, Case 65-1529.

32. Ibid.

33. Ibid.

34. Klaus memorandum to Bernstein, August 8, 1941, RG 131, NARA.

35. Goda, "Banking on Hitler."

36. Ibid.

37. Ibid.

38. Ibid.

39. Ibid.

40. Ibid.

CHAPTER SIX: WIRES AND BUGS

1. Memorandum of conversation, May 20, 1940, Morgenthau Diaries, Microfiche 562 (New York: Clearwater Publishing Company); Dallek, *Franklin D. Roosevelt and American Foreign Policy,* 225; Roosevelt memorandum to Jackson, May 21, 1940, Official and Confidential Files, Report 163, FBI Reading Room.

2. David Kahn, *The Reader of Gentlemen's Mail* (New Haven, Conn.: Yale University Press, 2004), 11–12.

3. Herbert O. Yardley, *The American Black Chamber* (Indianapolis: Bobbs-Merrill, 1931), 20–30.

4. Ibid.

5. Howard K. Beale, *Theodore Roosevelt and the Rise of American World Power* (Baltimore: Johns University Hopkins Press, 1956), 8–9.

6. Stimson served as secretary of war from 1911 to 1913, secretary of state from 1929 to 1933, and secretary of war again from 1940 to 1945. Stimson's 685-page memoir make no mention of Yardley, MI8, or the legislation passed in the wake of Yardley's exposures. Henry L. Stimson and McGeorge Bundy, *On Active Service in Peace and War* (New York: Harper and Brothers, 1947), xxi.

7. "In a period of twelve years, this Secretary (Henry L. Stimson) was the first diplomatist who, well aware that all great powers have their Black Chambers, had the courage—or was it naivete?—to announce that diplomatic correspondence must be inviolate, thus renouncing the secret practices of the American Cryptographic Bureau. Now that the Black Chamber has been destroyed there is no reason for withholding its secret." Yardley, *American Black Chamber,* foreword.

8. Yardley specifically identified Dr. S. W. Collins, "England's foremost secret-ink chemist," as the specialist sent to the United States to assist MI8. In another move that undoubtedly caused questions about the adequacy of British and U.S. security, Yardley included a photo in the book that he described as the "British Secret-Ink Laboratory, responsible for the capture of many German spies." Yardley, *American Black Chamber,* 250.

9. Ibid., 332.

10. "State Department Discredits Statements in the Book, *American Black Chamber,*" *New York Times,* June 2, 1931, 18; David Kahn, *The Codebreakers* (New York: Scribner, 1996), 364.

11. Kahn, *The Codebreakers,* 363–367; Communications Act of 1934, *U.S. Statutes at Large* 48, pt. 1 (1933–1934): 122–123.

12. Communications Act of 1934, 1064–1105.

13. This is a direct quote from Section 605 and was certainly written with Yardley in mind. It is no coincidence that the section is entitled "Unauthorized Publications of Communications." Ibid., 1104.

14. The Court's ruling stated that "the statute forbidding anyone, unless authorized by the sender to intercept a telephone message and directing that 'no person' shall divulge or publish the message or its substance to 'any person' comprehends federal agents and in prosecution of violation of statutes relating to smuggling, barred testimony of such agents concerning substance of defendant's interstate communications overheard by agents who had intercepted messages by tapping telephone wires." *Nardone et al. v. United States,* 58 S. Ct. 302–304 (1937).

15. *Nardone et al. v. United States,* 60 S. Ct. 308–310 (1939).

16. Ibid.

17. "Blow for Liberty," *Boston Globe,* December 12, 1939, 18; "Court Widens Ban on Wire Tapping," *Washington Post,* December 12, 1939, 1; "Supreme Court's Decision on Wiretapping," *New York Times,* December 12, 1939, 20; "Wire Tapping Ruled Out," *Los Angeles Times,* December 12, 1939, pat 2, 4.

18. Hoover's report to President Roosevelt was sent by Brigadier General Edwin Watson (his military aide) to Colonel E. R. W. McCabe, the army's assistant chief of staff for intelligence, for his views. McCabe characterized it as "a very accurate picture of Japanese propaganda methods, as verified by our reliable sources. The present trend of Japanese efforts is apparently away from cultural and educational lines toward more practical and effective approaches." McCabe letter to Watson, December 14, 1939, Report 12, OF10b, FDR Library. "Fugitive Spy Suspect Found in Nazi Crew," *Washington Post,* January 15, 1940, 2; "FBI Seizes 18, Arsenal in Revolt Plot," *New York Times,* January 15, 1940, 1.

19. "Norris Gives Senate Plea to Probe FBI," *Washington Post,* February 27, 1940, 3; "Federal Spying Hit in Senate Report," *New York Times,* March 13, 1940, 24.

20. "Prosecution Seen Sired by Politics," *New York Times,* April 7, 1940, 2; Hoover memorandum to Connelley, January 30, 1940, Connelley Personnel File.

21. "Attack on the FBI Laid to 'Left Wing,'" *New York Times,* April 26, 1940, 14; "OGPU Unthinkable Says Hoover," *New York Times,* March 17, 1940, 15; "FBI Attacks Laid to Reds by Hoover," *New York Times,* May 4, 1940, 6.

22. From 1931 until Jackson's order, the official FBI policy on wiretapping was that "telephone and telegraph wires shall not be tapped unless prior authorization of the Director of the Bureau has been secured." The new policy read: "Wiretapping, entrapment, or the use of any other improper, illegal, or unethical tactic in procuring information in connection with investigative activity will not be tolerated by the Bureau." Press release, March 18, 1940, Official and Confidential Files, No. 164, FBI Reading Room.

23. "White House Hails Neutrality Unit," *New York Times,* April 20, 1940, 8.

24. Morris Ernst, "Why I No Longer Fear the FBI," *Readers' Digest,* December 1950; Curt Gentry, *J. Edgar Hoover: The Man and the Secrets* (New York: W. W. Norton, 1991), 231; "FBI Is No OGPU, Jackson Asserts," *New York Times,* March 31, 1940, 19.

25. Hoover letter to Jackson, April 13, 1940, Box 94, Jackson Papers.

26. Morgenthau memorandum of conversation with Margaret LeHand, June 25, 1940, Microfiche 593; Morgenthau memorandum of conversation with General Edwin Watson, June 26, 1940, Microfiche 594. In 1940 Admiral Anderson, director of the ONI, described President Roosevelt as "quite intelligence minded," Anderson oral history interview, 230. Stimson Diary, May 23, 1941, Henry L. Stimson Diaries, Reel 6, 58–59. "When Congress dawdled and diddled about his [President Roosevelt's] request for authority for the FBI to tap wires of aliens and persons engaged in sabotage, he simply ordered that it be done." Jackson, *That Man,* 48, 68.

27. Years later, in a memoir (unfinished) he was writing shortly before his death, Jackson noted that the president's wiretap memorandum "limited the cases" of wiretapping under his authority and fixed responsibility "pretty clearly" for enforcing those limitations. Hoover regularly reported the taps to Jackson and usually obtained advance authorization from the attorney general. In Jackson's view, "Hoover had no desire to abuse it [wiretapping authority]. He was interested in those major offenses, and not in minor ones. The fact that he refused to go into labor matters at the request of the War Department and supervise labor conversations showed a restraint in the use of his powers for which, I may say, he was never given credit outside." Jackson, *That Man,* 69.

28. Hoover letter to Watson, September 28, 1940, with attachment entitled "Re: Washington Embassies," and Watson memorandum to Roosevelt, October 8, 1940, OF10b, Box 11, FDR Library.

CHAPTER SEVEN: OPPORTUNITIES MISSED

1. Walter Krivitsky, *In Stalin's Secret Service* (New York: Harper and Brothers, 1939), 109.

2. Ibid., xii–xvii.

3. Gordon Brook-Shepherd, *The Storm Petrels* (New York: Harcourt, Brace, Jovanovich, 1977), 140; Robert Conquest, *The Great Terror* (New York: Oxford University Press, 1990), 179–180.

4. "Together with his childhood friend Walter Krivitsky, 'Ludwig' was a mainstay of Russian intelligence and has been so since the 1920s." Robert Lamphere and Tom Schactman, *The FBI-KGB Wars* (New York: Random House, 1986), 52.

5. Ibid., 52–53. Massing was convinced by Reiss to stop attending local Communist Party meetings and consider espionage as a career. Appealing to her romantic nature and

political naiveté, he persuaded her that spying for the Marxist cause was a noble pursuit and that she should use her talents for Stalin and the party. On Reiss's instructions, Massing began providing him and his NKVD associates with the identities of potential recruits and evaluations of their susceptibility to espionage approach. She also located safe apartments for agent meetings, served as a mail drop, and later acted as a courier. In the late 1930s, while serving as a courier between the United States and Europe, she began actively recruiting agents on her own initiative. Her zeal and commitment resulted in the successful recruitment of Lawrence Duggan, a foreign service officer with the State Department. He later served as head of the department's Latin American Section. Hede Massing, *This Deception* (New York: Duell, Sloan and Pearce, 1951), 34.

6. Lamphere and Schactman, *The FBI-KGB Wars*, 54.

7. "Alexander Barmine, a senior GRU officer stationed in Athens, Greece defected from the Soviet Union. He secretly made his way to France and eventually to the United States in 1939. He later served in the Office of Strategic Services during the Second World War. After the war he became the head of the Russian Section of the Voice of America network." Brook-Shepherd, *Storm Petrels*, 144.

8. "When news of Reiss' death reached me on September fifth I realized that my own situation was truly desperate." W. G. Krivitsky, "My Flight from Stalin," *Saturday Evening Post,* August 5, 1939; Nigel West, *MI5: British Security Operations 1909–1945* (New York: Stein and Day, 1982), 72; FBI interview of Paul Wohl (date unknown), FBI report, March 19, 1941, File No. 100-11146, Walter Krivitsky File, FBI Reading Room.

9. Isaac Don Levine, *Eyewitness to History* (New York: Hawthorne Books, 1973), 184–185.

10. W. G. Krivitsky, "Stalin Appeases Hitler," *Saturday Evening Post,* April 29, 1939.

11. Fletcher Warren memorandum to Messersmith, May 19, 1939; Congressman John McCormick letter to Secretary of State Cordell Hull, April 22, 1939, loaned by Vern Newton, director of the FDR Library, who obtained them from the Department of State under the Freedom of Information/ Privacy Act (hereafter, Newton Papers); Loy Henderson, memorandum of conversation: General Krivitsky, March 15, 1939, Newton Papers.

12. W. G. Krivitsky "Stalin's Hand in Spain," *Saturday Evening Post,* August 15, 1939; Warren memorandum, Newton Papers.

13. "Stalin's Foe Pleads for Asylum Here," *New York Times,* July 7, 1939.

14. Adolf Berle wrote as follows: "I asked Levine whether he knows the names; Levine did not, but he would get them from Krivitsky and give me a personal and confidential memorandum as to who they were. I said when I had this I could determine how to proceed." Berle memorandum, May 19, 1939, Newton Papers.

15. Strong corroboration of Krivitsky's 1939 revelations emerged in April 1997 when the National Security Agency declassified the so-called Mask communications. These communications consisted of Comintern radio messages decrypted and reported by the British Government Code and Cypher School. The messages were enciphered using an encoded alphabet derived from a book held by both correspondents (usually a dictionary, but telephone directories and other books were also referred to in the messages). Messages were transmitted from Moscow and clandestine radio stations abroad. The correspondents abroad were agents or national Communist Party officials in Austria, China, Czechoslovakia, Denmark, France, Great Britain, Greece, Holland, Spain, Swe-

den, Switzerland, and the United States. The messages covered a wide variety of subjects, ranging from policy, propaganda, and publications to finance, demonstrations, training courses in the USSR, security, clandestine courier arrangements, and travel visas to the Soviet Union. A complete set of the translated messages is on file at the National Cryptologic Museum, Fort George G. Meade, Md., and in the PRO, London. Ruth Shipley memorandum, July 11, 1939, Newton Papers.

16. Shipley memorandum, Newton Papers.

17. Ibid.

18. "Mysterious Krivitsky Hunted for Deportation," *New York Times,* July 12, 1939.

19. Krivitsky, "Stalin's Hand in Spain"; FBI report, "Moishe Stern with aliases," August 11, 1939, Krivitsky File. Krivitsky's value as a source of information can be discerned from the fact that fifteen days before he was interviewed by the FBI, Levine was removed from the FBI's mailing list because "of his association with W. G. Krivitsky the former 'Red Army General' who recently accused Josef Stalin of seeking an alliance with Hitler." L. B. Nichols memorandum to Clyde Tolson, July 11, 1939, Krivitsky File.

20. Krivitsky, "Stalin's Hand in Spain." The FBI agent who interviewed Krivitsky concluded that "he accepts his own conclusions as facts and so relates them and in reply to a question he would state his opinion as fact rather than admit a lack of definite knowledge." Krivitsky File.

21. Krivitsky, "My Flight from Stalin"

22. Hoover letter to Warren, November 14, 1939; Messersmith letter to Hoover, November 18, 1939, Newton Papers.

23. In the fall of 1939 the British government spirited Krivitsky out of the United States by submarine and interviewed him intensively for a number of weeks. He provided valuable information concerning Soviet intelligence penetrations of the British defense establishment and the Foreign Office. His information led to the conviction of Francis Herbert King, a Foreign Office code clerk, who received a lengthy prison sentence. D. Cameron Watt, "Francis Herbert King: A Soviet Source in the Foreign Office," *Intelligence and National Security* 3, no. 4 (October 1998): 63–83; Vern Newton, *The Cambridge Spies* (New York: Madison Books, 1991), 14–19, 23.

24. Krivitsky's body was discovered in his locked hotel room in Washington, D.C., on February 10, 1941. He died of a gunshot wound to the head that was officially ruled a suicide. Despite the absence of any physical evidence suggesting foul play, conspiracy theories continue to proliferate even today. Hoover, in an apparent attempt to avoid being swept up in the controversy, claimed that the FBI was "not interested in whether he was murdered or committed suicide." He then washed his hands of the matter, claiming that Krivitsky's death was "primarily a local matter within the District of Columbia over which the Bureau exercises no jurisdiction." Hoover letter to SAC, New York office, March 15, 1941, Krivitsky File.

25. Edward Gazur, *Alexander Orlov: The FBI's KGB General* (New York: Carroll and Graf, 2002), 186–189.

26. Ibid.

27. Ibid., 182–202.

28. Ibid., 201.

29. John Costello and Oleg Tsarev, *Deadly Illusions* (New York: Crown, 1993), 318.

30. Ibid., 318, 319.

31. Gazur, *Alexander Orlov*, 291–292.

32. Ibid., 294.

33. Orlov later claimed that the flat-pack film contained photos of his daughter, Vera, and her governess in Spain. Costello and Tsarev, *Deadly Illusions*, 322–323.

34. Gazur, *Alexander Orlov*, 580.

35. Joseph Albright and Marcia Kunstel, *Bombshell* (New York: Times Books, 1997), 244–253.

36. Costello and Tsarev, *Deadly Illusions*, 313–314.

CHAPTER EIGHT: SPECIAL OVERSEAS ASSIGNMENTS

1. Foxworth memorandum to J. Edgar Hoover, May 8, 1940, FBI file 65-10347, "Carl Norden, with aliases, Espionage." The file was provided to the author by Dr. Stephen Mc-Farland, Auburn University, Auburn. Ala.; Dorwart, *Conflict of Duty*, 163.

2. Dorwart, *Conflict of Duty*, 164; Kermit Roosevelt Papers, Box 7, Manuscript Division, LOC.

3. Dorwart, *Conflict of Duty*, 165.

4. Foxworth letters to Hoover, May 8, 1940, June 4, 1940, FBI file 65-10347.

5. Stephen McFarland, *America's Pursuit of Precision Bombing, 1910–1945* (Washington, D.C.: Smithsonian Institution Press, 1995), 59.

6. Reminiscences of Admiral John S. Thach, 114–115, Special Collections Division, Chester Nimitz Library, USNA.

7. McFarland, *America's Pursuit of Precision Bombing*, 113–114; reminiscences of Admiral Daniel V. Gallery, 33–34, Special Collections Division, Nimitz Library, USNA; reminiscences of Admiral Frederick Stanton Withington, 41–42, ibid.; Kirk letter to Admiral Walter Anderson, January 4, 1940, Box 2, Admiral Alan G. Kirk Papers, Naval Historical Center, Washington Navy Yard, Washington, D.C.

8. McFarland, *America's Pursuit of Precision Bombing*, 53–54.

9. Ibid.

10. Ibid., 116. "In view of the evident importance attached to obtaining this Bomb Sight by the Air Ministry. . . ." Kirk letter to Admiral Anderson, January 4, 1940, Box 2, Kirk Papers.

11. Stark described the situation facing the United States as the gravest crisis "since the winter of Valley Forge." Stark letter to Senator Claude Pepper, May 13, 1940, Box 1, Admiral Harold R. Stark Papers, Naval Historical Center; McFarland, *America's Pursuit of Precision Bombing*, 118.

12. Crosby interview; Foxworth letter to Hoover, May 8, 1940, FBI file 65-10347.

13. Hoover memorandum, May 9, 1940, FBI file 65-10347.

14. Ibid.; Gentry, *J. Edgar Hoover*, 265.

15. Memorandum, May 10, 1940; Foxworth letter to Hoover, June 4, 1940, FBI file 65-10347.

16. Ibid.

17. Ibid.

18. Ibid.

19. Foxworth letter to Hoover, June 4, 1940, FBI file 65-10347.

20. Hoover letter to General Edwin O. Watson, June 11, 1940, FBI file 65-10347.

21. Ibid.

22. Ray Bearse and Anthony Read, *Conspirator: The Untold Story of Tyler Kent* (New York: Doubleday, 1991), 10–18.

23. Ibid.

24. Dallek, *Franklin D. Roosevelt and American Foreign Policy*, 79–81; Bearse and Read, *Conspirator*, 20–21.

25. Martin C. Weil, *A Pretty Good Club* (New York: W. W. Norton, 1979), 47.

26. Andrew and Gordievsky, *KGB: The Inside Story*, 126.

27. Charles E. Bohlen, *Witness to History* (New York: W. W. Norton, 1973).

28. Charles W. Thayer, *Bears in the Caviar* (Philadelphia: J. B. Lippincott, 1950), 95–97; Bohlen, *Witness to History*, 68; Weil, *A Pretty Good Club*, 55.

29. Bearse and Read, *Conspirator*, 25; Thayer, *Bears in the Caviar*, 148.

30. Bearse and Read, *Conspirator*, 36; FBI interview of Tatyana Richardson, January 23, 1947, RG 65, Entry 37G, Box 7, NARA.

31. Andrew and Gordievsky, *KGB: The Inside Story*, 89; Bohlen, *Witness to History*, 71–72; John R. Deane, *Strange Alliance* (New York: Viking Press, 1946), 154.

32. Andrew and Gordievsky, *KGB: The Inside Story*, 85; "Deception on a Grand Scale," *Journal of Intelligence and Counterintelligence* 1, no. 4 (1986–1988): 87.

33. Andrew and Gordievsky, *KGB: The Inside Story*, 173–174.

34. Ibid., 227–228; Bohlen, *Witness to History*, 20–21.

35. Bearse and Read, *Conspirator*, 83.

36. Ibid.

37. McClintock memorandum to Minister of Legation (undated), Box 2, Bearse Papers, FDR Library.

38. Ibid.

39. Breckinridge Long, *The War Diaries of Breckinridge Long* (Lincoln: University of Nebraska Press, 1966), 111.

40. Bearse and Read, *Conspirator*, 83.

41. Liddell letter to Johnson, February 7, 1940, and Johnson cable to Dunn (marked "Personal and Strictly Confidential"), February 4, 1940, Box 2, Bearse Papers; Weil, *A Pretty Good Club*, 270.

42. Welles memorandum to Long, May 6, 1940, Box 65, Sumner Welles Papers, FDR Library; Benjamin Sumner Welles, *Sumner Welles: FDR'S Global Strategist* (New York: St. Martin's Press, 1997), 268.

43. Long, *War Diaries*, 74–75.

44. Johnson memorandum, May 28, 1940, Box 2, Bearse Papers (hereafter, Johnson memo).

45. Ibid.

46. Johnson cable to the Secretary of State (marked "Secret"), May 30, 1940, Box 2, Bearse Papers.

47. Ibid.

48. Johnson memo; Francis Lowenheim, Harold D. Langley, and Manfred Jonas, *Roosevelt and Churchill: Their Secret Wartime Correspondence* (New York: Saturday Review Press/E. P. Dutton, 1975), 97.

49. Lowenheim et al., *Roosevelt and Churchill*, 97.

50. Johnson memo.

51. Long, *War Diaries*, 96.

52. Ibid.

53. Ibid.

54. Lowenheim et al., *Roosevelt and Churchill*, xv.

55. Johnson memo.

56. Long, *War Diaries*, 100–101.

57. Sam Tannenhaus, *Whittaker Chambers* (New York: Random House, 1997), 374.

58. Long, *War Diaries*, 100.

59. Ibid.

60. Edward Tamm memorandum to Hoover, June 18, 1940, Tamm Personnel File 67-1585-1280.

61. Interview of former FBI special agent Horton Telford, September 11, 1996, Rehoboth Beach, Del.

62. Ibid.

63. Ibid.

64. "Folders on Individuals," U.S. vs. Herman Lang, CR-38425, RG 21, Box 27, FRC, N.Y.

65. Hoover letter to General Edwin O. Watson, December 16, 1940, Box 22, President's Secretary's File, FDR Library.

66. Author interview of John Fox, FBI historian, March 14, 2006.

67. Hoover letter to Watson, December 16, 1940.

68. Ibid.

69. Ibid.

70. Ibid.

71. Ibid.

72. Ibid.

73. Ibid.

74. D. M. Ladd memorandum to Tamm, May 25, 1944, RG 65, Box 2, NARA.

75. Ibid. Ladd informed Tamm that the State Department files contained a note on President Roosevelt's stationery and signed "F.D.R." The note expressed satisfaction that copies of the messages between Churchill and himself had been found in Kent's possession, as well as the president's views on the importance of these messages: "These messages, together with others, might well be called the precursors of two subsequent logical developments. First, the sale for cash to Great Britain, at the time of and subsequent to Dunkirk, of various Army and Navy equipment which we considered at the time either surplus and out of date—such as field guns which so greatly helped Britain to bulk up its defense against probable invasion in July, August, and September, 1940. These messages were also precursors of the arrangement for the sale of fifty old American destroyers in exchange for eight naval bases which extend our defense across a long distance to seaward, northward and southward."

76. "History of the Operations of M.S. during the War 1939–1945," KV4/227, 47, PRO, Kew, England.

77. Report of special agent R. W. Wall, April 17, 1941, RG 65, Box 2, NARA.

CHAPTER NINE: BRITISH SECURITY COORDINATION

1. The Roosevelt administration was sensitive to criticism by isolationists and went to great lengths to avoid even the appearance of not wholeheartedly supporting neutrality. As late as 1940, Professor Archibald Vivian Hill, the British scientific attaché to Ottawa, Canada, warned his Foreign Office superiors that no scientific attaché should be assigned to Washington because of problems with isolationist elements in the United States. David Zimmerman, *Top Secret Exchange* (Montreal: McGill-Queens University Press, 1996), 68.

2. Anthony Cave Brown, *"C," The Secret Life of Sir Stewart Menzies* (New York: Macmillan, 1987), 263.

3. Christopher Andrew, "Churchill and Intelligence," *Intelligence and National Security* 3, no. 3 (July 1988): 181–193; Richard C. Thurlow, "British Fascism and State Surveillance, 1933–1945," *Intelligence and National Security* 3, no. 1 (January 1988): 77–99; David Kahn, *Seizing the Enigma* (New York: Houghton Mifflin, 1991), 184–185, 281; Brown, *Secret Life of Sir Stewart Menzies*, 263. For a detailed analysis of Great Britain's efforts to draw the United States into the war in Europe, see Nicholas John Cull, *Selling War* (New York: Oxford University Press, 1995).

4. Among Stephenson's air combat victims was Lothar von Richtofen, the brother of the famous German air ace Baron Manfred von Richtofen. He also served as one of Churchill's sources of information on international business and financial matters during the 1930s, when the future prime minister was alone and out of office. H. Montgomery Hyde, *Room 3603* (New York: Farrar, Straus, 1963), 3–8. While a prisoner of war, Stephenson discovered a can opener in the camp and took it with him when he escaped. When he discovered that it was not patented, he wasted no time obtaining a patent for the gadget and earned his first fortune by manufacturing it. Thomas E. Mahl, *Desperate Deception* (New York: Brassey's, 1998), 9; "The Coordinators of Information and British Intelligence," *Studies in Intelligence* 18, no.1-S (Spring 1974): 15.

5. *Secret History of British Intelligence in the Americas*, xxv; Thomas F. Troy, *Donovan and the CIA* (Washington, D.C.: CIA, 1981), 31; Brown, *Secret Life of Sir Stewart Menzies*, 262. "Hoover, who was personally anti-Nazi, welcomed Menzies' approach." John Ranleigh, *The Agency* (New York: Simon and Schuster, 1987), 40.

6. *Secret History of British Intelligence in the Americas*, 4–5.

7. For the remainder of the war, the BSC would provide cover for the activities of the British Secret Intelligence Service and the newly formed Special Operations Executive, in addition to its overt function of safeguarding British interests in the United States. Ibid., 239–240.

8. David Stafford, *Churchill and Secret Service* (Woodstock, N.Y.: Overlook Press, 1998), 204; memorandum, "Forthcoming Tour of Latin American Countries by Representatives of the Director of Commercial and Cultural Relations between the American Republics," September 9, 1940, RG 38, ONI, Special Activities Branch, Special Intelligence, Box 1, Folder "OP-16-F-9 File SIS (General) 1940," NARA. Stephenson, in a telegram to Menzies in September 1941, described the relationship with the FBI. He told "C" that security coordination is the name given by the Americans to camouflage the purely SIS [MI6] organization in U.S.A., where, owing to friendly relations with

Americans, it goes slightly beyond its normal function of obtaining information and undertakes with permission of Americans, certain security and anti-sabotage questions." Timothy Naftali, "X-2 and the Apprenticeship of American Counterintelligence" (Ph.D. diss., Harvard University, 1992), 35.

9. Chapman Pincher, *Too Secret Too Long* (New York: St. Martin's Press, 1984), 45; *Secret History of British Intelligence in the Americas*, 466–467.

10. In January 1942 an RSS officer was assigned to the BSC to coordinate the full exchange of illicit wireless intelligence between Great Britain, the United States, and Canada. *Secret History of British Intelligence in the Americas*, 467.

11. Author interview of Paul Napier, August 20, 1989; interview of Hugh H. Clegg, October 2, 1974, Oral Histories, Civil Rights in Mississippi Digital Archives, University of Southern Mississippi, Hattiesburg; Hoover memorandum to Roosevelt, October 15, 1940, OF10b, Box 1, Report 365, FDR Library. Nine years later Clegg accompanied special agent Robert J. Lamphere to London to interview Soviet spy Klaus Fuchs at Wormwood Scrubs Prison. Fuchs identified Harry Gold as his U.S. contact, leading to Gold's arrest on charges of espionage. Gold later testified against Julius and Ethel Rosenberg. Hoover memorandum to Clegg, November 12, 1940, Official and Confidential Files.

12. Clegg interview.

13. "Law Enforcement Duties in Wartime Emergencies," Box 3, Folder 61, Lawler Papers.

14. Ibid.

15. Ibid.

16. Ibid.

17. Ibid.

18. Hoover letter to Watson, March 6, 1941, OF10b, Box 1, Report 671, FDR Library (hereafter, Clegg memorandum); Raymond E. Lee, *The London Journals of General Raymond E. Lee 1940–1941* (Boston: Little, Brown, 1971), 124.

19. Clegg memorandum.

20. Eventually, 1,200 British technicians were assigned to censorship duties in Bermuda, handling postal, telegraph, and radio traffic between Europe and the Western Hemisphere. William Stevenson, *A Man Called Intrepid* (New York: Harcourt, Brace, Jovanovich, 1976), 172. As the Germans' photographic technology improved, they introduced the microdot, which reduces a microphotograph to the size of a period at the end of a sentence. This breakthrough meant that the Abwehr could now communicate as many as 300,000 characters of information on a piece of film no larger than 70 millimeters long. Norman Polmar and Thomas B. Allen, *Spy Book* (New York: Random House, 1997), 367; "The Mexican Microdot Case #1," RG 165, Box 6, NARA; "German Espionage in Latin America," RG 319, Box 6, NARA; Leslie B. Rout Jr. and John F. Bratzel, *The Shadow War* (Frederick, Md.: University Publications of America, 1986). *The Shadow War* and Stanley Hilton's *Hitler's Secret War in South America* (Baton Rouge: Louisiana University Press, 1981) are still the most comprehensive studies on the activities of the Special Intelligence Service during the Second World War.

21. The Duquesne case was instrumental to the censorship education of the British. According to the official history of British intelligence during the Second World War, both MI5 and MI6 began a significant expansion in 1935. Due to "a lack of imagination or a lack

of funds and probably for both reasons," neither took the necessary steps to build and train a sufficient staff to meet the growing Nazi threat in Europe. By August 1939 MI5 had a staff of only 83 professional counterintelligence officers and a total complement of 336 people. Exact figures for MI6 are not available, but its relatively small size can be gleaned from the fact that it had only 6 officers posted in the Western Hemisphere before 1940. This neglect during the interwar years revealed the inadequacy of the British understanding of German intelligence methods and organization. As the official historian notes, before 1939, neither MI5 nor MI6 even knew the name of the German military organization; they were equally unaware that Admiral Wilhelm Canaris was the head of the Abwehr. Francis H. Hinsley and C. A. G. Simpkins, *British Intelligence in the Second World War,* vol. 4 (New York: Cambridge University Press, 1993), 9–12; Hoover letter to Watson, November 27, 1941, with attached showing locations of FBI personnel in Central and South America.

22. Hoover letter to Watson, September 4, 1941, OF10b, Report 909, FDR Library; Farago, *The Game of the Foxes,* 429–430.

23. FBI file, "Captain Frederick Wiedemann, Espionage–G," File 65-1649, RG 65, Box 98, NARA (hereafter, Wiedemann file); *Secret History of British Intelligence in the Americas,* 353–365.

24. Memorandum, "Ludwig Case," undated, Lawler Papers; Hoover letter to Watson, September 4, 1941, POF, FDR Library.

25. Ibid.

26. Ibid.; *Secret History of British Intelligence in the Americas,* 28. Ludwig was convicted of espionage in March 1942 and sentenced to a twenty-year prison term.

27. *Secret History of British Intelligence in the Americas,* 367–371.

28. Ibid.

29. Berle memorandum, "British Relations," September 14, 1940, Box 64, Berle Papers.

30. *Secret History of British Intelligence in the Americas,* 242.

31. Anonymous letter to Thomas Dewey, January 26, 1939; Hoover letter to Secretary of State Hull, February 27, 1939, Wiedemann file.

32. Ibid.

33. FBI report of special agent C. C. MacCartee, December 2, 1940, Wiedemann file; Christopher Andrew, *For the President's Eyes Only* (New York: Harper Perennial, 1995), 38.

34. Wiedemann file.

35. Ibid.

36. Ibid.

37. Ibid.

38. Ibid. The file clearly indicates that FBI suspicions were not limited to British reports of the meeting. By the fall of 1940 the FBI had wiretaps on Wiseman's home telephone and the office of the British Purchasing Commission in New York City.

CHAPTER TEN: SPECIAL INTELLIGENCE SERVICE

1. *History of the SIS Division,* vol. 1, 1, obtained by the author under the provisions of the Freedom of Information/ Privacy Act. The history is an 800-page, five-volume

internal study of the Special Intelligence Service prepared by the FBI after the Second World War. The objectives of its creation were threefold: (1) to have a "usable handbook concerning the [FBI] operations in the SIS which could be used a guide book in setting up a new SIS operation in the event it becomes necessary," (2) to present accomplishments "if needed for Congressional testimony or for any other similar hearing," and (3) "to outline in general the material contained in [FBI] files and to indicate its location in order that completely detailed data will be available on any phase of our SIS operations in the event it becomes necessary for any reason."

2. The agreement was equally important for another reason. The recent revelation of the Duquesne espionage ring and the president's authorization of the interception of embassy and consulate telephones calls marked a seismic shift in FBI responsibility. Rather than simply investigating violations of U.S. laws, the Bureau now contemplated full-time coverage of the foreign diplomatic presence in the United States. In a May 29, 1940, memorandum, Hoover outlined the FBI's counterintelligence future, including the inauguration of "a counterintelligence service for the purpose of keeping a close check upon the intelligence activities of representatives of all foreign governments." "Memorandum on the Division of Duties between Military Intelligence Division, Office of Naval Intelligence and the Federal Bureau of Investigation," May 29, 1940, RG 65, Box 3, NARA.

3. Rout and Bratzel, *Shadow Wars*, 113; memorandum, "Conference between Representatives of the State Department, Military Intelligence Division of the War Department, Naval Intelligence, and the Federal Bureau of Investigation," June 3, 1940, RG 38, General Files, Box 1, Folder SIS General, NARA.

4. "No snooping" memorandum, "Information," November 1, 1940, RG 38, Box 1, Folder A8-2, Collection of Information Admin Files, 40–43, NARA. Riheldaffer went on to note that by far the "largest number of AGENTS or EMPLOYEES are taken from the petty criminal class, mal-contents, revolutionary refugees or psychopaths. In general only the very highest in the organization work purely for patriotic or selfless reasons." Riheldaffer memorandum to Director of ONI, February 3, 1941, RG 38, Box 1, General Files, Folder SIS (Admin. Pol. Fin.), NARA.

5. Memorandum, "Special Intelligence Service," June 6, 1940, RG 38, Box 1, Folder SIS (General), General Files, 40–42, NARA.

6. Memorandum, "Committee Meeting of State Department, Military Intelligence Division of the War Department, Naval Intelligence and the Federal Bureau of Investigation on June 11, 1940," loaned by Dennis DeBrandt; "Memorandum Prepared by Assistant Secretary of State Berle June 24, 1940 and Approved by the President," SIS Administrative File.

7. Memorandum for the Director, May 25, 1940, SIS Administrative File.

8. Memorandum, "Conference between Representatives of Treasury Department, Military Intelligence Division of the War Department, Naval Intelligence and the Federal Bureau of Investigation on July 28, 1940," loaned by Dennis DeBrandt. Contained in the General Files of the ONI is a rough, handwritten note by an unknown author that refers to a July 23, 1940, letter from Miles to Hoover expressing his reservations about the scope of SIS activities. It reads as follows: "Re. SIS—see Gen Miles secret memo of July 23 '40 to Adm. Anderson (Foxworth, Clegg) suggests SIS activities be limited to Anti-Am in for. Countries unless otherwise requested—Adm A says dead issue—

presently because SIS to activities in Latin Am." RG 38, Box 1, General Files, Folder "General File 1940," NARA. Berle was also crystal clear concerning the SIS mandate. According to Tamm, during a recent meeting Berle had informed him that "absolutely no restrictions whatsoever should be placed upon the SIS operatives who should be expected and instructed to report all information of an economic, industrial, financial, or political nature or in any other category that is of present or potential interest to any branch of the government of the United States." Tamm memorandum to Hoover, August 1, 1940, SIS Administrative File.

9. *History of the SIS Division,* vol. 1, 48.

10. Ibid.

11. Ibid., 1; Letter of Appointment, U.S. Naval Reserve, April 30, 1937, Box 3, Percy Foxworth Papers, Special Collections Division, University of Mississippi, Oxford.

12. Foxworth memorandum for the Director, June 22, 1939, Box 88, Murphy Papers.

13. Hoover memorandum for Murphy, June 19, 1939, Box 88, Murphy Papers.

14. Ibid.

15. Harold Smith letter to Roosevelt, October 7, 1941, and undated draft letter from Roosevelt to Morgenthau, OF79, Box 101, Folder "Treasury Department Authorization, 1941, July–December," FDR Library.

16. Ibid.

17. *History of the SIS Division,* vol. 1, 5.

18. Rout and Bratzel, *Shadow War,* 72–73. In August 1941 Ambassador Josephus Daniels, with the blessing of the State Department and Hoover, appointed Gus Jones, the special agent in charge of the San Antonio, Texas, FBI office to the position of civil attaché at the U.S. embassy in Mexico City. Until his reassignment in 1943, Jones directed all SIS investigations against the Axis in Mexico. Gus T. Jones, "In Mexico" (unpublished autobiographical memoir, undated). The author is grateful to Robert Heibel for providing this unique source of information. One of the great mysteries of counterintelligence history swirls around the State Department career of Lawrence Duggan and his relationship with Berle. On the evening of September 1, 1939, Whittaker Chambers met for hours at Berle's Washington, D.C., home, where he related details of his career as an espionage agent for the Soviets. He identified dozens of GRU spies in the U.S. government, the most prominent of whom were Alger Hiss and Lawrence Duggan. For unknown reasons, Duggan remained at his State Department post until July 1944, when he was eased out of the government because of nagging questions concerning his communist affiliations. On December 11, 1948, he was questioned by FBI agents at his Scarsdale, New York, home concerning Chambers's allegations. Nine days later Duggan either fell or jumped to his death from his sixth-floor Manhattan office. Based on recent scholarship concerning Duggan's affiliation with the Soviets, it is reasonable to conclude that all facets of the SIS from its formation in 1940 were revealed to the Soviets. Weinstein and Vassiliev, *Haunted Wood,* 21; Tannenhaus, *Whittaker Chambers,* 161–162.

19. *History of the SIS Division,* vol. 1, 4; interview of Robert Guerin, October 7, 1994; SIS Administrative File.

20. *History of the SIS Division,* vol. 1, 3.

21. Ibid.

22. Miscellaneous letters of condolence to Susan Foxworth following the death of Percy Foxworth in January 1943, Box 2, Folders 1–6, Foxworth Papers.

23. Rout and Bratzel, *Shadow War,* 40; Mark Riebling, *Wedge* (New York: Alfred A. Knopf, 1994), 3; Guerin interview.

24. "Memorandum Outlining the Investigative Jurisdiction and Responsibility of the Federal Bureau of Investigation of the Department of Justice, the Military Intelligence Division of the War Department and the Office of Naval Intelligence of the Navy Department," February 7, 1941.

25. The XY-code ordinarily required approximately three large pages of closely spaced typing in the guise of a normal letter to encipher one line of information. The use of secret ink, which was still in the experimental stage, was not much more satisfactory. Considerable experience was required to attain any appreciable degree of success. *History of the SIS Division,* vol. 1, 5–6.

26. Foxworth memorandum to Hoover, "Suggested Changes in SIS Work," December 4, 1940, SIS Administrative File.

27. *History of the SIS Division,* vol. 1, 7–8. The assignment of FBI agent to the U.S. embassy at Bogota, Colombia, was the forerunner of the legal attaché system, consisting of a network of agents and employees operating under an FBI agent (the legal attaché) in each U.S. embassy.

28. Hoover memorandum to Foxworth, October 16, 1940, SIS Administrative File, NARA.

29. Ron Charnow, *Titan* (New York: Random House, 1998), 658; memorandum for the Director of ONI, "Forthcoming Tour of Latin American Countries by Representatives of the Director of Commercial and Cultural Relations between the American Republics," September 9, 1940, RG 38, ONI Special Activities Branch, Special Intelligence Section, Box 1, Folder OP-16-F-9, NARA.

30. "Forthcoming Tour."

31. Foxworth memo, "Suggested Changes."

32. Ibid.

33. Ibid.

34. Ibid.

35. Tamm memoranda to Hoover, July 26, 1941, and August 1, 1941, SIS Administrative File.

36. Foxworth memo, "Suggested Changes"; Hoover memorandum to Tolson, December 9, 1940; Carson memorandum, "Informal Minutes Interdepartmental Intelligence Conference Held in the Office of the Director of the FBI," August 27, 1941; Carson memorandum to Hoover, "Agenda Interdepartmental Intelligence Conference to be held in the office of General Miles September 2, 1941," September 2, 1941, SIS Administrative File. In March 1941 Hoover was informed that fear of publicity and exposure made it essential not to disclose to applicants for SIS positions or American businessmen that the FBI was operating in South America. Hoover again displayed his deep-seated concerns by noting, "I agree more heartily." Foxworth memorandum to Hoover, March 4, 1941, SIS Administrative File.

37. It is apparent that Hoover was approached informally by one of his deputies, perhaps Foxworth, who suggested that expenses could be offset by increasing the salaries

of agents assigned to foreign SIS posts. Hoover's fixation on certain legal exactitudes surfaced when he warned his staff "to grant an increase to our Agents or representatives, which may be used to pay such expenses would be accomplishing by subterfuge what is not allowed by law and I cannot, therefore, authorize any such procedure." Hoover memorandum to Tolson, December 9, 1940, SIS Administrative File.

38. *History of the SIS Division,* vol. 1, 15.

39. Ibid.; author interview of Kenneth M. Crosby, August 8, 1996. During the first year of the SIS's existence, the Spanish language was taught to SIS recruits on an ad hoc basis, with no formal curriculum. In June 1941 Hoover ordered special agent Joseph E. Santoiana Jr. to establish the FBI's first Spanish-language training course. Santoiana was a Bridgeport, Connecticut, native and cum laude graduate of Georgetown University. Before joining the FBI in 1940, his proficiency in Portuguese and Spanish (learned at home) took him to Algeria, where he taught English at a French college. Later he served as the supervisor of English instruction for all the elementary schools in Puerto Rico. Santoiana produced the first "Comprehensive Spanish Text" for the Bureau's use in September 1941; the same month, an intensive six-week course of instruction for SIS candidates began under his supervision in Washington, D.C. On October 2, 1942, Hoover commended Santoiana's efforts in "preparing the work book . . . used by you during the course of your Spanish language training" and praised his "excellent preparation for this course and for performance as an instructor." Later, during the war years, Santoiana served as the legal attaché at the U.S. embassy in San Jose, Costa Rica, and Caracas, Venezuela. During his thirty-three-year career with the FBI, he rose through the ranks, eventually serving as the special agent in charge of seven FBI field offices. The Spanish course he created remained in continual operation for many decades. Interview of Joseph E. Santoiana Jr. by Julian Koerner, Tampa, Fla., no date; Hoover letter to Santoiana, October 10, 1942, provided by Mr. Santoiana, together with a copy of the original 233-page "Comprehensive Spanish Text," which is currently in the author's possession. The author gratefully acknowledges the assistance of Mr. Koerner.

40. Crosby remained in Buenos Aires until 1943, when the arrest of special agent John Thomas, another SIS undercover agent, forced Crosby and a number of others to flee the country. A year later, in a rebuttal to public charges made by Spruille Braden, the U.S. ambassador to Argentina, President Juan Peron wrote a critique of U.S. policy entitled *Libro y Sule Blanco,* in which he described Crosby as the head of U.S. espionage in Argentina. In 1946 Crosby resigned from the FBI and joined Merrill Lynch Corporation. For the next fourteen years, he headed the Merrill Lynch office in Havana, Cuba, followed by another four years in Madrid and a year in Paris. For the next twelve years, until his retirement in 1977, he headed the Merrill Lynch office in Washington, D.C. Crosby interview.

41. Crosby interview.

42. Papich returned to the United States and was assigned to the San Francisco office; he was later promoted to FBI Headquarters. During the 1960s, he became embroiled in controversy when he was put in the unenviable role of FBI liaison with the CIA. He remained with the FBI until his retirement in March 1970. Interview of Papich by John McCaffrey, January 13, 1999. For details of Papich's CIA liaison days, see Riebling's *Wedge.*

43. *History of the SIS Division,* vol. 1, 8, 13, 149A.

CHAPTER ELEVEN: DUCASE

1. Art Ronnie, *Counterfeit Hero* (Annapolis, Md.: Naval Institute Press, 1995), 214–263; United States vs. Lang, RG 21, CR-38425, Box 10, Trial Transcript, vol. 83, 112–123, NARA, FRC, N.Y.; memorandum, "William Gottleib Sebold, et al.— Espionage," OF10b, Box 11, Report 34, FDR Library (hereafter, Sebold memo). Special agents Paul Napier and Ivan Conrad were both assigned to the Laboratory Section of the Bureau's Identification Division. Napier was a code specialist, and Conrad focused on the construction and makeup of radio equipment. Both were immediately dispatched to New York City to participate in the technical phase of Sebold's lengthy series of interviews. Sebold's disclosures provided the first revelations of this new type of espionage and secret communication technique. Interview of Paul Napier, August 25, 1995.

2. Sebold memo.

3. Ibid.

4. Ibid.

5. United States vs. Lang, 232.

6. Sebold memo.

7. Interview of James C. Ellsworth, November 5, 1996; United States vs. Lang, 116.

8. Sebold memo.

9. Ibid.

10. Gentry, *J. Edgar Hoover,* 182; "Karpis, Public Enemy No. 1 Trapped in New Orleans," *Times Picayune,* May 2, 1936, 1.

11. Crosby interview; Connelley Personnel File.

12. Interview of Richard Millen, June 7, 1999.

13. Undated and unpublished memoir prepared by James C. Ellsworth and provided to the author (hereafter, Ellsworth memoir); interview of James C. Ellsworth, October 30 and November 14, 1996; testimony of James C. Ellsworth in United States vs. Lang.

14. Ellsworth memoir.

15. Sebold memo. MI5 conducted the most famous double-agent operation against the Germans during the Second World War. Rather than be hanged as spies, many German agents who parachuted into Great Britain and were captured chose to cooperate with MI5. With a large network of phony German agents sending a mixture of false and genuine information, the Abwehr eventually developed complete confidence in its Britain-based agent network. MI5's famous deception, known as the "Doublecross System," played a major role in sowing confusion among the German military leadership and giving Allied forces sufficient time in June 1944 to land troops in Normandy and consolidate their position. See John C. Masterman, *The Double-Cross System* (New York: Avon, 1972); Stafford, *Churchill and Secret Service;* and West, *MI5: British Security Operations.* For the use of double agents in support of strategic deception, see Michael Howard, *British Intelligence in the Second World War,* vol. 5, *Strategic Deception* (New York: Cambridge University Press, 1990).

16. Ellsworth memoir.

17. United States vs. Lang.

18. Ibid.

19. Sebold received a letter in May 1940 cautioning him to be patient if communications with Germany were not quickly established. They assured him that since "this long distance depends greatly on conditions of the atmosphere don't be impatient if it doesn't work for days. We will surely find each other. Until we hear each other again and greetings from the whole club." United States vs. Lang. Hoover's letter included the following instructions that had been sent to Sebold: "If Italy became engaged in the present conflict abroad, the informant should communicate with Germany through a named individual in Budapest, Hungary." Hoover letter to Watson, June 3, 1940, OF10b, Box 3, Report 110, FDR Library; Millen interview.

20. Regarding his shortwave communicating ability, Sebold's Abwehr instructors told him, "if you can do everything else that well you are O.K." U.S. Government Trial Brief, 14.

21. Ellsworth memoir; Ellsworth interview.

22. A sense of the unrelenting pressure on Sebold, Ellsworth, and Price can be deduced from a brief analysis of the large volume of traffic moving in and out of Centerport. Between May 19, 1940, and June 23, 1941, when the ring members were arrested, a total of 302 messages were transmitted to Germany, and another 167 were received. This averages approximately one message transmitted or received per day. United States vs. Lang.

23. Ibid.

24. In the message of September 16, 1940, replying to the bombsight inquiry, the FBI was clearly puzzled by the German request. "Proposed Congress investigation of German use of secret bombsight refers to newspaper reports that German planes shot down in France were equipped with secret American bombsight. I found nothing about any new bombsight. Is this the information you wanted?" There is no indication in the available records that the Centerport station ever received a reply from Hamburg concerning this matter. United States vs. Lang.

25. Ibid.

26. Ibid.

27. Report of special agent V. E. Criss, July 30, 1941, RG 118, Box 20, FRC, N.Y. "He [Irwin] later told us that it was a thrilling experience one night to take his equipment out onto a dirt road and when the broadcast began he followed the sound until looking through some brush across a field he could see an old farmhouse with a directional antenna which was the transmitter." Ellsworth memoir.

28. The Sicherheitsdienst (SD) was the Nazi Party's only authorized intelligence organization. Its domestic and foreign components were combined with the government police organizations to form the Reichsscherheitshauptamt (RSHA), or Reich Security Administration. Department III was domestic counterintelligence, Department IV was the dreaded Gestapo (the state police), and Department V was SD foreign intelligence. David Kahn, *Hitler's Spies* (New York: Macmillan, 1975), 6; Walter Schellenberg, *The Labyrinth* (New York: DaCapo Press, 1956), ix. The FBI later concluded that Retelsdorf's shortwave radio was the principal transmitting operation in Mexico during the Second World War. Nicolaus was arrested by agents of the Mexican government in March 1942. Two months later he was brought to the United States and turned over to immigration authorities to await repatriation to Germany. "Totalitarian Activities—Mexico Today, September 1942," RG 59, Box 3, NARA.

29. Axel Wheeler-Hill's brother, James, served as an assistant to Fritz Kuhn, the leader of the German-American Bund. When the case ended, Jahnke and Wheeler-Hill pleaded guilty to violating the Foreign Agents Registration Act (FARA); Klein was convicted of espionage; and Reuper was convicted of espionage and FARA violations (see appendix D). FBI memorandum, "Frederick Joubert Duquesne, et al., Espionage," May 5, 1948, RG 65, Box 5, NARA (hereafter, Duquesne memo).

30. United States vs. Lang.

31. Ibid., 126, 129.

32. Ibid., 139.

33. During their second meeting, Duquesne asked Sebold if he was acquainted with the characteristics of phosphorus. When he said that he was not, Duquesne, with obvious bravado, offered to teach him how to walk through an airplane factory and three hours later have the plant burst into flames. Ibid., 117, 123–124. The remarks about "Myron Taylor in Vatican" suggests that Abwehr agents did not always supply accurate information to Hamburg. Although Taylor did serve as President Roosevelt's special envoy to the Vatican, he was no "priest working for Catholic information." He was actually an Episcopalian born into a wealthy New York family. He had a law degree from Cornell University and served six years as chief executive officer of U.S. Steel. He remained in his post as U.S. envoy to the Vatican until Mussolini closed Rome in 1942. "Myron Taylor Dies; Ex-Envoy to Vatican," New York Times, May 7, 1959, 1.

34. Ronnie, Counterfeit Hero, 257–260; U.S. Government Trial Brief; "29 Are Held as Nazi Spies in Roundup by FBI, Ring Linked to Consuls," New York Herald Tribune, June 30, 1941. Weustenfeld was arrested on June 29, 1941. She later pleaded guilty and was sentenced to five years for espionage and two years for FARA violations. Duquesne memo.

35. Signed statement of Edmund C. Heine, June 29, 1941, United States vs. Lang.

36. Ibid.; "Greatest Spy Roundup in U.S. History Produces a Great Gallery of Faces," Life, July 14, 1941. Heine's ignorance of technical aviation terms, combined with his lackluster performance as a spy, probably saved him from a lengthy prison term (he received two years and a $5,000 fine). Although Heine's letters to Stein did not survive, they probably contained worthless or, at best, information of little importance to U.S. national security. Duquesne memo.

37. Ezima received "fourteen microphotographs . . . two .45 calibre and three .30 caliber bullets, and an original drawing from Sperry Gyroscope Company, No. 644832-B entitled 'Hydraulics Unit with pressure Switch A-5 Pilot' and an original drawing from Lawrence Engineering & Research Corp., R-12280, entitled 'Installation Drawing Soundproofed-5KW.'" Report of special agent V. E. Criss, July 30, 1941, FBI file 65-1819, United States vs. Lang.

38. Ibid. Following the arrest of the Duquesne ring, the State Department quietly ordered Ezima to leave the United States. "The State Department adopted the attitude that to arrest [Ezima] would greatly hinder and affect the relationship then being built up between the United States and Japan to prevent a state of war." Ladd memorandum to Hoover, April 30, 1946, FBI file 65-13868, "Itaru Tachibana with aliases et al., Espionage (J)." The file was made available by Kenneth Ringle, who obtained it from the FBI under the provisions of the Freedom of Information/Privacy Act.

39. "We request recommendations as to how payments can be made unsuspiciously or would you (plural) rather receive large payments in through Mexico?" United States vs. Lang.

40. Duquesne wrote to Sebold on March 1, 1940, that "investment dangerous. Followed after meeting, stock bad, position hold off, Frank." Ibid.

41. Ibid.

42. Ibid.

43. Hoover letter to Watson, July 3, 1941, OF10b, Report 857, FDR Library; Duquesne memo; Ellsworth memoir.

44. Ibid.; "Foreign Spy Gets a Year in Prison," New York Times, April 2, 1941, 10. Mezenen was arrested with an American named Fred Mario and a Hungarian refugee named Arnold Weisz. Hoover letter to Watson, June 6, 1941, OF10b, Report 803, FDR Library.

45. U.S. Department of State, Foreign Relations of the United States, vol. 2, Europe (Washington, D.C.: Government Printing Office, 1941), 803; Hyde, Room 3603, 106–108; "U.S. Rejects Axis Ship Protests," New York Times, April 2, 1941; "Billions Allocated for Aid to Britain," New York Times, April 2, 1941, 9; "U.S. Asks Recall of Italian Attaché," New York Times, April 4, 1941; "Danish Ship Plan," New York Times, April 9, 1941; "Ban on Transferring Axis Vessels to Britain Beaten 43–38," New York Times, May 16, 1941.

46. In 1942 Ovakimian was assigned the responsibility for coordinating all Soviet intelligence efforts to steal atomic bomb secrets, and in 1945 he was appointed head of the newly reconstituted NKGB. Pavel Sudaplatov and Anatoliy Sudaplatov, Special Tasks (Boston: Little, Brown, 1994), 76, 177, 213, 406, 472; Lamphere and Schactman, FBI-KGB Wars; FBI report 61-7574, "Armand Labis Feldman, Willy Brandes, Gaik Badalovich Ovakimian," June 23, 1942. FBI file provided to the author by Robert Lamphere.

47. FBI report, "Feldman, Brandes, Ovakimian"; Andrew and Gordievsky, KGB: The Inside Story, 169–170, 281. Ovakimian was nicknamed the "Wily Armenian" by FBI agents who attempted to follow him on the streets of New York City. Ever wary of FBI surveillance, Ovakimian would frequently taunt his followers and engage in provocative behavior to elude them. In one instance he got on a subway and then hopped out as the doors closed, trapping his pursuers on the moving train. Crosby interview.

48. Ellsworth memoir.

49. Duquesne memo; Jackson memorandum to Roosevelt, undated, Box 2, Francis Biddle Papers, FDR Library.

50. Cordell Hull, The Memoirs of Cordell Hull (New York: Macmillan, 1948), 2:945; Foreign Relations of the United States, 1941, 2:629.

51. "29 Are Held as Nazi Spies"; "FBI Rounds Up 29 as Spies," Washington Post, June 30, 1941; "Counter-Espionage in U.S. 29 Suspects Arrested," Times of London, June 30, 1941.

52. Nikolaus Ritter, Deckname Rantzau (Hamburg: Hoffman und Campe, 1972), 292. In 1913 a young Canaris served as an officer aboard the cruiser Dresden in the Tampico, Mexico, area. In December 1914 his ship was scuttled to avoid capture by a larger British force, and he and other German seamen were imprisoned by the Chilean government. He managed to escape and, with his command of Spanish, made his way across the mountains to Argentina. There he obtained a forged Chilean passport in the name

of Reed Rosas, a widower. He then boarded a Dutch steamer bound for Europe. En route his ship was stopped by British security and ordered into Plymouth, England, for inspection. Brazenly maintaining his false identity, Canaris duped the British and safely completed his journey back to Germany. Karl Heinz Abshagen, *Canaris* (London: Hutchinson, 1956), 27–29, 186.

53. Thomsen telegram to Foreign Ministry, May 22, 1940, Documents on German Foreign Policy, vol. 9 (series D), no. 299, 411.

54. Documents on German Foreign Policy, vol. 13 (series D), no. 81, 98.

55. John Weitz, *Hitler's Diplomat* (New York: Ticknor and Fields, 1992), 271. Lohr then lined up with his own bureaucracy by concluding that the criticism of Thomsen "does not appear justified on the basis of the results of the discussions." Documents on German Foreign Policy, vol. 13 (series D), no. 266, 433.

SELECTED BIBLIOGRAPHY

AUTHOR INTERVIEWS

Robert Louis Benson, Fort Meade, Maryland
Margaret Carbo, Silver Spring, Maryland
Cleveland Cram, Washington, D.C.
Kenneth M. Crosby, Washington, D.C.
William Doyle, San Francisco, California
James C. Ellsworth, Pasadena, California
Julian Englestad, Annapolis, Maryland
Dennis Flinn, Alexandria, Virginia
Frank Garvey, Babylon, New York
Rudolph Gomez, Washington, D.C.
Robert Guerin, Chicago, Illinois
Richard Millen, Fern Park, Florida
Clarence Moore, Washington, D.C.
Paul Napier, Arlington, Virginia
John Neely, Arlington, Virginia
Al Pearce, Springfield, Virginia
Cecil Phillips, Silver Spring, Maryland
Ken Ringle, Washington, D.C.
Eugene Rinta, Silver Spring, Maryland
Joseph Santoiana, Tampa, Florida
Daniel Sullivan, Parchment, Michigan
Horton Telford, LaJolla, California
John Thomas, Lancaster, Pennsylvania
Arthur Thurston, Shelbyville, Indiana
Robert Wall, Raleigh, North Carolina
John Walsh, Silver Spring, Maryland
Raymond Wannall, Silver Spring, Maryland
John West, Asheville, North Carolina

UNPUBLISHED SOURCES

Manuscript Collections: Franklin D. Roosevelt Library, Hyde Park, New York

Ray Bearse Papers
Adolf Berle Papers
Francis Biddle Papers
Steve Early Papers
Harry L. Hopkins Papers
Henry J. Morgenthau Papers
Franklin D. Roosevelt Papers
Harold Smith Papers
Edwin O. Watson Papers
Sumner Welles Papers

Manuscript Collections: Library of Congress, Manuscript Division, Washington, D.C.

Vincent Astor Papers
Homer Cummings Papers (microfilm)
Josephus Daniels Papers
Cordell Hull Papers
Harold Ickes Papers
Robert Jackson Papers
Frank Knox Papers
Breckinridge Long Papers
Nelson Appleton Miles Papers
Frank Murphy Papers (microfilm)
Robert Patterson Papers

Other Archival Papers

United States Navy Historical Center, Washington, D.C.: Admiral Alan Kirk Papers, Admiral Harold Stark Papers
United States Navy Historical Foundation, Washington, D.C.: Admiral Walter S. Anderson Papers
University of Delaware, Newark: George Messersmith Papers
University of Michigan, Ann Arbor: Frank Murphy Papers
University of Mississippi, Oxford: Percy E. Foxworth Papers
University of Virginia, Charlottesville: Homer Cummings Papers
Virginia Commonwealth University, Richmond: J. Edward Lawler Papers
Yale University, New Haven, Connecticut: Henry L. Stimson Papers

Other Library and Archival Sources

Bode Collection, Georgetown University, Washington, D.C.
Federal Bureau of Investigation, J. Edgar Hoover Photographic Collection, National Archives and Records Administration, College Park, Maryland
National Archives and Records Administration, College Park, Maryland
Public Records Office, Kew, England

Oral History Transcripts

Admiral Walter S. Anderson, Special Collections, Admiral Chester Nimitz Library, U.S. Naval Academy, Annapolis, Maryland
Hugh Clegg, Special Collections, University of Mississippi, Oxford

Dissertations

Bell, Leland. "Anatomy of a Hate Movement." Ph.D. diss., University of West Virginia, 1968.
Gerard, Christopher J. "A Program of Cooperation: The FBI, the Senate Internal Security Subcommittee, and the Communist Issue, 1950–1956." Ph.D. diss., Marquette University, 1993.
Mahl, Thomas. "'Forty-eight Land': British Intelligence and the American Isolation." Ph.D. diss., Kent State University, 1993.
Naftali, Timothy. "X-2 and the Apprenticeship of American Counterintelligence." Ph.D. diss., Harvard University, 1992.
Noakes, John Allen. "Enforcing Domestic Tranquility: State Building and the Origins of the Federal Bureau of Investigation, 1908–1920." Ph.D. diss., University of Pennsylvania, 1993.
Sokoll, Cartl A. "The German-American Bund as a Model for American Fascism 1924–1945." Ph.D. diss., Columbia University, 1974.

Other Unpublished Material

Undated memoir of James C. Ellsworth
Undated memoir of Gus T. Jones, "In Mexico"

BOOKS

Abshagen, Karl Heinz. *Canaris*. London: Hutchinson, 1956.
Acheson, Dean. *Present at the Creation*. New York: W. W. Norton, 1969.
Albright, Joseph, and Marcia Kunstel. *Bombshell*. New York: Time Books, 1997.
Alverez, David. *Secret Messages*. Lawrence: University Press of Kansas, 2000.
Andrew, Christopher. *For the President's Eyes Only*. New York: Harper Perennial, 1995.

Andrew, Christopher, and Oleg Gordievsky. *KGB: The Inside Story.* New York: Harper-Collins, 1990.

Andrew, Christopher, and Vasili Mitrokhin. *Mitrokhin Archives.* New York: Basic Books, 1999.

Arthey, Vin. *Like Father Like Son: A Dynasty of Spies.* New York: St. Ermin's Press, 2004.

Bales, James, ed. *J. Edgar Hoover Speaks.* Washington, D.C.: Capitol Hill, 1971.

Barron, John. *Operation Solo.* Washington, D.C.: Regnery Books, 1996.

Bearse, Ray, and Anthony Read. *Conspirator: The Untold Story of Tyler Kent.* New York: Doubleday, 1991.

Benson, Robert Louis, and Michael Warner. *Venona.* Washington, D.C.: Central Intelligence Agency and National Security Agency, 1996.

Bentley, Elizabeth. *Out of Bondage.* New York: Ivy Books, 1988.

Berle, Adolf, and Beatrice Bishop Berle. *Navigating the Rapids, 1918–1971.* Edited by Travis Beal Jacobs. New York: Harcourt, Brace, Jovanovich, 1973.

Biddle, Francis. *In Brief Authority.* Garden City, N.Y.: Doubleday, 1962.

Bidwell, Bruce. *History of the Military Intelligence Division, Department of the Army General Staff: 1775–1941.* Frederick, Md.: University Publications of America, 1986.

Bird, Kai. *The Chairman.* New York: Simon and Schuster, 1992.

Blum, John Morton. *Roosevelt and Morgenthau.* Boston: Houghton Mifflin, 1970.

———. *V Was for Victory.* New York: Harcourt, Brace, Jovanovich, 1976.

Braden, Spruille. *Diplomats and Demagogues.* New Rochelle, N.Y.: Arlington House, 1971.

Brinkley, David. *Washington Goes to War.* New York: Ballantine Books, 1988.

Brisard, Andre. *Canaris.* New York: Grosset and Dunlap, 1974.

Brown, Anthony Cave. *"C": The Secret Life of Stewart Menzies.* New York: Macmillan, 1987.

Burnham, Frederick Russell. *Scouting on Two Continents.* New York: Doubleday, Doran, 1928.

Burns, James McGregor. *Roosevelt: The Soldier of Freedom 1940–1945.* New York: Harcourt, Brace, Jovanovich, 1970.

Burrough, Bryan. *Public Enemies.* New York: Penguin Press, 2004.

Chambers, Whittaker. *Witness.* Washington, D.C.: Regnery Gateway, 1952.

Charnow, Ron. *The House of Morgan.* New York: Atlantic Monthly Press, 1990.

———. *Titan.* New York: Random House, 1998.

———. *The Warburgs.* New York: Random House, 1993.

Childs, H. L., and John B. Whitton. *Propaganda by Shortwave.* Princeton, N.J.: Princeton University Press, 1942.

Colby, Carroll B. *FBI.* New York: Coward-McMann, 1970.

Collins, Fred. *The FBI in Peace and War.* New York: G. P. Putnam's Sons, 1943.

Colvin, Ian. *Chief of Intelligence.* London: Gallancz, 1951.

Conant, Jennet. *Tuxedo Park.* New York: Simon and Schuster, 2002.

Cook, Fred. *The FBI Nobody Knows.* New York: Macmillan, 1964.

Cooper, Courtney Riley. *Ten Thousand Public Enemies.* New York: Little, Brown, 1935.

Costello, John. *Mask of Treachery.* New York: William Morrow, 1988.

Crump, Irving, and John Newton. *Our G Men*. New York: Dodd, Mead, 1937.

Cull, Nicholas. *Selling War*. New York: Oxford University Press, 1995.

Culver, John C., and John Hyde. *American Dreamer: A Life of Henry Wallace*. New York: W. W. Norton, 2000.

Cummings, Homer S. *Selected Papers of Homer Cummings*. New York: DaCapo Press, 1972.

Current, Richard N. *Secretary Stimson: A Study in Statecraft*. New Brunswick, N.J.: Rutgers University Press, 1954.

Dallek, Robert. *Franklin D. Roosevelt and U.S. Foreign Policy, 1932–1945*. New York: Oxford University Press, 1979.

Dasch, George. *Eight Spies against America*. New York: McBride, 1949.

DeLoach, Cartha. *Hoover's FBI*. Washington, D.C.: Regnery Press, 1995.

Demaris, Ovid. *The Director: An Oral Biography*. New York: Harpers Magazine Press, 1975.

DeToledano, Ralph. *J. Edgar Hoover: The Man in His Times*. New York: Arlington House, 1973.

———. *Spies, Dupes and Diplomats*. New York: Duell, Sloan and Pearce, 1952.

Diamond, Sander A. *The Nazi Movement in the United States*. Ithaca, N.Y.: Cornell University Press, 1974.

Dobbs, Michael. *Saboteurs*. New York: Vintage Books, 2004.

Donner, Frank. *The Age of Surveillance*. New York: Alfred A. Knopf, 1980.

Dorwart, Jeffrey. *Conflict of Duty*. Annapolis, Md.: Naval Institute Press, 1983.

Downes, Donald. *The Scarlet Thread*. London: Derek, Verschoyle, 1953.

Dziak, John. *Chekisty*. Lexington, Mass.: D. C. Heath, 1988.

Ellis, George. *A Man Named Jones*. New York: Signet, 1963.

Farago, Ladislaw. *The Broken Seal*. New York: Random House, 1967.

———. *The Game of the Foxes*. New York: David McKay, 1971.

———. *War of Wits*. New York: Funk and Wagnalls, 1954.

Felt, Mark. *The Pyramid from the Inside*. New York: Putnam, 1979.

Floherty, John J. *Inside the FBI*. New York: J. B. Lippincott, 1943.

Fowler, W. B. *British-American Relations, 1917–1918: The Role of Sir William Wiseman*. Princeton, N.J.: Princeton University Press, 1969.

Frank, Gary. *Struggle for Hegemony in South America*. Coral Gables, Fla.: Center for Advanced International Studies, 1979.

Frye, Alton. *Nazi Germany and the American Hemisphere: 1933–1941*. New Haven, Conn.: Yale University Press, 1967.

Gaddis, John Lewis. *The United States and the Origins of the Cold War*. New York: Columbia University Press, 1972.

Garlinski, Jozef. *The Enigma War*. New York: Charles Scribner's Sons, 1979.

Gazur, Edward. *Alexander Orlov: The FBI's KGB General*. New York: Carroll and Graf, 2002.

Gehlen, Reinhard. *The Service*. New York: World Publishing, 1972.

Gellman, Irving. *Good Neighbor Diplomacy: United States Policies in Latin America*. Baltimore: Johns Hopkins University Press, 1979.

———. *Secret Affairs*. Baltimore: Johns Hopkins University Press, 1995.

Gentry, Curt *J. Edgar Hoover: The Man and the Secrets*. New York: W. W. Norton, 1991.

Gimpel, Erich, and Will Berthold. *Spy for Germany*. London: Robert Hall, 1957.

Gitlow, Benjamin. *The Whole of Their Lives*. New York: Scribner's Sons, 1948.

Goodwin, Doris Kearns. *No Ordinary Time*. New York: Simon and Schuster, 1994.

Graff, Frank Warren. *Strategy of Involvement: A Diplomatic History of Sumner Welles*. New York: Garland, 1988.

Gross, Peter. *Gentleman Spy*. Amherst: University of Massachusetts Press, 1994.

Halperin, Morton H. *The Lawless State: The Crimes of the U.S. Intelligence Agencies*. New York: Penguin, 1976.

Hamilton, Nigel. *JFK: Reckless Youth*. New York: Random House, 1992.

Heardin, Patrick. *Roosevelt Confronts Hitler: American Entry into World War II*. De Kalb: Northern Illinois University Press, 1987.

Hilton, Stanley. *Hitler's Secret War in South America*. Baton Rouge: Louisiana University Press, 1981.

Hinsley, Francis H., and C. A. G. Simpkins. *British Intelligence in the Second World War*. Vol. 4. New York: Cambridge University Press, 1993.

Hinsley, Francis H., and Alan Stripp, eds. *Codebreakers*. New York: Oxford University Press, 1993.

Hodges, Andrew. *Alan Turing*. New York: Touchstone Books, 1983.

Holt, Thaddeus. *The Deceivers*. New York: Scribner, 2004.

Hoover, John Edgar. *J. Edgar Hoover on Communism*. New York: Random House, 1969.

———. *Masters of Deceit*. New York: Henry Holt, 1958.

———. *Persons in Hiding*. New York: Little, Brown, 1938.

———. *A Study of Communism*. New York: Holt Rinehart and Winston, 1959.

Howard, Michael E. *British Intelligence in the Second World War*. Vol. 5. New York: Cambridge University Press, 1990.

Hull, Cordell. *The Memoirs of Cordell Hull*. New York: Macmillan, 1948.

Hyde, H. Montgomery. *Room 3603*. New York: Farrar Straus, 1963.

Hynd, Alan. *Betrayal from the East*. New York: Robert McBride, 1943.

———. *Passport to Treason*. New York: Robert McBride, 1943.

Ickes, Harold. *The Secret Diaries*. 3 vols. New York: Simon and Schuster, 1954.

Israel, Fred. *The FBI*. New York: Chelsea House Publishers, 1986.

Kahn, David. *Codebreakers*. New York: Scribner, 1996.

———. *Hitler's Spies*. New York: Macmillan, 1975.

———. *The Reader of Gentlemen's Mail*. New Haven, Conn.: Yale University Press, 2004.

———. *Seizing the Enigma*. New York: Houghton Mifflin, 1991.

Kennedy, David. *Freedom from Fear*. New York: Oxford University Press, 1999.

Kern, Gary. *A Death in Washington*. New York: Enigma Books, 2004.

Koch, Stephen. *Double Lives*. New York: Free Press, 1994.

Koestler, Arthur. *Darkness at Noon*. New York: Macmillan, 1941.

Krivitsky, Walter. *In Stalin's Secret Service*. New York: Harper and Brothers, 1939.

Kutler, Stanley. *American Inquisition*. New York: Hill and Wang, 1982.

Lamphere, Robert, and Tom Schactman. *The FBI-KGB Wars*. New York: Random House, 1986.

Lavin, Earl. *Fifth Column in America*. New York: Doubleday, 1940.

Levine, Isaac Don. *Eyewitness to History.* New York: Hawthorne Books, 1973.

Liddell, Guy. *The Guy Liddell Diaries.* Vol. 1. Edited by Nigel West. London: Routledge, Taylor and Francis Group, 2005.

Loewenheim, Francis, and Harold D. Langley. *Roosevelt and Churchill: Their Secret Wartime Correspondence.* New York: Saturday Review Press, 1975.

Long, Breckinridge. *The War Diaries of Breckinridge Long.* Lincoln: University of Nebraska Press, 1966.

Lowenthal, Max. *The Federal Bureau of Investigation.* New York: William Sloan Associates, 1950.

Lyon, Eugene. *Red Decade.* Indianapolis: Bobbs-Merrill, 1941.

MacDonald, Bill. *The True Intrepid.* Vancouver, B.C.: Raincoast Books, 2001.

Mahl, Thomas. *Desperate Deception.* New York: Brassy's, 1998.

Manville, Roger, and Heinrich Fraenkel. *The Canaris Conspiracy.* New York: McKay, 1969.

Masterman, John C. The *Double-Cross System.* New York: Avon, 1972.

McCullough, David. *Truman.* New York: Simon and Schuster, 1992.

McDonnell, Francis. *Insidious Foes: The Axis Fifth Column and the American Homefront.* Guilford, Conn.: Lyons Press, 2004.

Mitchell, Thomas, and Marcia Mitchell. *The Spy Who Seduced America.* Montpelier, Vt.: Invisible Cities Press, 2002.

Morgan, Ted. *FDR: A Biography.* New York: Simon and Schuster, 1995.

Morris, Edmund. *The Rise of Theodore Roosevelt.* New York: Ballantine, 1979.

Ollstead, Norman. *Inside the FBI.* New York: Lancer, 1968.

O'Reilly, Kenneth. *Hoover and the Un-Americans.* Philadelphia: Temple University Press, 1983.

Packard, Wyman. *A Century of Naval Intelligence.* Washington, D.C.: Department of the Navy, 1996.

Paine, Lauren. *German Military Intelligence in World War II.* New York: Stein and Day, 1984.

Pincher, Chapman. *Too Secret Too Long.* New York: St. Martin's Press, 1984.

Pomerein, Reiner. *Das Dritte und Lateinamerika: Die Deutche politik Gegenuber Sud und Mittleamerika 1939–1945.* Dusseldorf, Germany: Droste Vertag, 1977.

Popov, Dusko. *Spy/Counterspy.* New York: Grosset and Dunlap, 1974.

Power, Richard Gid. *The Boss: J. Edgar Hoover and the Great Inquisition.* New York: Free Press, 1995.

———. *Not without Honor.* New York: Free Press, 1995.

Prange, Gordon. *Pearl Harbor: The Verdict of History.* New York: McGraw-Hill, 1986.

Preston, William Jr. *Aliens and Dissenters.* Cambridge, Mass.: Harvard University Press, 1963.

Radosh, Ronald, and Joyce Milton. *The Rosenberg File.* New York: Holt Rinehart and Winston, 1963.

Reiss, Curt. *Total Espionage.* New York: John Day, 1941.

Riebling, Mark. *Wedge.* New York: Alfred A. Knopf, 1994.

Ritter, Nikolaus. *Deckname Rantzau.* Hamburg, Germany: Hoffman und Campe, 1972.

Romerstein, Herbert, and Eric Breindel. *The Venona Secrets.* Washington, D.C.: Regnery Press, 2000.

Ronnie, Art. *Counterfeit Hero.* Annapolis, Md.: Naval Institute Press, 1995.

Rout, Leslie B. Jr., and John F. Bratzel. *The Shadow War.* Frederick, Md.: University Publications of America, 1986.

Sayers, Michael, and Albert E. Kahn. *Sabotage: The Secret War against America.* New York: Harper Brothers, 1942.

Schellenberg, Walter. *The Labyrinth.* New York: DaCapo Press, 1956.

Schwartz, Jordan A. *Liberal: Adolf Berle and the Vision of an American Era.* New York: Free Press, 1987.

The Secret History of British Intelligence in the Americas, 1940–1945. New York: Fromm International, 1999.

Sherwood, Robert. *Roosevelt and Hopkins.* New York: Harper and Row, 1948.

Sibley, Katherine A. S. *Red Spies in America.* Lawrence: University Press of Kansas, 2004.

Smith, Bradley. *The Shadow War.* New York: Basic Books, 1983.

Smith, Richard Norton. *An Uncommon Man.* New York: Simon and Schuster, 1984.

Stafford, David. *Churchill and Secret Service.* Woodstock, N.Y.: Overlook Press, 1998.

Stevenson, William. *A Man Called Intrepid.* New York: Harcourt, Brace, Jovanovich, 1976.

Stimson, Henry, and McGeorge Bundy. *On Active Service in Peace and War.* New York: Harper and Brothers, 1947.

Stinnett, Robert B. *Day of Deceit.* New York: Free Press, 2000.

Sudaplatov, Pavel, and Anatoliy Sudaplatov. *Special Tasks.* Boston: Little, Brown, 1994.

Talbert, Ray Jr. *Negative Intelligence: The Army and the American Left 1917–1941.* Jackson: University of Mississippi Press, 1991.

Tannenhaus, Sam. *Whittaker Chambers.* New York: Random House, 1997.

Theoharis, Athan. *The Truman Presidency: The Origins of the Imperial Presidency and the National Security State.* New York: Coleman, 1979.

———, ed. *FBI Wiretaps, Bugs, and Break-ins: The National Security Electronic Surveillance Card File and Surreptitious Entry File.* Bethesda, Md.: University Publications of America, 1979.

Thomas, Evan. *Robert Kennedy.* New York: Simon and Schuster, 2000.

Troy, Thomas. *Donovan and the CIA.* Washington, D.C.: Central Intelligence Agency, 1981.

———. *Wild Bill and Intrepid.* New Haven, Conn.: Yale University Press, 1996.

Tully, Andrew. *The FBI's Most Famous Cases.* New York: Dell, 1971.

Turner, Henry Ashby. *Big Business and the Rise of Hitler.* New York: Oxford University Press, 1985.

Turrou, Leon. *Nazi Spies in America.* New York: Random House, 1939.

———. *Where My Shadow Falls.* New York: Doubleday, 1949.

Ungar, Sanford. *FBI.* Boston: Little, Brown, 1979.

Valtin, Jan. *Out of the Night.* New York: Alliance, 1941.

Volland, Klaus. *Das Dritte und Mexiko: Studien zur Entwicklungdes Deutsche Mexikanischen Verhaltnises 1933–1942 unter Besonder Besusksightgung der Olpolitik.* Frankfurt-am-Main, Germany: Peter Lang, 1976.

Weinstein, Allen. *Perjury: The Hiss-Chambers Case.* New York: Alfred A. Knopf, 1978.

Weinstein, Allen, and Alexander Vassiliev. *The Haunted Wood.* New York: Random House, 1999.

Welles, Sumner. *Seven Decisions that Shaped the World.* New York: Harper, 1951.

West, Nigel. *MI5: British Security Operations, 1940–1945.* New York: Stein and Day, 1982.

———. *MI6: British Intelligence Operations.* London: Weidenfeld and Nicholson, 1983.

———. *Mortal Crimes.* New York: Enigma Books, 2004.

———. *Mortal Enemies.* New York: Enigma Books, 2003.

Whitehead, Don. *The FBI Story.* New York: Random House, 1956.

Winks, Robin. *Cloak and Dagger.* New York: William Morrow, 1987.

Wright, Peter. *Spycatcher.* New York: Viking, 1987.

Young, Desmond. *Rutland of Jutland.* London: Cassell, 1963.

ARTICLES

Bahrendt, Richard. "Fascist Penetration in Latin America." *American Council on Public Affairs,* 1941.

Beals, Carlton. "Swastika over the Andes." *Harpers Magazine* 17 (1938): 166–186.

———. "Totalitarian Inroads in Latin America." *Foreign Affairs* 17 (October 1938): 78–89.

Belknap, Richard. "The Mechanics of Repression: The Bureau of Investigation and the Radicals 1917–1925." *Crime and Social Justice* 7 (Spring–Summer 1977): 49–58.

Bidwell, Percy. "Getulio" *Time* 36 (August 12, 1940): 18–20.

———. "Latin America, Germany and the Hull Program." *Foreign Affairs* 17 (July 1939): 373–396.

Bratzell, John, and Leslie Rout. "Pearl Harbor, Microdots and J. Edgar Hoover." *American Historical Review* 87 (December 1982): 1346–1347.

Candeloro, Dominic. "Louis F. Post and the Red Scare of the 1920s." *Prologue* 11 (Spring 1979): 40–55.

Carleton, John Ray. "The Case of Tyler Kent." *This Month* (August 1946).

Clarens, Carlos. "Hooverville West: The Hollywood G-Man 1934–1945." *Film Comment* 3 (May–June 1977): 10–16.

Clifford, George. "The FBI's Greatest Cases." *Argosy* (September 1974).

Coben, Stanley. "A Study of Nativism: The Red Scare of 1919–1920." *Political Science Quarterly* 79 (March 1964): 52–75.

Cole, Wayne S. "American Entry into World War II: Historiographical Approach." *Mississippi Valley Review* 42 (March 1957): 142–161.

Crawford, Kenneth G. "J. Edgar Hoover." *Nation* (February 27, 1937): 232–234.

Culenare, A. "A Short History of Microphotography." *Journal of Forensic Sciences* 4 (January 1959): 38–54.

Dorwart, Jeffrey. "The Roosevelt-Astor Espionage Ring." *New York History* 62 (July 1981): 38–54.

Flanigan, Kerriann. "Nazi Spy Ring Rediscovered in Centerport." *Long Islander* (August 1, 1991).

Gaddis, John Lewis. "Intelligence, Espionage and the Origins of the Cold War." *Diplomatic History* 12 (Summer 1988): 193–209.

Hall, Melvin, and Walter Peck. "Wings for the Trojan Horse." *Foreign Affairs* 19 (January 1941): 347–369.

Hewitt, Steve. "Royal Canadian Spy: The Secret Life of John Leopold/Jack Esselwein." *Intelligence and National Security* 15, no. 1 (Spring 2000): 1444–1468.

Hoover, John Edgar. "The Enemy's Masterpiece of Espionage." *Reader's Digest* 48 (April 1946).

———. "The FBI on Guard." *Kiwanis Magazine* (February 14, 1943).

———. "Hitler's Spying Sirens." *American Magazine* 138 (December 1944).

———. "The Spy Who Doublecrossed." *American Magazine* 141 (May 1946).

Hoover, John Edgar, and Frederick L. Collins. "Hitler's Spies Are Experts." *Colliers* 3 (April 24, 1943).

Hoover, John Edgar, and Robert M. Grant. "Spy Trap." *Popular Mechanics* 80 (December 1943).

Irving, David. "The Many Motives of a Misguided Cypher Clerk." *Focal Point* (November 23, 1981).

Jenkisson, John. "The FBI Versus the New York Spies." *New York World Telegram* 25 (June 1945).

Kimball, Warren, and Bruce Bartlett. "Churchill and Roosevelt: The Personal Equation." *Prologue* 6 (Fall 1981).

Kingsley, Donald J. "Spies and Saboteurs." *Current History* 2 (August 1942).

Klehr, Harvey, and Ronald Radosh. "The Untold Story of the Amerasia Case." *New Republic* 194 (April 21, 1986): 18–21.

Kris, Ernst. "German Propaganda Instructions." *Social Research* 9 (February 1942): 48–81.

Leab, Daniel J. "Anti-Communism in the FBI and Cvetic: The Ups and Downs of a Professional Informer." *Pennsylvania Magazine of History and Biography* 115 (October 1958).

Leutze, James. "The Secret of the Churchill-Roosevelt Correspondence." *Journal of Contemporary History* 10, no. 3 (July 1975).

Martin, L. "Nazi Intrigues in Central America." *American Mercury* 53 (July 1941).

Miles, Sherman. "Pearl Harbor in Retrospect." *Atlantic* (July 1948).

O'Reilly, Kenneth. "A New Deal for the FBI: The Roosevelt Administration, Crime Control and National Security." *Journal of American History* (December 1969): 638–658.

Remak, Joachim. "Friends of the New Germany, the Bund and American Relations." *Journal of Modern History* 29 (1957): 38–41.

Salisbury, Harrision E. "The Strange Correspondence of Morris Ernst and J. Edgar Hoover, 1939–1944." *Nation* 239 (December 1, 1984): 575–589.

Sibley, Katherine A. S. "Soviet Industrial Espionage against American Military Technology and the U.S. Response." *Intelligence and National Security* 14, no. 2 (Summer 1999): 94–123.

Smith, Gerald. "The Strange Case of Tyler Kent." *Cross and the Flag* (1944).

Theoharis, Athan. "The FBI and the American Legion Program, 1940–1966." *Political Science Quarterly* 100 (Summer 1985): 271–286.

Trefousse, Hans L. "Failure of German Intelligence in the United States 1935–1945." *Mississippi Valley Historical Review* (June 1955).

Watt, D. C. "Hitler Comes to Power." *History Today* 13 (March 1963): 152–159.

Weinberg, Gerhard L. "Hitler's Image in the United States." *American Historical Review* 69 (July 1972): 1008–1021.

Whalen, Richard J. "The Strange Case of Tyler Kent." *Diplomat* 17, no. 186 (November 1965).

Wilson, Charles H. "Hitler, Goebbels and the Ministry of Propaganda." *Political Science Quarterly* (January 1939).

Wilson, James Q. "Buggings, Break-ins and the FBI." *Commentary* 65 (June 1978): 52–58.

NEWSPAPERS

Baltimore Sun
Boston Globe
Chicago Tribune
Hartford Courant
Los Angeles Times
New Orleans Times Picayune
New York Herald Tribune
New York Journal American
New York Times
New York World Telegram
San Francisco Examiner
Times of London
Washington Post

INDEX